(Not) Kidding

Studies in Critical Social Sciences Book Series

Haymarket Books is proud to be working with Brill Academic Publishers (www.brill.nl) to republish the *Studies in Critical Social Sciences* book series in paperback editions. This peer-reviewed book series offers insights into our current reality by exploring the content and consequences of power relationships under capitalism, and by considering the spaces of opposition and resistance to these changes that have been defining our new age. Our full catalog of *SCSS* volumes can be viewed at https://www.haymarketbooks.org/series_collections/4-studies-in-critical-social-sciences.

Series Editor
David Fasenfest (York University, Canada)

Editorial Board
Eduardo Bonilla-Silva (Duke University)
Chris Chase-Dunn (University of California–Riverside)
William Carroll (University of Victoria)
Raewyn Connell (University of Sydney)
Kimberlé W. Crenshaw (University of California–LA and Columbia University)
Heidi Gottfried (Wayne State University)
Alfredo Saad-Filho (Queen's University, Belfast)
Chizuko Ueno (University of Tokyo)
Sylvia Walby (Lancaster University)
Raju Das (York University)

(Not) Kidding

Politics in Online Tabloids

Helena Chmielewska-Szlajfer

Haymarket Books
Chicago, IL

First published in 2024 by Brill Academic Publishers, The Netherlands
© 2024 Koninklijke Brill NV, Leiden, The Netherlands

Published in paperback in 2025 by
Haymarket Books
P.O. Box 180165
Chicago, IL 60618
773-583-7884
www.haymarketbooks.org

ISBN: 979-8-88890-517-3

Distributed to the trade in the US through Consortium Book Sales and Distribution (www.cbsd.com) and internationally through Ingram Publisher Services International (www.ingramcontent.com).

This book was published with the generous support of Lannan Foundation, Wallace Action Fund, and the Marguerite Casey Foundation.

Special discounts are available for bulk purchases by organizations and institutions. Please call 773-583-7884 or email info@haymarketbooks.org for more information.

Cover design by Jamie Kerry and Ragina Johnson.

Printed in the United States.

Library of Congress Cataloging-in-Publication data is available.

For my friends
Dla przyjaciół

Contents

Acknowledgements IX
List of Figures and Tables XI

1 How Did We Get Here?
   Tabloidization of News and the 2015–16 Elections in Poland, UK, and the US 1
   1 What Happened? The Unexpected Results of 2015 Elections in Poland, 2016 Brexit Referendum and 2016 Presidential Elections in the United States 1
      1.1 Introduction 1
      1.2 Explanations of Flawed Polls 3
      1.3 Explanations of Flawed Media Coverage 4
      1.4 Politics in Online Tabloids as a Lens for Underrepresented Voices 5
      1.5 Tabloid Authority 8
      1.6 Popular Passions 9
   2 A Short History of the Tabloidization of News in Poland, the United Kingdom and the United States 10
      2.1 Tabloid Influence on News in the UK, US and Poland: In Brief 10
      2.2 United Kingdom 13
      2.3 United States 14
      2.4 Poland 16
   3 How Did We Get Here? Tabloidization of News-Making Today 19
      3.1 "Tabloidization," or a Definition of Power 19
      3.2 Default Online Tabloid Style: Backstory 22
      3.3 Tabloid Influence: Political Scandal 25
      3.4 The Cultural Frame for Politics in Online Tabloids 28
   4 Short Note on Methods and the Following Chapters 29

2 Politicians Are Crooks, Votes Are Rigged, and Other Visions of an (Un)just World 37
   1 Background on Gawker, Mail Online, and Pudelek: The Rise of Online News, and News Media Struggles for Profit 37
      1.1 Introduction 37
      1.2 Emergence and Rise of the Three Online Tabloids 37
   2 Politics of Online Tabloid Attention 45

	2.1	Game Frame, Scandal Frame, "Elite" Insult 47
	2.2	Entertaining Politicians 52
	2.3	The Commenters 54

3   What's Popular in Online Tabloid Political Coverage? A Close Look at Campaign News   56
  3.1   Numbers and Themes   56
  3.2   Poland 2015 Presidential Campaign   66
  3.3   United Kingdom 2016 EU Referendum Campaign   86
  3.4   United States 2016 Presidential Campaign   135
4   A Brief Summary, and Moving on to the Next Chapter   184

3 Backoffice, or How Online Tabloid Journalists Write on Politics   193

1   Getting to Talk to Online Tabloid Writers. A Personal Methodological Note on Finding Sources in Different Journalistic Cultures   193
2   Content and Comments   196
  2.1   Content 101: Newsworthy, Entertaining, Reactive   196
  2.2   Comments, Commenters, Language   201
  2.3   Journalists on Commenters   205
  2.4   Commenters on Journalists   211
3   Newsroom Agendas   214
  3.1   Newsworthiness and Traffic   215
  3.2   Newsroom Routines   221
  3.3   Newsroom Changes   226
  3.4   Professionalism   235
  3.5   Politics, Principles, and Secrets   240

4 Conclusion
Online Tabloid Voices and Democracy   254
1   Producing Knowledge and Inclusion in Journalistic Authority   256
2   Voicing Popular Passions and Exposing (Im)morality   257
3   The L(e)ast Credible Source and Democracy   259

Index   265

Acknowledgements

The idea for this book came to me several years ago, at my Department's summer barbeque party. I was casually talking with colleagues about my fascination with political coverage in online tabloids, especially the connections between news articles and readers' comments, which I found unique. Dariusz Jemielniak, the Head of the Department of Management in Networked and Digital Societies (MiNDS) said matter-of-factly, "You should write about it." First we laughed, then I decided it was a great idea. This conversation took place after the 2015 spring presidential elections in Poland, which had been won by Andrzej Duda from the right-wing party, PiS (Law and Justice), and fall parliamentary ones, which had also brought victory to PiS. To broaden the scope, I decided to focus on the EU membership (Brexit) referendum campaign in the United Kingdom, which was still several months ahead when I started my research, and on the presidential campaign in the United States, which was even further away. Three is a magic number and, given the relatively short time span between the three events, as well as the extraordinary online-tabloid-style intertwining the different local right-wing, nationalist tendencies that came to light in the three campaigns, it made sense to compare the Polish, British, and US cases. The research turned out to be a thrilling experience, even though finishing this book took me much longer than I had originally anticipated, and as I was writing the chapters I was worrying whether my findings wouldn't become outdated by the time I completed it. But today, in the spring of 2024, Poland is after parliamentary and local elections which managed to break PiS's power, yet it remains the second most popular party; the United Kingdom is suffering from the negative consequences of Brexit after more years of Tory government; and in the United States, Donald Trump, charged in criminal cases, is the Republican candidate for the 2024 presidential election. Thus, slow writing has proven rewarding – although these political developments are not exactly good news for democracy. Nonetheless, the findings presented in this book may help understand some of the reasons behind them.

I would have not been able to conduct the research, not to mention writing a book, without the immense help of many people who had supported me along the way. It goes without saying that it would have never come to life without the enormous trust of journalists, many of whom decided to remain anonymous. I am extremely grateful for their support and insightful conversations. I want to thank Alice Marwick, Matthew Kaminski, and Jakub Krupa, who opened many doors to online-tabloid newsrooms, which otherwise would have remained shut. I am also grateful to Koźmiński University for faith in this project (the

Covid pandemic was not a great time to be productive), and administrative support in obtaining funding and figuring out extended research travels; I am particularly thankful to Robert Rządca, Dariusz Jemielniak and, for the indispensable back-office support, to Andrzej Krzyżewski. My research in New York was made possible thanks to Eric Klinenberg at NYU Institute for Public Knowledge and Rod Benson at NYU Department of Media, Culture, and Communication; I am especially grateful for Rod's thoughtful suggestions which helped me formulate the key arguments for this book. Moreover, I am hugely indebted to LSE Department of Media and Communications, particularly to Nick Couldry, Nick Anstead, and Charlie Beckett, who have been instrumental in the British part of the research. The seminars I took part in at NYU and at LSE were illuminating and helped me explore additional avenues in my study of politics in online tabloids. Finally, this book would have looked quite differently (worse) without the brilliant comments made by Roch Dunin-Wąsowicz, and without the infinite support and patience of my editor, David Fasenfest.

Figures and Tables

Figures

1. Ex-Gawker Jezebel layout (fragment). A Gizmodo Media Group website where Gawker authors moved after Gawker was shut down; comments can be arranged by newest, oldest, and most popular   38
2. Pudelek layout (fragment). Top reader comments are at the top and highlighted in yellow   41
3. Mail Online layout (fragment). A bright-blue box with additional information is visible in the center. Comments can be arranged by newest, oldest, best rated, and worst rated   44
4. Map of associations between topics mentioned in Pudelek, Mail Online, and Gawker articles   60
5. Assessment of professionalism in online tabloids   236

Tables

1. "Member of the elite" and "People's person" labels used in Pudelek, Mail Online, and Gawker in the three campaigns   49
2. Number of articles in Pudelek, Mail Online, and Gawker in the three campaigns   58
3. The most popular themes on Pudelek, Mail Online, and Gawker during the three campaigns (numbers in parentheses indicate how many articles mention a given theme out of the total number of articles analyzed in depth using MAXQDA)   63

CHAPTER 1

How Did We Get Here?

Tabloidization of News and the 2015–16 Elections in Poland, UK, and the US

1 What Happened? The Unexpected Results of 2015 Elections in Poland, 2016 Brexit Referendum and 2016 Presidential Elections in the United States

1.1 *Introduction*

When one thinks of tabloids, including online ones, it usually goes along the lines of "downgrading of hard news and upgrading of sex, scandal and infotainment" (Esser 1999, p. 292). The typical topics range from "New 'Miss Euro' attends match with Ukraine (PHOTOS),"[1] and "I hate that man more than any other who has ever lived,"[2] to "My 14-Hour Search for the End of TGI Friday's Endless Appetizers."[3] Yet during the 2015 and 2016 elections, and referendum, held in Poland, the United Kingdom and the United States that led to some of the most important political shifts in the second decade of the 21st century, these outlets proved to have a sharp eye for public emotions – in contrast to most political surveys and expert analyses, which turned out to be wrong. Indeed, according to polls, at the beginning of 2015 the Civic Platform (PO), the then ruling center-conservative party in Poland, had reasons to feel confident about the coming presidential and parliamentary elections. The incumbent president, Bronisław Komorowski, a longtime PO member, maintained a clear lead before the May elections and his competitors were hardly noticeable. The spring presidential elections were also supposed to pave the way to the party's third victory in a row in the parliamentary elections, scheduled for the fall. This would have been a major feat for any political party in Poland since the fall of the Iron Curtain, given that the political scene generally tended to shift with each election since 1989. The nationalist right-wing Law and Justice (PiS), the main opposition party, put Andrzej Duda, a relatively

---

1 See: https://www.pudelek.pl/artykul/94296/nowa_miss_euro_na_meczu_z_ukraina_zdjecia/ (all websites accessed 3rd of October 2023; all translations have been done by the author).
2 See: https://www.dailymail.co.uk/news/article-2665099/I-hate-man-lived-Feud-Clintons-Obamas-laid-bare-author-claims-Michelle-calls-Hillary-Hildabeest.html.
3 See: https://gawker.com/my-14-hour-search-for-the-end-of-tgi-fridays-endless-ap-1606122925.

unknown politician in the presidential race. At the time, he was a Member of the European Parliament and had been a member of the Polish parliament before, but until 2015 he was rarely visible in the media. Komorowski expected an easy win; according to polls, in January the incumbent president enjoyed well over 60 percent support, while Duda had barely over 20 percent. Yet in the four months leading to the May elections as Duda's popularity climbed up to 30 percent, Komorowski's dropped below 50 percent. Nonetheless, the PO candidate was viewed as a clear leader right up until the May 10th election results rolled in: Duda received 34.76 percent of the votes and Komorowski 33.77. For one thing, this meant that a second round had to be scheduled, since none of the candidates received 50 percent of the votes. But more importantly, these unexpected results revealed that a newcomer (at least for the general public) from the main opposition party managed to beat the sure-to-win incumbent president from the governing PO, who had seemed beyond the reach of any of his competitors just a few months earlier. (Adam Michnik, the famous Polish Communist-era dissident and since 1989 editor-in-chief of the largest Polish opinion daily, *Gazeta Wyborcza* memorably, and incorrectly, predicted that Komorowski would lose the election only "if, drunk, he ran over a pregnant nun at a zebra crossing" (WP 2015).) In the runoff between Komorowski and Duda held two weeks later, the PiS candidate again proved more convincing for the voters and won the presidential elections by a margin of two percent. What's more, Duda's surprise triumph marked the beginning of a landslide victory for PiS; in the parliamentary elections held in October 2015, five months later, the main opposition party beat PO by almost 14 percentage points: PiS received 37.58 percent of the votes, while PO came in second with only 24.09 percent. This was a result few would have predicted at the beginning of 2015. Polls had clearly overlooked Duda. The question is: how could this have happened?

In the United Kingdom, the European Union membership referendum, otherwise known as the Brexit vote, was announced on 27th of May 2015, coincidentally three days after the victory of Andrzej Duda in the presidential elections in Poland. The date of the referendum itself was set several months later for 23rd of June 2016. It was called by the Tory Prime Minister, David Cameron, whose Conservative Party had won, unexpectedly in light of election polls, the general election in May 2015, promising to give "the British people" a say about membership in the European Union. Those who wanted to stay in the EU, the so-called Remainers – a group Cameron was a member of – held a clear lead in the polls against the so-called Leavers the entire time, once again until the results of the referendum rolled in. Still, according to these polls, throughout 2015 Remainers enjoyed around 45 percent support, while Leavers hovered around 39 percent, with 16 percent voters undecided whether to leave or remain in the EU. Even in June 2016, the month of the referendum, on average the polls showed a narrow win for the Remainers: 45 percent against 43 percent for Leavers. Nonetheless, the final result of the Brexit referendum held on June 23rd, with voter turnout above 72 percent, was 51.89 percent of votes to leave the EU and 48.11 percent to stay. Once again polls had missed the winner. What happened?

Across the pond, less than five months later, on 8th of November 2016 US citizens elected Donald Trump as the president of the United States, to the surprise of anyone who had tracked election surveys. The Republican candidate won even though throughout 2016 Hillary Clinton had maintained a lead of around four to five percentage points. She fared better in polls also after each of the three presidential candidates' debates – usually treated as an important indicator of voter sympathies – that were held in September and October, as well as in the very last surveys published in the final days before the election. And indeed, on November 8th in the popular vote Clinton did beat Trump by two percentage points, 48.2 to 46.1. But she lost in the electoral votes, which in the end determined the election results. Why were the polls wrong again?

1.2 *Explanations of Flawed Polls*

One question begging for an answer was how could have the expert analyses got voter sympathies so wrong? Some blamed deliberate misinformation on social media, most notably Cambridge Analytica and Russian influence, particularly in the UK and the US (US Senate Report 2018, 2019; Wylie 2019), but if so, such manufactured opinions should also have become visible in the polls. Others focused on the issues with polling itself, and the two main explanations of the flawed polls discussed in the media were as follows: firstly, voters kept their opinions to themselves (Levy, Aslan and Bironzo 2016).[4] This view echoed the theory of the spiral of silence (or shy voters), according to which people hide their views since they fear they might be unpopular (Noelle-Neumann 1974). Others pointed at experts' wishful thinking, or the "unthinkability bias," as Sean Trende (2016a, 2016b), an elections analyst aptly put it (see also: Cohn 2016). Their mistake was to focus on the fact that one side – the one they favored – was winning in the polls, instead of paying attention to how narrow the margin was. Researchers, however, tried to understand what made the polls flawed in the first place. A central argument concerned the ambivalent social role of political surveys in general (Guzik and Marzęcki 2015; Matuszewski 2016; Prendecki 2015). On the one hand, their role is to inform what the public

---

4 See also: Cassino 2016; Cohn 2017; Edwards 2016; Nowak 2015; past 2019.

opinion is; on the other hand, polls influence the sympathy of voters who tend to align with potential winners. In addition, they help to amplify the most popular opinions which are then discussed by experts in the media, while ignoring views that fared less well in the surveys – this was particularly noticeable in the Polish 2015 presidential elections. Furthermore, focusing on the technical aspects of election polling, one often-voiced argument made by researchers concerned the fact that especially in the case of the Brexit referendum online polls proved more accurate than phone polls (Sayers 2016). Another issue raised was that too many people, the so-called shy voters, had escaped surveys, which led to an overrepresentation of highly educated respondents who were more confident about sharing their thoughts (Wells 2016). Interestingly, these explanations were echoed by researchers in reference to the US presidential elections as well, both in terms of phone-call polling deficiencies as well as underrepresenting voters with low education levels (Kennedy et al. 2017, 2018; Mercer, Deane and McGeeney 2016). However, there was an additional important argument that focused on voter turnout: voters who wanted change were more likely to vote. Indeed, the winners promised change: Duda's and later PiS party's slogan was "Good Change" ("Dobra Zmiana"); Leavers campaigned with "Take Back Control"; and Trump promised to "Make America Great Again." Thus, the high turnouts, which had not been anticipated by polls, worked in their favor.

1.3 *Explanations of Flawed Media Coverage*

Explanations of the failed predictions focused not only on polls but on news media as well, predominantly newspapers and television. Scholars pointed out the political slant of news outlets, which, in a manner of a self-fulfilling prophecy, during the campaigns paid more attention to – and, in doing so, amplified the visibility of – those candidates who eventually came out as the winners: Duda and PiS in the Polish elections (Klepka 2016); Leavers in the UK Brexit referendum (Levy, Aslan and Bironzo 2016); and Donald Trump in the US presidential elections (Trende 2016b). The key argument concerning this bias was threefold: firstly, that news media, particularly newspapers, were themselves political actors (Firmstone 2016) and presented surveys and expert analyses in a way that supported their own agenda (Klepka 2016; Prendecki 2015). In many ways this problem is not new; well over half a century ago the political scientist Bernard Cohen wrote that the press "may not be successful much of the time in telling people what to think, but it is stunningly successful in telling them what to think about." (Cohen 1963, p. 13) This approach not only puts into question the very principle of news media impartiality but opens up additional ones, starting with: Impartiality in relation to what? Is it an impartiality towards the representativeness of candidates and issues, which are themselves based on polls? Is it an impartiality towards the distribution of power measured in parliamentary representation? Is it an impartiality as equal focus on all topics and candidates, regardless of their popularity? Or perhaps it is an impartiality to facts? Cushion and Lewis (2016) suggest the latter and blame Brexit campaign coverage for replacing the objectivity of facts with an impartiality towards issues. At the same time, as others point out (e.g. Daddow 2016) the logic of media attention advises precisely that, since objectivity draws in less viewers than letting the candidates talk, all in the name of impartiality. Thus, a related argument concerns the fact that news media focused almost entirely on the key players and issues, while ignoring the less popular candidates and more complex topics. As such, it is a vicious circle: the popularity of the candidates is dependent both on polls and media coverage. Thirdly and finally, news outlets were accused of focusing mainly on the so-called horse race or game frame aspect of the campaigns (Dunaway and Lawrence 2015). This type of framing of news stories made the campaigns look as if they were merely contests with winners and losers, rather than complex, far from black-and-white choices with fundamental political, social and economic consequences.

Yet an even stronger opinion on election polling in general was voiced by a statistician. On the pages of *Gazeta Wyborcza,* Mirosław Szreder argued that surveys are simply not enough to understand public opinion, as it is "not the sum of individual views" (an opinion Durkheim would have certainly appreciated). Szreder went even further, claiming that polling is largely transient, dependent on a particular moment and mood: "Social opinion and attitudes are shaped also when an opportunity to voice them arises, to meet and confront individual stances and beliefs." He then added, "emotions are significant too, but phone and internet surveys lack them entirely" (Szreder 2015). This last sentence is particularly significant in the context of this book, since if there is something that online tabloids are particularly good at it is the ability to swiftly adapt to readers' emotions. After all, more than one of the Mail Online journalists I talked to calls his own paper simply: "reactive."

1.4 *Politics in Online Tabloids as a Lens for Underrepresented Voices*

To understand voter sympathies that had been missing in polls and major media coverage, I decided to ask a basic question: Where should one look for open spaces for political discussion to find these voices that had been unaccounted for? Unlike major debates concerning fake news and micro-targeting on social media (Caplan and boyd 2016), I was not searching for closed groups of target audiences locked in their filter bubbles (Pariser 2011) but, on the contrary, for easily accessible, open spaces for people to discuss politics, as well as to vent their political emotions. This led me to pay closer attention to a particular feature of today's mainstream media, something of an elephant in the room surprisingly ignored in studies of the public sphere: online tabloids. While widely read, and generally blamed for the tabloidization of media as well as political bias (e.g. Conboy 2006; Esser 1999; Gripsrud 2000), they are otherwise often overlooked in the current debates concerning the state of news and democracy (e.g. Fenton 2010; Lowrey and Gade 2011; McNair 2000; Peters and Broersma 2013, 2017). Those are more centered either on so-called hard news – using Gaye Tuchman's (1972) now classic term – more nuanced and thus more demanding for readers; radio and television broadcasters; or social media, most notably Facebook and Twitter (renamed X), now considered a prime battleground for bots and trolls spreading misinformation to polarize opinion and, in consequence, instill conflict among their audiences, the potential voters.

In stark contrast to this inattention, the online progeny of old tabloids remains impressive both in scale of readership and political influence (e.g. Collins 2012; Mahler and Rutenberg 2019; Mance 2019; Toobin 2017), successfully cultivating the catchy, emotional, black-and-white, easily accessible style. What's more, these online outlets provide a key feature unavailable to paper tabloids, namely unlimited space for readers' comments. These two fundamental characteristics – one concerning the broadly understood public sphere (vide: Habermas 1974), the other concerning basic technological affordances – are the reason why in my search for the underrepresented voices of voters in Poland, the United Kingdom and the United States, I turned to major online tabloids that cover political issues: Polish Pudelek (in Polish the name means poodle, as a reference to the pet popular with old-Hollywood celebrities); British Mail Online, the most-read English-language online tabloid in the world and at the same time the online version of the paper, *Daily Mail*; and US Gawker, which despite its popularity went bankrupt in August 2016. The surprise closure was a result of a court case that concerned the invasion of privacy of a celebrity wrestler, Hulk Hogan, who was secretly supported by the Gawker-despising Silicon Valley entrepreneur, Peter Thiel. (What remained of Gawker Media's other websites, including the website's distinctive mischievous style, was later bought by other media entities.) Although these online tabloids are often dismissed in discussions concerning relations between news media and the public sphere, other than being blamed for political bias, given the actual reach of these scandalizing outlets it is perhaps a bit of a paradox to consider them spaces for voicing *underrepresented* voices: Mail Online attracts almost 25 million unique visitors per month (and many of the journalists from Mail Online I talked to emphasize that it is the most popular news website in the world); Gawker was visited by around 14.5 million unique visitors per month before it ceased operations at the end of August 2016; and Pudelek draws around 6.6 million unique visitors per month.[5] At the same time, because of the news these online tabloids offer – filled with celebrity gossip and scandalizing human-interest stories, where political news coverage is only part of the daily mix – they reach people who do not have to be necessarily interested in nuanced hard political news. Instead, they might just as well get their updates from sources that are more entertaining or infotaining, that is offering a blend of entertainment and news. And this is quite likely, since according to Wojcieszak et al. (2024), most people get political information from non-hard news outlets. What's more, online tabloid stories lend politics a lighthearted show-business appeal, which makes these topics look more like yet another celebrity or human-interest story, similarly black-and-white, scandalizing, but also detached from everyday life. Conversely, the fact that celebrity gossip neighbors with political coverage lends the former some gravitas of the latter. Presented using sarcastic language and imagery, political online tabloid stories seem both important and trivial, serious and joking. This is why I argue that in their political coverage these outlets use a crucial and ambiguous frame that makes these outlets both exceptional and popular with readers, namely: "(not) kidding." While it will be discussed in more detail further in the book, briefly put, the (not) kidding frame is essentially conversational, relying on readers' comments to the journalistic pieces to determine whether the meanings of political stories are serious, or perhaps they are merely jokes. What is particularly important here is that people engaging in this passionate and emotional, rather than rational, plebeian public sphere of the poorly educated[6] – as Habermas (1991, 1992) called it (predicting the current polling errors on the way) – take part in elections, too. What they see in online tabloids at least in part informs their knowledge about the world; because of this, these outlets are powerful actors in democracies. This is another reason why the articles and reader comments published there provide such an exciting and important lens, which allows to uncover political sympathies and more general outlooks on the public sphere that were lost – as the cases of 2015 and 2016 vote campaigns showed – both in the hard news media and in the polls.

---

5   Sources: https://www.mailmetromedia.co.uk/brand/mailonline/ (Mail Online); https://www.businessinsider.com/univision-buys-gawker-traffic-2016-8 (Gawker); https://www.wirtualnemedia.pl/artykul/pudelek-z-mniejsza-przewaga-nad-plotkiem-mocno-w-gore-sekcje-o2-pl-i-radiozet-pl (Pudelek).
6   In fact, Pudelek, Mail Online, and Gawker readers are predominantly well educated. This will be discussed in the next chapters.

1.5 Tabloid Authority

All three countries discussed in this book, Poland, the United Kingdom and the United States, share at least two common traits that are particularly important in the context of tabloids: they are highly polarized in terms of politics and their media systems are considerably commercialized. Both these characteristics have historically proven a fertile ground for tabloid journalism (Hallin and Mancini 2004). Thus, in the entertaining, scandalizing style of these online tabloids I discovered a remarkable space for sociological inquiry, found in the interactions between online articles written by journalists and readers' comments published directly below. Thanks to this simple, intuitive online page design established back in the 1990s – the Web 1.0 era – and the responsiveness of online tabloids to the views of their readers, these websites can be explored as platforms where it is possible to openly voice opinions to other readers but also directly to the journalistic, even if "merely" tabloid, authority. Moreover, I consider these online tabloids spaces of authority for several reasons: firstly, because they are websites where articles are written by journalists who bear the authority of professionals bound by press regulations. Secondly, these online platforms are visibility authorities (see: Dayan 2013) – they select what is worth showing as news to the readers. Thirdly, unlike in other online forums, the commenting readers on these websites speak not only to each other but also to the journalists and editors who read and occasionally react to such opinions in their subsequent stories. In addition, because of the online tabloids' intellectually undemanding, emotional style of covering politics, the readers' often passionate comments fall well in line with the scandalizing and frequently moralizing tone of the news pieces themselves. This makes the interactions between the articles and the readers' comments appear more equal, perhaps even more democratic than they would be in a hard news outlet. There, journalistic pieces look more polished and detached than comments written by the readers, who most likely spend far less time writing them than journalists do on refining their pieces.

Each of these three online tabloids has its own stance on politics that is easily noticeable in the articles – the British Mail Online is generally known for its right-wing slant, US Gawker (and its successors) was moderately left-wing, while the Polish Pudelek tends to stick to the political center but strongly supports certain progressive issues such as LGBT+ rights – yet the comments voiced by readers can sometimes be unexpectedly profound and irrespective of the outlet's own political agenda. Still, what is particularly important in the context of broader political consequences, is that in the articles written by professionals next to comments written by laypersons during the 2015 and 2016 election campaigns, one could find voices that remained hidden from the polls, including those contrary to the particular outlet's political line. In contrast to the flawed surveys which missed voters who had been unwilling to discuss their views on the phone, the combination of these online outlets' tabloid authority together with their inclusivity "by design" made it possible for such ignored voices to be heard. This is why it is important to explore the political coverage of these highly popular online tabloids: the lens they offer allows to uncover the emotional and normative, value-laden features of the everyday, the laypersons' public sphere that can be easily lost in news media that tend to focus on more nuanced and less impassioned coverage. Thus, the following study is based on over 2,000 online tabloid articles and the most popular (i.e. upvoted) anonymous comments posted directly below concerning the 2015–2016 election campaigns in Poland, the United Kingdom, and the United States. In addition, to get a better understanding of how online tabloid political coverage is made, I conducted interviews with twenty journalists and editors who worked (some of them continue to work) for Pudelek, Mail Online, and Gawker. Interestingly, only Gawker writers decided to speak under their own names; the other interviewees (with one notable exception of a former Mail Online reporter) agreed to talk only under the condition of anonymity.

1.6 *Popular Passions*

In her famous argument about agonism, Chantal Mouffe (2000, 2013) draws a fundamental distinction between the modern liberal concept of a rational public, most famously described by Habermas, and the reality of political life. Unlike the German scholar, she views it as full of passions that are both inherent to and constitutive of any political reality, while not being necessarily detrimental to it. According to Mouffe, "[i]f there is anything that endangers democracy nowadays, it is precisely the rationalist approach, because it is blind to the nature of the political and denies the central role that passions play in the field of politics" (2000, p. 146). Instead, she proposes "agonistic pluralism," the possibility of conflict, not only rational, but also emotional, that guards against the radicalization of political stances within a democracy. I treat Mouffe's concept as a point of departure to focus on such agonistic attitudes voiced online, treating them as a helpful indicator of the every-person's political emotions rather than as a sign of the decline of democracy. I am also inspired by Daniel Dayan's (2013) idea of media visibility (see also: Brundidge and Rice 2012) according to which news media can be seen as spaces for public deliberation. I find his approach important in understanding the power of showing (and, respectively, hiding) particular agendas – here, offered by online tabloids – which may lead to considerable political effects. In addition, this work is also indebted to Zizi Papacharissi's idea of affective politics that are made possible thanks to the internet's power to "presence" viewpoints underrepresented elsewhere (Papacharissi 2015, p. 130). Finally, I believe that in this particular context online tabloids, and the readers' comments sections in particular, provide spaces where such viewpoints are not just "presenced" but amplified: firstly, on a technological level by highlighting the most upvoted comments so that they appear directly below the original articles for other readers to see and, secondly, on an editorial level by adapting to the tone of the comments in subsequent articles.

These instructive theoretical approaches serve as the starting point for my own exploration of political coverage in online tabloids, based on the basic premise that people's opinions on politics are formed both by rational calculations of their own interests (vide: Tocqueville's (2003) classic take on the matter) as well as by their political passions connected to their notions of a shared common ground. Or, at times, it is the other way round: the paradox between the emotional need to be heard and cool calculation what is a better choice for the country was strikingly voiced by a Leave voter after the Brexit referendum: "I didn't think my vote would count," he admitted after the announcement of the referendum results, and wished he had voted Remain instead.[7] These two central, intertwined, occasionally conflicting elements make society alive. Given the recent wave of populism in these and other Western countries it is crucial to take a closer look at political issues covered by such widely-read news outlets, which cater to readers who do not necessarily go there for "hard" coverage of "serious" issues but who influence political reality as voters, nonetheless.

2   A Short History of the Tabloidization of News in Poland, the United Kingdom and the United States

2.1   *Tabloid Influence on News in the UK, US and Poland: In Brief*

The origins of the word "tabloid" are appropriately tabloidy. According to Örnebring and Jönsson, it was coined in 1896 by Alfred Harmsworth (Lord Northcliffe), the founder of the British newspaper *Daily Mail*. Harmsworth "stole a term trademarked by a pill manufacturer[8] (tabloid was a combination

---

7 Mail Online labeled such people "Bregretters"; source: http://www.dailymail.co.uk/news/article-3658563/Meet-Bregretters-Public-backed-Leave-vote-say-want-STAY-EU-one-adm its-didn-t-think-vote-count.html. The topic was also covered by the Polish online tabloid: https://www.pudelek.pl/artykul/94409/brytyjczyk_glosowal_za_brexitem_teraz_jest_w _szoku_myslalem_ze_zostaniemy_w_ue/.
8 The name of the company was Burroughs Wellcome and Co.

of the words tablet and alkaloid)," since he wanted the paper "to be like a small, concentrated, effective pill, containing all news needs within one handy package, half the size of a conventional broadsheet newspaper" (2004, p. 287). Indeed, compared to broadsheet papers the tabloid format, which was half the size, was easier to read in transit – both in form and in content – for a growing number of new lower and middle-class city dwellers coming from the country. Unlike broadsheets, tabloids, originally labeled "New Journalism" in Britain, targeted non-elite readers by offering less political news and more scandalizing and human-interest stories, a playful style of writing, as well as novel layouts, all in order to appeal to the reader's eye (Griffen-Foley 2008, p. 303). Still, it is worth noting that this emotional, oversimplifying style of writing emerged even earlier in the United States, with the so-called penny press which gained popularity in the 1830s. In contrast to elite newspapers which, as Schudson puts it bluntly, "provided a service to political parties and men of commerce," the penny press offered readers a news product and at the same time turned readers into a product to be sold to advertisers (1978, p. 25). While both New Journalism in the United Kingdom and the penny press in the United States were broadly criticized for offering lowbrow content, from the onset tabloids on both sides of the Atlantic catered to a new public that was disregarded by the broadsheet, elite press. Örnebring and Jönsson go so far as to argue that tabloids constituted an alternative public sphere, "where a grassroots-based populist critique against established corporate and governmental elites could come to the fore" (2004, p. 290). An anecdotal case in point, the first interview, meaning that the "exact words" of a person in power, rather than a revised summary, were "put into print," is attributed to John Brown, a reporter at the *New York Herald*, who published the conversation in the tabloid in 1859 (see: Shuman 1903, pp. 47–48). In short, from the start tabloids were dangerous to the existing elite-centered public sphere. This was not only because they provided coverage that was scandalizing, dumbing down, and sometimes openly dishonest, as Örnebring and Jönsson emphasize, but also because tabloids challenged the audience of the elite broadsheets by choosing to speak to – and thus create – a new readership. As it turned out, this approach proved effective.

In their seminal book, *Comparing media systems: Three models of media and politics*, Hallin and Mancini (2004) describe the history of three models of media dominant in Western Europe and North America, where tabloids have also been playing a significant part. The first of the three, the Liberal model is most prominent in the United Kingdom, Ireland, and North American countries. It is a considerably commercialized media system, in which journalists share a strong sense of independence and professionalism, as well as believe in the importance of neutral reporting. In the Democratic Corporatist model – found in Nordic countries, in addition to Germany and Austria – one can notice far more activity of the state in media than in the Liberal Model, albeit legally limited, next to the influence of organized professional bodies, including journalists. Finally, the third model is the Polarized Pluralist one, found most notably in Europe's Mediterranean countries. There, the media – as the model's name suggests – are largely polarized across political party lines and are financially supported by political organizations. Moreover, journalism is not well developed as an independent profession and the roles of politician and journalist tend to be intertwined. As a consequence, in the Polarized Pluralist model political commentary is more important than neutral reporting, since readers are considered to be in need to be "pushed" to support particular views. Yet, unlike in the Democratic Corporatist model or the Liberal model, readership is low and generally limited to the elites. Notably, according to Hallin and Mancini tabloids are rarely found in the Polarized Pluralist model, while being prominent in the Liberal model – especially in the UK – as well as in the Democratic Corporatist model, although in the latter case they cater to a more middle-brow audience than the British tabloids (p. 158f).

The United States and the United Kingdom are prime examples of the Liberal model. Not only did the news industry develop there earliest as a commercial enterprise replacing newspapers as political parties' mouthpieces. Along with it came the professionalization of journalism and the general, increasingly influential concept of the job as that of a neutral reporter or watchdog who keeps an eye on people in power, in the name of ordinary citizens. Because of early commercialization, in the Liberal model journalists were freed from party alliances but instead became dependent on advertising and subscriptions. Obviously, this commercial focus has also been fundamental to the development of tabloids which, filled with scandal and entertainment, claim to adopt the stance of their readers, the average Joes and Janes. Poland, however, is more difficult to pinpoint within Hallin and Mancini's categories. It is mentioned by the authors only briefly, given the country's geographical location in Central-Eastern Europe but also, perhaps more importantly, because of her postwar history marked by forced membership in the Soviet Bloc until 1989.[9] Poland's media grew considerably before 1939, in many ways following the Polarized Pluralist model with politicized journalists and a relatively small readership. At the same time, however, since the 19th

---

9   In *Comparing media systems* ... Hallin and Mancini place Poland within the Democratic Corporatist model, a choice I find debatable. However, in a follow-up to the original book the scholars published an edited volume, *Comparing media systems beyond the Western*

century the Polish press had been influenced by the Democratic Corporatist model coming from Austro-Hungary and Prussia, which together with Russia had ruled over different parts of the partitioned country from the end of the 18th century until the end of the First World War. After further media growth throughout the two interwar decades, in the 1945–1989 Communist period that followed, journalism, under virtual state monopoly, developed differently in Poland than in her Western-European counterparts. Nonetheless, because Polish journalism's strong pre-1939 heritage also influenced journalists under Communism, today the country's media landscape presents an interesting mix of all three models: professionalized journalists as in the Liberal and Democratic Corporatist models; a relatively low readership and visible presence of the state in media typical for the Polarized Pluralist model; yet accompanied by significant commercialization of the industry, much like in the Liberal model (Dobek-Ostrowska 2012). Bearing in mind this general systemic outlook on the development of media, in the following paragraphs I present brief outlines of the changes in readership of tabloids in the United Kingdom, the United States and Poland, since their emergence until today, in a news industry profoundly transformed by the internet.

2.2 United Kingdom

In the UK, for over a century tabloids enjoyed the highest circulation among all dailies, with papers such as *Daily Mirror*, *Daily Express*, *Daily Mail*, and *The Sun* surpassing the best-performing broadsheet papers at least twofold and running millions of copies each day.[10] *Daily Mirror*, intended for the working class, and also founded by Harmsworth, was UK's best-selling daily for three decades, from its launch in 1903 until the 1930s, when it was surpassed by the more right-wing tabloids *Daily Express* and *Daily Mail*,[11] as well as by the *Daily Herald*. The paper regained its top position after the Second World War and was the most-read daily for almost twenty years (with peak circulation above 5 million) until the lead was taken by Rupert Murdoch's *The Sun*, a relative newcomer launched only in 1964, which replaced the closed *Daily Herald*. The successor achieved its highest circulation of around 4 million in

---

 world (2012), where the case of Poland is discussed in detail by Dobek-Ostrowska who offers a more nuanced take on the country's media system.
10 Compare e.g. *The Sun's* more than 3.7 million copies with the best-selling broadsheet paper *The Daily Telegraph's* less than 1.5 million copies in the 1980s, which were still considered good times for newspaper circulation in the UK.
11 Although *Daily Mail* is one of the most famous tabloids in the world, the paper kept its broadsheet format until 1971.

the 1980s. Interestingly, at the end of the 1990s the more Conservative-leaning *Daily Mail* replaced the Labour-oriented *Daily Mirror* in second place. *Daily Mail* came close to *The Sun*[12] in 2020, over two decades later, but with both papers' circulation dropped, around a mere 1.2 million. A general decline in print circulation has been observed since the aughts and has been universally blamed on the internet. Paradoxically, thanks to the internet circulation counted in the millions has broadened beyond tabloids: for example, digital subscriptions have significantly helped the old broadsheet, *Financial Times*, which reported over 1.2 million in total circulation and digital subscriptions in 2020.[13] Still, *Metro*, the free daily launched in 1999, which is also owned by *Daily Mail's* publisher, but with a far more neutral political stance, has been enjoying the highest circulation among all British dailies since 2018 when it topped *The Sun*; in 2020 *Metro's* circulation was around 1.4 million copies. To put these numbers in perspective, *Mail Online* boasts 12 million unique visitors per day, which is ten times more than its print version, and claims to be the most-read news website in the world. At the same time, in terms of both online and offline reach, half of the British newspaper landscape is divided between three players: the tabloids *The Sun* and *Daily Mail*, and the daily *The Guardian*. In terms of newspaper revenue, the market is even more consolidated as only two companies comprise half of the British newspaper market share: News Corp, owned by Murdoch, which publishes the tabloid *The Sun* and the broadsheet *The Times*; and DMG Media, owned by Lord Rothermere, which publishes *Daily Mail*. As for the top news websites in the UK, the website of *The Guardian* and *Daily Mail's* Mail Online top the charts in terms of total monthly visits, both well above 300 million, while the digital-native news website Buzzfeed comes in third place with 109 million visits per month. There are some swaps, too: in contrast to print circulation, the online version of *The Mirror* ranks higher than the online *The Sun*, with 91.3 million and 86.8 million monthly visits respectively.[14]

2.3 United States

In the United States tabloids have been more successful in weekly rather than daily editions, particularly the "supermarket tabloid" versions – as the name suggests, papers sold in large food stores instead of newsstands. The most popular one among them, *National Enquirer* enjoyed the highest

---

12 Pun not (entirely) intended.
13 Data from July 2020; see: https://www2.fipp.com/global-digital-subscription-snapshot-2020-q3.
14 Data from January 2019; see: Ramsay 2019.

circulation in the 1970s, when it reached over 5 million copies (see: Sloan 2001, p. 218). Its current circulation is a mere shadow of its former tabloid glory, around 240 thousand copies, less than five percent of the circulation enjoyed half a century ago. Interestingly, *National Enquirer* was originally founded in 1926 as a broadsheet, and was turned into a hugely successful tabloid in 1952 by its new owner, Pope Generoso Jr. While in 1995, four decades later, the weekly enjoyed a circulation of around 2.5 million copies, it dropped significantly in the aughts (blame the internet) and has been plummeting ever since. The trends have been similar with *Globe*, *National Enquirer's* main competitor, which was launched in 1954. However, *Globe* had a somewhat stronger focus on politics. Since the 1990s, both tabloid weeklies had been owned by the same company, American Media Inc., and despite the pessimistic statistics they were bought by Hudson News in 2019. Although in general the supermarket tabloids, replaced by the internet, have been clearly losing out in the 21st century, two daily tabloids, both located in New York – *Daily News* and *New York Post* – remain prominent. Of the two, *Daily News*, the US tabloid most influenced by its British counterparts, was launched after the end of the First World War. Although it was directly inspired by the left-wing *Daily Mirror*, the paper became more right-leaning later on, and when *Daily News* achieved its peak popularity in the late 1940s its circulation was over 2.4 million copies. In the 1970s, *Daily News* was challenged by another daily tabloid from the Big Apple, *New York Post*. The latter had an impressive pedigree, having been founded as an elite broadsheet in 1801 by one of the United States' Founding Fathers, Alexander Hamilton. 175 years later it was bought by Murdoch and turned into a tabloid. While in its broadsheet era in the late 1960s *New York Post* enjoyed a circulation of up to 700 thousand copies, it reached its all-time high of over a 1.1 million copies in 1977, a year after it had become an outlet for scandalizing stories. Still, it is worthy to put these numbers in perspective and compare them with other US dailies: the much younger general-interest paper, *USA Today*, launched in 1982, has been one of the top-selling US dailies, and reached its peak circulation of 6.6 million copies in 1991. The top tabloid at the time, *National Enquirer* shared less than a half of *USA Today's* circulation. Fast forward twenty years later, the finance-focused broadsheet *Wall Street Journal*, originally launched in 1889 – and currently owned by Murdoch – gained top position among US dailies at the beginning of the 2010s, and claimed print circulation above 1 million in 2019. As in the UK, the internet has helped some US papers and online subscriptions have been significantly impacting readership rankings, with *The New York Times* being the recent winner. In 2020 the "Gray Lady" reported circulation close to 5.5 million including digital subscriptions, compared to *Wall Street Journal's* 3.2 million, *Washington Post's* 2.2 million, and

USA Today's 1.6 million.[15] In comparison, before its closing in late August 2016, Gawker claimed 30 million unique visitors per month. In terms of newspaper revenue, the most successful companies include Gannett, the publisher of *USA Today* and other papers; Advance Publications, which owns Condé Nast, in addition to a number of local newspapers, and is the largest shareholder of the website Reddit.com; and Tribune Publishing, the largest newspaper publisher, measured by circulation, owner of *Chicago Tribune* and *New York Daily News*, as well as other papers.[16] As for US top news websites, Yahoo News comes in first place with 175 million monthly visitors, followed by Google News with 150 million, and Huffington Post comes in third, with 110 million visitors per month. All of the top three outlets are digital-native websites, and Google News does not even produce original content. The website of the CNN television channel is ranked fourth (95 million monthly visitors), while the most popular online version of a newspaper, *The New York Times* is the fifth most visited news website in the United States (70 million). Still, the US version of the British Mail Online is also highly popular and is currently visited in the US by 53 million visitors per month. However, it is also worth noting that websites of the dailies *USA Today* and *LA Times* – ranked 14 and 15 respectively – attracted similar numbers of visitors in 2020 as the online tabloid Gawker did at the time of its closure in 2016.[17]

2.4 Poland

Although the Polish press did not play such a significant part in creating the tabloid genre as the United Kingdom or the United States, the scandalizing format was successfully adopted in the interwar period in Poland, after she had regained independence in 1918, in consequence of the First World War. Called "czerwoniaki" ("reddies," a Polish version of "red tops"), or "revolver press" because of the crimes regularly reported on their pages, Polish tabloids quickly became hugely popular, most notably *Kurier Czerwony* ("Red Dispatch")[18] and *Express Poranny* ("Morning Express"), both of which were launched in 1922 by

---

15   Data from July 2020; see: https://www2.fipp.com/global-digital-subscription-snaps hot-2020-q3.
16   Data from 2018; see: https://www.freepress.net/issues/media-control/media-consolidat ion/who-owns-media; see also: Abernathy 2016.
17   Data from August 2020; see: https://www.statista.com/statistics/381569/leading-news -and-media-sites-usa-by-share-of-visits/.
18   *Kurier Czerwony*, launched in 1922, was originally titled *Kurier Informacyjny i Telegraficzny* ("Information and Telegraphic Dispatch") but the name was changed in 1925 (Paczkowski 1983, p. 194). After the paper merged with *Dobry Wieczór* ("Good Evening") in 1932, the name was changed again, this time into *Dobry Wieczór! Kurier Czerwony*.

the same public company, Prasa Polska SA (Polish Press Co.).[19] As was the case in the UK and the US, unlike more elite dailies Polish tabloids aimed primarily at generating profit. This was achieved by creating news fit to be read "by any man on the street and any woman in the kitchen" (Władyka 1982, p. 13), but tabloids were also generally considered pro-government (Paczkowski 1983, pp. 198, 200). The need to attract readers was the driver of technological innovation and, for example, *Kurier Czerwony* was the first Polish newspaper to use what we would today call infographics; these came in handy especially when describing crime scenes (Osęka 2015). The sensationalism next to technical advancements in printing photos and fresh layouts undeniably worked, and by the mid-1930s *Kurier Czerwony* had the highest circulation – up to 83 thousand copies – among dailies published in Warsaw, Poland's major press hub and market. *Express Poranny* came in third place, with circulation close to 59 thousand. However, the middle spot was taken by a general-readership newspaper, *Wieczór Warszawski* ("Warsaw Evening") with over 66 thousand copies, making it one of the top-selling dailies in Warsaw throughout the 1930s (Paczkowski 1976, pp. 78–95). Nevertheless, the top daily in terms of circulation in interwar Poland was a Catholic one, *Mały Dziennik* ("Little Daily"), headed by Maximilian Kolbe, a Franciscan friar, and published at the monastery in Niepokalanów, a small town close to Warsaw. Bearing a style inspired by tabloids but with a strongly right-wing and traditionalist agenda, *Mały Dziennik* enjoyed circulation up to 120 thousand, a quarter more than *Kurier Czerwony*. Still, it is worth remembering that the paper's popularity was significantly aided by distribution in Catholic churches and by the free labor of priests in the daily's printing house. Particularly the latter sparked accusations of dumping, made by other presses (Paczkowski 1983, p. 226f). In the Communist period that came as a result of the Second World War and lasted till 1989, the press was almost single-handedly managed by the Polish Communist Party's Robotnicza Spółdzielnia Wydawnicza "Prasa-Książka-Ruch" (Workers' Publishing Cooperative "Press-Book-Movement"),[20] and prewar-style tabloids disappeared. The daily that came closest to sensationalism at the time was *Express Wieczorny* ("Evening Express") but it was far more tame than the prewar or post-1989 tabloids in Poland. Nonetheless,

---

19 The company, owned by Henryk Butkiewicz, Antoni Lewandowski and initially also by Adam Nowicki, Jerzy Plewiński and Jan Zagleniczny, changed its name to Dom Prasy SA (House of the Press Co.) after changes in ownership in 1934 (Paczkowski 1983, pp. 197, 204).
20 From 1948 the press was managed by RSW "Prasa"; it was turned into RSW "Prasa-Książka-Ruch" as a result of a merger with the book publisher "Książka i Wiedza" and the monopolist press distributor "Ruch" in 1973 (Drygalski and Kwaśniewski 1992, p. 230).

it was a bestseller, with circulation around 800 thousand in the 1970s and 450 thousand in the 1980s (Mielczarek 1998, p. 172). One of the reasons for the popularity of *Express Wieczorny* was that it employed highly popular writers, including Stefan Wiechecki "Wiech," one of the most known authors of the prewar tabloid, *Kurier Czerwony*. After the fall of the Iron Curtain and start of Poland's democratic transition, in 1991 journalists from *Express Wieczorny* founded *Super Express*, this time a proper sensationalist and celebrity-filled tabloid. It proved a huge success and has been one of the top-selling dailies in Poland ever since, reaching its peak circulation around 480 thousand in the mid-1990s. Yet the daily with the highest circulation is the tabloid *Fakt*, launched over a decade later, in 2003. Interestingly, it was also the first daily to top the circulation of the opinion daily *Gazeta Wyborcza*, which had been the most popular daily since its launch by pro-democratic dissidents in 1989 (this being yet another example of the difficulty in pinpointing Poland's media model). *Fakt's* peak circulation was around 700 thousand, and was reached in its first year, with *Gazeta Wyborcza's* over 600 thousand at a similar time. Since then, the Polish dailies have been experiencing a comparable decline in print circulation to that in the United Kingdom and the United States, caused by the rise of the internet. Today, the tabloid *Fakt* still tops the charts with print circulation close to 300 thousand.[21] However, with online subscriptions of newspapers on the rise, *Gazeta Wyborcza* recently reported 218 thousand online subscriptions, landing in 23. place for dailies worldwide.[22] This gives the opinion daily an estimated total of over 360 thousand copies, but so far combined measures for online and offline newspaper circulation in Poland have been lacking.[23] At the same time, the number of unique visitors on Pudelek is around 5 million. In terms of news media concentration, over half of the Polish press market is divided between three major players: Ringier Axel Springer Polska (RASP), a German, US and Swiss-owned company, the publisher of *Fakt* in addition to other magazines, as well as of the top Polish news website, Onet. pl; ZPR Media, publisher of the second most-popular tabloid, *Super Express* as well as other magazines and associated websites, in addition to owning several radio stations; and Agora SA, which publishes the most-read opinion daily, *Gazeta Wyborcza*, a number of specialist magazines, besides books, music and films, and owns popular news websites Gazeta.pl and Wyborcza.pl (the latter

---

21 Data from May 2020; see: www.teleskop.org.pl.
22 Data from July 2020; see: https://www2.fipp.com/global-digital-subscription-snapshot-2020-q3.
23 Unfortunately, information about digital subscriptions of dailies is patchy, hence the circulation of print and online editions is only an estimate.

an online version of the opinion daily), a cinema chain, several radio stations, and a major outdoor advertising company.[24] As for Polish news websites, the most popular is Onet.pl, owned by RASP, with over 12 million monthly viewers, followed by wp.pl (Wirtualna Polska) and o2.pl, each viewed by over 10 million users per month, and both owned by Grupa Wirtualna Polska (Virtual Poland Group), which also publishes Pudelek. Se.pl, the online version of the paper tabloid, *Super Express* is ranked fourth with well over 9.5 million views, while the online version of *Fakt*, fakt.pl (also owned by RASP), comes in tenth with over 7 million monthly viewers – 2 million more than Pudelek.[25]

In sum, as circulation numbers from these three countries show, availability in both physical and digital forms has been helping papers' readership, with significant gains for broadsheets, such as *The New York Times*, *Financial Times*, and *Gazeta Wyborcza*, although, unsurprisingly, because of the language the latter reaches far less readers. Nonetheless, the recent years and the 2020 coronavirus pandemic in particular have shown that people continue to read daily news offered by newspaper publishers, but are increasingly doing so online. Then again, it is worth noting that the three online tabloid news providers, Pudelek, Mail Online and Gawker offer their content free of charge and enjoy (in the case of Gawker: enjoyed) a viewership several-fold greater than most opinion dailies. Traditional newspapers, though increasingly successful in their digital versions, are still forced to compete for people's eyeballs and for their wallets with entertaining, sensationalizing online competitors.[26]

3 How Did We Get Here? Tabloidization of News-Making Today

3.1 *"Tabloidization," or a Definition of Power*

Although the accusations of "tabloidization" are over a century long, almost as old as the daily press itself, the word has been around for only about three decades (Rowe 2011, p. 452). The most common definition of tabloidization goes something like this: "a downgrading of hard news and upgrading of sex,

---

24 Data from 2020; see: https://www.pbc.pl/rynek-sprzedazy/; in addition, Dzierżyńska-Mielcarek (2018) provides a more detailed view of the recent changes in ownership in the Polish news media market.
25 Data from November 2020; see: https://www.wirtualnemedia.pl/artykul/serwisy-informacyjno-publicystyczne-top-10-listopad-2020-onet-i-wp-ze-spadkami-o2-pl-i-se-pl-przed-naszemiasto-tvn24-pl-i-wyborcza-pl.
26 This is particularly interesting in the case of the British Mail Online, a digital spinoff of *Daily Mail*, which shares the paper's offline news but includes its own online editorial staff. This will be further discussed in the following chapters.

scandal and infotainment" (Esser 1999, p. 292). Essentially, it boils down to pointing a finger at tabloid style as the culprit for the overall deterioration of quality across media platforms, from newspapers to radio and television – not to mention the internet, which has been "tabloidized" from the very beginning (Magin 2019), with its focus on attracting attention e.g. by using "clickbait." Gripsrud is only slightly more generous in his understanding of the term "tabloidization" when he writes, "some forms of popular and tabloid journalism may be good for some purposes and not for others, while some other forms are probably good for nothing much" (2000, p. 285). Still, as scholars point out (e.g. Esser 1999; Otto, Glogger and Boukes 2017), the word itself is "diffuse." By lacking clarity, it allows anything that does not meet the criteria of hard news (a comparatively vague term) to be jumbled under the wide umbrella of "tabloidization." This is why, instead, Otto, Glogger and Boukes propose to look at the different characteristics of news that make them to a greater or lesser extent "tabloidized." This includes adopting a commercial focus; mixing information and entertainment (i.e. infotainment); covering non-political topics or paying attention to personal stories within the broader framework of political coverage (i.e. soft news); and using emotional language and extensive visuals to cause an impassioned reaction from readers (i.e. sensationalism) (2017, p. 140f). Another popular distinction, that between soft and hard news, is not any less blurry. Briefly put, hard news focuses on politics, the economy and social issues; in contrast, soft news focuses on gossip and human-interest stories (Lehman-Wilzig and Seletzky 2010, pp. 37–38). Accordingly, the distinction between elite and popular press is equally vague, centering on educational levels and social class of the readers, which indicate their access to power and therefore their interest in particular news topics. As Magin writes pointedly, "[i]n the case of the elite press, the small, but powerful readership results in major importance of the newspapers in the public discourse. (…) In the case of the popular press (and particularly the tabloids as one of its subtypes), the influence results from their mass readerships and their campaign journalism" (2019, p. 2). Another argument that further complicates the unclear lines between hard/elite and soft/popular news, concerns the very definition of political coverage, which is at the heart of the former. Two decades before Magin, Sparks wrote that "if one broadens one's notion of politics from the traditional concern with the state and its works to include a much wider range of life experiences, then one would find that the popular press is indeed stuffed with politics" (1988, p. 214). This observation emphasizes the fact that from the point of view of political coverage the difference between tabloid and non-tabloid press is not just the quantity of political news items but what counts as politics in general. Seaton and Pimlott, quoted by Sparks, emphasize that in fact, "non-political media coverage is politically more important in the long run than overtly political material because of the role of the media in establishing or modifying acceptable values" (1987, p. x). In this sense, anything visible in the media is potentially political. To illustrate this, the authors point out that entertainment-writing about positive black characters in soap operas has possibly more power in the fight against racism than hard-news coverage of political debates on the issue. Gripsrud (2000) suggests a still different take and reverses the usual argument about the tabloidization of hard-news press. Instead of looking top-down from hard news to soft news, he poses a somewhat meta-question whether it is at all possible for a tabloid to not be "trash" (p. 291). For Gripsrud the answer is: yes. He states, "Tabloid may sometimes be useful and relevant popular journalism; trash may at best be brutal entertainment." The author then goes on to explain the meaning of trash journalism, which he defines as journalism lacking values: "Trash is on the whole probably best defined by its disregard of ethics – both ethics in general (exploitation of sources, participants, and so on) and the professional ethos of journalism" (p. 292).

Thus, taking these different arguments together, if not all hard news is necessarily *good*, in that it struggles to appeal to broader audiences, not all tabloid news is necessarily *bad*, when personalization and sensationalist style serve to inform, not merely entertain. Gans (2009) echoes this notion, arguing that tabloidization is in fact a way of popularizing news among the non-elites. Bastos (2019) goes even further by pointing out that the black-and-white distinction between hard-news broadsheets and soft-news tabloids is merely ostensible, and that "the polarity would be better represented as a spectrum rather than a gap between tabloids and quality newspapers." This stark opposition between hard and soft news has also been critiqued from a feminist perspective. For example, according to Lumby (1997), quoted by Turner, accusing tabloids of the deterioration of the public sphere in the end serves to protect "traditional definitions of what matters in 'public affairs' – business, parliamentary politics, economics, the law and so on." Lumby argues that such an agenda should be "challenged by the private, the domestic – above all, by the feminine" (Turner 1999, pp. 61–62). According to this concept, hard news can be seen as "masculine" while tabloid news as "feminine" – and indeed, readership statistics show that tabloids are more often read by women than men (see e.g.: Johansson 2007; Rosentiel 2008). Finally, Sparks makes a valid, even if often overlooked, point when he states the seemingly obvious:

> [P]olitical and economic power in a stable bourgeois democracy is so far removed from the real lives of the mass of the population that they have

no interest, in either sense, in monitoring its disposal. The infrequent rituals of elections apart, there exist few if any channels whereby any opinion that anyone might hold can be implemented or even heard. Football matches take place every week in winter and anyone who cares to pay for a ticket can go along and cheer. Consequently, it should not come as a surprise to find that political life is most fully covered in just those periods when people get a say, however limited, in political life, whereas football matches get reported in detail with great regularity.

1988, p. 217

This comparison is particularly illuminating because in the stark opposition between readership (class) interests – hard-news politics versus tabloid football – one can also find the key issue lying at the intersection of tabloid news entertainment and elite news political coverage: the sense of personal agency. Readers of broadsheets are assumed to be interested in the nuances of power, be it political, economic or cultural, because they feel they are able to influence it. In contrast, readers of tabloids show interest in entertainment and human-interest stories because they are assumed to feel and thus be powerless (see: Couldry, Livingstone and Markham 2007).

The sensationalizing, entertaining and simplifying style has certainly proved effective in grabbing audience attention. Still, the broader reasons for the overall success of the tabloidization of news lie in the fact that the desire for greater profits – which tabloids have generally shown to be good at generating – has been competing with other issues, such as political agenda particular news outlets have been standing for. In short: if fighting for workers' rights (as done e.g. by *Daily Mirror* and *Kurier Czerwony*) won't cut it financially, then sex and crime stories, preferably of the rich and famous, probably will. Esser sees tabloidization as a form of "contamination" of "quality press." Thus, for him tabloidization manifests something much more profound: it "can be seen as a social phenomenon both instigating and symbolizing major changes to the constitution of society," where successful political marketing is more important than education. The consequence of this is "an increase in political alienation" (1999, p. 293). This means that tabloidization relates not just to the sphere of news media but to people's general interest in the public sphere, and according to Esser the outcome is rather grim.

3.2   *Default Online Tabloid Style: Backstory*
Although tabloids are often perceived as broadsheets' ugly sisters, many characteristics of tabloids – including paper size, attention-grabbing headlines and images, story length, human-interest and celebrity content – have not

only proven inventive, but a number of tabloid features have been embraced by non-tabloid papers (Rowe 2011). Today, it is even more difficult to pinpoint straightforward tabloids on the web, as the style has been widely adopted on the internet, which in turn has become the personalized, emotional, attention-grabbing, many-to-many medium *par excellence*.[27] ("The information superhighway is a two-way street" as the popular saying goes.) After all, Bingham and Conboy stress that "tabloid values [have] colonized the media landscape" (2015, p. 228) in its entirety, and this includes digital media. One such early example of tabloid style finding its way on the internet – and later in online versions of mainstream media – was the Drudge Report. The "strange brew of media, political and showbiz tidbits," as Allan (2006, p. 39) described it, broke the story about the Monica Lewinsky scandal in 1998.[28] The website was created by Matt Drudge, an online writer without journalistic training who had worked at a gift shop at Studio City in Los Angeles, a place which proved perfect for media-related gossip. As the Drudge Report grew in popularity, its readers became the site's sources of tips, next to late-night news and radio shows, a mix of sources now often found in online tabloids. If the Drudge Report was the first online tabloid, Allan argues that the 1995 Oklahoma City bombing could be labeled as the first event in which "the potential of news sites for providing breaking news became readily apparent to advocates and critics alike within journalism's inner circles" (2006, p. 18). News commentary blogs, these chronologically organized online diaries, began to be noticed by journalists in the second half of the 1990s, even if with some initial disdain (pretty much directed at the internet as such). Among them, MediaGossip.com was one of the more popular, and focused specifically on "juicy tidbits about newspurveyors" (Allan 2006, p. 51). In its form and scope this site was the precursor of Gawker, which was launched in 2002. However, the world wide web's tabloid potential became undeniable in the aftermath of Princess Diana's death in a car crash in Paris in 1997, blamed on tabloid paparazzi. Although the photo of the fatal crash was rejected by newspapers and television stations, it emerged on Rotten.com, another tabloid website, a few days after the event. So many people clicked on the website where the image – which later turned out to be fake – had been posted, the site broke down (Allan 2006, p. 28). A 'Web expert' commented at the time, "The Net always contains the most scandalous,

---

27 In fact, the term "tabloidization" has been used to describe the deterioration of quality and growing role of entertainment across different media, notably television talk and reality shows. See e.g.: Bingham and Conboy 2015; Turner 1999.
28 See archived version: https://australianpolitics.com/1998/01/17/original-drudge-reports-lewinsky-scandal.html.

dubious and exploitative information you might possibly want or stumble into" (McNamara 1997, p. 65). Many would still agree with this today.

Fast-forward to 2005, during a speech to the American Society of Newspaper Editors the media mogul Rupert Murdoch of News Corporation lamented, "Scarcely a day goes by without some claim that new technologies are fast writing newsprint's obituary" (Allan 2006, p. 2). Online versions of newspapers started popping up in the mid-1990s, competing with web portals (e.g. Yahoo, America Online, MSN, as well as Onet.pl and Wirtualna Polska in Poland) and websites of other traditional news media (e.g. CNN, BBC, Fox News) which emerged with the spread of the world wide web in people's households. By the mid aughts, as BBC's Director of Global News Richard Sambrook (2006) admitted, news organizations did "not own the news any more," and the possibility of tailoring online news items to one's own individual taste meant that hard news on current affairs was often replaced with celebrity gossip and sports. According to Nielsen people have been spending no more than three percent of their time on the internet following the news (2016, p. 53). At the same time, the tabloid style of catchy headlines and big photos proved particularly well suited for the online world, including social media such as Facebook and Twitter, which in the last decade have become major entry points for people to access the news (Roston 2015). Thus, it was no surprise that clickbait turned out to be the tabloid-style invention tailored for the online world (e.g. Munger 2020). As the name suggests, the aim of such a news piece is to attract attention (i.e. clicks) and generate revenue thanks to ads placed on the webpage. Bastos goes even further, arguing that clickbait news sites are examples "of extreme tabloidization, with celebrity news as an endemic phenomenon that has found a place across the entire news business and beyond the niche market of tabloid media" (2017, p. 223). It is then no surprise that online tabloids including Gawker, Mail Online and Pudelek have been fighting for attention by producing clickbaity, infotaining, sensationalizing pieces using punchy headlines and large-sized photos, often reusing content from other sources to keep the production costs low, all the while being able to attract large audiences by offering content for free (Nielsen 2016, pp. 60–61).[29]

---

29 Nevertheless, Nielsen notes that although "[d]igital advertising is growing rapidly, (...) legacy platforms still account for three quarters of global advertising spending." (2016, p. 61).

3.3 Tabloid Influence: Political Scandal

Discussions about the role of tabloids in the Habermasian (1974) public sphere, or more specifically in the spheres of civic engagement and politics,[30] have been generally going in two very different directions: according to the first one, tabloids are responsible for dumbing down publics and making people disinterested in matters of civic concern by offering a steady flow of entertainment drivel. According to the other one, tabloids are platforms for inclusion of non-elite voices and their interests; in so doing tabloids broaden the sphere of civic engagement, however broadly understood. Regardless of one's stance towards tabloids, they have been operating in an increasingly tabloidizing (sic) environment of "churnalism," the cutting and pasting of news items written by other journalists, without attribution (Davies 2009); "newszak," or poor-quality news (e.g. Allan 2010; Franklin 1997); and infotainment (e.g. Otto, Glogger and Boukes 2017), which all have been transforming news media. What's more, from the beginning tabloids have been playing a powerful role in the sphere of politics, not only by adopting more liberal or more conservative positions tailored to their readers, but also by influencing politics directly, such as playing a vital part in uncovering political scandals (e.g. Tumber 2004).

One such prime example of online tabloid influence is the previously mentioned Clinton-Lewinsky sex scandal in the US, uncovered by Drudge Report. The heavily covered story, which nearly cost Bill Clinton his presidency, came to haunt Hillary Clinton eighteen years later during her own unsuccessful presidential campaign against Donald Trump (McNair 2019). In the UK, a largely discussed recent case in which a tabloid became both the subject and the object of scandal, concerned phone hacking conducted by *The News of the World*,[31] at the time of the event a Sunday sister paper of *The Sun*. The story of the paper's illegal phone tapping of politicians, celebrities, families of murder victims, and members of the British royal family developed throughout the second half of the aughts, closely covered by *The Guardian*, and led to the tabloid's closure in 2011, after 168 years in print. The subsequent judicial public inquiry, named the Leveson Inquiry after its chair, Lord Justice Leveson, was carried out to reveal the practices and ethics of the British press. As a result, the so-called Leveson Report was published in 2012. It offered a number of

---

30   I understand them broadly as spaces of communication, including both rational discussion (vide: Habermas) and emotions (vide: Mouffe).
31   It is worth noting that the weekly tabloid was mostly known for its paper version, which was twice as popular as the website. Before *The News of the World* closed down on 10th of July 2011 the paper's print circulation was around 2.5 million, while its online viewership was only around 1.1 million unique visitors. See: Lovett 2011; Mediatique 2018.

recommendations, including creating a new commission for press complaints. However, adequate legislation was never introduced. In Poland, too, an interesting recent case of visible political influence could be found in the online tabloid, Pudelek. At the end of 2011 the website became strongly involved in the anti-ACTA (Anti-Counterfeiting Trade Agreement) protests and encouraged people to take part in demonstrations against the proposed EU bill. Many feared the proposed legislation would limit access to content on the internet and was labeled by its critics as a threat to the freedom of speech. Unlike the previously mentioned cases in the US and the UK, the focus of this particular scandal was not individuals but cyberspace; the untransparent way the legislation was passed in the EU also fueled people's outrage. ACTA aggravated people, particularly younger ones for whom the internet played a major part in their lives as a place for acquiring (not always legal) content, as well as for creating and sharing material. The article against the ACTA legislation posted on Pudelek[32] which, as I learned later, had been written by one of the site's co-founders, was the first non-ironic, earnest political piece published there, and one of the most commented on the site until today. It was one of the few times when Pudelek's editorial team straightforwardly voiced its liberal and anti-establishment views: the EU regulation would significantly benefit companies which owned the copyrights, at the cost of citizens. As a result of the large protests that took place throughout the country, ACTA was not ratified by the Polish parliament and was later dropped by the European Union. This came as a blow particularly to large companies, which had hoped to use the legislation to curb online piracy. In this sense, Pudelek won. Paradoxically, online piracy has been falling since then, although this is largely attributed to the development of legal streaming services providing access to vast libraries of music and films for a fee (see e.g.: BSA 2018).

Scandals not only uncover the values shared by the public, they are also "analytically rich events for understanding dynamics and structures in public communication" (Tumber and Waisbord 2019, p. 19). Such events point at the numerous roles played by the news media, from calling truth to power to providing entertainment. Because of this, scandals fit in the realm of journalism perfectly since they offer novelty, which is a newsworthy deviation from the norm (Just and Crigler 2019). In addition, the coverage of scandals generally tends to be negative, and bad news is known to gather more attention than good news (see e.g.: Harcup and O'Neill 2017). What's more, scandals are

---

32 See: https://www.pudelek.pl/artykul/38176/acta_czyli_jak_celebryci_stracili_kontakt_z_rzeczywistoscia/.

often focused on individuals rather than institutions, which makes them easier to follow; in this sense, scandals are tailor-made for tabloids. Thompson (2000), in his important work on political scandal identifies five characteristics that make an occurrence a "scandal": firstly, it transgresses values, norms and moral codes; secondly, it is concealed but is strongly believed to exist by non-participants; thirdly, some of these non-participants are offended by this transgression; fourthly, some non-participants publicly denounce these occurrences; and, finally, revealing these occurrences may damage the reputation of those responsible for them (pp. 13–14). In addition to this list, McNair (2019) points out the importance of another feature: for a scandal to happen it requires hypocrisy first. A person who commits a scandalous act not only has to be caught going against commonly shared norms, but in so doing has to contradict the values he or she publicly professes.[33] Tumber and Waisbord (2019) adopt a broader stance, arguing that the focus on scandals is a typical feature of democracies but also an indicator of the mediatization of the public sphere, especially politics. In short, democracy and scandal go hand in hand. However, research conducted by Umbricht and Esser (2016) shows that while the growing commercialization and tabloidization of news has led to more scandal-focused coverage, not all countries are equally prone to producing news coverage of political scandals. Significant markers of whether political news in a particular country will skew towards scandal are high levels of polarization of political and media systems, and a liberal model of journalism. Unlike e.g. Germany and the Nordic countries, the United States, the United Kingdom, and Poland are thus prime examples of such scandal-prone news environments (Hallin and Mancini 2004; 2012).

How is scandalizing online tabloid news done? In the case of Pudelek, Mail Online and Gawker, but possibly also other such outlets, firstly, this includes presenting political news items by emphasizing both text and image; secondly, the online layout of news pieces appears to work seamlessly together with the readers' comments; and thirdly, the meanings and values presented in the stories – the heroes and the villains, deeds good and bad – are shaped, negotiated, and occasionally shifted in a continuous online interaction between journalists and the commenting readers. Political stories inform readers about issues that may influence their actions as citizens, including their decisions at the ballot box – even if, contrary to popular opinion, online tabloid readers are generally well educated and claim to add other, more hard-news sources to

---

33   According to McNair (2019), this is why allegations of sexual misconduct made against Donald Trump during the US 2016 presidential campaign did not tarnish his reputation – he never claimed not to be sexist.

their news diet. While the tabloid style of writing has largely permeated the news industry because of its effectiveness in attracting attention and generating profit, the conversational, inviting, tongue-in-cheek, entertaining style of online tabloids that will be discussed in further detail in the following chapters, is something often absent in other, more hard-news focused outlets. This particular language, too, is an integral feature in the online-tabloid cultural framing of politics.

3.4 The Cultural Frame for Politics in Online Tabloids

When we set politics within a cultural frame, we discuss political heroes and villains, those who are morally right and those who are morally wrong, and we place these conversations within the structure of cultural norms that bind society together. This is precisely why Polish Pudelek, British Mail Online and US Gawker are analyzed here: to illuminate the cultural framing of politics. In order to do so, I adopt a standpoint of cultural sociology, echoing Alexander's reading of Durkheim's project for the social sciences as a "cultural logic for society" (1988, p. 188). Political scandals depicted on these websites present deviations from the norm that reinforce community, by highlighting shared values as well as the notions of what is right and wrong in the public sphere (Alexander 1988; Brenton 2019). After all, the language of morality is integral to civil society. Alexander (2006) describes it as a cultural sphere of shared solidarity and notions of justice, with institutions built to enforce them. This is not the public sphere of pure rational deliberation described by Habermas where emotions pose as a mere distraction; on the contrary, the public sphere is filled with popular passions that need to be taken into account. For this reason, in addition to Alexander's cultural frame of civic practices, the following chapters are strongly inspired by Mouffe's idea of politics, which "always operate within a terrain of conflictuality informed by 'the political;'" it forms the general "dimension of antagonism" (2013, p. 2) that is inherent to society. I adopt this concept in a broader cultural sense, focusing on the ways online tabloids present voices that are invisible in other major, albeit less scandalizing and more highly-regarded outlets. While online tabloids are considered lowbrow entertainment barely posing as news, within the logic of 'agonism' they increase the pluralization of viewpoints vis-à-vis the more established outlets. In doing so, online tabloids help to reveal a conflict that would otherwise be hidden in the name of a consensus that is both merely alleged and exclusionary, as Mouffe writes. Nonetheless, the role played by online tabloids is paradoxical: they tend to describe politics in terms of morality, yet according to Mouffe moral language is only used when it is impossible to form political identities (2013, p. 139f). This impossibility of turning values into political action leads a potential 'agonistic' adversary with whom debate is possible to become an 'antagonistic' enemy which should be destroyed. Following Mouffe, this suggests that by covering politics in a scandalizing manner, online tabloids may bring the sphere of politics to publics less interested in hard news but depoliticize it on the way. Still, the audiences of online tabloids make political choices, too. In the 2015–2016 elections that were held in Poland, the UK and the US the general atmosphere was of voting for change, in the hope that it would make people's lives better. At the end of the day, the language of the public sphere is a language of values, even if attempts are made to depoliticize politics in the manner of 'We have a vote, but we do not have a voice' (2013, p. 119). A case in point, in the years following these elections people have been taking to the streets *en masse* for political and moral reasons including defending the independence of the judiciary (in Poland); against racism (Black Lives Matter, in the US and the UK); protecting the climate (Extinction Rebellion, in all three countries); and most recently in defense of women's reproductive rights (Women's Strike, in Poland). Given the popularity of online tabloids, it is hard to imagine that the demonstrators could have ignored them.

4   Short Note on Methods and the Following Chapters

The research conducted for this book was twofold: Chapter 2 is based on a qualitative analysis of articles and comments published on Pudelek, Mail Online and Gawker (and later, after its closure on 28th of August 2016, by ex-Gawker authors on other Gizmodo Media sites), which mentioned the Polish 2015 presidential election, the 2016 UK Brexit referendum, and the 2016 US presidential election, starting two months before each vote date. In addition, up to thirty most commented articles (some outlets posted less than thirty articles on a given topic) and five most upvoted comments for each of these articles concerning the Polish, British, and US elections were also analyzed using MAXQDA to tease out connections between the topics. Chapter 3 focuses on the interviews I conducted with twenty writers and editors at Pudelek, Mail Online, and Gawker, whom I asked about work in these outlets. Their opinions offer a broader view on journalistic professionalism and on the objectives that drive online tabloid writers to reveal topics ignored by others, and to embrace the specific tabloid tone. In Chapter 4 I bring together the findings from the previous chapters, pointing at the exceptional (not) kidding frame adopted by online tabloids. Finally, I discuss how certain features of online tabloid political coverage can be used to strengthen journalism and democracy, the shared space for negotiating conflicting passions.

References

Abernathy, P. (2016). *The rise of a new media baron and the emerging threat of news deserts.* Chapel Hill, NC: University of North Carolina Press.

Alexander, J. C. (1988). Culture and political crisis: "Watergate" and Durkheimian sociology. In: Alexander, J. C. ed. *Durkheimian sociology: cultural studies.* New York: Cambridge University Press, pp. 187–224.

Alexander, J. C. (2006). *The civil sphere.* Oxford, UK: Oxford University Press.

Allan, S. (2006). *Online news: journalism and the internet.* Maidenhead, UK: Open University Press.

Allan, S. (2010). *News culture.* Third edition. Maidenhead, UK: Open University Press.

Bastos, M. T. (2017). Digital journalism and tabloid journalism. In: Franklin, B. and Eldridge II S. A. eds. *The Routledge companion do digital journalism studies.* New York: Routledge, pp. 217–225.

Bastos, M. T. (2019). Tabloid journalism. In: Vos, T. P. and Hanusch, F. eds. *The international encyclopedia of journalism studies.* Hoboken, NJ: John Wiley & Sons.

Bingham, A. and Conboy, M. (2015). *Tabloid century: the popular press in Britain, 1986 to the present.* Oxford, UK: Peter Lang.

Brenton, S. (2019). Scandal and social theory. In: Tumber, H. and Waisbord, S. eds. *The Routledge companion to media and scandal.* New York: Routledge, pp. 25–33.

Brundidge, J. and Rice, R. E. (2012). Political engagement online: do the information rich get richer and the like-minded more similar?. In: Chadwick, A. and Howard, P. N. eds., *Routledge handbook of internet politics.* New York: Routledge, pp. 144–156.

BSA. (2018). *BSA global software survey. Software management: security imperative, business opportunity.* Washington, DC: Business Software Alliance. Available at: https://gss.bsa.org/wp-content/uploads/2018/05/2018_BSA_GSS_Report_en.pdf.

Caplan, R. and boyd, d. (2016). *Who controls the public sphere in an era of algorithms? Mediation, automation, power.* New York: Data & Society Research Institute.

Cassino, D. (2016). Why pollsters were completely and utterly wrong. *Harvard Business Review*, 9 November. Available at: https://hbr.org/2016/11/why-pollsters-were-completely-and-utterly-wrong.

Cohen, B. (1963). *The press and foreign policy.* Princeton, NJ: Princeton University Press.

Cohn, N. (2016). Why the surprise over 'Brexit'? Don't blame the polls. *The New York Times*, 24 June. Available at: https://www.nytimes.com/2016/06/25/upshot/why-the-surprise-over-brexit-dont-blame-the-polls.html.

Cohn, N. (2017). Election review: Why crucial state polls turned out to be wrong. *The New York Times*, 1 June, p. A12.

Collins, L. (2012). Mail supremacy. The newspaper that rules Britain. *The New Yorker*, April 2, pp. 50–59.

Conboy, M. (2006). *Tabloid Britain. Constructing a community through language.* New York: Routledge.

Couldry, N., Livingtone, S. and Markham, T. (2007). *Media consumption and public engagement: beyond the presumption of attention.* New York: Palgrave MacMillan.

Cushion, S. and Lewis, J. (2016). Scrutinising statistical gains and constructing balance: television news coverage of the 2016 EU referendum. In: Jackson, D., Thorsen, E. and Wring, D. eds., *EU referendum analysis 2016: media, voters and the campaign.* Poole, UK: The Centre for the Study of Journalism, Culture and Community, Bournemouth University, p. 40.

Daddow, O. (2016). UK newspapers and the EU referendum: Brexit or Bremain? In: Jackson, D., Thorsen, E. and Wring, D. eds., *EU referendum analysis 2016: media, voters and the campaign.* Poole, UK: The Centre for the Study of Journalism, Culture and Community, Bournemouth University, p. 50.

Davies, N. (2009). *Flat Earth news: an award-winning reporter exposes falsehood, distortion and propaganda in the global media.* London: Vintage.

Dayan, D. (2013). Conquering visibility, conferring visibility: visibility seekers and media performance. *International Journal of Communication,* 7, pp. 137–153.

Dobek-Ostrowska, B. (2012). Italianization (or Mediterraneanization) of the Polish media system? Reality and perspective. In: Hallin, D. C. and Mancini, P. eds. *Comparing media systems beyond the Western world.* New York: Cambridge University Press, pp. 26–50.

Drygalski, J. and Kwaśniewski, J. (1992). *(Nie)realny socjalizm.* Warsaw, Poland: PWN.

Dunaway, J. and Lawrence, R. G. (2015). What predicts the game frame? Media ownership, electoral context, and campaign news. *Political Communication,* 32, pp. 43–60.

Dzierżyńska-Mielcarek, J. (2018). *Rynek mediów w Polsce. Zmiany pod wpływem nowych technologii cyfrowych.* Warsaw, Poland: ASPRA-JR.

Edwards, J. (2016). Pollsters now know why they were wrong about Brexit. *Business Insider,* 24 July. Available at: https://www.businessinsider.com/pollsters-know-why-they-were-wrong-about-brexit-2016-7.

Esser, F. (1999). 'Tabloidization' of news. A comparative analysis of Anglo-American and German press journalism. *European Journal of Communication,* 14(3), pp. 291–324.

Fenton, N., ed., (2010). *New media, old news. Journalism & democracy in the digital age.* London: Sage.

Firmstone, J. (2016). Newspapers' editorial opinions during the referendum campaign. In: Jackson, D., Thorsen, E. and Wring, D. eds., *EU referendum analysis 2016: media, voters and the campaign.* Poole, UK: The Centre for the Study of Journalism, Culture and Community, Bournemouth University, p. 36.

Franklin, B. (1997) *Newszak and news media.* London: Arnold.

Gans, H. J. (2009). Can popularization help the news media? In: Zelizer, B. ed. *The changing faces of journalism: tabloidization, technology and truthiness.* New York: Routledge, pp. 17–28.

Griffen-Foley, B. (2008). From *Tit Bits* to *Big Brother*: a century of audience participation in the media. In: Biressi A. and H. Nunn H. eds. *The tabloid culture reader*, Maidenhead, UK: Open University Press, pp. 303–313.

Gripsrud, J. (2000). Tabloidization, popular journalism and democracy. In: Sparks, C. and Tulloch, J. eds. *Tabloid tales: global debates over media standards.* New York: Rowman & Littlefield, pp. 285–300.

Guzik A. and Marzęcki R. (2015). Instrumentalne wykorzystywanie sondaży w dyskursach medialnych i politycznych. *Polityka i społeczeństwo*, 2(13), pp. 58–74.

Habermas, J. (1974). The public sphere: an encyclopedia article. *New German Critique*, 3, pp. 49–55.

Habermas, J. (1991). *The structural transformations of the public sphere.* Massachusetts, CA: The MIT Press.

Habermas, J. (1992). Further reflections on the public sphere. In: C. Calhoun, ed., *Habermas and the public sphere.* Massachusetts, CA: The MIT Press, pp. 421–461.

Hallin, D. C. and Mancini, P. (2004). *Comparing media systems: three models of media and politics.* New York: Cambridge University Press.

Hallin, D. C. and Mancini, P. eds. (2012). *Comparing media systems beyond the Western world.* New York: Cambridge University Press.

Harcup, T. and O'Neill, D. (2017). What is news? News values revisited (again). *Journalism Studies*, 18(12), pp. 1470–1488.

Johansson, S. (2007). *Reading tabloids. Tabloid newspapers and their readers.* Huddinge, Sweden: Södertörns Högskola.

Just, M. R. and Crigler, A. N. (2019). Media coverage of political scandals: effects of personalization and potential for democratic reforms. In: Tumber, H. and Waisbord, S. eds. *The Routledge companion to media and scandal.* New York: Routledge, pp. 34–45.

Kennedy, C., Blumenthal, M., Clement, S., et al. (2017). *An evaluation of 2016 election polls in the United States.* Oakbrook Terrace, IL: American Association for Public Opinion Research.

Kennedy, C., Blumenthal, M., Clement, S., et al. (2018). An evaluation of 2016 election polls in the United States. *Public Opinion Quarterly*, 82(1), pp. 1–33.

Klepka, R. (2016). Informowanie, krytyka i agitacja w wybranych tygodnikach opinii o kandydatach w wyborach prezydenckich w 2015 roku. In: Batorowska, H. and Kwiasowski Z., eds., *Kultura informacyjna w ujęciu interdyscyplinarnym. Teoria i praktyka*, Krakow: Uniwersytet Pedagogiczny im. Komisji Edukacji Narodowej w Krakowie, vol. 2, pp. 140–152.

Lehman-Wilzig, S. N. and Seletzky, M. (2010). Hard news, soft news, 'general' news: the necessity and utility of an intermediate classification. *Journalism*, 11(1), pp. 37–56.

Levy, D. A. L., Aslan, B. and Bironzo, D. (2016). *UK press coverage of the EU referendum.* Oxford, UK: Reuters Institute for the Study of Journalism.

Lovett, G. (2011). News of the World website dismantles paywall. *Marketing Week*, 8 July. Available at: https://www.marketingweek.com/news-of-the-world-website-dismantles-paywall/.

Lowrey, W. and Gade, P. J., eds. (2011). *Changing the news. The forces shaping journalism in uncertain times.* New York: Routledge.

Lumby, C. (1997) *Bad girls: the media, sex and feminism in the 90s.* Sydney, Australia: Allen and Unwin.

Magin, M. (2019). Elite versus popular press. In: Vos, T. P. and Hanusch, F. eds. *The international encyclopedia of journalism studies.* Hoboken, NJ: John Wiley & Sons.

Mahler, J. and Rutenberg, J. (2019). How Rupert Murdoch's empire of influence remade the world. *The New York Times*, April 3. Available at: https://www.nytimes.com/interactive/2019/04/03/magazine/rupert-murdoch-fox-news-trump.html.

Mance, H. (2019). Geordie Grieg: 'Provocation is a good thing'. *Financial Times*, October 4. Available at: https://www.ft.com/content/16b7c032-de20-11e9-9743-db5a370481bc.

Matuszewski, P. (2016). Czy można wierzyć sondażom przedwyborczym? Wykorzystanie podejścia bayesowskiego do analizy rozbieżności między wynikami wyborów parlamentarnych w Polsce a danymi z badań sondażowych. *Studia socjologiczne*, 4(223), pp. 253–276.

McNair, B. (2000). *Journalism and democracy.* London: Routledge.

McNair, B. (2019). Scandal and news values. In: Tumber, H. and Waisbord, S. eds. *The Routledge companion to media and scandal.* New York: Routledge, pp. 76–85.

McNamara, P. (1997). A crying shame: princess Di's death brings out the worst of the web. *Network World*, 8 September, pp. 1, 65.

Mediatique. (2018). *Department for Digital, Culture, Media & Sport: overview of recent dynamics in the UK press market.* London: Mediatique Limited. Available at: https://assets.publishing.service.gov.uk/government/uploads/system/uploads/attachment_data/file/720400/180621_Mediatique_-_Overview_of_recent_dynamics_in_the_UK_press_market_-_Report_for_DCMS.pdf.

Mercer, A., Deane, C. and McGeeney, K. (2016). Why 2016 election polls missed their mark. *Pew Research Center*, November 9. Available at: https://www.pewresearch.org/fact-tank/2016/11/09/why-2016-election-polls-missed-their-mark/.

Mielczarek, T. (1998). *Między monopolem a pluralizmem: zarys dziejów środków komunikowania masowego w Polsce w latach 1989 – 1997.* Kielce, Poland: Wyższa Szkoła Pedagogiczna im. Jana Kochanowskiego.

Mouffe, C. (2000). *The democratic paradox.* London: Verso Books.

Mouffe, C. (2013). *Agonistics: thinking the world democratically.* London: Verso Books.

Munger, K. (2020). All the news that's fit to click: the economics of clickbait media, *Political Communication*, 37(3), pp. 376–397.

Nielsen, R. K. (2016). The business of news. In: Witschge, T., Anderson, C. W., Domingo D. and Hermida, A. eds. *The SAGE handbook of digital journalism*. London: Sage, pp. 51–67.

Noelle-Neumann, E. (1974). The spiral of silence. A theory of public opinion. *Journal of Communication*, 24(2), pp. 43–51.

Nowak, D. (2015). Sondaże a powyborcza rzeczywistość. Diabeł tkwi w szczegółach. *TVN24*, 18 October. Available at: https://tvn24.pl/polska/dlaczego-sondaze-wybor cze-odbiegaja-od-wynikow-wyborow-ra5869893315578.

Örnebring, H. and Jönsson A. M. (2004). Tabloid journalism and the public sphere: a historical perspective on tabloid journalism. *Journalism Studies*, 5(3), pp. 283–295.

Osęka, P. (2015). Newsy Czerwoniaków. *Gazeta Wyborcza. Ale Historia*, 26 October, p. 6.

Otto, L., Glogger, I. and Boukes, M. (2017). The softening of journalistic political communication: a comprehensive framework model of sensationalism, soft news, infotainment, and tabloidization. *Communication Theory*, 27, pp. 136–155.

Paczkowski, A. (1976). Nakłady dzienników warszawskich w latach 1931–1938. *Rocznik Historii Czasopiśmiennictwa Polskiego*, 15(1), pp. 65–97.

Paczkowski, A. (1983). *Prasa codzienna Warszawy w latach 1918–1939*. Warsaw, Poland: Państwowy Instytut Wydawniczy.

Papacharissi, Z. (2015). *Affective publics: sentiment, technology, and politics*. New York: Oxford University Press.

Pariser, E. (2011). *The filter bubble. What the internet is hiding from you*. New York: The Penguin Press.

past. (2019). Sondaże i exit poll niezgodne z wynikiem wyborów. Skąd błąd? "Więcej odmów odpowiedzi." *Gazeta.pl*, 28 May. Available at: https://wiadomosci.gazeta.pl /wiadomosci/7,114883,24835385,sondaze-i-exit-poll-niezgodne-z-wynikiem-wybo row-skad-blad.html.

Peters, C. and Broersma, M., eds. (2013). *Rethinking journalism. Trust and participation in a transformed news landscape*. London: Routledge.

Peters, C. and Broersma, M., eds. (2017). *Rethinking journalism again. Societal role and public relevance in a digital age*. London: Routledge.

Prendecki, K. (2015). Sondaże wyborcze – socjologia w służbie polityki. *Humanities and Social Sciences*, 22(1), pp. 193–207.

Ramsay, G. (2019). *Who owns the UK media?*. London: Media Reform Coalition, Goldsmiths Leverhulme Media Research Centre. Available at: https://www.medi areform.org.uk/media-ownership/who-owns-the-uk-media.

Rosentiel, T. (2008). Where men and women differ in following the news. *Pew Research Center*, 6 February. Available at: https://www.pewresearch.org/2008/02/06/where -men-and-women-differ-in-following-the-news/.

Roston, M. (2015). Don't try too hard to please Twitter – and other lessons from The New York Times' social media desk. *Nieman Lab*, 22 January. Available at: https://www.niemanlab.org/2015/01/dont-try-too-hard-to-please-twitter-and-other-lessons-from-the-new-york-times-social-media-desk/.

Rowe, D. (2011). Obituary for the newspaper? Tracking the tabloid. *Journalism*, 12(4), pp. 449–466.

Sambrook, R. (2006). How the net is transforming news. *BBC News*, 20 January. Available at: http://news.bbc.co.uk/2/hi/technology/4630890.stm.

Sayers, F. (2016). The online polls were right, and other lessons from the referendum. *YouGov*, June, 28. Available at: https://yougov.co.uk/topics/politics/articles-reports/2016/06/28/online-polls-were-right.

Schudson, M. (1978). *Discovering the news: a social history of American newspapers*. New York: Basic Books.

Seaton, J. and Pimlott, B. eds. (1987). *The media in British politics*. Aldershot, UK: Gower.

Shuman, E. L. (1903). *Practical journalism: a complete manual of the best newspaper methods*. New York: D. Appleton and Company.

Sloan, B. (2001). *"I watched a wild hog eat my baby!" A colorful history of tabloids and their cultural impact*. Amherst, NY: Prometheus Books.

Sparks, C. (1988). The popular press and political democracy. *Media, Culture and Society*, 10, pp. 209–223.

Szreder, M. (2015). Badania ankietowe nie wystarczą. *Gazeta Wyborcza*, September 1, p. 7.

Thompson, J. B. (2000). *Political scandal: power and visibility in the media age*. Cambridge, UK: Polity.

Tocqueville, A. (2003). *Democracy in America*. New York: Penguin Books.

Toobin, J. (2017). Feeding the beast. David Pecker's reign at the National Enquirer and the rise of Trump. *The New Yorker*, July 3, pp. 38–47.

Trende, S. (2016a). Trump, Brexit, and the state of the race. *Real Clear Politics*, June 28. Available at: https://www.realclearpolitics.com/articles/2016/06/28/trump_brexit_and_the_state_of_the_race_131036.html.

Trende, S. (2016b). It wasn't the polls that missed, it was the pundits. *Real Clear Politics*, November 12. Available at: https://www.realclearpolitics.com/articles/2016/11/12/it_wasnt_the_polls_that_missed_it_was_the_pundits_132333.html.

Tuchman, G. (1972). Objectivity as strategic ritual: an examination of newsmen's notions of objectivity. *The American Journal of Sociology*, 77(4), pp. 660–679.

Tumber, H. (2004). Scandal and media in the United Kingdom. *The American Behavioral Scientist*, 47(8), pp. 1122–1137.

Tumber, H. and Waisbord, S. (2019). Introduction. In: Tumber, H. and Waisbord, S. eds. *The Routledge companion to media and scandal*. New York: Routledge, pp. 1–9.

Turner, G. (1999). Tabloidization, journalism and the possibility of critique. *International Journal of Cultural Studies*, 2(1), pp. 59–76.

Umbricht, A. and Esser, F. (2016). The push to popularize politics: understanding the audience-friendly packaging of political news in six media systems since the 1960s. *Journalism Studies*, 17(1), pp. 100–121.

US Senate Report. (2018). *Putin's asymmetric assault on democracy in Russia and Europe: implications for U.S. national security*. Washington D.C.: U.S. Government Publishing Office. Available at: https://www.foreign.senate.gov/imo/media/doc/FinalRR.pdf.

US Senate Report. (2019). *Report of the Select Committee on Intelligence, United States Senate on Russian active measures campaigns and interference in the 2016 U.S. election. Volume 2: Russia's use of social media, with additional views*. Washington D.C.: U.S. Government Publishing Office. Available at: https://www.intelligence.senate.gov/sites/default/files/documents/Report_Volume2.pdf.

Wells, A. (2016). What we can learn from the referendum polling. *UK Polling Report*, July 19. Available at: https://ukpollingreport.co.uk/blog/archives/9738.

Władyka, W. (1982) *Krew na pierwszej stronie: sensacyjne dzienniki Drugiej Rzeczypospolitej*. Warsaw, Poland: Czytelnik.

Wojcieszak, M., Menchen-Trevino, E. and von Hohenberg, B. C. et al. (2024). Non-News Websites Expose People to More Political Content Than News Websites: Evidence from Browsing Data in Three Countries. *Political Communication*, 41(1), pp. 129–151.

WP. (2015). Adam Michnik: Komorowski przegra wybory tylko, jeśli pijany przejedzie na pasach zakonnice w ciąży. *Wirtualna Polska*, 5 January. Available at: https://wiadomosci.wp.pl/adam-michnik-komorowski-przegra-wybory-tylko-jesli-pijany-przejedzie-na-pasach-zakonnice-w-ciazy-6027669969146497a.

Wylie, C. (2019). *Mindf*ck: Cambridge Analytica and the plot to break America*. New York: Random House.

CHAPTER 2

Politicians Are Crooks, Votes Are Rigged, and Other Visions of an (Un)just World

1 Background on Gawker, Mail Online, and Pudelek: The Rise of Online News, and News Media Struggles for Profit

1.1 *Introduction*

This chapter presents a close study of political campaign coverage on Pudelek, Mail Online, and Gawker, preceding the 2015 and 2016 votes in Poland, the United Kingdom, and the United States. Based on a qualitative analysis of 193 articles and 965 comments, starting two months before each vote date and ending on election day (with exceptions), I show a detailed analysis of coverage of the Polish 2015 presidential campaign, the 2016 British EU referendum campaign, and the US 2016 presidential campaign. The first part of this chapter discusses the background of the three online tabloids; the second part focuses on the main frames, themes and attitudes voiced in articles and readers' comments in the three outlets, sometimes predictable, other times surprising, and often ambiguous. In particular, I point out game and scandal frames that are used to discuss the campaigns and the candidates; the positive labeling of candidates as non-elite and, conversely, negative labeling as elite; the focus on political scandals that do not question the *status quo*; the emphasis on entertainment features; as well as, finally, the tone and role of reader comments, located directly under the journalistic pieces. After providing this contextual setup, in the succeeding sections I present a detailed study of the articles and comments published during the three campaigns.

1.2 *Emergence and Rise of the Three Online Tabloids*

Gawker, Mail Online and Pudelek emerged at a time when traditional news media were not paying much attention to the internet. Print circulation was high, papers often either did not have their proper websites, or they were heavily paywalled, and mimicked paper issues. The internet was mostly used on desktop computers, and smartphones were not yet introduced to mass consumers. At the same time, the early aughts were the heyday of blogs, simple, usually personal websites that were easy to edit and enabled posting content arranged in a diary format (see e.g.: Siles 2019).

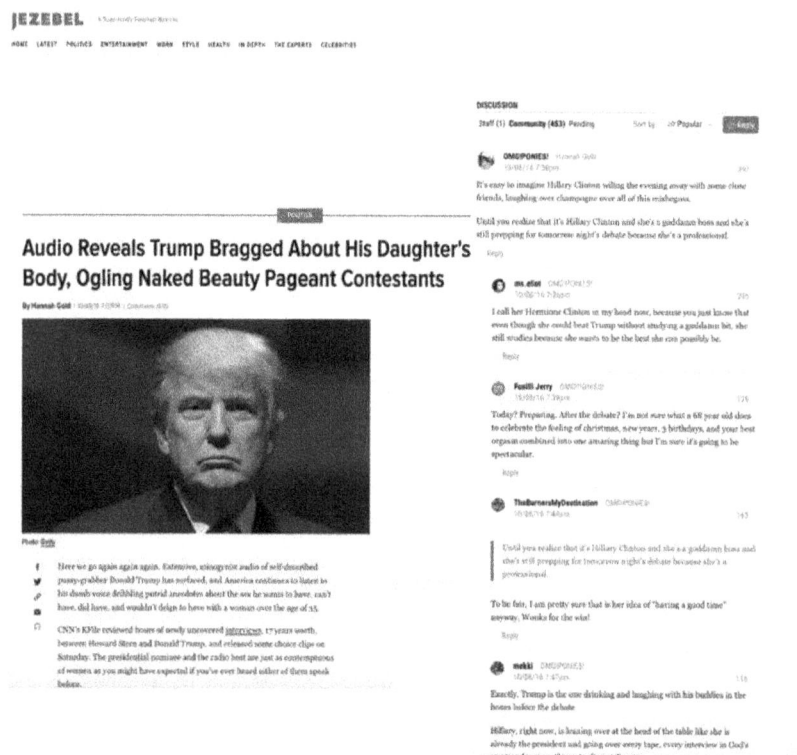

FIGURE 1   Ex-Gawker Jezebel layout (fragment). A Gizmodo Media Group website where Gawker authors moved after Gawker was shut down; comments can be arranged by newest, oldest, and most popular

SOURCE: HTTPS://WEB.ARCHIVE.ORG/WEB/20210726164748/HTTPS://JEZE
BEL.COM/NEW-AUDIO-EMERGES-OF-TRUMP-BRAGGING-ABOUT-HIS-VOLUP
TUO-1787578389

Enter Gawker. The online tabloid, the brainchild of Nick Denton, a former *Financial Times* journalist and later a tech entrepreneur, was launched in December 2002. Created as one of several blogs within the Gawker Media platform, the site was intended to fill the gap between outlets such as *The New York Times* and *National Enquirer*. In contrast to the United Kingdom where Denton hails from, these types of media were pretty much nonexistent in the United States. David Galbraith, Denton's business partner argued that in the UK, "you had quite sophisticated tabloids with large presence that weren't written by morons. So Nick's idea was to do the postmodern thing, something that superficially looks crappy but actually is doing something deep underneath" (Abrams 2015). (Another British trope: the name *Gawker* was intended to rhyme with

The New Yorker, but it works only if you say it in Received Pronunciation.) Some of the few American exceptions with a knack for picking on the media industry included the satirical New York-based monthly, *Spy*, which closed after 12 years in 1998, and the weekly, *The New York Observer*. The magazine, launched a year after *Spy*, was bought by Jared Kushner in 2006. Interestingly, it was turned into an online-only outlet titled *Observer* on 9th of November 2016, the day after Donald Trump, Kushner's father-in-law, won the US presidential election. Back in 2002, with little competition, Gawker directed its attention to the media industry itself, from Condé Nast to the stars of Page Six, and New York City itself. Denton "brought that crazy English publishing sensibility," according to Meg Hourihan, the co-founder Gawker Media's news aggregator Kinja (Abrams 2015). The basic format for Gawker and other Gawker Media websites was that of a blog. Different writers – at the beginning all of them bloggers who already had their own blogs – created articles that could be scrolled through chronologically. While blogs were already widely popular at the time, the question was how to make them generate revenue. (Elizabeth Spiers, Gawker's first editor-in-chief, and one of several Gawker writers and editors I talked to, describes the first stages of making the website profitable; this is discussed in Chapter 3.) Gawker quickly became something of an *enfant terrible* of the newly emerging online media scene, with its attitude of "attacking up" people the writers deemed as having power, be it financial, political, or the power of media influence. On average, Gawker published around 30 posts per day while individual Gawker writers wrote up to 12 stories daily, which were published across Gawker Media. On Gawker itself, the posts predominantly focused on media, politics, and crime.[1] As far as numbers go, according to statistical data, six months after the launch of Gawker the website was visited over 500 thousand times per month (Holiday 2018), whereas in 2007 the number of unique visitors was around ten times higher (Smith 2010), climbing up to 10 million in 2012 (Spangler 2016), and reaching 14.5 million in 2016, the year of its closing (Dunn 2016). To put these statistics in perspective, the best-selling newspaper in the US in the early 00s was *USA Today*, with peak print circulation above 2.2 million. However, in 2015 the top position was held by *Wall Street Journal*, with print circulation over one million. Online subscriptions were rarely disclosed at the time but, as an example, *The New York Times*, the bestseller daily

---

1 An interesting overview of Gawker internal statistics can be found in a now archived post "Closing the Book on Gawker.com," published by Josh Laurito on 21st of August 2016; see: https://web.archive.org/web/20160822222925/https://gawkerdata.kinja.com/closing-the-book-on-gawker-com-1785555716; see also: Abrams (2015).

in 2018 claimed close to 5.5 million combined print and digital subscriptions.[2] This means that the top-selling newspaper was viewed by only a third of the audience that Gawker had reached two years earlier.

The fact that Gawker was independent from outside funding helped it maintain its snarky, unkind style, or "one glint of nastiness per post," as its writers described it (New York Magazine 2008). Independence was a key factor for the company to the point that Denton decided to sell a minority stake only in early 2016, to an investment fund owned by the Russian billionaire, Viktor Vekselberg, in order to cover the legal expenses of the Hulk Hogan trial. Even so, Gawker Media went bankrupt several months later (Ingram 2016), ostensibly because of having abused a celebrity's right to privacy, and of having publicly outed a powerful gay man years earlier. Before this happened, however, numerous controversies sparked by the Gawker website included Gawker Stalker, a frequently updated Google map that showed where celebrities – for the most part actors and television personalities – had been spotted in New York; an article outing the CFO of Condé Nast, a married man with children, who was being extorted by a male prostitute; a Scientology recruitment video with Tom Cruise which had been deleted from YouTube; screenshots of Sarah Palin's emails leaked by pranksters associated with the infamous anonymous discussion forum 4chan; and many others. Still, the two posts that proved most consequential for Gawker appeared several years apart: first, in 2007, the Silicon Valley investor and PayPal founder Peter Thiel was outed in an article titled "Peter Thiel is totally gay, people"[3] (it was originally published on the Silicon Valley gossip site, Valleywag, which was also part of Gawker Media). According to Spiers but also Owen Thomas, Valleywag's managing editor, the public outing of Thiel by Gawker ruined talks between Clarium Capital, a hedge fund that Thiel owned, and Saudi Arabian investors (Thomas 2016). Upset, he promised a vendetta. Second, in 2012, Gawker published a post under the telling title, "Even for a Minute, Watching Hulk Hogan Have Sex in a Canopy Bed is Not Safe For Work but Watch it Anyway,"[4] which included a video with the American celebrity wrestler Hulk Hogan (Terry Bollea) having sex with the wife of his best friend, the shock jock radio host Bubba the Love Sponge (Todd Clem). According to Hogan, the sex video had been made without his knowledge, not to mention consent, and so in 2013 he decided to sue Gawker for infringement of privacy.

---

2 In 2016, the year Gawker went bankrupt, the number of unique visitors who accessed the limited content on *The New York Times* website without a subscription reached over a 100 million; see: Doctor 2016.
3 https://www.gawker.com/335894/peter-thiel-is-totally-gay-people.
4 The video has been since taken down as a result of the lawsuit.

According to numerous commentators (e.g. Holiday 2018), the lawsuit was successful because of the generous, and secret, funding provided by Peter Thiel. As a result, after the jury awarded Hogan over $100 million in compensation in 2016, Gawker was forced to file for bankruptcy. The Gawker site was closed in the end of August, and its writers were dispersed among other Gawker Media websites. Thus, my analysis of the three election campaigns includes articles written by Gawker authors who spent most of the final months of the US presidential campaign as former Gawker writers, publishing in the remaining Gawker Media outlets, in particular Deadspin, Gizmodo and Jezebel.

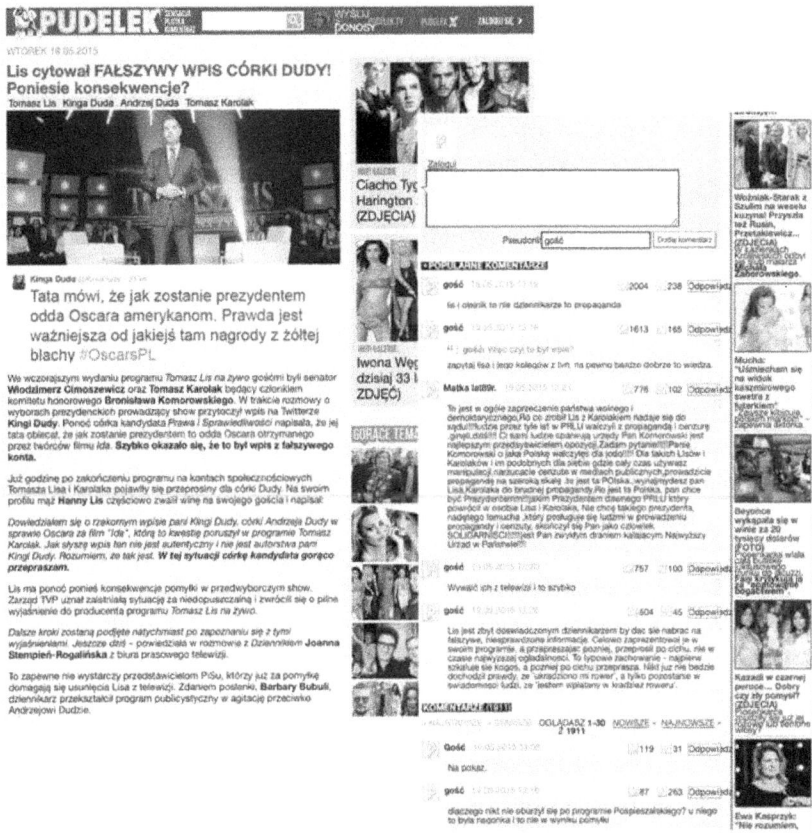

FIGURE 2 Pudelek layout (fragment). Top reader comments are at the top and highlighted in yellow
SOURCE: HTTPS://WEB.ARCHIVE.ORG/WEB/20150520232757/HTTP://WWW
.PUDELEK.PL/ARTYKUL/79379/LIS_CYTOWAL_FALSZYWY_WPIS_CORKI_DUD
Y_PONIESIE_KONSEKWENCJE/

Pudelek (Poodle), the Polish online tabloid, was launched three years after Gawker, at the beginning of 2006. It was inspired by the most popular online gossip website at the time, TMZ, as well as Perez Hilton and Gawker. Michał Brański, one of Pudelek's founders admitted that the inspiration came from his wife who liked to read online gossip on US celebrities (Socha-Jakubowska 2015). Pudelek quicky became popular for its sarcastic style of writing about Polish and international celebrities, be it actors, reality-show stars, or politicians – until then, a style mostly unheard of in popular Polish media. The online tabloid was created as a part of the Polish online company o2, founded in 1999 by three students from the Warsaw School of Economics, Michał Brański, Jacek Świderski and Krzysztof Sierota. Fifteen years later, in 2014 o2 bought the oldest and one of the most popular Polish online portals, Wirtualna Polska, and renamed the combined companies Grupa Wirtualna Polska (erka 2014). The merger led to changes in the organizational structure of the company, including the staff of Pudelek. (This will be discussed in more detail in Chapter 3.) As in Gawker, Pudelek's layout was simple and blog-like, with chronologically organized posts and lots of pictures often unfavorable to the people portrayed in the articles. Unlike Gawker, however, since the launch of Pudelek its writers have been anonymous, using individual *noms de plume* instead. Thanks to these qualities Pudelek, a novel medium on the Polish web, quickly became the most popular celebrity-focused online tabloid in Poland. Two years after its launch, the website was visited by over 1.7 million unique visitors per month; in 2012 there were a million more; while in 2016 Pudelek attracted close to 3.3 million unique visitors per month. In 2021, fifteen years after its launch, the number of unique visitors on Pudelek was twice as high, around 6.6 million (tw 2021). To put these numbers in perspective, in 2007 the best-selling print daily was *Fakt*, a tabloid with circulation close to 690 thousand; in 2012 *Fakt* was still at the top but with circulation shrunk to 505 thousand; five years later it went further down to less than 388 thousand. At the same time, however, until 2020 the online version of the tabloid was free of charge, reaching 2.1 million unique users in 2012 and over 3.6 million in 2016 – fairly similar numbers to the online-only Pudelek (bg 2020).

For Pudelek, its first openly political moment came in late 2011, when the online tabloid published an article condemning ACTA, the Anti-Counterfeiting Trade Agreement.[5] In the post, the author (as I learned later, one of Pudelek's

---

5 The article is available here: https://www.pudelek.pl/artykul/38176/acta_czyli_jak_celebryci _stracili_kontakt_z_rzeczywistoscia/; see also the European Parliament's analysis of factors that led to the rejection of ACTA: https://www.europarl.europa.eu/RegData/presse/pr_g ran/2012/EN/03A-DV-PRESSE_FCS(2012)02-20(38611)_EN.pdf.

founders) argued that ACTA was an infringement not only of the freedom of speech but also of access to culture. In addition, the post accused well-off Polish journalists who were in favor of ACTA of being out of touch with most young people in Poland – many of them being their own audience. Young Poles were often simply too poor to pay for the films and music, which were priced similarly or even higher than in Western European countries while Polish wages were, and still often are, several times lower. Accordingly, the mass anti-ACTA demonstrations in Poland were framed by Pudelek not as organized by "pirates" who "steal" other people's work, as mainstream Polish journalists and artists would have it, but as protests of people fighting against exclusion from culture, which they saw as a basic right for any member of society. Ironically, Paweł Wroński (2012), a journalist from the main Polish opinion daily, *Gazeta Wyborcza*, penned an unusually snide comment in response to the post of snarky-by-definition Pudelek, implying that a website which publishes articles such as "Brilliant bottoms – weigh in" has little credibility in defending people's right to culture. Yet in his opinion piece the journalist ignored Pudelek's main argument about young people's poor finances. Remarkably, however, Poland's former President Aleksander Kwaśniewski proved more sympathetic to the online tabloid. He rightly observed that "*Gazeta Wyborcza* and online portals are directed towards entirely different audiences. The problem is precisely that we are living in completely different worlds, which are in poor communication with each other. (...) Pudelek has its army of supporters, and it is interesting that the discussion [about ACTA] started there" (Kwaśniewski 2012). Poles were not alone in their objections concerning the proposed legislation. Demonstrations were attended by thousands of people in several EU member states, eventually leading policymakers to drop the ACTA bill. For Pudelek, the support for anti-ACTA protests was a significant turning point in the website's coverage of politics. If, earlier, political topics had been mentioned on the website only in passing, after ACTA politicians and political events became a mainstay on the celebrity gossip website. According to its writers, since 2015 around one third of posts published on Pudelek have been devoted to political topics, many of them providing not just (snarky) opinion but also some form of news coverage (see: Socha-Jakubowska and Krawiec 2015; Walecka-Rynduch 2016). And indeed, with each campaign season one could clearly notice a spike in posts concerning politicians.

The third online tabloid, the British Mail Online is a year younger than Gawker, having been launched at the end of 2003. However, unlike the other two online tabloids, it is an internet version of the paper tabloid, *Daily Mail*, the second most popular British daily, after *The Sun*, which is also a tabloid. The print version of the *Daily Mail* dates back to the beginning of the 20th century.

FIGURE 3   Mail Online layout (fragment). A bright-blue box with additional information is visible in the center. Comments can be arranged by newest, oldest, best rated, and worst rated
SOURCE: HTTPS://WEB.ARCHIVE.ORG/WEB/20160604125623/HTTPS://WWW
.DAILYMAIL.CO.UK/NEWS/ARTICLE-3624338/GOVE-SLAMS-SNEERING-ELI
TES-TRYING-BRITAIN-EU-URGES-VOTERS-CONTROL-REFERENDUM.HTML

It was founded by Associated Newspapers in 1905 (the company was renamed DMG Media in 2013), almost a century before the launch of the online version. From the beginning Mail Online was headed by Martin Clarke, its editor-in-chief known for being both successful in terms of circulation and ruthless with his staff (Addison 2017); however, after thirteen years, in 2022 Clarke stepped down (see: Tobitt 2022).[6] Although born out of a print daily, since 2006 the online outlet has been operating with its own staff of reporters and editors. Still, the website mixes articles written specifically for Mail Online with online "reprints" from *Daily Mail*. Perhaps because of this mix Mail Online is the most-read online newspaper in the world, which is a fact its writers point out gladly. It reported around 2.5 million unique visitors per month in 2006; 6.5 million in 2012;[7] and close to 15 million unique visitors per month in 2016.

---

6   Martin Clarke was replaced by Danny Groom, who had previously been the UK editor of the website, while the editor in chief position was renamed "Acting Global Editor of MailOnline."
7   That year, Mail Online overtook *The New York Times* as the top-viewed online newspaper; see: BBC 2012.

At the end of 2021 the number was around 10 million higher, reaching almost 25 million unique visitors per month.[8] Interestingly, from the start the tone of Mail Online has been different from that of the paper, more liberal – as one of my interviewees put it – catering to younger, more online-savvy audiences than *Daily Mail* readers. It is also worth noting that while until recently the website was entirely free of charge, in 2019 *Daily Mail* launched an additional paywalled online version of the print daily, named Mail+. (A similar move was also made, for instance, by the Polish tabloid, *Fakt*.) Nevertheless, Mail Online has remained free and its editorial strategy has proven successful both in terms of attracting audiences and revenue, which have been steadily growing (Alpert 2019).

To sum up, since their launch in the 00s, the three online tabloids have been faring well in a changing journalistic environment, troubled by the falling numbers of audiences of traditional media who, in turn, have been increasingly switching to internet and social-media content. In contrast, online tabloid readers have been slowly growing in each of the three local settings, although in the case of Gawker this growth was brought to a rapid halt. Still, it was not a result of diminishing viewership but of a lawsuit that led to the website's closing – an alarming precedent that will be analyzed in more detail in Chapter 3. Meanwhile, this chapter centers on the content published in Pudelek, Mail Online, and Gawker during the three campaigns – two presidential, and one referendum – which led to major right-wing shifts.

2 Politics of Online Tabloid Attention

The devil is in the details, and in the case of online tabloids it often hides in the headlines, photos, highlighted sections, and readers' comments. A seemingly neutral, non-partisan piece of reporting can be fundamentally transformed by adding unfavorable photos of a particular candidate, whether from the event discussed or from a different context entirely. The tone can also be shifted by emphasizing particular phrases, usually using bold font or capitalized letters, or by selectively including historical contexts. These techniques are visible in all three analyzed tabloids. In a helpful typology of dimensions of journalistic role performance, Mellado (2015) points out the differences between interpretative and opinion-writing styles, the latter comprising value judgement. However,

---

[8] See: https://www.mailmetromedia.co.uk/brand/mailonline/. All data on Mail Online viewers is based on information provided by the UK Audit Bureau of Circulations (ABCs). According to ComScore, which uses different measurements, the numbers are several times higher.

the style adopted in online tabloids, such as using the neutral third person but also strong, emotional adjectives, shows that the seemingly clear line between the two styles can be very blurry. A uniquely Mail Online approach is to insert subheadings which suggest political sympathies (and antipathies), as well as copying and pasting fragments from previous articles. These can be particularly found in bright-blue boxes inserted in the posts, offering background on concrete topics, which, too, are positioned in a way that hint at the favored political views. At times, these editorial written and graphic "interventions" in the articles all but contradict the main body of the text. This is no coincidence, as some of my interviewees from Mail Online admit. What's more, Kelsey, a media scholar, argues that newsmakers do not even need to be consistent across their stories, and the "immediate purpose that a story serves often overrides discursive 'contradictions'" (2019, p. 252; see also: Kelsey 2015). Nonetheless, the overall meaning is coherent on an *ideological* level, he emphasizes. This can indeed be noticed in the political sympathies and antipathies visible in the three outlets. And so, while Mail Online was pro-Brexit, even if only because of a "reactiveness" to its audience, as its writers emphasize, Gawker adopted a stance that was clearly pro-Clinton (or, perhaps, anti-Trump). Contradicting voices, if shown, for the most part appeared in the comments, although most often as attempts at analysis of what "the other side" might be thinking or doing. Pudelek adopted a still different strategy from the other two tabloids; it is one which many of its authors describe as "against the elites" and "in favor of the underdog." (This, too, will be further examined in Chapter 3). As follows, for Pudelek and its commenters the incumbent President Bronisław Komorowski represented the elites to a far greater extent than fresh-faced Andrzej Duda. At the same time, the online tabloid pointed out that this relative newcomer was supported by PiS – the main opposition party at the time – which also made him a member of the "elite." Nevertheless, most of the commenters thought otherwise. This sentiment was similar to that voiced by commenters on Mail Online. They cheered the Republican-nominated outsider Trump under articles in which reporters admitted that Clinton – the epitome of "the elite" to many – had won an argument with the businessman-cum-reality TV celebrity. Such reactions confirm the findings of Engell (2005), who studied scandals on German television. The scholar argues that when television celebrities are concerned, scandals not only do not tarnish but in fact strengthen their careers. It is likely that Trump's reality-show experience, in The Apprentice, made him appear to the public more like a TV celebrity than a politician running for office. The anti-elite argument was important in Mail Online articles, too, especially in opinions favoring Brexit – again regardless of the fact that the Leave campaigners, perhaps most notably the Tory, Boris Johnson and Nigel

Farage from United Kingdom Independence Party (UKIP), had been members of "the elite" for decades. In the case of Clinton mentions on Gawker, a reverse pattern could be noted: she was the nerdy top-student "underdog" fighting against a candidate representing both the Republican elites and patriarchal privilege. Thus, what seems to have played a key role in the outlets' and commenters' sympathies was not so much being an "underdog," as unabashedly claiming to be one, no matter the facts; it is a strategy sometimes labeled political gaslighting (Rietdijk 2021). Within this logic only the ostensibly non-elite "underdogs" can claim to fight for the average Joes and Janes – in contrast to the elites, accused of being solely interested in maintaining their own privilege. Perhaps this is why Komorowski, Remainers, and Clinton, all successfully branded as "elite" by their opponents and unsympathetic media, struggled to show that they indeed had something to offer to the "non-elite." However, if we look at tabloids it turns out that, paradoxically, this form of political gaslighting quite fittingly describes their own general setup: tabloids are usually owned by powerful publishers yet insistently claim to be writing for "ordinary people." This has been the case ever since the emergence of the penny press in the mid-19th century.

2.1 *Game Frame, Scandal Frame, "Elite" Insult*

In the campaign coverage on Pudelek, Mail Online and Gawker one can notice the dominance of two types of framing, the intentional structuring of facts, used in the articles and in the comments: the game frame (sometimes also called a horse race) and the scandal frame. Since it is a key element of the journalistic shaping of reality, framing deserves special attention. According to Baden (2019), a communications scholar, it "synchronizes the meanings available to large and dispersed audiences." Moreover, by using frames journalists "manage the bandwidth of meanings" available in public debate (e.g. Entman 1993). In short, frames shape importance for the audience. In the case of the game frame, nuanced political issues are reduced to simple, easily-understandable developing stories on the question who (or what) is leading in the race (Dunaway and Lawrence 2015). A game frame is also strategic in the sense that news outlets cover campaigns as calculated endeavors aimed to win the vote, rather than discussions on issue-driven political agendas, where the vote result would be a consequence of such deliberation. On a more general level, this type of strategic framing leads to audience cynicism, a phenomenon Capella and Jamieson describe in their illuminating book, *Spiral of cynicism* (1997). Even though they analyzed this phenomenon before the internet transformed the news landscape, this aspect of news coverage and its effect on audiences generally – and voters specifically – has remained markedly unchanged. Thus, when the game frame is used, the weight of the articles lies not in the issues that make a particular candidate lead (or fall behind) but in the very fact of being at the top – or, respectively, bottom – of the polls. Coverage of this kind is also less expensive to produce than in-depth analyses of issue proposals, as Rosenstiel (2005) aptly points out. Still, the game frame is not the only clearly noticeable frame used by journalists during campaign season. Closely connected to it is the scandal frame, the second dominant frame in the analyzed publications. It is a tabloid specialty, although it is not limited to tabloids. For example, according to Baum (2002), the scandal frame can also be found in so-called soft-news outlets – located somewhere between tabloids and hard-news elite media – in the "cheap-frame" variation, which emphasizes "dramatic and sensational human-interest stories, intended primarily to appeal to an entertainment-seeking audience" (p. 94). On the whole, like the game frame, the scandal frame obfuscates complex political agendas, but unlike the game frame it does so by putting personalities and their individual, outrage-inducing traits, in the limelight. This last feature is key, making the scandal frame distinct from the general entertainment-centered cheap frame. Thus, when looking at the 2015–2016 campaigns from the point of view of the scandal frame, Komorowski could be seen as associated with Military Information Services; Leave campaigners Johnson and Farage with inflammatory comments and publicity stunts; Clinton with dishonesty; and Trump with sexism. At the same time, Duda, a newcomer, was instead "non-scandalously" framed as an untarnished fresh face of "Good Change" (PiS party's slogan), while the Remain campaign, most notably Cameron, was often portrayed as bland and unconvincing – individual dullness and no past to dig into are non-scandals. Nonetheless, scandal framing is not always equally effective and some instances of such framing stick better than others. This is because a scandal requires not only a violation of norms by a public person, but also hypocrisy. McNair (2019) maintains that a politician who is known for violating norms and who does not hide this fact, is no material for a news scandal. This is possibly why Trump's "grab them by the pussy" did not tarnish his overall image among his voters, similarly to Johnson's antagonizing statements, such as those comparing the European Union to Hitler, which did not dissuade Leave sympathizers.

The "elite" label deserves a deeper look as it presents an interesting paradox. On the one hand, all of the discussed candidates clearly fall into the category of elites, if one cares to look at their political and financial backing. On the other hand, in the eyes of online tabloids, and especially in the eyes of commenters, some of the hopefuls managed to elude the quintessentially populist accusation of belonging to the (corrupt, disconnected etc.) elite better than others. This is briefly summarized in Table 1:

TABLE 1 "Member of the elite" and "People's person" labels used in Pudelek, Mail Online, and Gawker in the three campaigns

Campaign	"Member of the elite" label	"People's person" label
Poland 2015 presidential election main candidates		
Bronisław Komorowski	x	
Andrzej Duda		x
United Kingdom 2016 EU referendum		
Remain (David Cameron)	x	
Leave (Boris Johnson and Nigel Farage)		x
United States 2016 presidential election		
Hillary Clinton	x	
Donald Trump		x

SOURCE: AUTHOR

During the 2015–2016 election campaigns, being referred to as a member of the elite was itself something of an insult, which triggered online tabloids to use the scandal frame. For these ostensibly anti-elite, populist outlets, and for their commenters, the mere fact that a politician could be associated with the elite was reason for outrage. And since scandal framing relies on people's notions of morality and justice, in the studied campaigns the "elite" marker became a sign of a politician's depravity. This exposes an important contradiction in the popular view of the role of a politician; after all, being a politician implies (at least a desire to) access to power – and power is one of the key features of the elite. The online tabloids, however, did not attempt to eliminate or justify this paradox. One of the reasons may be that the tension focused on the notions of elite status and power inspire hundreds of comments, which generate revenue for these outlets. A different explanation, however, is offered by Fiske who writes, "[t]he last thing that tabloid journalism produces is a believing subject. One of its most characteristic tones of voice is that of a skeptical laughter which offers the pleasures of disbelief, the pleasures of not being taken in" (1992, p. 49). Indeed, a close study of articles and comments on Pudelek, Mail Online, and Gawker that is presented further in this chapter, reveals that scandal frames are shaped and shared in a perpetual negotiation, and suspension, of disbelief between journalistic articles and user comments. This very process informs the (not) kidding frame. Still, next to the profit-driven and (not) kidding approaches, a more Durkheimian take on scandal is also worth noting. For example, Thompson (2000) views it as a transgression of norms which, after being punished, reinforces the values of a community. Tumber and Waisbord (2019) set this idea in a political reality and stress that scandal can only take place in democracies, since only in a democratic system change inspired by public opinion is possible. While this is enticing in principle, Entman (2012) remains skeptical of the power of scandal to strengthen moral (or democratic) ideals. Instead, in his instructive book, *Scandal and silence*, the author carefully analyzes how politicians who had been the perpetrators of scandals have remained mostly unpunished, simply waiting for the popular outrage to fade before they reemerge on the political scene. In contrast to Thompson's optimistic and democracy-strengthening interpretation of scandal, Entman adopts a somber look at the media tasked with covering it: the bigger the scandal, and the more threatening it is to "to existing structures of power and distributions of resources," the less likely it is that news outlets will cover it. This is because major scandals concerning "grave misconduct," as he writes, "are difficult for media to initiate and virtually impossible for them to sustain on their own" (p. 7). The response of government institutions, other political actors, as well as public opinion (usually demonstrated in the form of polls) to the alleged wrongdoing are indispensable for a scandal to be punished and lead to a reinstatement of norms (see: Tumber 2004). Additionally important is the fact that, at the end of the day, unlike prestige and profit, uncovering political scandals is not necessarily the goal of media. Even if particular outlets choose to cover a scandal, without outside support they not only prove ineffective in restoring violated norms but risk tarnishing their own reputation.[9]

As a result, issues covered as scandalous tend to be relatively minor and do not fundamentally threaten the status quo. Indeed, campaigns analyzed in online tabloids demonstrate this particularly well: neither accusations of elitism nor of unacceptable sexual and racist behavior led to major changes in the already existing political setup, such as the choice of candidates (e.g. for Bernie Sanders in the US or Paweł Kukiz in Poland) or in their general conduct. Scandals that are ultimately revealed – and are often long-known to journalists, as both Entman and Gawker's creator Nick Denton confirm – are treated

---

9 For this reason, Entman views the resignation of President Richard Nixon in consequence of the Watergate scandal not as a rule but as an exception.

by media outlets as a feature of entertainment which quickly bores audiences. This means that there is little incentive to investigate them in depth and for longer periods of time. As an exception to this rule, sex scandals of political actors are especially interesting because they pertain to the private sphere, and because the candidates are generally expected to adhere to traditional moral values that are supposed to extend to their conduct offstage. The "presidential" look, while naïve and spectacle-oriented, may attract swing voters, Entman argues. Marshall (2014) adds that being the head of the family helps maintain this appearance, too, as it symbolically extends to the entire nation. Hence the dozens of family photos of presidential hopefuls published in online tabloids – in the US campaign typically shot during presidential debates, and in the Polish campaign chiefly during rallies – are anything but accidental. Remarkably, the issue how this "presidential" quality translates into carrying out political agendas is rarely raised by journalists. Thus, this exposes another paradox concerning the expected performance of the chief of state: the individual should be an anti-elite yet grounded head of the nation, who is powerful but also relatable to ordinary Janes and Joes. It is an intrinsically self-contradicting combination. Still, it remains largely unquestioned because it reflects the populist stance of online tabloids, which, in turn, claim to be reactive to their readers.

The flip side of powerful, stately gravitas are humiliating sex scandals, which bring the private to the public eye. It should be emphasized, however, that although right-wing politicians are just as likely as those in the center and on the left side of the political spectrum to engage in scandalizing sexual behavior, such as extramarital affairs, the former are much better at deflecting the scandal label, Entman observes. They achieve this by unanimously denying accusations while redirecting attention to the scandalous behavior of their competitors, and providing fresh content to further promote scandal coverage hurting their opponents. Clinton and Trump campaigns are perfect illustrations of this mechanism, which Entman names a "scandal cascade." At the same time, right-wing politicians who promise to deliver on the conservative (e.g. religious) agenda are more likely to be forgiven for unconservative behavior in their personal lives than to disappoint voters enough for them to switch political allegiances. Trump, Johnson and numerous PiS politicians in Poland are good examples of this trend, where individual hypocrisy of politicians is accepted as long as they instate conservative rules intended to bind all citizens – while putting a blind eye on the politicians who enforce them. Considering this context, the two-faced conservative moral push appears as the tails to the heads of general political cynicism.

Finally, the scandal frame is arbitrarily used by journalists who choose which stories to present as scandals and which stories to hide, based on the imagined expectations of their audience. The author of *Scandal and silence* offers five such "media decision biases" which influence if and how a political scandal is covered: the stereotype-confirming novelty, meaning who is more likely to be involved in a scandal; the likeability of a particular politician; pressure relief over truth-seeking, for instance in word choice (e.g. "locker room banter" vs. "sexist behavior"); popularity and power of a given politician; as well as the person's cultural congruence and symbolism (e.g. anti-Communist hero). These biases are repeatedly applied in media coverage, which makes them "stick" to the individual described. This is why in online tabloids, for example, Duda was continually characterized as a promising newcomer, Clinton as hiding something shameful, and Cameron as a disappointment. Such labeling is cheap to produce, easy to understand, and is emotionally gratifying to audiences, as Entman argues – and online tabloids show.

2.2 Entertaining Politicians

If journalists tend to write about politics using the scandal frame, Van Zoonen (2005) offers a more general argument, that we are living in an "entertainment-political complex," where politics are intrinsically entwined with entertainment. More than Weber's charismatic leader, a politician today is something of a performer who borrows attention-grabbing techniques from show business. This is why, especially during campaigns, one can find politicians in front of eye-catching stage setups at rallies, appearing on late-night talk shows, not to mention receiving endorsements coming directly from show-business personalities (Street 2004). Although the focus on the online visibility of these performances is recent, van Krieken (2012) finds the beginnings of the celebritization of politics already in the 16th century, such as Machiavelli's teachings on princely appearance. From this perspective, online tabloid portrayals of politicians as celebrities seem not so much an invention of the penny press but rather a continuation of a centuries-old feature of public life. Blurring the lines between politics, understood as activities concerning power and the state, and political entertainment, understood as everything else a politician does in public, makes separating news from entertainment increasingly difficult. In line with this, Delli Carpini and Williams (2001) assert that in today's reality of infotainment the differences between news and entertainment are in many ways arbitrary. For the most part, they are based on the reputation of a given outlet, the types of audiences it attracts, and the prominence of a journalistic story on the page (or the timeslot in the case of radio and television news). In short, the authors write, it is the elite audiences who define which news is serious – the news they consume – but these news sources tend to be less accessible to a broader audience. In contrast, the popular press targeted at the latter attracts the audience by offering more human-interest, crime, and show-business stories or, briefly put, entertainment. Finally, tabloids add a scandalizing twist to the mix, and given that they thrive on entertaining their audiences, it is no surprise that politics and politicians are, too, portrayed as entertainment. As a result, politicians are molded in a similar emotional vein as other celebrities featured in these non-elite outlets, and special attention is paid to their (im)moral behavior, looks, as well as detachment from average people, which puts them in a bad, but well-selling, light.

Street emphasizes yet another crucial feature, namely the importance of "political style" and political aesthetics. The scholar convincingly argues that they, too, are borrowed directly from celebrities. Because of this relatability to show-business, emphasis on political style offers audiences a shortcut – easy explanations of a complicated political reality. Politicians are supposed to visually "look" the part, hence the detailed descriptions of outfits and extensive photo galleries of the candidates posted in the online tabloids. However, the detachment of politicians from people's ordinary lives is a disadvantage when they attempt to win votes. This is why a politician who appears to be an approachable person "of the people" – even if the image is entirely manufactured – is particularly valued by tabloids, which generally applaud familiarity, homeliness, and a down-to-earth attitude. Van Zoonen offers a helpful four-fold typology of politicians' approaches towards celebrity, which is particularly worth mentioning here: the ordinary political insider; the special (or unconventional) political insider; the ordinary political outsider; and the special political outsider. And so, according to the author,

> The ultimate celebrity politician, then, the one who is able to balance the contradictory requirements of politics and celebrity, is located right in the middle of the plot. He or she projects a persona that has inside experience with politics but is still an outsider; his (or, in some cases, her) performance builds on a unique mixture of ordinariness and exceptionality.
> p. 84

Indeed, one can notice the effectiveness of this balancing act in online tabloid readers' enthusiastic comments concerning Duda, Trump and the Leave campaign. These candidates proved more persuasive than their competitors in selling themselves to the voters as one of their own, as outsiders fighting for ordinary Janes and Joes from the inside. At the same time, it is hard to ignore that the tabloid celebrity frame administered on politicians is a stark departure from the formal, statesman style found in hard-news outlets which focus on politicians' public performance rather than their personalities and private lives. Nonetheless, elite outlets fighting for audience attention have been increasingly embracing this type of soft news, and political sex scandals provide a transgressive moment where the private realm becomes public in the public's interest, not merely for tabloid entertainment. Thus, while one can imagine accusations of political corruption garnering popular outrage, tabloids know well that sex sells but accusations of fraud require lengthy explaining, even if people are more likely to condemn the latter, as Warren and Barton (2019) argue. In contrast, sexual misdeeds are usually understandable to everyone. This may be the reason why Trump's "grab them by the pussy" remark was one of the most covered and commented features of the US campaign in the three online tabloids. Inconsistencies concerning his finances proved far less attractive news material.

2.3 The Commenters

Readers commenting under articles on online news websites have received some scrutiny from social scientists, notably in the context of participatory journalism (Graham 2013; Lewis et al. 2017) and consumer behavior (Phillips 2015; Wahl-Jorgensen 2016).[10] According to these approaches, the commenters, while not directly cooperating with journalists in creating news stories, nonetheless shape a sense of online community on the websites. Moreover, from a financial point of view they generate profit for the outlets, for instance through ad views, each time other users engage in conversation. In a rare example of qualitative analysis of comments on news websites – albeit focused on the articles rather than readers' replies – Boczkowski and Mitchelstein (2013) found that around the 2008 US presidential election the most commented articles were commentaries on "controversial, high-profile public affairs topics." In a study of a French online news outlet, Christin (2015), too, found that commenters tended to comment on controversial topics such as racism, sexism, and religion under articles concerning politics. These studies point at political news' focus on high-stakes normative issues, which makes it easier for opinions to concentrate not so much on facts as on their moral significance. Boczkowski and Mitchelstein's, as well as Christin's descriptions of comments relate well to the articles on politics that were published in the three online tabloids analyzed here. Though for tabloid writers the scholars' discoveries might

---

10   However, people who comment on news articles linked on social media, most notably Facebook and Twitter, have been receiving significantly more attention from researchers in the social sciences. See e.g.: Anspach and Carlson 2020; Hanusch and Tandoc Jr 2019; Su et al. 2018.

not strike as particularly surprising, the readers' comments on Pudelek, Mail Online and Gawker reveal an important yet ignored, third dimension. More than just saleable commodities (each comment and comment "like" or "unlike" is a click which translates into revenue) or civic journalism (the comments are predominantly emotional opinions, not factual discoveries) they extend the journalistic pieces beyond the final, professionally edited period. For many people, reading online articles includes reading user comments; online "vox pop" opinions have become almost seamless extensions of journalistic writing. After all, it is enough to scroll down the page. Right after the article ends, the comments begin, and the option to add a comment is conveniently located at the top of the section. As for the comments sections themselves, they are embedded by default on each article webpage, and the comments are not merely an addition, they are expected to be there. In the three online tabloids, comments vary from compliments or insults – towards journalists, towards people and institutions discussed in a given piece, or both – to asking questions related to the topic (or not), and providing additional information. Von Sikorski and Hänelt (2016) conducted an interesting experiment on online readers' comments, which relates to commenter sympathies and to scandal framing discussed earlier. Using a German case, the scholars found that online news readers who saw positive comments concerning a public figure accused of scandal felt more sympathetic towards that person. However, it did not work the other way round, audiences were not affected by negative comments concerning the individual. This may suggest why Komorowski's negative depictions of Duda as Kaczyński's puppet, Remain campaign's arguments about UK's gloomy future outside the European Union (dubbed "Project Fear" by the Leave side), not to mention Clinton's focus on Trump's sex scandals did not sway voters enough to vote in their favor.

Although von Sikorski and Hänelt's findings are intriguing, the category of a snarky (Denby 2009) and paranoid commenter (Sedgwick 2003; see also: Ricoeur 1970) may be more helpful in understanding comments under articles on political campaigns in online tabloids. Snark is an oft-found feature in readers' comments and is not uncommon in the online tabloid articles. This type of ironic, often exaggerating, and usually offensive remark has been largely attributed to Gawker and, according to Denby, was treated as the outlet's official style. However, snark did not end with the journalistic pieces but was successfully adopted by readers in the comments section. What's more, snark is often mixed with paranoid reading, a term proposed by Sedgwick, which assumes that stories include hidden messages that need to be revealed to get to the truth of the matter. This idea is inspired by Ricoeur's concept of hermeneutics of suspicion, where "to seek meaning is no longer to spell out the consciousness of meaning, but to *decipher its expressions*" (p. 33). This consciousness of meaning thus becomes a compound, a multifaceted relation between "hidden-shown" or "simulated-manifested." Such an interpretation of consciousness, which Ricoeur attributes to Freud, Marx, and Nietzsche, is taken a step further by Sedgwick in her psychoanalytical take on the paranoid outlook. The scholar defines it in a manner I find particularly illuminating in this context: "In a world where no one need be delusional to find evidence of systemic oppression, to theorize out of anything but a paranoid critical stance has come to seem naïve, pious, or complaisant" (p. 125–126). What this implies is that from the paranoid point of view bad news is not just expected but already known. Furthermore, within its own tautological logic, a paranoid reading proves that negative expectations are always correct. Nonetheless, there is, again, a paradox: according to the paranoid view described by Sedgwick, public exposure of such negative knowledge could potentially lead to change – it is a radical belief in the power of visibility – but bad news, which by paranoid definition is always anticipated, always prevails. This way, it completes the perfect circle of paranoia. For instance, the "elite" discussed earlier is a prime example of such paranoid focus: it always wins, regardless of particular individuals who take power. Besides, if snark – "parasitic, referential, insinuating," often faking shock to expand into "superfluous" anger, as Denby describes it – was not as widespread in the readers' comments on Pudelek and Mail Online as it was on Gawker, the paranoid readings of the journalistic pieces were manifest throughout. They could be found in the conviction that elections would be "rigged" in favor of Remain and Clinton, even though they were won, respectively, by Leave and Trump. Paranoid readings could also be noticed in the certainty that Komorowski and Clinton were not just corrupt individuals but members of secret powerful associations ranging from the Bilderberg Group to the Illuminati, not to mention being Jews, a staple of global conspiracy theories. In this sense, the votes became a triumph of agency in paranoid reading: the "anti-elite" elite won.

3   What's Popular in Online Tabloid Political Coverage? A Close Look at Campaign News

3.1   *Numbers and Themes*

How did the political coverage of the 2015 and 2016 election campaigns look like in these widely popular online tabloids? For the purpose of this analysis,

I collected articles published on Pudelek, Mail Online and Gawker[11] during the two preceding months for each vote: Polish presidential election in 2015, the British EU "Brexit" referendum in 2016, and the US presidential election in 2016. In the analysis I used the websites' internal search engines using keywords: Duda, Komorowski, PiS, Prawo i Sprawiedliwość, PO, Platforma Obywatelska, Brexit, Cameron, Johnson, Corbyn, Farage, Donald, Trump, Hillary, and Clinton.[12] Finally, since in the case of the Polish election the only article on Mail Online which mentioned the vote was published later, and since in the case of the EU referendum, all of the articles on Pudelek and all but one article on Gawker on the topic were published after the vote, I included them in the sample as well. The articles differed in length across the three outlets: on Pudelek the posts were typically 150–600 words long, Gawker posts were slightly longer, around 600 to 1,600 words-long. This remained in stark contrast to Mail Online where the articles were significantly lengthier, varying from anywhere around 3,000 words up to 13,000 words. It is also worth noting that Mail Online, by far the largest outlet of the three, published articles on the analyzed topics in several different sections of the website. The single article on the Polish election was published in the News section. Still, it focused on the parliamentary election that was held later in the fall that same year, and the post mentioned the May presidential election only in passing. However, references to the US election could be found not only in the News section but also in the Sport, Femail, and TV & Showbiz categories. Similarly, the British EU referendum while, too, mostly present in the News section, often appeared in other Mail Online categories, from TV & Showbiz, through Money, to Science. If not necessarily surprising, this shows that the local British topic was approached from significantly more angles, relating to more aspects of life than foreign issues, although the US election, too, received significant attention across different sections.

It is hard not to notice that the election campaign for the presidential seat in Poland, the first of the studied three, was completely invisible to Gawker and received just a single article from Mail Online, yet only after the election.

---

11 After the Gawker website was closed on 28th of August 2016, I continued collecting articles written by then already former Gawker authors who published on other Gizmodo Media Group (formerly Gawker Media) websites. For the sake of clarity, I use the name Gawker also when discussing articles published after that date.

12 It has to be noted, however, that the Mail Online search engine turned out to be unstable during my research. To deal with this issue, I cross-checked the records using the Factiva archive of Mail Online. This allowed me to establish and analyze the actual number of Mail Online articles published during the set periods.

TABLE 2 Number of articles in Pudelek, Mail Online, and Gawker in the three campaigns

	PL presidential campaign: 11 Mar–24 May 2015 (2nd round)[a]	After PL presidential election: 25 May 2015–31 Mar 2017	UK Brexit referendum campaign: 24 Apr–23 Jun 2016 (election day)	After UK Brexit referendum: 24 Jun 2016–30 Jun 2018	US presidential campaign: 9 Sep–8 Nov 2016 (election day)
No. of articles on Pudelek	30	7	0	17	29
No. of articles on Mail Online	0	1	984	[not included]	1,485
No. of articles written by Gawker writers	0	0	1	18	171[b]

Note:
a The first round was held on 10th of May 2015 but none of the candidates received more than 50 percent of the votes to win without a runoff
b Gawker authors who were included in the detailed analysis: Gabrielle Bluestone, Ashley Feinberg, Hannah Gold, Hudson Hongo, Hamilton Nolan, Brendan O'Connor, Alex Pareene, Jordan Sargent, Kelly Stout, and J.K. Trotter. After the Gawker website was closed, articles written on the US campaign by other authors within the Gizmodo Media Group were also included in the total number. 554 articles were written by all Gizmodo Media Group authors during the period

SOURCE: AUTHOR

The British EU referendum held a year later gained more attention: one post on Gawker during the campaign, and over a dozen articles on both Gawker and Pudelek after the vote, not to mention 984 articles published in the British online tabloid, a whopping number in comparison to the two other outlets. However, the US presidential election was the most popular in all three tabloids, an indication of its significance for the audiences. For example, Pudelek posted just one article less on the US presidential campaign than on the Polish one. The importance of the election across the Atlantic was even more notable on Mail Online; the number of articles published there was around one third higher compared to pieces written about the EU referendum campaign. As could be expected, the US online tabloid was most interested in its own local affairs, though they garnered the most attention in the other two outlets as well. Even before going into the details of the published articles, and judging solely by the numbers, one can notice that the rate of foreign coverage in the three online tabloids reflects common notions concerning the power of the three states. The scandalizing and emotional tabloid-style treatment of the campaigns does not undermine these broadly shared views. Thus, based on the articles in the three outlets, the United States is confirmed as a superpower, with the US presidential elections having a major impact on the rest of the world. The United Kingdom is, too, shown as an important international player; after all, the 2016 referendum concerned its departure from the European Union, a powerful regional economic and political structure. In contrast to the two, the influence of Poland is presented as much smaller, hence the limited attention paid to the country's election. However, numbers alone only tell part of the story, and the significance of the three countries can also be noticed in how foreign vote campaigns are mixed into local contexts. Despite the different levels of interest in specific elections, similarities and recurring patterns can be observed in online tabloid coverage across all three political campaigns. In the next sections, I present a close look at the articles and readers' comments to bring a better understanding of how these outlets present matters in which their audiences have a final say by the ballot box.

In order to uncover the recurring topics and relations between them, I analyzed the top thirty most commented articles for each of the three election campaigns in each online tabloid.[13] In the case when less than thirty articles were published by an outlet on a particular campaign, all of the posts were analyzed. A general overview of the main topics and the relations between them on Pudelek, Mail Online, and Gawker taken together is presented in Figure 4. The map shows associations between topics mentioned in the articles and in the readers' comments, as well as their popularity – the larger the bubbles and the lines between them, the more frequent their mentions and co-occurrences.[14] The strongest connections can be noticed between posts and

---

13 The analysis and coding of topics was performed using MAXQDA software.
14 It should be noted that the same topic could be mentioned more than once in different parts of the same article; the map reflects this.

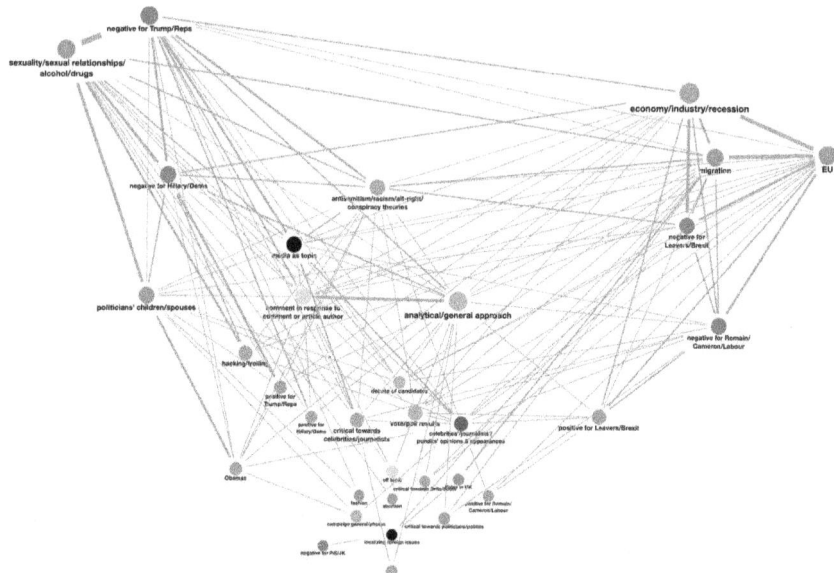

FIGURE 4   Map of associations between topics mentioned in Pudelek, Mail Online, and Gawker articles
SOURCE: AUTHOR

comments that are negative towards Donald Trump and the Republican Party, and mentions of sexual topics, particularly related to the scandal that broke out after a recording was revealed with Trump stating he likes to grab attractive women "by the pussy." Another strong connection can be observed in the EU referendum campaign between mentions of the European Union and migration, usually its negative effect on the UK emphasized by Leavers. A different prominent connection is that between the EU and its impact on the UK economy. This second connection was frequently mentioned both by Leavers and Remainers. The argumentation, however, used by the two sides was markedly different: for Remainers the EU had a positive influence on the British economy, Leavers claimed the opposite. In addition, the map highlights the differences in popularity of US and UK-related topics, compared to the lesser visibility of topics connected to the Polish presidential campaign; this also reflects the generally smaller number of articles published on the Polish election. Yet the third clear link between the different topics is a meta-connection of sorts. It does not so much focus on concrete issues mentioned in the articles but, instead, it ties general analyses presented in the articles and readers' comments in response to the journalistic pieces and to other commenters. This connection is crucial as it indicates the vital importance of the conversational relationship between journalistic pieces and the reader comments, which so far has been largely overlooked in research studies.

In the following sections, I present an in-depth qualitative analysis of the three most popular themes published on Pudelek, Mail Online, and Gawker during each campaign. Within these themes three of the most commented articles are closely examined alongside five most upvoted comments for each of these articles. Some of the studied posts and comments received thousands of upvotes, while others got far less. This is largely dependent on the familiarity of a story, since the closer the topic to home the more comments and upvotes it receives. Gurevitsch, Levy and Roeh (1991) call this "domesticating the foreign." In their analysis of global television news, the authors argue that it "simultaneously maintains both global and culturally specific orientations. This is accomplished, first, by casting far-away events in frameworks that render these events comprehensible, appealing and 'relevant' to domestic audiences; and second, by constructing the meanings of these events in ways that are compatible with the culture and the 'dominant ideology' of the societies they serve." They then add aptly, "[t]he meaning of a concrete news story is always produced in the public space of culture, and in the framework of a relevant family-of-stories, already familiar to the members of a given society" (pp. 206–207). While such contextualization can be found in different news outlets, it is particularly noticeable in campaign coverage published in the three online tabloids, where the aspect of familiarity is often what makes foreign news attractive to report in the first place. However, familiarizing outside news is not just applied to make it more attractive for the audience. It can also serve as an internal "protectionist strategy," which Clausen describes as "a means of protection of national identity [that] may be at work in the international newsrooms" (2004, p. 29). In this sense, domesticating foreign news serves not to bring them closer but to reinforce the distinction between us and others, those who are inside and outside the community. This idea is corroborated by Gans (2004) in his famous work on news on television and in weeklies in the United States. The scholar argues that foreign news reveals general value judgements that are presented in local news far less explicitly. Indeed, whereas online tabloids are not shy about using moral(izing) language, the coverage of national political campaigns vividly shows how such value-laden familiarization is done, and how the domestication of foreign stories is achieved by immersing them in familiar moral perspectives. In this context, it is worth noting Galtung and Ruge's (1965) seminal study on foreign news, since it highlights the power imbalance in foreign news selection, which can be observed in online tabloid coverage as well. Their list of twelve factors influencing news selection includes one that is especially important here: "reference to elite nations," meaning countries influential enough to be worthy of other states' attention. The scholars explain that such nations can be mostly found in the "elite northwestern corners of the world" (p. 73). This implies that not all nations are considered worth reporting in the local news, not to mention doing the additional work of domesticating foreign issues. Gans offers a blunt explanation of this:

> Foreign events are also of interest when they represent convergences with American phenomena. England is newsworthy simply because it is thought to converge culturally with the United States; but when other countries adopt American election strategies, incorporate American words into their language, or establish American-type goods and stores, the event is likely to be reported.
>
> 2004, pp.32–33

Over fifty years later O'Neill and Harcup (2019) reinterpret Galtung and Ruge's category less geographically, and describe elite nations as those whose actions "are seen as more consequential than the actions of other nations" (p. 217). While this is a departure from the emphasis on Western dominance, some national power relations remain the same. Thus, it is impossible to ignore that in online-tabloid coverage of the three national campaigns held in the mid-2010s in countries in the northern hemisphere, the US presidential campaign was clearly the most written about, followed by the EU referendum campaign in the UK, whereas the Polish presidential campaign barely received any coverage in the two popular foreign outlets. It is a telling illustration of the position of "elite northwestern corners of the world" which has not changed much in the last half century, even if during this period Poland successfully transitioned from a crumbling Communist country to a strong EU member state, while the United Kingdom lost control over its overseas possessions.[15]

Still, regardless of the influence of international powers, domestic news prevails. The most popular pieces and the most upvoted comments on Pudelek concerned Polish topics, accordingly, British issues were the most popular on Mail Online, and US matters received the most attention on Gawker. At the same time, Mail Online articles received the most comments and comment

---

15   For example, the domestication strategy applied to reporting on the fall of the Iron Curtain is described by Gurevitsch, Levy and Roeh as follows: "US television coverage of recent events in Eastern Europe has been consistently couched in the terminology of the triumph of 'freedom' and 'democratization', thus conveying a sense of America's triumph in the cold war" (1991, p. 206).

votes. This is not surprising given that the audience of the outlet is much bigger compared to the two other websites. A technical issue worth noting is that while Gawker only offered upvotes in the form of clickable stars, Mail Online and Pudelek allow both upvotes and downvotes – on Pudelek these are thumbs up and thumbs down, on Mail Online readers can click on upward and downward facing arrows. The most upvoted posts often also happened to be the most downvoted, though the number of positive reactions to a given post surpassed negative ones. However, to maintain consistency across all three outlets, only upvotes were considered in the analysis. A breakdown of the main campaign themes is presented in Table 3. Finally, the following sections can be read in two ways: either chronologically or by jumping from one top theme to another.

TABLE 3　The most popular themes on Pudelek, Mail Online, and Gawker during the three campaigns (numbers in parentheses indicate how many articles mention a given theme out of the total number of articles analyzed in depth using MAXQDA)

Campaign	Online tabloid	Most popular themes
Poland 2015 presidential election	Pudelek	1. *criticism towards celebrities and journalists* (21/30) 2. *negative attitudes towards Bronisław Komorowski* (15/30) 3. *general comments* (14/30) 4. *mentions of Paweł Kukiz* (11/30) 5. negative attitudes towards Andrzej Duda (10/30) 6. opinions of pundits and celebrities (10/30) 7. positive attitudes towards Andrzej Duda (8/30) 8. focus on media (8/30) 9. polls and vote results (7/30) 10. conversations between commenters (7/30)
	Gawker	-
	Mail Online	*single article on the parliamentary election held in Poland later that same year, mentioning the May presidential election, published on 25th of October 2015*
United Kingdom 2016 EU referendum	Mail Online	1. *European Union* (27/30) 2. *immigration* (26/30) 3. *negative attitudes towards Leavers/Brexit* (26/30) 4. negative attitudes towards Remainers/Cameron/Labour (25/30)

TABLE 3 The most popular themes on Pudelek, Mail Online, and Gawker (*cont.*)

Campaign	Online tabloid	Most popular themes
		5. positive attitudes towards Leavers/Brexit (24/30)
		6. economy/recession (24/30)
		7. polls and vote results (18/30)
		8. general comments (13/30)
		9. focus on media (12/30)
		10. candidates' debates (11/30)
	Gawker/ Gizmodo	1. *general comments* (16/19)
		2. *conversations between commenters* (13/19)
		3. *economy/recession* (9/19)
		4. hacking and trolling (8/19)
		5. European Union (8/19)
		6. negative attitudes towards Leavers/Brexit (6/19)
		7. negative attitudes towards Donald Trump/Republicans (5/19)
		8. antisemitism/racism/alt-right/conspiracy theories (5/19)
		9. negative attitudes towards Hillary Clinton/Democrats (3/19)
		10. polls and vote results (3/19)
	Pudelek	1. *general comments* (12/17)
		2. *European Union* (11/17)
		3. *Poles in the United Kingdom* (10/17)
		4. domesticating foreign issues (9/17)
		5. negative attitudes towards British citizens (8/17)
		6. immigration (8/17)
		7. focus on media (7/17)
		8. polls and vote results (6/17)
		9. negative attitudes towards Leavers/Brexit (5/17)
		10. negative attitudes towards pundits and celebrities (5/17)
United States 2016 presidential election	Gawker/ Gizmodo	1. *negative attitudes towards Donald Trump/Republicans* (25/30)
		2. *conversations between commenters* (20/30)
		3. *sex and sexism* (17/30)
		4. focus on media (15/30)

TABLE 3 The most popular themes on Pudelek, Mail Online, and Gawker (cont.)

Campaign	Online tabloid	Most popular themes
		5. general comments (11/30) 6. antisemitism/racism/alt-right/conspiracy theories (10/30) 7. immigration (8/30) 8. negative attitudes towards Hillary Clinton/ Democrats (7/30) 9. polls and vote results (7/30) 10. economy/recession (6/30)
	Mail Online	1. *negative attitudes towards Hillary Clinton/ Democrats (24/30)* 2. *negative attitudes towards Donald Trump/ Republicans (20/30)* 3. *sex and sexism (20/30)* 4. general comments (19/30) 5. focus on media (18/30) 6. hacking/trolling (16/30) 7. positive attitudes towards Donald Trump/ Republicans (16/30) 8. antisemitism/racism/alt-right/conspiracy theories (14/30) 9. politicians' families (12/30) 10. Barack and/or Michelle Obama (11/30)
	Pudelek	1. *general comments (17/29)* 2. *photo galleries (images) (15/29)* 3. *negative attitudes towards Hillary Clinton/ Democrats (13/29)* 4. negative attitudes towards Donald Trump/ Republicans (12/29) 5. politicians' families (12/29) 6. sex and sexism (11/29) 7. antisemitism/racism/alt-right/conspiracy theories (9/29) 8. Barack and/or Michelle Obama (8/29) 9. conversations between commenters (8/29) 10. opinions of pundits and celebrities (8/29)

SOURCE: AUTHOR

3.2 Poland 2015 Presidential Campaign

Although the Polish presidential election was the first of the three votes in the discussed 2015–2016 period that led to a major political right-wing shift, at the time British and US online tabloid audiences did not find Poland's presidential election particularly exciting: it received barely one mention in Mail Online, and that only long after the vote. For this reason, the main themes are based on articles and comments from Pudelek. Despite this, US and British influences were present in the Polish campaign. Still, the lack of interest in the Polish presidential election on the part of Mail Online and Gawker may, on the one hand, speak of Poland's minor international role at the time. But, on the other hand, the increasing focus on Poland that came after PiS gained presidential and parliamentary power in 2015 was the effect of Poland's growing internal and EU-related conflicts concerning, among other things, the rule of law, media freedom, and women's rights. In this sense, the lack of attention to the Polish presidential election was also a reflection of the country's international "non-troublemaker" status. It was only later that the poster child of post-1989 successful democratic transition became famous as a rule of law-breaking *enfant terrible* of the European Union, next to Hungary which has been led by the authoritarian-leaning Prime Minister, Viktor Orbán since 2010. However, in the spring of 2015, for an outsider Polish politics was stable and boring. Yet the sensationalizing online tabloid articles, and especially the emotional comments, revealed a different picture. It was one in which people were fed up with the elite, the incumbent President Komorowski being its prime example. Hence, the endorsements he received from famous artists, journalists, and celebrities only fueled Pudelek readers' anger, since they appeared to confirm their suspicions about members of the elite supporting each other at the cost of average Joes and Janes. In contrast, the previously largely unknown Duda, younger and inexperienced in big politics, could be presented as a fresh alternative to Komorowski, and as a person not depraved by power – despite the fact of being supported by PiS, then the major opposition party. In short, Duda was shown as a non-elite agent of change, even though he was backed by powerful politicians, and on 24th of May he succeeded in winning the presidential vote. Branding politicians as non-elite even if facts prove otherwise is a pattern that also became apparent in the subsequent British and American campaigns. In fact, Johnson and Farage in the United Kingdom, next to Trump in the United States are perfect examples of populist anti-elite framing of elite politicians to gain popular support. They turned out to be much more effective than actual non-elite, outsider politicians, such as Sanders in the US and Kukiz in Poland. Thus, from the point of view of chronology, the portrayal of Duda and his campaign in online tabloids reveals an anti-elite style that later proved successful for Leavers and for Republicans.

3.2.1 Pudelek

Unlike Gawker and Mail Online, Pudelek does not require commenters to sign up to write comments, and until the website's redesign in 2019 the prefilled name in the comment form was "gość" (guest).[16] Most of the commenters used this alias or other random ones, making it impossible to identify a particular person behind the comments. Conversations between commenters were rare, although not entirely invisible; the comments were for the most part statements of opinion or replies to the articles rather than conversation pieces – similarly to Mail Online but in contrast to Gawker. The three most popular themes in the two final months leading to the May 2015 presidential election were: criticism towards celebrities and journalists; negative attitudes towards the incumbent president from the PO party, Bronisław Komorowski; and general comments made by Pudelek's anonymous readers. Especially the first two highlight anti-elite sentiment – towards individuals with media influence and towards the head of state, with direct political power. The third most popular theme shows that Pudelek commenters shared the desire to present their own broader views on politics, offering additional contexts to the topics discussed in the journalistic pieces.

3.2.1.1 *Criticism towards Celebrities and Journalists*

And so, in terms of *criticism towards celebrities and journalists* voiced in the articles and comments, it has to be noted that most of the celebrities described in relation to the campaign endorsed the incumbent President Komorowski, who was supported by PO, the ruling party at the time. Although celebrity endorsements are popular in Polish politics, studies question their effectiveness in persuading voters to change their party sympathies or their values. Nonetheless, Kollman and Jackson (2021) argue that party loyalties may shift if a party's position on key issues is transformed (for example, regarding abortion rights or membership in the European Union). In addition, according to Atkinson and DeWitt (2016) celebrity support may be successful when entertainment-focused outlets are used to influence people who do not pay much attention to politics, when celebrities support specific politicians within the same party – for instance, when they are competing for a nomination – or when celebrities

---

16 At present, commenters have to manually enter a name in the comment form but some still stick to "gość," possibly out of sentiment.

support public policies rather than people. One such post on Pudelek, which touched on a celebrity – in this case a celebrity-journalist – bore the headline "New 'Newsweek' cover: 'ELECTORAL FRAUD!'"[17] (2,161 comments), and was published on 11th of May, right after the first round of the presidential election, won by Duda. The piece analyzed the cover of the Polish edition of *Newsweek* weekly, which was then headed by Tomasz Lis, a well-known news journalist and commentator.[18] On the cover, one could see Jarosław Kaczyński, the leader of PiS, take off a mask of Andrzej Duda from his own face. The piece briefly explained the sudden ascent of previously unknown Duda, a "fresh face" who according to opposition politicians was Kaczyński's "puppet." Despite this, in an anti-elite vein, the most upvoted readers' comments were highly critical of Lis and of other journalists supporting Komorowski:

"lis, kuzniar, are biased journalists, not reliable"[19] (1,385 upvotes);

"Lis is a fake both in professional and private life" (245 upvotes).

The "fake" comment likely referred to Lis's marital infidelity in the past, but other top comments emphasized his possible future struggles after Duda's victory:

"lis are you afraid?" (1,230 upvotes);

while also playing with the name "lis," which means "fox":

"The foxhole is burning, time to run" (1,290 upvotes).

One top comment, however, looked into the bright Duda-led future, directly referring to PiS's campaign slogan:

"finally some cheerful air in Poland ,,,Poland is rising from her knees!!!!!!!" (571 upvotes).

The "puppet" theme could also be found in another top commented post, published on 18th of May. This one focused on a popular sports

---

17 https://www.pudelek.pl/artykul/79094/nowa_okladka_newsweeka_falszerstwo_wybor cze/. Original use of letter case, punctuation, and spelling errors has been kept were possible.
18 Lis left the post in 2022 after a bullying scandal.
19 Jarosław Kuźniar is another liberal-leaning journalist.

celebrity: "Michalczewski pleads: DUDA IS A MATRYOSHKA DOLL, Macierewicz and Kaczyński are standing behind him! Vote with your heads!"[20] (1,986 comments). Dariusz Michalczewski, a famous boxer, joined Komorowski's campaign and appealed for voters to "uncover" the hidden "puppet masters" behind Duda. These were Jarosław Kaczyński, the leader of PiS party, and the party's high-ranking member and chief conspiracy theorist Antoni Macierewicz. The latter is known, among other things, for claiming that the 2010 plane crash near the Russian town, Smolensk, in which 96 state officials including Poland's president, Lech Kaczyński (Jarosław's twin brother) died, had been a coup orchestrated by Russia, possibly together with the then ruling party PO. Macierewicz and other PiS party members have been making these claims for over two decades despite overwhelming evidence that the crash had been the result of human error. An additional layer provided by Michalczewski that was cited in the article was the mention of a matryoshka doll, which was a clear allusion to Russian influence in the presidential campaign. In doing so, he was pointing a finger at the usual suspect in the popular Polish imagination – and not without historical reason – namely Russia, and linked it with PiS. Still, the commenters were unconvinced by Michalczewski's arguments. The most upvoted comments referred to "asses":

"they [celebrities] are nobodies so I can wipe my ass with their 'authority'. I am voting for Duda." (301 upvotes);

„so thanks to this he should like Komorowski's and PO's ass out of gratitude?" (197 upvotes).

Another popular comment focused on the differences between "haves" and "have nots," another variation of elite vs. non-elite:

"He [Michalczewski] is saying this because he is rich when he was poor and lived from paycheck to paycheck his attitude towards komor [Komorowski] was different, and Komorowski had his five years [presidential term] for which he should, begging your pardon, f*** off ...!" (241 upvotes).

---

20 https://www.pudelek.pl/michalczewski-apeluje-duda-to-matrioszka-za-nim-stoi-macierewicz-i-kaczynski-glosujcie-z-glowa-6366069304505985w.

This was followed by a scathing comment concerning the boxer's looks:

"face unclouded by intelligence" (217 upvotes).

Still, a different comment posed a rhetorical question about Komorowski's powerful supporters, as if to balance out such accusations made against Duda:

"And who's standing behind Komorowski? WSI [Military Information Services], Communist secret agents, pro civili?[21] Vote who you want for but check first" (77 upvotes).

A different post along the same theme, again mentioning the journalist, was: "Lis quoted a FAKE POST OF DUDA'S DAUGHTER! Will he suffer the consequences?"[22] (1,976 comments), which was published the next day, 19th of May. Lis mentioned the fake quote in a popular television news show he used to host, Tomasz Lis na Żywo (Tomasz Lis Live), aired on the public channel, TVP 2. The fake quote was based on a tweet, in which a person pretending to be the presidential candidate's daughter claimed that if Duda were to win the election, he would return the Oscar prize that had been awarded to the Polish movie "Ida" that year. The film was criticized by right-wing commentators for highlighting the troubled relations between Poles and Jews during the Second World War. While such a tweet would not have been very surprising for a right-wing commenter, Kinga Duda kept mostly silent throughout the campaign and stayed away from controversial topics. As it turned out, Lis, a vocal supporter of Komorowski, was peddling fake news, and the readers' comments reflected the article's unsympathetic attitude towards the journalist. One such popular comment was:

"lis and olejnik are not journalists but propaganda" (2,037 upvotes).

Monika Olejnik, also a popular liberal-leaning political journalist had nothing to do with this particular story but was tied together with Lis since, in the view

---

21 Pro Civili Foundation was a foreign criminal organization which, according to right-wing media, infiltrated Poland's Military Information Services and the Military University of Technology. The foundation defrauded funds from Poland's largest bank, PKO BP. During the 2015 presidential campaign Bronisław Komorowski was accused of involvement in the organization, but the accusations were never confirmed. See e.g.: Czuchnowski and Jałoszewski 2016.

22 https://www.pudelek.pl/artykul/79379/lis_cytowal_falszywy_wpis_corki_dudy_poniesie_konsekwencje/.

of the commenter, she was another example of the same type of journalistic dishonesty. Other commenters were no less outraged:

"This is a travesty of a free and democratic state,What Lis and Karolak [a popular actor who was also part of the show] did should end up in court!!!! (...) What Poland did you fight for Mr Komorowski!!!!." (799 upvotes);

"They should be kicked out of television, and fast" (777 upvotes).

However, two commenters speculated about the use of the fake tweet. The first one analyzed,

"Lis is too experienced a journalist to fall for fake, unverified information. He deliberately showed it in his program, and when he apologized later he did so quietly, not during primetime" (526 upvotes).

The second referred to the popular private television channel TVN, whose stars by and large endorsed Komorowski:

"ask lis and his friends from tvn. they certainly know this very well" (1,636 upvotes)

– it was a reply to another commenter's question,

"so whose [Twitter] post was it?"

3.2.1.2   *Negative Attitudes towards Bronisław Komorowski*
Given the unenthusiastic opinions described above, it is no surprise that the second most popular theme presented a *negative attitude towards the incumbent President Bronisław Komorowski*. (Negative opinions of Andrzej Duda came in fifth place, after mentions of Kukiz.)[23] A prime example of this was an article titled "Komorowski on TVP: 'I am an independent person. I don't have any chairman above me!'"[24] (1,520 comments), published on 18th of May. The title's second sentence was a thinly veiled allusion to Kaczyński's

---

23   Topics negative for Duda were mentioned in 10 out of the 30 analyzed articles; Kukiz was mentioned in 11 out of 30 articles.
24   https://www.pudelek.pl/komorowski-w-tvp-jestem-czlowiekiem-niezaleznym-nie-mam-zadnego-prezesa-nad-soba--6366069394671745w; TVP is a Polish public television channel.

power over Duda. The post discussed the presidential debate held a day earlier, which according to most public commenters was won by Komorowski. As Pudelek wrote, it was at times quite "heated," particularly when the topics turned to IVF (Komorowski favored subsidies for couples in need of IVF, Duda was against them) and the 2010 Smoleńsk plane crash, for which Duda blamed Komorowski in particular, and PO in general. Nevertheless, again, the top upvoted commenters were less than convinced about the incumbent president's debate triumph, openly disagreeing with the opinions of elite-experts:

"The debate will not help you, Bronek.[25] You came out against Poles. We remember this!!!" (566 upvotes);

"This debate uncovered Komorowski's true face. Total failure" (518 upvotes);

"Talked bullsh** like crazy, and links between his daughters and foundations financed by the state and Agora[26] came to light. Didn't he surprise ... Got a dose of his own medicine" (403 upvotes);

"[Komorowski] doesn't have a chairman in front of him???/when Donald [Tusk, leader of PO] hears this he will show him ha ha ha" (403 upvotes).

In addition, Komorowski was perceived as a manipulator:

"K*******I" – propaganda straight from Communist Poland they must have consulted this with Urban" (330 upvotes).

Jerzy Urban, mentioned in the comment, was a widely known journalist who became equally infamous for his work as the Communist government's spokesperson in the 1980s, including the 1981–1983 period of martial law. For many, he remains a symbol of government propaganda and arrogance. Though Komorowski had always been on the anti-Communist side of the political spectrum, this did not bother the commenter or those who upvoted the comment. The "elite" label proved more important and more "sticky" than historical evidence.

---

25   "Bronek" is short for Bronisław, Komorowski's first name.
26   Agora S.A. is the owner of *Gazeta Wyborcza*. The daily supported Komorowski in the presidential election.

"Poniedziałek: 'Duda is Kaczyński! An Iran-style Catholic heritage park'"[27] (4,463 comments), also published on 18th of May, offers another example of a negative attitude towards the incumbent president, albeit this time predominantly in the comments. The article quoted a Facebook post written by Jacek Poniedziałek, a celebrated and openly gay Polish actor, who appealed to his followers to vote for "predictable security" embodied by Komorowski. Instead, Duda was described as "Kaczyński, and Kaczyński is Smoleńsk [plane crash] insanity, (...) destruction of the freedom of media, freedom to create, personal freedom, moral Middle Ages (...)." Earlier in the piece, the journalist reported that many people turned away from Poniedziałek after he had outed himself, and because he openly discussed many popular artists, musicians and politicians as being closeted gays. In fact, one such prime alleged example is Jarosław Kaczyński, who has been rumored to be gay at least since the early 1990s. For example, in 1993 Lech Wałęsa, then president of Poland, stated that he could invite Jarosław Kaczyński to his birthday party "with his husband" (see e.g.: Głuchowski 2022). Although the Pudelek piece included photos of Kaczyński making different faces, from scary to pleased, the commenters focused on their dismay towards Komorowski and elite celebrities who endorsed him, accusing them of lacking knowledge about politics and the reality of ordinary people:

> "Komorowski is supported by Warsaw celebrities who are out of touch with reality" (3,229 upvotes);

> "He [Poniedziałek] said this as if he knew anything about the topic" (2,382 upvotes).

Other top comments under the article openly criticized the PO party for accepting refugees from Syria and Afghanistan, and echoed PiS party's anti-Muslim slogans:

> "I prefer a Catholic Church state than an Islamic one" (785 upvotes).

The commenters spoke unfavorably of other PO policies as well, including the introduction of earlier school age and later retirement age, which Komorowski had signed into law:

---

27 https://www.pudelek.pl/artykul/79422/poniedzialek_duda_to_kaczynski_katolicki_sk ansen_w_stylu_iranu/.

"I don't want to work till [I'm] 67 and I don't want my child to go to school when it's 6 years old so I will vote for Duda" (950 upvotes).

Nonetheless, one of the top comments was happily off topic:

"Have a nice day everybody :)" (782 upvotes).

Yet another negative article for the incumbent president bore a quote from a soap-opera actor as its title, "Mroczek: I am DISAPPOINTED WITH KOMOROWSKI! Duda guarantees change"[28] (1,099 comments). The article was published on 22nd of May, two days before the second round, and reported a last-minute celebrity endorsement of Andrzej Duda. Marcin Mroczek, an actor, became famous for his role in the top Polish soap, "M jak miłość" ("L for Love"). He has been starring in the show together with his twin brother since its launch in 2000, when they were teenagers. A much-liked TV celebrity, he gave his endorsement in an interview for a right-wing online portal, wPolityce (inPolitics), in which he criticized Komorowski for having ignored referendum pleas submitted by citizens, proposing to introduce single-member districts. The idea was first introduced by Paweł Kukiz, the popular outsider presidential candidate who came in third place in the first round of the 2015 presidential election (see: Chmielewska-Szlajfer 2018). However, after initially rejecting the pleas, in the middle of the presidential campaign Komorowski suddenly changed his mind about the referendum. Under Kukiz's influence and after having narrowly lost the first round of the election to Duda, Komorowski decided to hold a vote on creating single-member districts in Poland. Held in September that same year, the referendum was a complete fiasco, with turnout below 8 percent.[29] Interestingly, in the article Mroczek's account was countered by an endorsement in favor of Komorowski offered by a popular comedy-film director, Andrzej Saramonowicz. In contrast to Mroczek's enthusiasm for the newcomer from PiS, Saramonowicz pointed out Duda's poor performance in the two presidential debates, and his likely dependence on PiS party's leader. The most upvoted comment summed up the opinions reported in the article, coming to a bitter conclusion about the state of politics:

---

28   https://www.pudelek.pl/artykul/79499/mroczek_jestem_rozczarowany_komorowskim_duda_gwarantuje_zmiane/.
29   The referendum, held on 6th of September 2015, included three questions: on single-member districts; on financing political parties; and whether tax laws should be interpreted in favor of the taxpayers. The turnout during the referendum, under 8 percent, was the lowest such result in post-1945 Europe.

"Is it just me who thinks that by voting we are choosing a lesser evil? : |" (688 upvotes).

Another top comment shared the sentiment, although less pessimistically:

"Let people vote who they want for, it's their business" (445 upvotes).

Still, a different popular comment agreed with the soap-opera actor's opinion, stressing his non-elite appearance:

"Mroczek is no longer such a celeprity as he used to, he doesn't gain any profit from supporting PO and Mr. Komorowski. He is right because he is not dependent on regime stations" (518 upvotes).

(Contrary to this statement, "M jak miłość" in which Mroczek stars has been aired on Polish public television.) A subsequent comment also agreed with Mroczek, but the commenter adopted a more analytical – and loquacious – approach, discussing the economic situation of non-elite people in Poland:

"PO's only [political] program is to threaten [people] with PiS. Let us ask ourselves the question how is it to live in this country and if it can be worse than it has been until now? Think if you live well, or whether it is our neighbors who live well. I go abroad once in a while for work, my neighbor does too. I don't want this. This is my Country! I want to live fairly. I don't need excess! I want to work, for decent money, not to worry if I can pay the bills! Look around and check how others live! Our country is not for everyone, not only for the chosen people who cannot survive for less than 6 thousand złoty"[30] (457 upvotes).

Lastly, in another top comment a user disagreed with a commenter who questioned Mroczek's credentials. The initial comment was:

---

30   This number is an allusion to a statement made in 2014 by the minister of infrastructure and development, Elżbieta Bieńkowska, in a secretly recorded conversation, one among many such recordings of private talks held by politicians in expensive restaurants. In the recording, Bieńkowska said, "Six thousand ... You understand? Either an idiot, or a crook ... It's impossible anyone would work for this money." The release of these recordings by the weekly, *Wprost* sparked the so-called "tape scandal" that same year, which proved a significant blow to the PO government. To put this salary in perspective, the average monthly wage in Poland in 2015 was around 3,900 złoty.

"Indeed,Mroczek an authority figure for sure, it's an embarrassment to read this !!!!!!!!!!!!" (no votes given)

Yet it was not the questioning of the soap-opera actor's expertise but the snub in the reply which agreed with Mroczek's political opinion, that turned out to be popular among Pudelek readers:

"It's an embarrassment to read your scribbles" (324 upvotes).

3.2.1.3 *General Comments*
More general, contextualizing and not necessarily political comments were, too, one of the most recurring themes during the 2015 presidential campaign, an indication that the comments section was appreciated as a space for more open and wide-ranging opinions. In fact, such general commentary was highly popular in all three campaigns and in all three online tabloids. This shows that treating online-tabloid websites as spaces to speak out on broader issues, at times only loosely related to the articles, is shared by commenters across political and journalistic cultures. For example, on Pudelek this could be found in comments under an article titled, "TVP cancels Pospieszalski's program with Kukiz! 'THIS IS WAR!'"[31] (20th of May, 891 comments). The piece described the unexpected scrapping of a political show which was supposed to be aired on public television, and hosted by the openly right-wing journalist, Jan Pospieszalski. Paweł Kukiz, the outsider who came in third place in the first round of the election having earned a surprisingly high number of votes, was invited as a guest. In a previous episode of the show, Pospieszalski had asked the viewers in a text-message survey whether they would "vote for a candidate supported by the secret service," which was a thinly-veiled allusion to Komorowski. In reference to this, the article on Pudelek mentioned the opinion of Krzysztof Luft, a member of Poland's National Broadcasting Council, who claimed that Pospieszalski's program was not journalism but primitive political propaganda. Kukiz, on the other hand, argued that canceling the show only proved the power of "the System to manipulate reality." (A year later, Trump would be talking about the "deep state" in a similar tone.) Surprisingly, given the anti-Komorowski attitudes noticeable elsewhere, four of the five most upvoted comments written in response to the article adopted more of a general approach, which included two statements of disappointment:

---

31 https://www.pudelek.pl/artykul/79403/tvp_odwoluje_program_pospieszalskiego_z_ku kizem_to_jest_wojna/.

"What is going on in this country :(" (1149 upvotes)

and "This is terrible ☹" (178 upvotes);

a sarcastic comment about the law:

"But we are living in a country governed by the rule of law, for sure.";

and a comment pointing out a non-existing factual error:

"Lubin is not Kukiz's hometown" (299 upvotes).

There was no mention of the town in the article. Instead, the piece cited Kukiz's offer to host an additional, third debate between Komorowski and Duda there. One of the replies to this last comment offered a helpful explanation why that particular town was chosen, demonstrating the conversational, and occasionally informative style, linking the articles and the comments:

"[Lubin] is not [Kukiz's hometown] but it supports him. A rally was organized in Lubin for Kukiz's team after the first round."

"Duda to Komorowski: 'You walked around with a chocolate eagle. Cotillion, balloon, a party-owned president!'"[32] (836 comments), another instance of the theme, was published two days before the second round, on 22nd of May. The title was a direct quote from the final presidential debate. Pudelek described the discussion as "heated" and focused on the candidates' exchanges concerning the Polish national symbol. Komorowski accused Duda of abstaining from voting on a presidential bill that would add the crowned white eagle to the outfits worn by the Polish national sports team, while Duda accused Komorowski of a "pathetic" and "ridiculous" celebration of Poland's National Flag Day in 2013, which included a huge eagle made of white chocolate. Indeed, the initiative was immediately met with criticism, particularly from right-wing media.[33] The incumbent president responded to the accusation defensively, "So you can see, the eagle can only be a PiS eagle." The commenters, once more, were

---

32 https://www.pudelek.pl/duda-do-komorowskiego-pan-wychodzil-z-czekolado wym-orlem-kotylionik-i-balonik-partyjny-prezydent--6366068939753601w.

33 The chocolate eagle was one of many features in an all-Poland campaign, titled "The Eagle Can" under the patronage of the president, which promoted happy patriotism instead of gloomy commemorations of war battles. The campaign was supported by

unconvinced by Komorowski's performance. One of the top comments ridiculed Komorowski, alluding to his spelling mistakes:

> "and illiteracy?" (128 upvotes),

other comments were more general. One stated ambiguously,

> "I feel pity" (197 upvotes),

as it was unclear for whom the commenter felt pity. Another popular comment referred to a reader's statement that people who do not have proper – that is big – families have no idea how to manage. It was an allusion to the fact that Duda is a father of one, while Komorowski has five children. A much-upvoted reply countered this position:

> "Not a very logical statement, what does having a family have to do with management? Having a family only signifies being married and procreating. Balecerkowkie [misspelled Balcerkowie] from Alternatywy 4 and Kiepscy (…) have families, but management … you know :)"[34] (100 upvotes).

A different comment appealed to others to stop spreading fear:

> "You [Pudelek writer or another user – unclear], too, are pathetic with such posts! Zero facts, only pure propaganda and fearmongering. Cut it out!!!!" (82 upvotes).

Finally, another popular comment presented the choice between the two candidates as one between a rock and a hard place. The remark was also spiced with a popular conspiracy theory mixing money with antisemitism, which can be often found on Pudelek and other Polish online forums:

Gazeta Wyborcza daily and Trójka, then a widely popular public radio station (its audience dropped to dismal numbers after changes were introduced by PiS-nominated management, starting 2015). The involvement of these media outlets was criticized by many, particularly on the right, as an undercover campaign in support of Komorowski's reelection. See e.g.: Gąsior 2013.

34   *Alternatywy 4* (the title is a fictitious street address, which means Alternative 4) and *Kiepscy* (the title, a family name, can be translated as "Losers") are both popular Polish family comedy series. The former was originally aired in the 1980s, the latter has been running since the end of the 1990s.

"Kaczyński is standing behind Duda and behind Komorowski are oligarchs of Jewish origin such as Walter Solorz Kulczyk"[35] (31 upvotes).

An additional example of this theme could be found in an article from 24th of May, which was the day of the second round of the presidential election. The piece was titled "Election silence extended till 22:30!"[36] (362 comments), instead of the usual closing time at 8pm. The article reported that the election silence was extended because of the death of an 80-year-old woman at a polling station. This forced the station to close for an hour and a half, hence the added time. In response to the article, two of the most upvoted comments were identical, short and to the point:

"Silence" (405 and 111 upvotes, respectively).

One comment complained about the lack of unofficial exit poll results:

"They are saying on television tvn24[37] that everyone already knows the results online – but no one is saying anything here" (56 upvotes).

Another top upvoted comment voiced surprise about the factuality of the Pudelek article:

"wooow never thought pudel would write abut this:p" (213 upvotes).

Yet a very different type of comment was upvoted, too, even though – or perhaps because – it was completely off topic and suggested the commenter's young age on a day centered on those over 18 years old:

"jeez how I don't want to go to school tomorrow." (295 upvotes).

3.2.1.4 Mentions of Paweł Kukiz

Paweł Kukiz, the outsider candidate who came in third place in the first round of the presidential election, was ranked fourth in terms of mentions

---

35 Mariusz Walter, Zygmunt Solorz and Jan Kulczyk (the latter died in July 2015) are among the richest and most known businessmen in Poland; they began making their fortunes in the 1980s as the Communist economy was collapsing.
36 https://www.pudelek.pl/artykul/79564/cisza_wyborcza_przedluzona_do_2230/.
37 TVN24 is the main private news channel in Poland, owned by the same company as the popular television channel TVN.

on Pudelek, but nonetheless deserves a closer look. In stark contrast to the two main candidates, he received predominantly positive coverage in the articles, and even more so in the comments. His fresh, outsider status helped, as did the fact that he had been a popular punk-rock musician since the 1980s. Appropriately, a post from 29th of April zoomed in on rock-star celebrities, including the presidential candidate. Kukiz was described there as attacking other highly popular musicians by using the elite insult: "Kukiz on Kazik and Muniek: 'They made a lot of money and NOW THEY ARE PROTECTING MEDALS from Komorowski!'"[38] (511 comments). However, to add another layer of celebrity context, Kukiz made this statement during his appearance on a popular talk show hosted by Kuba Wojewódzki, a celebrity in his own right, known for polarizing audiences with his scandalizing behavior, particularly sexism.[39] In the program Kukiz presented himself as an anti-system candidate and accused his rock-star friends of having abandoned punk-rock values, by making money (which Kukiz has also been doing) and accepting state medals (which Kukiz has not been offered) instead. "This whole Jarocin is looking after its apartments on Tenerife," Kukiz summed up his fellow formerly-punk artists with a reference to a legendary punk-rock festival held in the 1980s, which openly confronted Communist rule. Again, top comments sided with the outsider candidate.

> "Paweł is brave ... Brave people are in short supply in Poland!Bravo Paweł!" (1,827 upvotes),

and other popular comments followed suit:

> "Finally a presidential candidate who makes sense!!!" (1,327 upvotes);

> "He is saying the truth" (1,244 upvotes);

> "I like him" (993 upvotes).

---

38 https://www.pudelek.pl/artykul/78718/kukiz_o_kaziku_i_munku_zarobili_ogromne_pieniadze_a_teraz_pilnuja_medali_od_komorowskiego/; Kazik Staszewski and Muniek Staszczyk are popular rock musicians who have been famous in Poland since the late 1980s. Kukiz belongs to the same generation of Polish rock artists as Staszewski and Staszczyk, and all three have known each other for decades.

39 The show is aired on TVN.

Last but not least, one of the most upvoted comments expanded enthusiastically on Kukiz's anti-system stance, while condemning the biggest parties, PO and PiS:

> "People, how can you vote for Po, PiS, parties which are milking us, stealing our money, which are anti-Polish Unfavorable regulations, tax hikes. Yet people still vote [for them]! They should go to jail, not vote! We are the world's laughingstock!" (1,119 upvotes).

Still, the most commented post on Kukiz was published a day later, on 30th of April, titled in an exclamatory fashion, "Kukiz already in third place in election polls!"[40] (1,595 comments). The piece focused on Kukiz's sudden rise from relative obscurity, which became visible in the polls, next to the presidential campaign's major celebrity figure, Magdalena Ogórek. The latter had been endorsed by the left-wing party, Democratic Left Alliance (SLD) but instead of campaigning she was more often found at show-business-related parties and fashion events.[41] Although Ogórek was perfect political online-tabloid material, the commenters focused on Kukiz, and all the top upvoted comments voiced enthusiasm towards his candidacy, the outsider proposing the creation of single-member districts in Poland as a solution to democratic ills. One such example was:

> "I will vote for kukiz too :)" (4,200 upvotes);

> "Kukiz probably won't win but I will vote for him to cut those old dogs to size!" (3,713 upvotes)

was another, the "old dogs" indicating PO and PiS parties' candidates.

> "I am supporting Kukiz too, the only one outside the system, he has a good and realistic program! HE HAS MY VOTE" (3,476 upvotes).

Other popular comments echoed this sentiment:

---

40 https://www.pudelek.pl/artykul/78748/kukiz_juz_na_trzecim_miejscu_w_sondazach_wyborczych/.
41 In an unexpected twist, after the election Ogórek quickly switched political allegiances and became a vocal supporter of Duda and PiS. She has since turned into a host on news commentary programs on public television, which after the 2015 presidential and parliamentary elections became a mouthpiece of the PiS government.

"Bravo Mr. Paweł! My president!!" (2753 upvotes);

"I will vote for Paweł in the first round! If there is a second one and he gets in, I'll vote for him again!" (411 upvotes).

A different post concerning Kukiz was published on Pudelek on 14th of May, after the first round of the presidential election, in which PiS and PO candidates received most of the votes. Titled "Skiba on Kukiz: 'They compare him with Wałęsa and Lepper. Platforma's [PO] drivel and derelict SLD helped him!'"[42] (139 comments), the article focused on remarks made by Kukiz's rock-star friends, Maciej Maleńczuk and Krzysztof Skiba; a short video with the two musicians was also included. In the piece, Maleńczuk and Skiba were shown voicing their continued support for Kukiz and complimented him on his unexpectedly high result in the first round, which totaled 20.8 percent of the votes. Maleńczuk called Kukiz a "walking single-mandate district," while Skiba emphasized his charisma, his ability to talk to people frustrated with the state of politics, and the fact that he had been ignored by the two major candidates, Komorowski and Duda. The post ended with a question (a regular style of ending articles on Pudelek): "Do you agree with them?," "them" referring to Maleńczuk and Skiba. Indeed, the dominant answer in the comments was: yes. For example, the most upvoted comment stated,

"Kukiz is very well fit [for the part]" (158 upvotes).

Another went into conspiracy theory, with hints of antisemitism:

"Kukiz interesting fella[;] Duda-kosher puppet For some reason you can't see His bosses Shorty [Kaczyński,] Maciarewicz[43] and company" (197 upvotes).

---

42   https://tv.pudelek.pl/video/Skiba-o-Kukizie-Porownuja-go-do-Walesy-i-Leppera-Pomo glo-mu-dziadostwo-Platformy-i-lajzostwo-SLD-8798/; Lech Wałęsa was the leader of the Solidarity movement which ended Communist rule in Poland in 1989; he was elected Poland's president in 1991 in the first free democratic elections since the end of the Second World War. Andrzej Lepper was the leader of the populist-agrarian and Euroskeptic party, Self-Defense (Samoobrona), and deputy prime minister in the first PiS-led coalition government in 2006–2007.

43   Antoni Macierewicz (the name is misspelled in the comment) is an extreme-right member of PiS, former minister of national defense and former head of military counterintelligence service. A major figure in the anti-Communist opposition, after 1989 he became known, among other things, for destabilizing Poland's counterintelligence and

A different popular comment mentioned the candidate's education:

"Kukiz studied 2 faculties but didn't finish any" (29 upvotes),

although it is hard to tell whether it was complimenting Kukiz on his university experience or admonishing him for not completing his studies. Interestingly, two of the most upvoted comments were openly critical of the two rock-star celebrities despite their endorsement of Kukiz. According to one commenter,

"For a long time Skiba has been a super sad frustrated guy who's been forcing himself to act like a joker ... :(((" (62 upvotes).

The other, named NieStokrotka[44] harshly summed up celebrities – although it is not clear whether the commenter meant Skiba and Maleńczuk or celebrities in general – who appeared on TVN24, implying their Communist ties and being sellouts:

"Some of the PRL24 celebrities are similar to the world's oldest profession" (61 upvotes).[45]

Ultimately, when one looks at Pudelek's comments section during the 2015 presidential campaign, it is impossible to ignore the fact that the election was as much about the present state of politics as about grievances concerning the consequences of Poland's Communist past. A good illustration of this are the often-voiced allegations of collaboration with the Communist secret services. They point to a more general belief that much of the economic and political elite in post-1989 Poland is fundamentally corrupt, as it has been shaped by people who had ties with the previous regime. This is why, in contrast with Komorowski, Duda positioned himself as a young unblemished politician deserving to be given a chance because, as a minor player in politics, he had

---

propagating the conspiracy theory that the 2010 plane crash near Smoleńsk in which President Lech Kaczyński and 95 other people died had been orchestrated by Russia.

44 The commenter's name means NotDaisy. "Stokrotka" is, allegedly, a pseudonym of the journalist, Monika Olejnik given to her by the Communist secret service after shed had been signed up as a secret collaborator. Lech Kaczyński, when he was the president of Poland, called Olejnik by this pseudonym after an interview, but apologized later; see: https://wiadomosci.wp.pl/zlote-usta-lecha-kaczynskiego-6038677585257089g/3.

45 PRL is the abbreviation for the Polish People's Republic, the official name of Poland under Communist rule. Accordingly, PRL24 is an allusion to the private news channel TVN24, which employs journalists critical of PiS.

not become corrupted by power (yet). Not having political experience turned out to be an advantage in the run for the presidential post. Poles chose "a good change," trusting PiS's slogan.

3.2.2   Gawker & Mail Online
3.2.2.1   *PiS Victory in the Fall 2015 Parliamentary Election*
Although the Polish presidential campaign was filled with a variety of local celebrities, from popular news-show hosts, through rock stars, to soap-opera actors, it failed to attract attention from the two foreign online tabloids. Neither Polish politics nor Polish show-business proved attractive enough for Gawker or Mail Online to pay attention. Nonetheless, the British outlet did publish one article about the topic: it reported on *the victory of PiS in the parliamentary election,* which was held on 25th of October that same year, and referred in passing to Duda's victory in the May presidential election. Perhaps the reason for this mention was the almost million-strong Polish minority living in the United Kingdom at the time, making it the largest non-British nationality in the country.[46] However, the fact that Poles could find only a single article about the Polish presidential election in the highly popular outlet proves that in the United Kingdom little attention was paid to the political choices faced by its largest minority. This is particularly ironic given that Polish migrants played a significant role in the Leave campaign, pointed out as one of the prime reasons why the UK should leave the European Union. Still, back in 2015, the single Mail Online piece, titled "Poland takes a turn to right after Eurosceptic social-conservative party claim victory in country's parliamentary elections,"[47] was written a day after the vote in a neutral, reporting tone by Euan McLelland. The article received 221 comments, and the most upvoted ones echoed the pro-Brexit and anti-EU sentiments. As such, it is a perfect illustration of the typical online-tabloid fashion of domesticating foreign issues, setting them in familiar contexts, and using them as arguments in non-related or loosely-related internal conflicts. (Unless, of course, one adopts the paranoid outlook according to which everything is connected, and for the worse, as was discussed earlier in this chapter). For example,

---

46   See: Dunin-Wąsowicz 2013.
47   https://www.dailymail.co.uk/news/article-3289360/Poland-takes-turn-right-Eurosceptic-social-conservative-party-claim-victory-country-s-parliamentary-elections.html.

"So Poland can see the danger of letting loads of people into their country, it really is a no brainier" (MG Worcester, Worcester, UK,[48] 694 upvotes).

It was a reference to PiS's reluctance to accept refugees from Syria and Afghanistan during the 2015 migrant crisis, which affected many countries in the European Union. Other comments centered on EU policies, which were not met with enthusiasm:

"People everywhere are getting fed up with the EU. Again and again eurosceptic parties are winning in national elections. Next EU election will see more eurosceptic meps [Members of European Parliament] in farage's group. Hopefully enough to give them real power." (Mika, Brooklyn, US, 504 upvotes);

"Why can't Dave [Cameron] see the obvious??? Who says that the Poles are dumb?" (kp, Adelaide, Australia, 406 upvotes);

"People are starting to realise what a disaster the EU has become." (John, London, UK, 395 upvotes).

In one popular comment Euroskepticism was complemented by a desire for more nationalist politics and Christian values – a mix also found in comments on Pudelek and Gawker concerning the EU referendum and, later, the 2016 US presidential election:

"First Portugal and now Poland, the anti-EU Nationalist parties are on the rise. This is a fight back for Christianity in Europe by our Eastern countries. Well done Poland. Are you listening Merkel and Juncker?" (Claire, Swindon, UK, 435 upvotes).

When one pays attention to the comments, one can notice that the tone of Mail Online readers' opinions on the Polish election presaged the Euroskeptic attitudes that would be loudly voiced during the EU referendum campaign held in the UK several months later. In the Mail Online comments section in 2015, local foreign politics served as a pretext to reveal and feed anti-EU views

---

48 Mail Online requires its readers to sign up, and provide an alias and location in order to post comments. While the location can be invented, it gives an idea where the commenters want to be seen as coming from.

regarding UK's home affairs. These attitudes came in full force later, in Mail Online coverage and in the comments on the EU referendum campaign.

3.3 United Kingdom 2016 EU Referendum Campaign

Unlike Poland's presidential election, the EU "Brexit" referendum campaign in the UK attracted significant interest from all three online tabloids. On the one hand, already then the implications of the referendum were considered potentially seismic not just for the United Kingdom but for the entire European Union – much more so than the Polish elections. On the other hand, this shows that, in contrast to Poland, the UK is viewed as one of the "elite northwestern corners of the world," described by Galtung and Ruge (1965), and for this reason is worth writing about. Nevertheless, in Mail Online, Gawker and Pudelek the most recurring themes were those concerning the European Union, pointing at UK's relations with a larger international body; general and analytical approaches to the campaign; negative opinions about the Leave campaign and Brexit (negative opinions concerning the Remain campaign were, too, more visible than positive ones); migration; as well as opinions on poll and vote results.

3.3.1 Mail Online

3.3.1.1 European Union

The *European Union* was the most popular theme on Mail Online, which was predictable given that membership in the international organization was the focal point of the referendum campaign. For example, a post full of EU references was published at midnight on 3rd of June, under the title "'Follow your heart and not scaremonger Cameron': Michael Gove twists the knife into his friend as he urges voters to defy 'sneering elites' and the 'undeserving rich' – and tell the EU 'You're fired'"[49] (5,259 comments), written by James Tapsfield together with Tim Sculthorpe. The piece discussed a television debate with Michael Gove, the Tory Justice Secretary. According to the authors, Gove "launched a savage attack on the 'sneering' elites trying to keep Britain in the EU as he urged voters to 'take back control.'" To make his point, the Justice Secretary attacked Cameron, the Remainer Prime Minister from his own party, arguing that "the people of this country have had enough of experts from organisations with acronyms saying they know what is best and getting it consistently wrong." Given the anti-elite sentiment voiced by Gove, it should be noted that the

---

49   https://www.dailymail.co.uk/news/article-3624338/Gove-slams-sneering-elites-trying-Britain-EU-urges-voters-control-referendum.html.

debate host used Donald Trump as a negative point of reference in the British context, and he labeled Gove an "Oxbridge Trump" who uses "post-truth." In doing so, the host exposed Gove's elite anti-elite strategy, which had been used earlier by Duda in the Polish election and would be used by the Republican presidential candidate later. In addition, the article highlighted that a member of the audience had "grilled" Gove "over 'lies' by the Leave campaign," including the topic of immigration. Still, Gove managed to turn the Trump reference around. He paraphrased the US presidential candidate's catchphrase from the reality TV show, "The Apprentice" in which he had starred: "Unelected, unaccountable elites, it's time to say 'you're fired' – we're going to take back control," Gove declared. Further, the journalists criticized Cameron's performance on the same television show the day prior, during which, according to the authors, he had been "mauled by audience members over his failure to tackle immigration, his Project Fear tactics and 'waffling.'" Like in many other Mail Online pieces, the article comprised several eye-catching bright-blue columns scattered throughout the page. The first was titled "MICHAEL GOVE'S BEST LINES" and included "'sneering' Remain supporters," "firing Eurocrats," and "being on the side of workers," among others. In another such highlighted section Gove was described as "THE INTELLECTUAL HEAVYWEIGHT OF VOTE LEAVE." In yet a different one, titled "LEAVE DISMISSES BANK WARNING," the head of JP Morgan bank alerted about likely job losses in the UK as a result of Brexit; the next such box explained who was eligible to vote in the referendum. Finally, at the very bottom of the piece Donald Trump appeared for a third time, this time as a presumed Leave supporter: "Donald Trump reveals he will fly into Britain BEFORE voters go the polls and give their verdict on Brexit – but Remain campaigners insist Britons will reject him." However, despite the article's sympathetic tone towards the Leave campaign, the readers' comments were mixed, and the two top upvoted ones were anti-Leave:

"One thing is now clear, Gove is a LIAR!" (Neil Loot, London, UK, 10,151 upvotes);

"Yet again the BREXIT economic case is in tatters" (Dave, London, UK, 8,514 upvotes).

Nonetheless, the next top three comments were favorable towards Gove and Brexit, suggesting that even on Mail Online the race for the votes was tight:

"Faisel [Faisal Islam, the debate host] is getting on my nerves. Mr Gove is making a good, concise argument. Vote out" (jonothan, somewhereintheuk, UK, 7,286 upvotes);

"Top man handles the pressure well and I have absolute confidence that a Vote LEAVE is the best decision for this country." (common sense, Essex, UK, 5,931 upvotes);

and

"Unlike last night's man [David Cameron], this Michael Gove chap knows his onions. A confident, assured performance so far. He believes in Britain, he believes in us. We should believe in ourselves and vote OUT." (unvisible man, England, UK, 4,733 upvotes).

One more highly commented EU-focused article was published in the evening that same day by Matt Dathan and Martin Robinson. Titled "'You're literally not giving me the chance to answer!': The extraordinary moment David Cameron snaps at Kate Garraway as she interrupts him to ask about his record on immigration during EU discussion"[50] (4,694 comments), it concerned the moment David Cameron lost his temper towards the host of a subsequent television debate. The piece stressed the Prime Minister's inability to give concrete answers to questions on migration during the television show, and the authors pointed out that he "sounded croaky." What's more, not only were Cameron's answers insufficient, according to Mail Online he was also visibly nervous. For instance, the Prime Minister was reported to have "appeared to have a sheen of sweat on his upper lip" during another television program aired the previous evening, in which he had been "accused of 'waffling' and 'scaremongering' by a member of the audience." In proper tabloid style, Mail Online included the woman's photos, which were taken from her Facebook profile. In most of the pictures she posed in party dresses, and Mail Online labeled them "racy," adding a hint of sexual innuendo. The possible reason behind this was that in one of photos the woman was making a gesture as if she were tearing her shirt off, but she was fully clothed underneath. In short, in the online tabloid piece the head Remainer was unfit and the woman who attacked him was hot. The article also described, among other things, and with dozens of photos: Cameron's

---

50 https://www.dailymail.co.uk/news/article-3623371/A-defiant-David-Cameron-claims-leaving-EU-terrible-way-cut-immigration-morning-savaged-public-live-TV-waffling-scaremongering-Brexit.html.

reserved approach to Boris Johnson; the fact that "Foreign voters HAVE been wrongly sent polling cards for the EU referendum, admits elections watchdog;" Jeremy Corbyn's, the Labour Party leader's worries about the high levels of immigration to the UK, though at the same time he was reluctantly telling "people to vote In anyway;" and a claim made by Gove that he was forced to let in criminals because of EU rules. Adding still another layer to the story – this time an unfavorable private context – a separate, long, bright-blue-colored column placed alongside the main article recapped how a couple of days earlier Cameron had forgotten his own twentieth wedding anniversary. There were more such columns in the piece: one presented Cameron's key debate points; another was a copied section from a previous article, explaining who was eligible to vote in the referendum; a still different column showed polls according to which Labour party voters did not know the party's position on the referendum; and one focused on a "Brexit-backing economist" who nonetheless admitted that leaving the EU would lead to higher tariffs. Despite this openly anti-Brexit argument placed at the end of the article, the top user comments were unanimously critical of Cameron and of staying in the European Union:

"Dave [Cameron] – the man who promises everything and delivers NOTHING." (Tony, Petersfield, UK, 8,488 upvotes);

"I would rather be a Poor UK Pensioner and OUT, than be a Poor UK Pensioner and Subservient to Brussels !!! I won't mess about, but just Vote OUT !!!" (RevoltingPensioner, Up NORF, UK, 5,081 upvotes);

"Sorry DC [David Cameron], your increasingly tenuous grasp on reality is starting to make me wonder if you need to visit a shrink. Having promised to reduce the flow, you presided over a flood, and your answer seems to be more of the same" (LofADay___, London, UK, 4,201 upvotes).

Two of the five top comments were written by the same person, who clearly showed skill in voicing negative opinions about Prime Minister Cameron that proved popular among other Mail Online readers:

"A PM [Prime Minister] who is never positive or backs up legitimate reasons for staying in the EU – cannot trust!" (So so, [no town name provided], UK, 3,250 upvotes);

"Just QUIT and let someone else rebuild the mess you've caused – no one cares about your plans for the UK!" (So so, [no town name provided], UK, 3,037 upvotes).

However, the article in which the EU was mentioned the most was published as the clock struck midnight after the day of the vote, 23rd of June 2016. Written by five journalists, James Tapsfield, Tim Sculthorpe, Martin Robinson, James Slack, and Jason Groves, titled "David Cameron QUITS in the wake of the historic Brexit vote in EU referendum"[51] (31,996 comments), it also happened to be one of the longest articles published on Mail Online concerning the EU referendum: it was over 12,800 words-long. Apart from the vote result itself, the piece reported on the reactions of politicians from the UK as well as those from other EU countries, their families, the stock market, and, as expected in an online tabloid, celebrities. The piece ended with Cameron's resignation letter, which was published in full. In line with the vote, most of the top upvoted comments at the bottom of the page were enthusiastic about the preliminary result:

> "I pray we are OUT..Give my grandchildren HOPE!! GOOD LUCK BREXIT!!" (Northern Chap, Manchester, UK, 18,967 upvotes);

> "Historic times, this could be Independence Day. Or we could all be doomed." (bababooey, Coventry, UK, 10,760 upvotes);

> "Hope with all my heart that OUT wins, that so many millions of us really truly want and believe in." (SWLady, London, UK, 6,501 upvotes).

One of the top comments, however, voiced suspicion about the vote-counting process, implying that a "remain" result would be the effect of manipulation, as other similar comments suggested, of the EU-favoring elite. Given that it was written by a person claiming to be from the United States, it could be seen as prophetic – the theme of "rigging" elections would be exploited in the US several months later, in favor of Trump:

> "BREXIT if tonite the voters say REMAIN you know this election has BEEN RIGGED!" (Joshua_USA17, NY, USA, 7,226 upvotes).

Finally, one of the best-rated comments was a grassroots survey of sorts:

> "Quick exit poll … green for leave … red for stay" (Francis, Birmingham, UK).

---

51   https://www.dailymail.co.uk/news/article-3657160/David-Cameron-QUITS-Prime-Minister-voters-Brexit-EU-referendum.html.

The result: 11,541 green upward-facing arrows signifying upvotes and 3,729 red downward-facing arrows signifying downvotes. If in the actual referendum the Leavers won by less than four percentage points, in the comment poll they won over threefold.

3.3.1.2 Immigration

Directly related to the European Union, *immigration* was another top theme in Mail Online, and the issue was prominent enough on its own to be featured as a separate topic in the outlet.[52] While political debates were the prime events in which migration appeared as a key issue, one could also find it in the context of celebrity endorsements. For example, "'That's a lovely question': Angelina Jolie's admiration for Polish schoolgirl, 12, who wants to improve integration of young immigrants in Britain"[53] (3,842 comments), written by Matt Dathan, Daniel Martin and Laura Lambert was published on 16th of May. The article discussed a BBC interview on global migration with the American actress and at the same time the UN special envoy for refugees. Jolie criticized European leaders for their "isolationist" response to the refugee crisis, which emerged in consequence of the war in Syria. Remarkably, the headline singled out a 12-year-old Polish immigrant, one of almost one million Poles who had moved to the UK since the country's accession to the European Union in 2004. The girl asked Jolie how to "improve the integration of young immigrants," a remark which according to the article pleased the actress. The issue set Jolie's interview in the specific context of the British EU referendum campaign. And indeed, the journalists stressed Jolie's "hinting" that "she wanted British voters to back staying in the EU in the June referendum," as well as her "attack" on "Tory Eurosceptics" who accused the actress of trying to "tell us how to vote." One of them, the MP Peter Bone went on to say, possibly in an attempt to appease Jolie, that "Britain would have the capacity to take in more vulnerable migrants if we were no longer part of the EU's freedom of movement rules." Still, a bright-blue box on the side of the main text was very different in tone, "BBC ACCUSED OF SUPPORTING MASS MIGRATION TO BOOST TV LICENCE FEE REVENUE" – a thinly veiled counterargument to Jolie's claim. According to Mail Online, the British public broadcaster was covertly encouraging immigration for its own financial gain. This, the piece suggested, revealed BBC's biased stance on the

---

52 According to research conducted by Goodwin and Heath (2016), immigration was in fact the most important issue for voters in the EU membership referendum.
53 https://www.dailymail.co.uk/news/article-3592880/Angelina-Jolie-blasts-EU-race-bottom-response-refugee-crisis-sends-message-British-voters-reject-Brexit-gives-BBC-lecture.html.

topic. Beyond the blue box, in the main part of the article, the journalists further reported that while the EU "boasted the number of migrants arriving in Greece has dropped by 90 percent," it was less vocal about the "vast numbers (...) pouring into Italy." The piece included dozens of photos, mainly of Jolie speaking about immigration, and of migrants crowding in front of wire fences. The top comments, again from both sides of the Atlantic, were critical of Jolie's involvement in the matter, viewing her as a non-expert unfit for the job:

> "Good heavens, you are just an actress. Shut up and mind your own business" (Catherine, Chicago, US, 7,785 upvotes);

> "SHUT IT ANGIE." (Bonny1, Scotland, UK, 5,389 upvotes);

> "We don't want them [immigrants] here! Ange just because you live in England now doesn't mean we'll listen to your opinion" (Kuato Lives, Venusville [sic], UK, 4,360 upvotes).

Interestingly, one of the top comments was aimed not at Jolie but at Angela Merkel, then the German Chancellor, whom the former had criticized for opening Germany to refugees without EU coordination:

> "This disaster has been made so much worse by big mouthed mother Merkel" (Nayen, Southampton, UK, 4,434 upvotes).

It must be noted, however, that it was not all criticism. One popular comment agreed with the actress, if only in terms of the deficiencies of the European Union, pointing out why the UK should leave:

> "This women is right the EU is not fit for purpose, that's why I want out before it ruins our country completely. VOTE OUT" (Future for UK, united kingdom, United Kingdom, 3,134 upvotes).

Another example of the immigration theme could be found in an article which described the first, youth-focused television debate on the EU referendum, published on 26th of May, titled "'Where are we going to put them all?': Furious row erupts during first EU referendum TV debate after Brexit voter accuses migrants of 'jumping the housing queue' ahead of her disabled mother"[54]

---

54   https://www.dailymail.co.uk/news/article-3611400/Alex-Salmond-admits-no-economic-apocalypse-Britain-quits-EU-live-TV-debate-Brexit-battle-begins.html.

(7,319 comments). The piece was written by Tim Sculthorpe and Martin Robinson, and started off with remarks made by an audience member about – as the headline suggests – her disabled mother. These comments were also recapped in a subsequent article (discussed in the next paragraph), and such "recycling," at times direct copy-pasting of entire paragraphs, was often found in Mail Online articles. On the one hand, it added context to the story but, on the other hand, it refreshed "yesterday's news," keeping it in a perpetual-present news cycle.[55] And so, the woman who complained about immigrants "jumping the housing queue" ahead of her mother was countered by another audience member who argued, "'the Government needs to build more council houses. The EU is not some kind of scapegoat for you to keep blaming for your problems. It's funny how you have selective memory." She then added, "Just remember how immigrants like my family and people in this audience have built this nation.'" Despite this matter-of-fact comment, a UKIP MEP present at the debate stressed that if the Leave vote wins, EU migrants, especially those from Eastern Europe, should not be accepted in the UK because "they do not speak English," unlike migrants from the Commonwealth countries, such as "qualified doctors." The bright-blue boxes embedded in the article focused on the debate lineup, offering helpful summaries, "THE BREXIT BATTLE: THE LINE UP OF TV CLASHES AHEAD OF POLLING DAY" next to "THE CONTENDERS: THE FOUR POLITICIANS SQUARING UP FOR THE FIRST TV DEBATE OF THE BREXIT BATTLE," and added three-sentence-long bios for each of them. The debate, however, was not a success. According to the journalists the audience members were upset by the politicians' "poor" and "petty" arguments, which made the event lack substance. To prove their point, the writers described how an audience member used the referendum discussion as an opportunity to ask the BBC host out on a date. While the scene was entertaining, it made the debate look even less serious. Nonetheless, most top-voted comments mentioned not so much the debate, as migration, albeit from different angles. For a change, the most popular comment was anti-Brexit:

"Pathetic Brexit only have one card left to play -immigration .What they dont seem to realise is two things: 1) a huge number of migrants come from outside the EU and the only way to control them is by cooperation with our EU partners 2) Even if left the EU we would still have to accept

---

55 Vorberg and Zeitler (2019) offer an interesting take on "re-actualizing" past events in their analysis of Clinton's "emailgate" and Trump's "trumptape(s)" during the US presidential campaign. On "recycling news" see also: Westlund and Ekström 2019.

EU migrants as part of any negotiated deal" (Don Maico, [no town name provided], UK, 8,286 upvotes).

In contrast, another top upvoted comment was pro-Brexit:

I watched a few minutes of it. I saw Alex Salmond [of the Scottish National Party] and turned it off. She [the woman who mentioned her mother's housing situation] is right. Where are they going to put all these people coming here. That lady only managed to get housed after 14 years, this week. She had waited 14 years and she was born here. I do not listen to the people who want to stay in the EU. Most of them are deluded about the situation (Sandy Brown, London, UK, 4,726 upvotes).

A different popular comment questioned the value of immigrant "qualified doctors," who had been praised by the UKIP MEP, suggesting that even such skilled immigrants do not present value to British society:

"Migrants working in our NHS? That would explain why it's on its knees year on year out" (You know 1T, San Diego, UK [US], 3,212 upvotes).

The same commenter scored another top comment, this time doubting the objectivity of the debaters:

"So why is a politician who wants independence from the UK but wants to stay in the EU doing this debate?" (You know 1T, San Diego, UK [US], 3,510 upvotes).

The comment alluded to Cameron, a Remainer who had won parliamentary elections on the promise that he would deliver the referendum. Finally, another top comment was unclear who it was referring to, and perhaps because of this it received several thousand upvotes:

"A politician told the truth, I nearly fell off the couch!" (George, Stockport, UK, 4,918 upvotes).

Possibly, the commenting voters chose the politician they thought this statement fit best. A still different example of the theme of migration appeared on 7th of June, in a piece written by James Tapsfield, Tim Sculthorpe and Martin Robinson, under the title "'I have no GP, I can't get on the housing ladder and have three kids in one room': David Cameron is taken to task for his immigration record by '40-year-old Brit who has been working full time since 16'"[56] (10,394 comments). The piece provided an account of a television debate with David Cameron and Nigel Farage, the leader of Euroskeptic UKIP. According to the journalists, Cameron was "mauled" and "battered" over immigration by an audience member, who complained he "could not get a GP, could not buy a house and had three children in one room because of 'uncontrolled' immigration," which also created "no-go zones." Farage, too, was criticized by other members of the audience, who accused him of racism by "scaremongering against non-white people." Next to numerous photos included in the article, one could find a chart showing the growth of immigration to the UK since 1970 which reached an all-time high in 2015, a year before the referendum. In addition, bright-blue boxes on the side highlighted "VOTER REGISTRATION WEBSITE CRASHES JUST TWO HOURS BEFORE REFERENDUM DEADLINE," and the UKIP leader's claim, "'WE WON'T BE BULLIED': FARAGE SLAPS DOWN JEAN-CLAUDE JUNCKER," who was the president of the European Commission at the time. The third attention-grabbing box at the bottom focused on the main theme: "IMMIGRATION STATISTICS REVEALING RECORD HIGHS SHIFT THE BREXIT DEBATE AND DOMINATE THE TV DEBATES;" a pro-Leave comment made by an audience member almost two weeks earlier, during the first television debate (discussed earlier) was also mentioned there. The quoted woman complained that "her disabled mother could not get the council house she needs because immigrants are given priority," strengthening Farage's argument. But even more context was added to the topic: at the end of the article Central-Eastern Europeans were mentioned again, unfavorably, in reference to migration, in the words of a Leaver Tory, Lord Astor: "We Conservatives made a mistake when we thought that the inclusion of the Eastern bloc countries in the EU, after they were freed from the shackles of centralised rule, would be a beneficial influence. Sadly most, with a couple of exceptions, have remained subsidy junkies beholden to Brussels in the same way they were once beholden to Moscow." In line with this rather hostile outlook, once more the top comments were evidently pro-Brexit:

> "Go for it Nigel! Make mincemeat out of the traitor and expose the lies and deceit of the remainiacs. Vote LEAVE, LEAVE, LEAVE" (jchw, London, UK, 9,640 upvotes);

> "Nige gets my vote !! Only says what most people are thinking !!" (shabsy, Sunderland, UK, 8,355 upvotes).

---

56   https://www.dailymail.co.uk/news/article-3630039/PM-Farage-battle-Brexit-primetime-referendum-special-Cameron-won-t-debate-EU-head-head.html.

Accordingly, the comments were also critical towards Cameron:

"A Prime Minister who won't debate an issue with the opposition? If his cause is just and his heart is pure, what's Mr. Cameron afraid of?" (Galahad, The Meadows, US, 11,582 upvotes);

"Cameron is used to poor opponents like Miliband and Corbyn,He trembles at the prospect of meeting an able debater so you can see why he is chicken and frit" (f.clarke, Chesterfield, UK, 6,931 upvotes).

Nonetheless, one top comment not only admonished the Prime Minister but, tellingly, exposed disapproval of the media in general:

"Cameron doesn't want anyone asking him awkward questions. He is safe with the media who treat him with kid gloves. Cameron is a coward and will do anything he can to avoid the exposure of his nonsense and lies – but he is happy to bully and threaten the British people from behind the closed doors of the elitist establishment." (peterr, glos [Gloucestershire], UK, 6,250 upvotes).

3.3.1.3   Negative Attitudes towards Leavers/Brexit

Despite the popularity of anti-EU opinions, *negative attitudes towards Leavers and/or Brexit* were, too, among the top themes in Mail Online. However, as listed in Table 3, topics negative towards Remainers, including the Prime Minister David Cameron and the Labour Party, but also positive views of the Leave campaign were not far behind – which is an order comparable to the results predicted in the polls. Positive views of the Remain campaign were much rarer. On the whole, similarly to the Polish presidential election, in the case of the EU referendum in the United Kingdom negative attitudes were more frequent than positive ones, regardless of one's political stance. This suggests a general frustration with politicians, clearly more prevalent than optimism concerning the promises they make. One example of the theme could be found in a top-commented article written by Matt Dathan and published on 26th of May, with the headline: "Remain campaign opens up new 13% lead in EU battle as Tory poll guru warns Boris's Brexit campaign is 'weak and dwindling'"[57] (5,981 comments). The piece was based on a poll showing

---

57   https://www.dailymail.co.uk/news/article-3606305/New-13-lead-Remain-campaign-Tory-poll-guru-warns-Brexit-campaign-getting-hammered-economy.html.

dismal predictions for the Leave campaign, and large charts with the results were posted under the headline. The campaign was described as "dwindling" and "was warned it is failing to combat economic fears of Brexit." What's more, according to the journalist, a majority of Tory voters suddenly decided to vote to stay in the European Union, while Johnson – who was a "mixed blessing" according to a quoted pro-Brexit Tory – was accused of the "weaknesses of the campaign's organisation." Johnson was featured in several photos, for example, sitting in a sports car with a big red sign "Take back control" on the door; but also posing wearing a safety mask, a neon yellow "high-vis" vest, and holding an angle-grinder. Further down, the piece discussed a document issued by the UK Treasury, which claimed that food prices would significantly rise and over 800,000 jobs could be lost because of Brexit. A bright-blue box on the side expanded on the topic: "COST OF HOLIDAYS COULD RISE BY £230 A YEAR IF WE LEAVE THE EU, DAVID CAMERON WARNS;" another box carried the headline "BREXIT WOULD SEND PRICES ROCKETING AND GROWTH PLUNGING, WARNS BANK CHIEF;" still another centered on the referendum debates: "CAMERON AND GOVE TO FACE EU QUESTION TIME CHALLENGE – BUT WON'T APPEAR TOGETHER." In addition, two eye-catching, page-width blue boxes were added to the article; one of them began with the question, "WHO ARE THE MAJOR PLAYERS IN THE VOTE LEAVE CAMPAIGN?" It was followed by a presentation of short bios of "The Beast" Boris Johnson, "The Intellectual" Michael Gove, "The Attack Dog" Duncan Smith, "The Maverick" Dominic Cummings, and "The Referendum Veteran" Matthew Elliott. They were set in contrast with Tony Blair, the former Labour Prime Minister, who was also highlighted close by in the main body of the article: "Tony Blair insists Europe NEEDS Britain to give it leadership as he claims David Cameron's 'strong and effective' campaign to stay in the EU is doing 'pretty well.'" Yet the final paragraphs of the article appeared exceptionally gloomy. The journalist mentioned Johnson using *reductio ad Hitlerum* in relation to the European Union, which according to the Tory "wanted the same goal as Adolf Hitler – but was pursuing it via 'different methods.'" Moreover, a second page-wide blue box, located at the very bottom, bore an end-of-the-world title, "THE APOCALYPSE IS COMING! IF YOU BELIEVE BOTH SIDES WHATEVER THE RESULT ON JUNE 23 WE'RE ALL DOOMED." It included a recap of the major arguments from Cameron's Remain and Johnson's Leave sides, with both men pictured. Respectively, the most-upvoted comments were split. One reader, in an example of anecdotal evidence, argued that the polls did not reflect reality:

"I have no idea where these polls come from save that they are another figment of Dave's [Cameron's] imagination: every person I speak to is voting to leave, not one person has even remotely suggested they will vote to stay !!" (p.s., south west, UK, 7,987 upvotes).

This sentiment was echoed by another commenter who, additionally, voiced suspicion about the fairness of the vote:

"Do not believe. It :: Anything that comes from the remainers. Especially from Cameron. Mouth regardless of the polls. And Cameron his cronies need booting out ... They are not to be trusted I am even dubious about the referendum. I have a postal vote but don't know if I can go and vote in person ... Don't. Trust the postal vote. I will be voting OUT" (thetruth, preston, UK, 3,042 upvotes).

Nonetheless, a different top-upvoted comment was less skeptical of the polls:

"To be honest I think most UK citizens want to stay in and are happy with the way thing are." (Mick Walker, Weston Turville, UK, 5,566 upvotes).

Others presented their negative stance towards the vision of Britain offered by the Leave campaign:

"I am, and the majority of people in this country will, because they want to live in an open, forward-looking, multi-cultural and prosperous UK and not some narrow-minded, selfish, nationalistic and impoverished Little England" (marcs2012, cheshire, UK, 6,699 upvotes);

as well as towards Leave voters:

"Don't worry Remainers. Most Leavers won't be able to pick up the pen on polling day due to their sore knuckles" (Bingster, Coventry, UK, 4,903 upvotes).

In sum, in the top comments the race between Leave enthusiasts suspicious of the polls as well as the Remain politicians, and Remain supporters deriding the Leavers was even.

A different article where various examples of negative attitudes towards the Leave campaign and Brexit could be found, accompanied, however, by a similar number of negative attitudes towards the Remain campaign, was published by James Tapsfield on 21st of June, two days before the referendum. The piece again reported on people's annoyance with the poor quality of the referendum campaign. Given that Mail Online journalists claim the outlet is reactive to its readers (which will be discussed in Chapter 3), here it was reacting by showing politicians as a disappointment. The piece bore a lengthy, summary-like title, typical for Mail Online: "'Make Thursday our Independence Day!' Boris Johnson issues rallying cry for Brexit after Sadiq Khan accuses him of 'big fat LIES' and running 'Project Hate' in bitter end to brutal EU debate"[58] (10,824 comments). This time, focus was laid on the final BBC debate with Boris Johnson and Sadiq Khan, the London mayor. Tellingly, Mail Online labeled the event a "bruising slugfest." According to the article, Khan "lambasted" the head of the Leave campaign "for 'scaremongering' about the prospects of Turkey joining the EU." He added that Johnson "should be 'ashamed' of the 'big fat lies' he had told." Furthermore, a Scottish pro-Remain Tory MP, Ruth Davidson claimed Johnson was trying to turn the debate into a "Boris show," and asked him – a rhetorical question – if he could name "'one country in the world' that had promised to give Britain a trade deal." A pro-Remain member of the audience, pictured close to the top of the post, asked "If we leave the EU will this be a slippery slope towards weaker employment and social rights in the UK?" This, according to Mail Online, led to an internal argument between Labour-Remainer Khan and Labour-Leaver Gisela Stuart about the role of the EU in securing workers' rights. Still, there was "blue-on-blue action" as well,[59] when the pro-Leave Tory Treasury minister Andrea Leadsom was taken "to task over Vote Leave's 'blatant untruths'" by pro-Remain Davidson. They concerned the alleged percentage of laws applicable to the UK that had been created by the EU. Leadsom claimed it was 60 percent, which meant that most of the laws were created outside the UK, but Davidson corrected the Treasury Minister that the actual number was a fraction of that, 13 percent. What's more, "In the last five year parliament," Davidson argued, "there were four bills out of 121 that came out of Europe," totaling 3.3 percent. Remainers accused Leavers of lying, to which, as Tapsfield reported, the audience responded with "applause and banging." "[T]hey lied about Turkey's entrance to Europe, they lied about the European army because we have a veto over that," Davidson continued. "They put this on their leaflets and they've lied about this tonight too and it's not good enough because you deserve the truth, you deserve the truth." The article followed with another blue-on-blue conflict, this time including the Tory MP Sarah Wollaston, who had switched to Remain a week before the referendum because of her concerns about the fate of the National Health Service

---

58 https://www.dailymail.co.uk/news/article-3653068/Boris-Johnson-leads-Brexiteers-battle-against-Sadiq-Khan-Remain-backers-live-TV-referendum-showdown.html.
59 The color blue is associated with the Tory party, while red is the color of the Labour party.

(NHS) in the event of Brexit. "There will be a very serious Brexit penalty for the NHS, make no mistake," Wollaston stressed, "and if people are caring about the NHS and research when they make their vote I would say vote to remain with our European partners." This was an implicit response to the Leave campaign's oft-repeated claim (and one that was painted on its campaign's bus) that the NHS would receive 350 million pounds a week – the amount Britain paid into the EU budget – if the UK were to leave the European Union. While Leavers were accused of lying, the Remain campaign was blamed for instilling "Project Fear" and having "nothing positive to say." Leavers, again, voiced the need to control immigration which Khan called "Project Hate" in return. To make the matter even more difficult, the article stressed that the debate was held "on the worst possible day for Mr Khan due to the Summer Solstice making it the longest day of the year," since "Muslims in London required to fast from 2.40am until 9.24pm." A bright-blue side box titled "SADIQ KHAN TOOK PART IN 2-HOUR DEBATE AFTER NOT EATING OR DRINKING DUE TO RAMADAN" explained the mayor's predicament in more detail. In the main section, however, the piece continued by pointing out the nervousness of the Remain camp whose head David Cameron "was under another torrid spell of pressure over his failure to curb immigration." Despite this, he argued that "the economic case for membership was 'paramount'" and "issued a desperate plea to older voters not to punish him for mistakes in government by sending Britain crashing out of the EU." Next, another big blue box presented a picture with the latest poll numbers: "A DIVIDED NATION WITH TWO DAYS TO GO: POLLING DATA REVEALS THE DEEP SPLITS BETWEEN YOUNG AND OLD, THE NORTH AND THE SOUTH." Interestingly, the pro-Leave Labour Party member Gisela Stuart appeared once again later in the article, but this time because of a bigoted accusation made in a tweet by Lord Sugar, a pro-Remain businessman. He posted that the Bavarian-born MP "'shouldn't tell us British what we should do' because she's from Germany." Predictably, Lord Sugar was quickly condemned – also in tweets – by members of both Leave and Remain campaigns, and was called out as racist. Yet there was more on the debate itself: a headline closer to the bottom of the piece announced sarcastically, "It's all fun and games! Boris Johnson and Ruth Davidson embrace minutes after mauling each other over Haggis in bruising EU referendum debate" (Johnson argued EU regulations made it impossible to export Haggis, a traditional Scottish meal, to the United States). A big photo showed the Tory pair hugging and laughing after the debate, as though implying that it had been just a show. Indeed, a good example of the game frame could be found in another bright-blue side box, the message strengthening the notion of the event as a frivolous punching fest: "THE BEST OF THE SLUGS: WHO LANDED THE HARDEST BLOWS." Nonetheless, the final push was offered to the Queen, who was also pictured in the article. Though the monarch is not supposed to take political sides, the headline of the final section sounded less than neutral: "Queen said to have been asking dinner guests for 'three good reasons' why Britain should be in EU," according to a "Royal author Robert Lacey." To avoid complaints about bias, the journalist emphasized that the main competitor of Mail Online (or rather *Daily Mail*), the paper tabloid *The Sun* had been "rebuked by the press regulator in March for suggesting that the Queen favoured leaving the EU." Moreover, according to Mr Lacey, "The Queen likes a healthy debate around the dinner table. It was just a question." Even if it was, the frame was an ambiguous (not) kidding one, and the commenters remained predominantly pro-Leave. Two of the top five most popular comments were almost identical:

"Vote BREXIT!" (Anonymous, [no town name provided], 11,441 upvotes)

and

"VOTE FOR BREXIT" (Username, EU Dictatorship, UK, 5,983 upvotes).

Another popular comment echoed this sentiment:

"It will be better for the UK out of the EU." (SuperDec, isle de murte [sic], UK, 7,413 upvotes).

The comments were openly anti-Remain, but one added the charge of elitism:

"Khan only represents a very narrow set of like minded metro elitist." (Ron, Leeds, UK, 8,372 upvotes);

while another offered a brief comparison of both campaigns:

"Boris and Brexit are holding their own! Remain camp have a lot to say, with no substance." (YESITSMEAGAIN, Northern Ireland, UK, 5,088 upvotes).

Astonishing news was published the next day, on 22nd of June, a day before the referendum: "What's he playing at? On the eve of the vote he's campaigned for his entire political life, Nigel Farage pulls out of crunch referendum TV debate 'to have dinner with his son'"[60] (7,060 comments), was written by Richard

---

60 https://www.dailymail.co.uk/news/article-3654977/Nigel-Farage-pulls-Channel-4-s-EU-referendum-debate-just-hour-start.html.

Spillett, Flora Drury, Stephanie Linning, and Gerri Peev. This article was critical of one of the Leave campaign leaders and, starting at the very top, the authors reported that "Farage was not present to defend it [the Leave campaign] after pulling out of debate at 2pm. He claimed it was for 'family reasons'." As they explained further, "It emerged last night he had gone for dinner with his City worker son, 27." The implicit argument made in Mail Online was that dinner with his son was not enough for the head of the main pro-Brexit organization to pull out from the final television debate at the last minute. "The announcement was met with surprise," the reporters wrote, "with many expressing concern for Farage and his family as many believed only something truly terrible would make the politician pull out of the key debate." Dinner did not sound as something "truly terrible," and as if to emphasize Farage's snub of the event, numerous photos of him smiling happily were added in the first paragraphs of the piece. According to "a source," the reason for Farage's absence was that had not seen his son for nine months since he had been working abroad, "so it was between that or being on against the founder of Ukip who calls him racist. It was a no brainer." Indeed, the journalists mentioned that the party's recent Brexit poster, which displayed "a snaking line of hundreds of immigrants arriving in Europe" was deemed "anti-human" and "the 'darkest moment' of the EU campaign" by Delia Smith, a popular pro-Remain television presenter and cook who sat in the audience during the debate. The photo of Farage standing in front of said billboard, with the caption "BREAKING POINT The EU has failed us all" was included further in the article. Smith might have had a point, since UKIP wanted its leader to apologize for the poster, the journalists reported. However, Farage refused and argued that he could not "apologise for the truth." Even though the anti-EU campaigner was a no-show at the debate, a blue side box exclaimed, somewhat paradoxically, "I'VE WAITED MY ADULT LIFE FOR THIS MOMENT, SAYS UKIP LEADER." Farage made this statement while walking towards the polling station, which means that the side box must have been added a day later, on 23rd of June. As has been mentioned earlier, this "recycling" technique was used more than once to keep yesterday's news fresh. (Indeed, one could find information at the top of the page that the article had been updated.) Sticking to the critical tone, the journalists stressed that Nigel Lawson, another Leave campaigner was accused of hypocrisy during the debate when he voiced his "fears" that Britain was "becoming a 'colony' of a United States of Europe;" the irony is he lives in France. A pro-Remain Tory Steve Hilton was labeled a hypocrite as well, for "having a go at 'unelected bureaucrats'," since he had been David Cameron's director of strategy. Nevertheless, the article ended with a shift in attitude, offering an excuse for the criticized UKIP leader: a big bright-blue box posted at the bottom was titled,

"FARAGE HAS PREVIOUSLY TOLD OF LONG RUNNING BACK PROBLEMS." The section listed Farage's health issues, including back pain issues for which he was "receiving hospital treatment twice a week;" his previous two cancer treatments; as well as a plane crash in 2010, which "left him with permanent nerve damage." An upsetting photo of Farage from the time of the accident was inserted in the blue box, an image strikingly different from the previous ones showing him smiling widely. In this particular photo the UKIP leader was standing in a field, in front of a small plane which was turned upside down. He was dressed in a suit and looking in pain, with a trickle of blood running down his face. If other pictures of Farage showed him acting lighthearted, in this one he appeared solemn, a well-dressed man suffering from a serious-looking accident. Finally, despite the less than enthusiastic coverage of Farage's dinner in lieu of the debate, but in line with the more empathic tone in article's final paragraphs, all the top comments were clearly on his side:

> "Nigel you have done us proud. WE WILL TAKE OUR COUNTRY BACK! WE WILL HAVE INDEPENDENCE DAY!!" (JammyJamesPrescott, Manchester, UK, 19,121 upvotes);

> "Nigel I hope all is ok Don't worry about the vote we are going to win and get out of the EU Thank you" (MAKEY, Sheffield, UK, 6,398 upvotes);

> "I hope everything is ok, love him or hate him, you can't say this guy doesn't have guts or will shy away from confrontation. I genuinely believe he's fought for what he believes in." (BoredMuffins, Wherever home is, UK, 3,934 upvotes);

> "Thank You Nigel for giving your all to Great Britain. We appreciate your efforts and your dream will hopefully be achieved. Thank you." (Plutopug, Shrewsbury, UK, 3,660 upvotes).

In addition, one of the top comments was spreading misinformation. However, it was in agreement with suggestions on EU's expansion plans made by the Leavers:

> "The Eu is opening new membership talks with Turkey next Thursday! 30th June 2016. Out Out Out." (joly1zzzz, Bristol, UK, 5,510 upvotes).

No such meetings were planned.

Overall, while the most-commented articles in Mail Online touched on different aspects concerning the referendum campaign, they were put in a simplifying game frame (not that online tabloids are the only outlets to use it; see: Capella and Jamieson 1997), with added hints of general dissatisfaction with the political class. Thus, politicians were often shown as disappointing, offering emotional slogans instead of serious discussion. At the same time, the context provided by Mail Online editors to the reporting, such as unflattering photos and carefully phrased background material in the bright-blue boxes, made some of the pieces suggest a pro-Leave position – this was not necessarily surprising given the openly pro-Brexit stance of *Daily Mail* paper. But even if the political bent in the online articles was subtle, readers' comments were for the most part unshakable in their enthusiasm towards the UK leaving the European Union. As follows, if we care to look at the articles and comments taken together, we can notice that the more neutral journalistic reporting molded in politically suggestive editing is almost seamlessly complemented by ideologically candid comments.

3.3.2   Gawker

In contrast to Mail Online, Gawker's position on the EU referendum was absolutely clear: Brexit was a bad idea. At the same time, the EU referendum was barely noticeable on the US website, as was the UK in general. Only one article mentioning the vote in any way was posted before 23rd of June, which indicates that the referendum campaign was found to be less interesting than its aftermath – until the end of June 2018, two years after the vote, 18 more posts referring Brexit, also merely in passing, were published. In contrast to Mail Online, the articles on Gawker were usually brief, and the most visible themes concerned not so much particular issues but rather general opinions on the referendum; conversations between commenters and article authors; but also, interestingly, the economy (and the European Union) – the latter apparently a more relatable issue to the US audience than the vote itself.

3.3.2.1   *General Comments*

A good example of the *general theme* was "'Rogue' Algorithm Blamed for Historic Crash of the British Pound"[61] (83 comments), written by George Dvorsky and published on 10th of October 2016. According to the writer, the crash was a political, financial, and technological consequence of the decision

---

61   https://gizmodo.com/rogue-algorithm-blamed-for-historic-crash-of-the-britis-178
       7523587.

made by British citizens four months earlier: "Normally, dramatic drops like this are triggered by major news events, such as declaration of war or a monumental political development. But experts say this incident was likely the result of trading algorithms in high-frequency stock trading that were reacting to recent comments made by French President Francois Hollande, who called for tougher Brexit negotiations." The "rogue algorithm" was likely caused by a "deluge of negative Brexit headlines," which "could have led to an algo[rhythm] taking that as a major sell signal for GBP." While the post was demanding to analyze, requiring a level of financial and technological expertise, in a manner not unusual for Gawker comments the most upvoted ones were remarkably in-depth. For instance, the top-rated observation expanded in detail – its length was about a quarter of the original post – on a quote from the article concerning high-frequency stock trading:

> "If you're trading in milliseconds you're going too slow. Just to give you an idea of the speeds we're dealing with here let's take the CME [Chicago Mercantile Exchange] in Chicago. The main matching engine for all the CME products (bonds, currencies, agricultural products) is located in a data center in Aurora even though the market itself is in downtown Chicago. With a fiber connection out to the data center you can get a signal out there in 150 microseconds. (...) High-frequency traders are operating black box servers hosted in the same data center. (...) If people are on black boxes they have a ton of money at their disposal. It's all an arms race at this point" (Arturo, 21 upvotes).

Other top comments, too, referred to the algorithm and its impact on the British economy:

> "Maybe the bot is right and it's us humans who are wrong? Seriously, a tough, years-long exit from European trade agreements would be terrible for the UK economy. Big companies would move a lot of their major HQs out eventually, I would imagine, which cuts down tremendously on commerce and tourism. mass exodusIt's not like British CEOs are planning a or anything" (Married with Chillum, 18 upvotes);

Tauromachy replied,

> "Agreed. It looks like a proper algorithm ... nothing rogue about it. The GBP has already taken a huge hit since Brexit, and the fallout is just getting worse." (Tauromachy, 11 upvotes).

However, another popular comment focused not on the analytical details but on the humorous aspect of the article:

> "I think it's nice that Wall Street programmed 'panic madly' into their trading computers" (Mud Dedoochka, 26 upvotes).

Finally, one commenter summed up the incident, and the commonsensical opinion found approval among several other readers:

> "This is equally interesting and terrifying" (RedRobin84, 6 upvotes).

A different example of the theme could be found in a piece published by Ryan F. Mandelbaum on 22nd of April 2017, ten months after the referendum in which British citizens decided to leave the European Union. Titled "Dr. Who Joins the March For Science in London"[62] (87 comments), the article was "partially supported by a grant from the National Science Foundation," as per statement added at the bottom – it was a sponsored post. The piece focused on a march in support of science that had taken place in London, as well as six hundred other cities. The aim of the march, Mandelbaum wrote, was to voice the need for evidence-based policies, fears concerning international cooperation after Brexit, solidarity with similar marches held in the United States, and for scientists to show themselves to the broader public in a less "Ivory tower" style. The journalist reported, "Donald Trump might not be the President, but solidarity, Brexit woes and a general love of evidence-based facts drew the excited crowd. Oh, and Doctor Who aka Peter Capaldi was there." (Capaldi played the part of the Doctor in "Doctor Who," a popular British science-fiction television show which has been aired since the 1960s.) The atmosphere at the event was largely critical of Brexit, and the reporter took photos of people holding anti-Brexit posters (e.g. "First step, BREXIT. Next step, CLEXIT," while "CLEXIT = Climate Exit = Climate Crisis") and donning cut-out face masks featuring Nigel Farage and Donald Trump. According to a nanochemist who took part in the rally, "Brexit is already negatively impacting the potential for international collaboration. (...) It can mean we lose access to the facilities we rely on, and will be losing out on funding." The location of the march was not accidental, which Mandelbaum noted: "Organizers and speakers hoped to send a message to the British government, given the rally's spot in front of the Parliament building." The writer added that the event ended in a distinctly playful British manner,

---

62   https://gizmodo.com/dr-who-joins-the-march-for-science-in-london-1794558615.

namely "with a group caroling of Monty Python's Galaxy Song." A YouTube video of the original comedy song – about the galaxy, as its name suggests – was embedded directly underneath. Despite the adoption of such unconventional methods to highlight the negative consequences of Brexit, but in line with Gawker's general disinterest with it, only one of the top-five comments focused on the topic of the article:

> "I read somewhere (the guardian maybe?) that between 10–15% of all scientists' salaries in the UK are funded by EU grants. Brexit will lead to a brain drain in the UK." (I made a pigeonrat, 12 upvotes).

Unlike this commenter, in a typical online-nerd fashion also characteristic of Gawker (see e.g.: Tocci 2009), others were quick to point out the reporter's mistake of misnaming the title character, the Doctor as Doctor Who. Thus, one example of such comment was:

> "How many people are going to skip the article just to tell you it's 'The Doctor' not 'Doctor Who'?" (Adamdoesthings, 31 upvotes).

But another commenter pointed out that this was not a mistake, and pasted stills of the series' credits from different decades as proof:

> "*cough* [images of stills] It's fine. 'Dr. Who' and 'Doctor Who' are both correct. Now let's move past it and pay attention to the content of the article" (Platypus Man, 52 upvotes).

A different popular comment was an enthusiastic direct reply to Platypus Man:

> "You win the internets today" (BlueTADIS, 14 upvotes).

As this piece demonstrates, in stark contrast to Pudelek and Mail Online where journalists did not react to readers' comments directly, on Gawker Mandelbaum posted a half-joking, half-apologizing response in the comments section, and his own comment landed in one of the top spots, too:

> "hi everyone just wanted to apologize for my utter lack of pop culture knowledge" (Ryan F. Mandelbaum, 23 upvotes).

The author's comment also included a pasted (and now deleted) tweet he had published that same day:

"everyone yelled when this guy showed up idk [I didn't know] he was the doctor in that show doctor whom #marchforscienceLDN #marchforscience."

As the post and comments show, this type of engaged discussion, rather than mere statements of opinion approved in upvotes, made Gawker markedly distinct from the other two online tabloids. Unlike Pudelek and Mail Online, the US outlet actively experimented with brining the readers closer to the journalists by encouraging conversation between the two parties. In doing so, Gawker attempted to tear down the wall that separated paid journalists from the freely (pun intended) commenting readers, and in consequence made the comments section worth checking more. After all, if the article's author converses with the commenting readers, the more reason there is to go through the comments section for additional information.

"Facebook Suspends Cambridge Analytica, Data Firm That Worked on Donald Trump's Campaign [Updated]"[63] (34 comments), written by Tom McKay on 17th of March 2018, is another example of a general take on Brexit. The piece discussed the Facebook ban of the UK-based company Cambridge Analytica, which was accused of influencing the 2016 US presidential elections in favor of Donald Trump and, earlier, aiding the Leave campaign in the UK by microtargeting potential voters on Facebook.[64] Brexit was mentioned in the post only briefly – "[Cambridge Analytica] also is being investigated for its possible involvement in the UK's Brexit referendum" – but a link to an investigative feature on the topic published by the UK Sunday paper, *The Observer* was embedded in the post.[65] Although both the British and American cases of microtargeting using social media, while not the first ones (see e.g.: Wylie 2019), are considered exceptionally far-reaching, the comments ignored Brexit

---

63   https://gizmodo.com/facebook-suspends-cambridge-analytica-data-firm-that-w-1823858305.
64   On psychometric targeting on Facebook, see: Kosinski et al. 2013. Contrary to popular opinion, in an article published after the EU referendum in the UK and the US elections, González (2017) questions Cambridge Analytica's claims about its power to effectively microtarget voters.
65   The opening sentence of the article in *The Observer* is worth noting as it illustrates the scale of Cambridge Analytica's operations: "The data analytics firm that worked with Donald Trump's election team and the winning Brexit campaign harvested millions of Facebook profiles of US voters, in one of the tech giant's biggest ever data breaches, and used them to build a powerful software program to predict and influence choices at the ballot box." See: Cadwalladr and Graham-Harrison 2018.

and went straight to US politics instead. The lengthiest one included several tweets to prove the commenter's argument:

"Commence the inevitable shitshow of Facebook execs claiming they didn't know (they knew), claiming they acted immediately (they did virtually nothing), arguing about the semantics around the word 'breach' (which is a meaningless distinction, like gun owners who carp about the AR-15 not really being a semi-automatic weapon after 30 people are killed by a random gun owner with an AR-15), and claiming to want to find out the truth (while threatening to sue news outlets trying to report the truth that FB was hiding all along), and then embarrassing themselves by making idiotic arguments on Twitter (because no one would see them on fucking Facebook) and re-tweeting dumb tweets that they believe somehow support their belief that as long as they can make money off of selling our data to anyone with a dime, they should be respected, admired, and rewarded" (gramercypolice, 16 upvotes).

Another commenter agreed with the disillusioned stance on Facebook's willingness to come clean:

"Spot on. These guys (and yes, they're mainly but not all guys) live in a high priced bubble where mission statements stand in for moral centers, and legal teams trump all. They're so deep in the business of dopamine drip tricking us into signing away our secrets, it's self congratulatory castle guarding or bust." (JoeBarleyCares, 5 upvotes).

A different popular comment followed the same trail, and added the Russian context of Cambridge Analytica's microtargeting voters, with President Putin being known for favoring Trump over Clinton:

"That feel when Zuck[erberg] sold out your country for a few rubles. Cambridge Analytica's connections to Russia have been known for almost a year, even to the layperson" (flyfunner5, 27 upvotes).

Still, one commenter pointed out the larger flaws in the US electoral system that allowed Cambridge Analytica to succeed in the first place:

"Can this not be the logical outcome of citizens united /money=speech? Did they really think that influence would stop at borders? And, has the democratic party only legitimized it by not opposing it outright, but competing for those corporate dollars?" (Meanwhile, Elsewhere, 8 upvotes).

The person received a reply with a matter-of-fact rhetorical question,

"Agreed on the first two points, on the last I would ask: what are Dems supposed to do, sit back and not raise money while the other party does?" (SetteOtto, 9 upvotes).

One can notice that the conversation shifted towards some of the broader contexts of the issue described in the article, such as the problematic accountability of Facebook, foreign influence carried out by using social media, and existing laws on financing elections. Unlike Pudelek and Mail Online comments, which frequently boiled down to emotional outbursts, on Gawker if the comments were ironic in tone, they were often substantive, too.

3.3.2.2 Conversations between Commenters

Because of this, it comes as no surprise that another recurring theme on Gawker was *commenting on other users' comments*. This conversational style was unique for the website, and the popularity of this theme on Gawker highlights the importance laid on interacting with each other rather than just making statements for others to see. An illustration of the conversational attitude can be found in the only article that was published on Gawker about Brexit ahead of the referendum. Posted on 20th of June, three days before the vote, the piece was titled "The Number of Stars on the EU Flag Means Absolutely Nothing"[66] (21 comments), and was written by Katharine Trendacosta.[67] The author elaborated on the symbols of the European Union flag using the flag of the United States as a point of reference. Thus, while on the US banner the number of stars signifies the number of states, in contrast, on the EU flag "[t]he stars are just the number that looks good in a circle, which is a 'symbol of unity'," the journalist reported. "Also the 12 stars somehow also represent the three ideals of 'unity, solidarity and harmony among the peoples of Europe.' Four stars for each one, I guess," she explained. It is hard to ignore the fact that the only aspect of Brexit presented in the article was the number of stars on

---

66 https://gizmodo.com/the-number-of-stars-on-the-eu-flag-means-absolutely-not-178 2306382.

67 Trendacosta's article was originally published on Gizmodo, not Gawker, which was still operational in June 2016. However, because it is the only article on Brexit that was published on Gawker Media before the referendum, it was included in the sample.

the flag of the European Union. The writer made a weak – even if mocking – attempt to fit the United Kingdom in the EU flag by mimicking the direct star-state symbolism of the US flag, wrongly suggesting the European Union was a federation with particular countries as states. Yet, in response, a commenter was quick to point out the inconsistencies of the star symbolism, even on US soil. "50 stars = 50 states," Trendacosta wrote, applied "since childhood," but

> "only (…) if you were a child on or after August 1959. Before that it was 49 or 48, etc. (The oldest American alive today was born in 1989, so there are no Americans alive who had anything smaller than 46 pounded into them.) You may now resume your regularly scheduled browsing" (Farquest de Jamal, 3 upvotes).

In line with Cunningham's Law,[68] a popular online adage according to which to get a good answer on the internet it is best to initially post a wrong one, the commenter's typo in the date sparked an interchange that made it to the top comments:

> "1989? You say? Dear Lord above, I suddenly feel old" (lostEngineer, 9 upvotes);

Farquest de Jamal replied,

> "** expletive deleted ** 1898. I deserve a dope slap," (Farquest de Jamal, 6 upvotes);

and lostEngineer continued,

> "No worries. I have sexdaily … er … dyslexia too" (lostEngineer, 5 upvotes).

Finally, in another reply to the "dope slap" response, a different commenter added,

> "request granted." (MaximilianMeen, 4 upvotes)

---

68 The "law" was named after Howard Cunningham, the author of a framework for online collaboration which served as the basis for Wikipedia.

and embedded the post with a gif of a man slapping another, while both are spectacularly spinning in the air. It was in fact a scene from an Indian 2011 blockbuster action movie, "Singham," serving as a perfect example of online cultural remix described by Shifman (2014) in her study of memes. Finally, although the conversation in the comments section had almost nothing to the with the topic of the original post, it vividly showed communal engagement in a joking-style conversation.

Other articles with conversational comments where Brexit was mentioned had even less to do with the referendum. For instance, on 22nd of August Christina Warren published a post titled, "Amazingly, Donald Trump's New App Is Not a Joke"[69] (22 comments), in which the author mockingly described Donald Trump's (as well as Hillary Clinton's) campaign smartphone app. In the last paragraph, the journalist pointed out that Trump's app looked very similar to one made earlier for Ted Cruz, his competitor in the Republican primaries. The explanation was that both apps had been created by uCampaign, a company also known for building apps for organizations such as the National Rifle Association, as well as one to support "the Brexit" (sic) – the app was called Vote Leave.[70] Predictably for Gawker commenters, they were highly suspicious of the app. One of them wrote a mock-quote:

> "'Here, be distracted by this while we data-mine your phone'" (OT.level7, 21 upvotes),

which started a conversation with the article's author. The journalist replied,

> "Totally why I signed-up with a burner email and the name 'Your Mom'" (Christina Warren, 3 upvotes).

The commenter continued:

> "Right but does it have access to your contacts and other data?" (OT.level7, 1 upvote).

Warren answered once again:

---

69 https://gizmodo.com/amazingly-donald-trumps-new-app-is-not-a-joke-1785592675.
70 See also uCampaign's CEO Thomas Peters's (2016) post on the topic (originally linked in the Gawker article).

"It asks but you don't have to grant. I didn't grant and iOS is good at sandboxing. Mileage may vary on Android" (Christina Warren, 3 upvotes).

As shown above, the exchange between author and commenter went into details about the differences in access to private content between Apple and Android smartphone operating systems. Yet, more broadly, the talk touched on suspicions – not entirely unfounded – that app developers and politicians wish to infringe on voters' privacy, for instance by mining data on their phones. In light of the US National Security Agency mass surveillance scandal, revealed by Edward Snowden in 2013, such doubts are justified (see: Greenwald 2013).[71] However, violations of privacy were not the only topic of discussion. Warren also commented on another reader's joking post, which mentioned the previous US presidential run: the commenter reminded of Mitt Romney's typo, "A Better Amercia" in the 2012 presidential candidate's campaign app (see e.g.: Gross 2012). Her sarcastic reply was,

"This is VERY, VERY true. That was truly a great moment for everyone" (Christina Warren, 4 upvotes),

Another example of dialog between commenters could be found in an article published on 9th of November, a day after the US presidential election. Although the piece referred to Brexit, among others, the date heavily influenced the post and comments. Thus, in "Trump's Troll Army Sets Its Sights on Europe"[72] (136 comments), Bryan Menegus reported on the excitement of the newly elected president's "internet army" on Reddit, a popular discussion website. As for Donald Trump himself, he was described as "a man who shares in common all the traits of burgeoning fascists through history." According to Menegus, the right-wing users of Reddit considered themselves the reason for both Trump's win and Leavers' success in the UK referendum held several months earlier. In light of such major victories, and in an attempt to keep fuel to the fire, they set a new goal: to get the far-right politician, Marine Le Pen elected in the French 2017 presidential election. The article suggests that right-wing US Reddit users believed that nationalist and conservative political shifts in different European countries had been, and would continue to be, the result

---

71 To put the matter in perspective, in 2017 the PiS-led government bought Pegasus spying software which it used to target political opponents in Poland. See: Czuchnowski and Szostak 2022.
72 https://gizmodo.com/trump-s-troll-army-sets-its-sights-on-europe-1788780523.

of US grassroots online propaganda of their own making. Though their conclusions were not entirely accurate (or effective), they nonetheless presented a vision of internet-forum enhanced US imperialism of right-wing nationalisms. While it was an anti-democratic caricature of the international ideals – if not always pragmatic goals – voiced by the United States (see e.g.: Holmes and Krastev 2020), it was nonetheless a grassroots, nationalist concept for America's continued global political domination. In reference to this, a commenter tellingly named Another Gawker Refugee (Gawker had disappeared at the end of August that year) started a conversation by drawing historical comparisons between voting in the US in 2016 and Germany in the 1930s or, in short, between Trump and Hitler:

> "I keep reading comments from people who voted Trump saying that they aren't rascists and that they voted for Trump because they are unhappy with jobs and the economy and want change. But they still voted for a racist, sexist xenophobe with fascist leanings. Germans in the 1930's who voted for Hitler would probably say much the same thing. They weren't necessarily rascist, but they were unhappy with the economy and jobs in the middle of the Great Depression and they wanted change. Sure, but they still voted for a racist xenophobe with fascist ideas. Hitler also never won a popular vote. He came into power through a coalition, and then managed to eliminate dissent and roll back civil rights. That 'brighter future' at the end of the article is chilling" (Another Gawker Refugee, 32 upvotes).

Done With This Site (another reference to Gawker), however, questioned the commenter's *Reductio ad Hitlerum,* using celebrity comparisons instead:

> "Why is every Republican President automatically compared to Hitler? Bush was accused of war crimes and compared to Hitler for example. (…) Trump is a Kardashian that managed to convince 59 million people to vote for him to be President. He thinks he can run the country as a business, he'll find out in the first week that he can't. (…) If you want to worry about something, worry about congress because that's where the REAL work is done. Trump is a figure head, not Hitler" (Done With This Site, 26 upvotes).

Still, some popular comments begged to differ:

> "Good straw man you have there. I've literally never heard of a single person comparing any Republican president to Hitler. It is just Trump. He's

hostile to the press, encourages his mobs to commit violence, convinces his followers that specific minorities (mostly Mexicans and Muslims, but sometimes blacks too) are to blame for crime and taking their jobs, promised to bring back torture even if it doesn't work. (...) Edit: Oh, I almost forgot. He also has the support of neo-Nazis and the KKK. If the brown shirt fits." (Dikt1, 31 upvotes).

VanMorbison, too, was critical of Done With This Site's comment, at least parts of it:

"Bush authorized, and thus committed, war crimes. How hard is it, then, to understand why he would be said to have committed war crimes?" (VanMorbison, 22 upvotes).

Nevertheless, among the most popular comments, one, rather than discussing the plausibly fascist inclinations of the newly-elected president, fact-checked the international right-wing propaganda context of the original post, including the images from Reddit that were embedded in the piece. One of them was titled "How to fix the West," and included party logos (in the case of the US and the UK, campaign logos), photos of their leaders, and country flags: the United States with the Republican Donald Trump, the United Kingdom with UKIP's Nigel Farage (both had green checkmarks underneath), France with Front National's (not) Marine Le Pen, Germany with Alternative für Deutschland's Frauke Petry, Australia with Kirralie Smith from the Australia Liberty Alliance, and Austria with Norbert Hofer from Freiheitliche Partei Österreichs. The subtitle in the image explained the checkmarks, "2 to down. 4 to go."[73] But a commenter bearing a French-sounding name, bitingly undermined the political savvy of the Reddit "internet army":

"Wow, those trolls need to do their homework. French presidents are elected for 5 years, not 4 and that's a picture of Marion Maréchal Le Pen, Marine Le Pen's niece who, although a major player in the National Front, is far from being its leader" (Etienne, 13 upvotes).

---

73   The image can be found on an archived version of the website: https://web.arch ive.org/web/20161111160307/https://gizmodo.com/trump-s-troll-army-sets-its-sights-on -europe-1788780523.

3.3.2.3   Economy/Recession

The economy was another recurring theme on Gawker related to Brexit and a post, "One of the Best Cheap Phones Might Get a Price Hike Thanks to Brexit,"[74] (19 comments), as the title indicates, reported on phone price hikes. In the piece which had the feel of an unmarked advertisement, published on 29th of June – six days after the EU referendum – the author, Daren Orf explained that the likely change in the price of a "surprisingly great" Chinese phone, called OnePlus 3 would be the result of the post-Brexit referendum "garbage" value of the British pound. Orf, openly enthusiastic about the phone brand, deliberated whether the price hikes in the UK could become a larger trend, and observed that "customers flooded the Apple store in southwest London in fear of impending price hikes as the pound continues at 31-year low." Meanwhile Samsung, Apple's major competitor in mobile phones, went so far as to consider leaving London because of Brexit, the journalist alarmed. The commenters, however, were more careful in their own analytical takes on the matter. For example, one commenter wrote,

> "Wouldn't the opposite be true for people outside Britain though (making the headline misleading)? Because the Pound is weak, it should be cheaper for those in the US using USD. (…) Also, there are already indications that the markets and currencies will bounce back. The hysteria is starting to subside and people are beginning to objectively evaluate the impact of Brexit" (B3815, 3 upvotes).

A sober reply followed:

> "Just for the record: Brexit hasn't happened yet. The UK is still a part of the EU so everything that happened until now isn't much more than a teaser" (beano, 5 upvotes).

Nevertheless, a counterargument on foreign exchange came next:

> "You would be right if OnePlus was based in the UK and used pounds for accounting purposes. But since they're Chinese selling to the US and the relative value of renminbi to dollars has remained constant the dollar value has remained the same Americans won't see any savings. If right now you in the US bought a phone and managed to pay them in pounds then

---

74   https://gizmodo.com/one-of-the-best-cheap-phones-might-get-a-price-hike-tha-1782824306.

it'd be cheaper but that's a very very edge case" (Unemployed Astronaut, 1 upvote).

In a reply to a comment concerning the economic implications of the UK referendum, one commenter empathized,

> "If I was the UK and my credit was just downgraded and I had effectively no Prime Minister – no national leadership, and I had racist assholes coming out of the woodwork, I'd be smashing that panic button right about now" (bourgeoisie, 3 upvotes).

bourgeoisie was also the author of another upvoted reply, in which they assumed it was an answer to a comment made by a Brit ("you" in the comment):

> "[We] 'may be' 'okay' is hardly a ringing endorsement. The UK is, in the eyes of the world, lesser today than it was before the vote. Not because you're all racists, or even because leaving the EU is fundamentally wrong but because the way that the vote came about empowered the undercurrent of racism and xenophobia. In turn it insulted all of Europe by essentially saying 'fuck you losers, we can do better on our own!'. (...) The financiers aren't wrong to be scared" (bourgeoisie, 1 upvote).

In sum, the online tabloid commenters offered a reasonably commonsensical take on the financial sector, particularly given the post-referendum UK-EU relations. But they were also unenthusiastic about the xenophobic reasons for Leavers' success.

Another good illustration of the theme could be found in the article, "What Is The Federal Reserve Trying to Hide About Donald Trump's Relationship With Reptilians?"[75] (35 comments), written by Matt Novak and published on 8th of March 2017. It was an unusually long piece for the website, over 5,500-words long, for the most part made up of extensive quotes from messages sent to the Fed. To write the article, Novak filed a Freedom of Information Act (FOIA) request for messages sent by the general public to the Federal Reserve with keywords such as Trump, Hillary, Democrats and Republicans, as well as "the kinds [of words] you'd find on conspiracy websites about the Fed, including

---

75 https://gizmodo.com/what-is-the-federal-reserve-trying-to-hide-about-donald-1793053793.

'lizard people,' 'reptilian,' 'Jewish,' and 'Alex Jones.'"[76] The quoted messages, written in 2015 and 2016, range from general opinions on the activities of the Federal Reserve and demands to bring jobs back to the United States as well as change interest rates, to numerous conspiracy theories, including foreign agents, Jews, and extraterrestrials. Many of the messages were written entirely in uppercase, which is popularly interpreted as the written equivalent of shouting. Interestingly, Brexit was mentioned in two of the quoted messages. In the first, from 13th of June 2016, ten days before the EU referendum, the author demanded that the Fed "RAISE THE DAMN INTEREST RATES 1/4 OF 1 PERCENT NOW!!!" In what turned out to be an example of poor judgement, the writer accused the institution of cowardice based, among other things, on "unrealistic fears of a BREXIT". In the other message, written a day after the referendum, its author compared the economic-nationalist sentiment of British Leave voters to those who had voted for Donald Trump and Bernie Sanders in the US presidential primaries: "BREXIT passing simply means that Great Britain's citizens believe in nationalism over globalization. Clearly, most of the people who voted for Bernie Sanders and Donald Trump believe that nationalism would be a better policy than globalization." Thus, when the authors mentioned Brexit, a decidedly foreign event, they stuck to the familiar US context. Yet the most upvoted comment focused neither on the UK vote nor on the Fed, but on anti-liberal conspiracy theories. In addition, it played with the genre found in many of the quoted messages in the article:

> "Honestly I'd be more surprised if it turned out that Donald Trump was secretly a human. Ted Cruz[77] is definitely one of the lizard people, though" (TheBurnersMyDestination, 21 upvotes).

A different commenter paid attention to the catchphrases chosen by the journalist in his FOIA request:

---

76   Alex Jones is a far-right conspiracy theorist and creator of a popular website, InfoWars which propagates his views. In 2022, Jones was fined almost one billion US dollars for deliberately spreading misinformation about an elementary school shooting that took place in Sandy Hook, Connecticut ten years earlier.
77   Ted Cruz, a Republican senator, is a religious conservative, known among other things for supporting the death penalty and gun rights. Cruz competed with Donald Trump in the 2016 presidential primaries, but later became his staunch supporter.

POLITICIANS ARE CROOKS, VOTES ARE RIGGED, AND OTHER VISIONS 119

> "I want them to release letters with the word 'libtard'[78] I know that would be a treasure trove of stupid. I'm going to file a request and see what they say" (MrCaligula, 14 upvotes).

In response, ProfessorChaos suggested adding the opening phrase of the preamble to the US Constitution to the journalist's request:

> "I'd include 'We the people' on that list as well. Can't ever have a good rant without it" (ProfessorChaos, 6 upvotes).

In another reply in the discussion thread, a commenter pointed out spelling and punctuation as a possible subject of analysis:

> "I think the ones [sentences] completely lacking upper case (and/or periods) would be very telling too" (Ellestra, 2 upvotes).

Lastly, in contrast to other popular comments, which centered on the Fed request, one top comment included a meme. The short introduction,

> "It's safe to say that conspiracy theories are officially mainstream. The President of the United States tweets out a new one every week. Introducing the latest in Presidential Haberdashery" (David E. Davis, 5 upvotes)

was followed by Trump's portrait, in which the President was shown wearing a Make America Great Again hat, albeit one made out of tinfoil. According to conspiracy theorists, the material protects against electromagnetic fields. The comment thus shifted attention from mocking messages sent to the Fed to a part sour, part sarcastic conclusion that with Trump in the presidential seat conspiracy theories would become a POTUS-approved way of perceiving the world.

A different piece, titled "Ryanair Scrambles to Solve Its Drunken Passenger Problem"[79] (111 comments), written by Adam Clark Estes on 15th of August 2017, concerned the low-cost airline's troubles with inebriated travelers. The piece

---

78   "Libtard" is short for "libertarian retard," a derogatory term used by radical Republican supporters in reference to their Democratic counterparts.
79   https://gizmodo.com/ryanair-scrambles-to-solve-its-drunken-passenger-proble-179 7857341.

began with a summary of potential difficulties people face when flying: "As Brexit threatens to turn its entire business upside down, passengers can't stop getting drunk on its flights, doing something stupid on camera, and causing all kinds of chaos when the video hits the internet." Because of this, "Ryanair is trying to restrict how much people drink at the airport." The author listed a number of recent incidents involving drunk British passengers on planes, concluding "[y]ou almost can't blame Ryanair for treating its passengers like college students who need extra supervision." He then went on to explain the Irish airline's proposal for airports to sell alcohol in bars only after 10 am, reasoning that while airports profit from it, crews on the aircrafts are left to deal with the consequences. However, Estes also pointed at the hypocrisy of the request, given that a Ryanair employee accused the company of pushing crews to sell drinks during flights, which the carrier denied. What's more, according to the journalist, in the past Ryanair had suggested charging for using restrooms next to selling standing tickets. This made the employee's claims about the company caring only about sales, rather than civility, sound credible. Consequently, the top comment criticized both the low-cost airline and its passengers:

> "Don't want low-rent passengers? Don't offer low-rent fares. Also, F Ryanair – they try to monitize everything. Ever seen Border Patrol?" (VictorH, 27 upvotes).

(The reference to Border Patrol is unclear: it could be the US law enforcement agency, a contemporary New Zealand reality show, an American television series from 1959, a Western from 1943, or still something else.) Another commenter criticized drunk passengers:

> "I've never understood why people get hammered at airports. If you're incapable of getting through a simple flight without alcohol, you've probably got issues that need sorting out" (Chiral_Spiral, 20 upvotes).

In contrast to this, a different commenter replied in defense of consuming alcohol when traveling by air:

> "I don't get hammered, but I do take the opportunity to drink a bit more than I usually do in public. Think of it: I'm not driving anywhere. I'm out of the office and away from home, so nobody expects anything of me. I've got limited mobility (in the airport or plane). So why not have a few drinks?" (ScreaminScott, 19 upvotes).

More sympathy towards drinking on the plane followed in the same thread:

> "Air travel sucks and a lot of people get anxiety over it. I'm not sure how people are confused why others might want to soften the blow" (COMT-NDRVR, 15 upvotes).

The exchange was summed up by a commenter who embedded a YouTube clip from the adult animated series "Family Guy," in which the family is on a plane about to land in Ireland. "You know, Ireland has more drunks per capita than people," the father explains as the plane descends to the runway buried under empty liquor bottles. The commenter captioned the video,

> "I am so going to hell for this" (The Devil Drives a Mustang (Rotary Pending), 17 upvotes).

To conclude, in most Gawker pieces the EU referendum served as a background for other stories referring to the United Kingdom, or it was mentioned in passing when discussing still different topics. What remains in stark contrast to Pudelek and Mail Online, however, is that the mocking tone of the articles trickled down to the comments, which happened almost seamlessly. There, the commenters further elaborated on the topics, often with levels of extraordinary expertise for an online-tabloid forum, or played with Gawker's snarky style, writing quips and embedding memes. It was thus a very different comments section from the predominantly outraged ones in the Polish and British outlets.

3.3.3   Pudelek

Judging by the number of comments, Brexit was a far more popular topic on Pudelek than it was on Gawker. This is understandable, given the large number of Poles who were living and working in the United Kingdom at the time, and the fact that for Poles the UK was considered the top country of immigration within the European Union. This made the EU membership referendum a matter of direct interest for many. Despite this, similarly to the US website, Pudelek articles on the topic were published only after the referendum took place.

3.3.3.1   *General Comments*

One of the features Pudelek shared with Gawker was the prevalence of *general opinions* concerning Brexit in the Polish online tabloid. "Great Britain after

Brexit: Brits ask Google what is the European Union!"[80] (523 comments), is a vivid example of this theme, and was published two days after the UK referendum, on 25th of June. The piece reported on the surprise and disappointment of British citizens with the vote result, including those who voted "leave." Pudelek also noted that questions such as "What is the EU?" and "What does it mean to leave the EU?" became top questions searched on Google in the UK – yet not until after the referendum.[81] The final sentence in the article was a bitter quote from a woman who had been interviewed by ITV, a British television station, after the referendum results rolled in. She admitted that "'reality' has now hit her and that given her chance again she would vote to remain."[82] Screenshots of mostly gloomy people in referendum t-shirts were added at the bottom of the post, and in keeping with the bleak tone of the article, the two top comments were highly critical of British voters. A likely reason for this was that for the Polish commenters the idea of leaving the EU sounded absurd – most Poles have been strong supporters of the European Union ever since the country's accession in 2004.[83] One commenter wrote,

> "Unfortunately the English[84] are retards ... And lack culture" (1,850 upvotes);

> "how can such people decide on matters important for the country?" (1,349 upvotes),

asked another. Interestingly, a different commenter considered "retards" a global phenomenon:

> "It's not just in Great Britain but in the whole world. Ignoramuses and retards everywhere. Sad but true" (1,496 upvotes).

> "[A]nd yet democracy is not a miraculous invention" (1,366 upvotes),

---

80 https://www.pudelek.pl/artykul/94415/wielka_brytania_po_brexicie_brytyjczycy_pytaja_googlea_czym_jest_unia_europejska/.
81 Link to the Google Trends tweet mentioned in the article: https://twitter.com/googletrends/status/746303118820937728.
82 Link to the ITV post: https://www.itv.com/news/update/2016-06-24/leave-voter-disappointed-and-wishes-to-vote-remain/.
83 In 2016, 84 percent of Poles declared they supported Poland's membership in the EU; since then the number has been rising. See: CBOS, 2022.
84 In the Polish language the term "English" is often used interchangeably with "British."

was another upvoted interpretation of the vote results, disappointed that democratic voting does not always translate into wise decisions. Nonetheless, one of the most popular comments praised the Prime Minister David Cameron for leaving his post after the result was announced. It was considered honorable behavior, very different from the actions of PiS government officials, who stayed in power despite being embroiled in numerous scandals during the party's rule:

> "I don't know whether this will be for better or for worse but respect to the Prime Minister who handed in his resignation. Can you imagine any of ours doing this? Everyone around would be guilty but no one would feel any guilt in himself" (426 upvotes).

"Another Pole beaten in the United Kingdom! By ... 30 teenagers!"[85] (454 comments), was an article published on 12th of September 2016. The piece, a different example of an article with a focus on general opinions, discussed the latest in a series of beatings of Polish citizens committed by British locals annoyed with migrants from Poland. This one took place in Leeds, and the article included Google Street View screenshots of the city's streets, a photo of the murdered Polish citizen taken less than a month earlier, in addition to a photo of a random anti-Muslim protest. Again, some of the most popular comments voiced broad, unfavorable remarks about the British – an expected tone given that it was not the first instance of a Pole having been beaten by the locals in the UK:

> "The English are pigs !!!! Look what is happening !!!!" (572 upvotes);

> "Total retards" (448 upvotes).

Still, a slightly longer comment pointed out the similarities between aggressive young Brits and Poles:

> "The stereotype in Europe is that they are a super cultured and progressive nation, but young Brits are the same vermin like Polish street hooligans" (478 upvotes),

while another top comment offered a generally pessimistic overview:

---

85 https://www.pudelek.pl/artykul/97776/kolejny_polak_pobity_w_wielkiej_brytanii_przez _nastolatkow/.

"This world is becoming more and more terrifying. We are driven towards self-destruction" (600 upvotes).

In spite of this, and similarly to the "familiarizing" Gawker comments, the most upvoted comment on the Pudelek article drew the foreign news piece closer to home by pointing out racism as a shared trait. At the same time, though, it revealed the commenter's own xenophobic attitudes:

"Someone shouted Poland for Poles in Poland recently, the English have the same thing. England for the English and I'm not even very surprised, but beating people is going too far. Of course they won't touch the Ahmeds on benefits because they're afraid." (1,112 upvotes).

This last comment was particularly telling, as it not only expressed outrage at the British for having beaten a Pole but added another layer, not of nationality but religion. In fact, according to a study from 2019, 45 percent of Poles share a negative stance towards Muslims, which is the lowest score among all religions (CBOS 2019). It is not uncommon for Poles to vilify Muslims, especially online, for example by using the name "Ahmed" instead of "Muslim." This is largely based on a sense of racial superiority (Poles are predominantly white) and at the same time fear, particularly since the start of the migrant crisis in 2015. This was successfully exploited by PiS in the fall 2015 parliamentary campaign. For instance, at a rally, Jarosław Kaczyński, the party's leader famously stated that if allowed to enter Poland, refugees, hailing mostly from Muslim countries, would spread "parasites and protozoa" (sk and mc 2015).

A different example of the general approach could be found in a piece titled "Londoners protest against Great Britain leaving the European Union (PHOTOS)"[86] (144 comments), published on 26th of March 2017, 9 months after the referendum. As the heading indicates, the post included a click-through "gallery," typical for Pudelek posts, with 28 photos from the London demonstration. A picture showing a mass of people standing close to Big Ben, holding numerous banners as well as UK, EU, and Polish flags was posted at the very top of the article, but a rhetorical question was added in the subheading: "Is it not a bit too late for this?" The article itself focused on Theresa May, David Cameron's successor in the Prime Minister's seat from the Tory party, and her declaration that the process of Brexit would begin in a matter of days. In line

---

86   https://www.pudelek.pl/artykul/107658/londynczycy_protestuja_przeciwko_wyjsciu_wielkiej_brytanii_z_unii_europejskiej_zdjecia_s/foto_1.

with this, British representatives were absent at the EU summit celebrating the 60th anniversary of the Treaty of Rome, which established the European Economic Community. The Pudelek article emphasized the contrast between this notable absence and the crowded demonstration on London streets. There, people marched under the "Unite for Europe" banner and gathered in front of the UK Parliament to protest against Brexit. The piece ended with the same sarcastic-sounding question posed in the subheading, this time written in bold: "Is it not a bit too late for this?" The commenters agreed, and the most popular comments included remarks such as:

> "An opinion of a certain Englishman that 'he voted Leave because he was sure it wouldn't happen and now he's shocked' says everything." (430 upvotes);

> "Most Brits don't know what the EU is" (292 upvotes);

> "Unfortunately, populists won there too!" (227 upvotes),

the "too" most likely referring to Poland. Another commenter offered an opinion on the plausible consequences of Brexit on the labor market in the context of Central-Eastern European workers (who had been mocked by a Tory MP in a Mail Online article discussed earlier):

> "I live in the UK and I have no idea who will do the dirty job that we, Poles but also Czechs and Slovaks currently do. For minimum [pay] … of course" (402 upvotes).

Then there was a top comment that brought Brexit back directly to the Polish political reality – another example of domesticating foreign topics, which is a trait found in all three online tabloids:

> "We won't leave, they will kick us out and szydło [Beata Szydło, the Polish Prime Minister at the time] will claim victory" (446 upvotes).

The comment offered a bitter take on the PiS government which, then in its second year of rule, already showed skill in turning key issues concerning the state on their head. An example of this was Szydło's refusal to publish a number of rulings of the Constitutional Tribunal because she did not agree with them, even though she was legally obligated to do so (see: Mazur and Żurek 2017). This marked the beginning of undermining the independence of the judiciary in Poland by PiS. In 2023, the Court of Justice of the European Union ruled these changes breached the EU law.

3.3.3.2   *European Union*
Unmistakably tied with Brexit (and Poland), the *European Union*, too, was a popular theme on Pudelek. The popularity of this topic is understandable given that Brexit meant the United Kingdom's departure from the EU. And so, two days after the UK referendum the former Polish President, during whose tenure Poland joined the Union, headlined one such piece: "Kwaśniewski on Brexit: 'Our Europe is worse from today on'"[87] (89 comments). The post had just three short paragraphs, the first a description of the UK referendum results, and the latter two a recap of the interview Aleksander Kwaśniewski gave on a private Polish news television channel, TVN24 BiŚ. Additionally, a minute-long clip from the interview was embedded at the top of the page. In it, the former President explained that Brexit showed nationalism was on the rise across Europe, and Denmark, next to the Netherlands, were countries "at risk." However, most of the top commenters were less interested in the consequences of Brexit for the EU and more in Kwaśniewski.

"Red Olek,[88] don't worry, liquor prices shouldn't go up" (120 upvotes),

referred to the former President's Communist past and his well-known fondness of vodka. Another comment was openly hostile:

"a Communist agent alias .Alek was the president of our country and passes for a person of authority . what world are we living in ?" (101 upvotes).

Still, one popular comment focused not on Kwaśniewski's words but on his figure:

"he sure got fat" (64 upvotes).

The former President has been known for his struggles with maintaining weight, to the extent that a diet cabbage soup he ate while in office was named

---

87   https://www.pudelek.pl/kwasniewski-o-brexicie-od-dzisiaj-mamy-gorsza-europe-6366090819024513w.
88   "Olek" is short for "Aleksander" in Polish.

"the presidential diet." Nonetheless, two other top comments did touch upon Brexit, and were skeptical of the former President's fears:

"if it doesn't go our way, it's bad – this is Kwaśniewski's thinking" (69 upvotes);

"You're overreacting, Switzerland and Norway aren't in the Union and they are rich. Wait and judge [then]" (145 upvotes).

Such examples show that depending on the framing of the topic – e.g. Brexit-centered or EU-centered – the sentiment in the comments could be very different. In the first case, which was discussed earlier, in response to an article on vote results and a sense of disappointment in the UK, the commenters deemed Brexit a mistake. Here, the opinions were far less unequivocal, possibly because they were juxtaposed with the views voiced by Poland's former President. This, too, was a case of familiarizing foreign issues, where local Polish contexts gained more attention than the consequences of the British vote.

Yet another example of the EU theme relating to Brexit, and to internal Polish political battles, could be found in an article published three days later, on 28th of June, titled "Kaczyński: Tusk is directly responsible for Brexit!"[89] (831 comments). Pudelek reported that Jarosław Kaczyński used Brexit as an excuse to attack Donald Tusk, his political nemesis, who was the President of the European Council at the time. Prior to that he had been the Prime Minister and leader of PO party,[90] which lost power to PiS in 2015. The article quoted Kaczyński stating, among other things, that the EU dislikes nation states, that increased European integration is an "awful principle," as it boils down to more power given to "Berlin," and that Tusk should "disappear from European politics." Again, a short video, this time with Kaczyński's interview in the news channel TVN24 was pasted directly under the article's heading, while two screenshots of Kaczyński's face during the interview, followed by a photo of Tusk with an angry expression were added at the bottom. Despite Tusk's cross face, the top comments were unconvinced by Kaczyński's arguments, for example:

"the black hole and world starvation must be Tusk's fault too." (920 upvotes).

---

89   https://www.pudelek.pl/kaczynski-bezposrednia-odpowiedzialnosc-za-brexit-ponosi-tusk-6366090124895873w.
90   Tusk became the leader of PO once again in 2021 and Prime Minister at the end of 2023.

Some discussed PiS leader's state of mind:

"This guy has an inferiority complex towards Tusk ... there is no other way you can name it" (979 upvotes);

"he is only spitting duck venom" (817 upvotes).

The latter was a play on the meaning of the name "Kaczyński," which in Polish is similar to the word "duck" (adjective "kaczy").

"sick head" (774 upvotes)

was another comment. However, a different upvoted comment offered an opinion about Kaczyński that was not unthinkable in the EU:

"An overlooked old goat. No one would elect this freak in Brussels, maybe he feels hurt" (669 upvotes).

While it has been Kaczyński's strategy to blame Tusk for all possible ills, at least at that point, in a country of EU-enthusiasts this seemed too much.

"'The Guardian' on William's and Kate's visit in Poland: duped into endorsing POLAND'S ugly NATIONALISM!"[91] (389 comments), revealed a different example of the EU theme. The article was published on 23rd of July 2017, over a year after the EU referendum, and this time the piece was largely based on an article written by Kate Maltby in the British daily, *The Guardian*.[92] The piece focused on the visit of the British royal couple to the site of the concentration camp in Stutthof, and Pudelek's title was a direct quote from the British paper. The article was fairly long for the online tabloid (nearly 750 words) and mostly comprised quotes and paraphrases from *The Guardian*. In Pudelek, the article began with a thinly veiled political accusation: "The visit of Prince William and Duchess Kate quite accidentally took place as Law and Justice was taking steps to change the law to curtail the independence of the Supreme Court. (...) While Kate and William's calendar was so full that they did not have a chance to see the demonstrations held in front of the Sejm or the Presidential Palace, the context of their visit, that is the political situation in Poland, was not lost

---

91 https://www.pudelek.pl/artykul/114134/the_guardian_o_wizycie_williama_i_kate_w_polsce_wkreceni_w_sankcjonowanie_brzydkiego_nacjonalizmu_polski/.
92 See: Maltby 2017.

on British [news] services."[93] The article emphasized the Polish government's manipulations in which the royal couple took part, consequently "strengthening a historical narrative promoted by Law and Justice, according to which Poles, and not Jews, had been in the center of the tragedy of the Second World War, as victims of genocide planned against them." This narrative was pushed by emphasizing the role of the Stutthof concentration camp where around 65 thousand prisoners had died out of starvation, disease, extreme labor conditions, and murdered in a gas chamber, rather than the concentration camp and death camp in Auschwitz where among the 1.1 million killed a million were Jews. Pudelek continued with another biting quote from *The Guardian*: "The [British] Foreign Office already knew that by sending our photogenic young royals – complete with cutesy Prince George and Princess Charlotte – we were whitewashing an appalling [Polish] government." Maltby argued, "Brexit has left us scrabbling for allies in Europe. (...) Poland has particular reasons for resenting the heavy hand of Brussels at present: this week's constitutional power-grab has led to condemnation by the EU, and even threats to strip Poland of its voting rights." In the Pudelek piece, official photos of the royal couple with President Andrzej Duda and the first lady, Agata Duda, followed. The final picture, with a close-up of Agata Duda making a hand gesture as if she were tapping herself on the head, looked particularly derisive. Even so, the top comments found the article anti-Polish, thus showing that PiS's strategy was effective. In contrast to the Second World War and Polish-Jewish relations, European Union sanctions, which were eventually implemented[94] and the large protests held in defense of the independence of Poland's Supreme Court did not spark the commenters' interest. For example, one commenter posted a long paragraph equating the scale of Jewish and non-Jewish deaths in Poland during the Second World War, which was a perfect illustration of a widely shared opinion among Poles:

> "It's not even about supporting one party [most likely Civic Platform] but about history. Tragic history. Both Jews and Poles died in concentration

---

93   The PiS government has been undermining the rule of law in Poland since it came into power in 2015. This has been causing major clashes with the European Union, and has provoked numerous demonstrations in Polish cities. See analyses in the 2015–2016 period: Szuleka, Wolny and Szwed 2016; Buras and Knaus 2018. For coverage of the demonstrations that took place a week before the British royal couple's arrival, see e.g.: Harper 2017.

94   In 2017, the European Commission launched Article 7 of the Treaty on European Union against Poland, a procedure intended to establish whether a member state is considered at clear risk of a serious breach of EU values, in this case the rule of law. If a country is

camps. Not just Jews but also Poles died on the streets of occupied Poland. (...) How are you not ashamed to write (with great pride) that you support the publication of this article? (...) Do you also support calling death camps Polish,[95] and not Nazi or German? How dare you call yourselves Poles if you have not even the slightest knowledge about the history of your own homeland?" (269 upvotes).

What the comment overlooked entirely was the difference in the sheer number of people murdered, or the fact that the Nazi the Final Solution was a plan to exterminate Jews, not Poles. Still, while this comment sounded earnest, other popular comments adopted a sarcastic tone:

"I am proud that Poodle reads the Guardian but it's even more leftie than GW [*Gazeta Wyborcza*], so 'it was expected'" (424 upvotes);

"'A rival site of Polish martyrdom'?[96] God, forgive [them] because I cannot" (191 upvotes).

What's more, some of the top comments shamed *The Guardian* writer as a Pole hater:

"a disgrace not a journalist. She has no clue about Poland" (125 upvotes);

and

"Who is sponsoring this pathetic pen pusher and her disgusting, anti-Polish rubbish?" (247 upvotes).

---

found to breach these core values, its voting rights on EU decisions may be suspended. See: https://ec.europa.eu/commission/presscorner/detail/en/IP_17_5367.

95 The term "Polish death camps" has been erroneously used for years to describe Nazi death camps on occupied Polish territory. For example, in 2012, US President Barack Obama used the term when posthumously awarding the Presidential Medal of Freedom to Jan Karski, a Polish Second World War hero who informed Western Allies about Nazi extermination camps and the destruction of the Warsaw Ghetto. President Komorowski and Prime Minister Tusk strongly protested against the use of the phrase, and Obama expressed regret for his mistake (see: https://www.president.pl/president-komorowski/news/president-on-barack-obamas-letter,38594). Six years later, President Duda signed a bill which makes it illegal to use the term "Polish death camps." At the same time, however, the new law makes it difficult to discuss any instances of Polish involvement in the persecution of Jews, and has been viewed by many historians as an act of censorship.

96 This is a quote from *The Guardian* article. Maltby described Stutthof as a "rival site" to Auschwitz.

Maltby's argument about the post-referendum reasons for the royal couple's visit to Stutthof, which was quoted by Pudelek, was lost on the commenters. Instead, they focused on defending the Polish victims of the Nazi occupation – in the view of the commenters, the suffering of Poles during the Second World War was overlooked and needed to be defended. At the same time, the international aspect of the trip and the "Brexit means Brexit" UK government's need to strengthen ties with the Polish law-breaking, right-wing counterpart was entirely omitted. Nevertheless, the fact that the most upvoted comment was enthusiastic about Pudelek taking note of the "leftie" *Guardian* should not be ignored. These comments, too, show the fundamental importance of framing: when commenters referred to Brexit, they were far more likely to voice enthusiasm towards the European Union than when responding to articles mentioning Polish political affairs, riddled by ideological fighting. Perhaps it felt easier to appreciate the EU when looking from a more international perspective. At the same time, the vote for Brexit meant that Poles would lose the chance of making a better life in the United Kingdom. This was no trivial matter; the UK had been the main destination for Polish economic migrants since the country's EU accession in 2004.

3.3.3.3 *Poles in the United Kingdom*

It is then no surprise that a third theme distinctly visible in Pudelek posts related to Brexit concerned *Poles living in the United Kingdom*. After all, Poles who lived in Britain before Brexit formed the largest minority in the country. "Great Britain will leave the European Union!"[97] (756 comments), published on the morning of 24th of June, just several hours after the end of the referendum, is an apt example of the topic. The article began with basic information on the outcome of the UK referendum: 51.9 percent voted to leave the EU, 49.1 percent voted to remain in the Union. It then went on to discuss "an exceptionally difficult morning for Poland," with a "weaker negotiating position" in "a weaker EU," while Poles living in the UK would potentially lose "the right to work and to benefits." Pasted lower on the page were a screenshot from a *New York Times* tweet[98] with the UK referendum results map, photos of a delighted woman holding the Union Jack, Nigel Farage making a victory sign with his fingers, and, lastly, faces of shocked and saddened people. The commenters touched on the Polish aspect of the British referendum results, and voiced fear of Poles forced to return to their homeland:

---

97 https://www.pudelek.pl/artykul/94381/wielka_brytania_wyjdzie_z_unii_europejskiej/.
98 See: https://twitter.com/nytimes/status/746225481490436096.

"This is a mess, now all these Polish degenerates will come back here." (1,791 upvotes);

"So now they won't be able to cough up 500plus when hordes of Poles come back" (1,580 upvotes).

The "500+ Family" is a popular child benefit program introduced by the PiS government in 2016, based on which parents receive 500 złoty (ca. 140 US dollars) per month for each child. (The new government has recently relabeled it "800+ Family" and raised the benefits to 800 złoty, ca. 200 US dollars.) While some commenters were concerned about Poles coming back, another top comment showed sympathy towards Poles abroad:

"I feel sorry for Poles working in the UK, tough times are coming :(" (1,325 upvotes).

Meanwhile, a different one worried about travel and work opportunities:

"This will be the end of trips to England :(" (1,093 upvotes).

One of the most popular, and possibly racist-sounding comments focused on migrants and refugees in Great Britain:

"European immigrants will leave, and they will remain with Syrian ones" (1,145 upvotes).

The topic stood out in public discussions, since the anti-refugee fear campaign fomented by PiS helped the party gain power in 2015. Here, it was carried over to post-Brexit immigration from non-EU countries, which many Pudelek commenters considered inferior.

Another Brexit-related post on the topic of Poles in the UK was published just two days later, on 27th of June, under the alarming headline "Brexit supporters to Polish emigrants: 'Go home Polish scum'"[99] (1,151 comments). The article described the "panic in Great Britain," next to plans made by Scotland and the city of London to hold their own separate referenda to stay in the European Union. The journalist contrasted these declarations with accounts of British citizens pleased with the results, who hoped to "get rid of refugees."

---

99   https://www.pudelek.pl/artykul/94452/zwolennicy_brexit_do_polskich_emigrantow_wrocic_do_domu_polskie_szumowiny/.

According to a quoted local Polish paper published in Huntingdon, an English town (the name was misspelled "Huntington" in the article), small laminated cards printed with slogans "Leave the EU No more Polish Vermin" and, in poor Polish grammar, "Wrócić do domu polskiego szumowiny" ("Going to Polish home scum") were placed on a number of entrance doors to houses in which Poles lived. According to Pudelek, the police responded immediately. The article was accompanied by different Brexit-related photos: a smiling woman holding the UK flag (the same picture was used in one of the previously mentioned posts); a jubilant man donning a Union Jack paper hat and a stack of small Union Jacks in his breast pocket; laminated cards with hateful messages targeting Polish migrants; and the back of a person covered in the EU flag, sitting on Parliament Square, in front of Big Ben. Once more, the top comments revealed strong discontent with the behavior of British voters. The most upvoted stated matter-of-factly,

"Soon you will do your own Brit dishes and cry over this scum" (3,020 upvotes);

while another asked rhetorically,

"I wonder how long the British economy will last without 'polacks'" (2,488 upvotes).

Other top comments were more general, offering opinions on history and nationalism:

"The English, a lazy nation. Lacking history or moral backbone" (2,055 upvotes);

"Here you go, nationalism is hate" (1,527 upvotes);

and summarized the xenophobic story in a single word:

"Rude" (1,392 upvotes).

"The audience BOOED at a Polish woman in a British program! 'I've lived here for 23 years and I had never been discriminated'"[100] (190 comments), published

---

[100] https://www.pudelek.pl/publicznosc-wygwizdala-polke-w-brytyjskim-programie-miesz kam-tu-od-23-lat-i-nigdy-nie-bylam-dyskryminowana-6366063405639809w.

on 22nd of October, presented a still different example of the theme, and one that was hard to pass over. According to the article, the incident took place at a BBC television show, Question Time, during which the Pole shared her feelings on Brexit with expert guests, Lisa Duffy, a member of UKIP, Conrad Black, a former publisher of the conservative daily, *Daily Telegraph*, and other members of the audience. With the slightest hint of a Polish accent, the woman stated that she had "never been discriminated until Brexit came about" and that "the majority of people voted against the Poles who work extremely hard for twelve hours seven days a week. They work in such conditions that most of the people would not want to work, and yet they are the ones you, the British population, want to get out." The woman was interrupted by Lisa Duffy, who explained, "We don't want to stop immigration, we want to control immigration." The Pudelek post ended by offering some comfort, that "The situation was later commented on by British MPs who reassured the woman and declared that she was welcome in their country." A short clip from the show was pasted directly under the article's headline, and photos of the Polish woman, sitting in a row filled with British-looking white men, were added under the article. This time, in line with PiS government's policies back home, some of the popular comments voiced support for UK's anti-immigration policies, even though they targeted Polish immigrants:

> "The British people voted against immigrant slackers who come to their country and take their money. Benefits, sending British money to the wife and children who are living in their home country. No one has anything against hard-working Poles. And certainly not against the wives of British men" (505 upvotes)

– the last part of the remark referred to the woman on the show, who said her husband was British. Another commenter wrote,

> "you yourselves don't want immigrants in Poland but you are surprised that the Eenglish don't want.. it's their country, it's their right" (862 upvotes).

In contrast to these comments, one was clear about the negative attitude towards British citizens:

> "I've always laughed at the British. Louts who think they are somebodies but the majority doesn't live on such a great level" (494 upvotes).

On a different note, another comment focused on the Polish woman's language skills:

> "Btw – she speaks English beautifully, almost no accent!" (752 upvotes).

Still, one of the most popular comments undermined the entire argument of the article:

> "You punched out a title as if she had been laughed at, but after watching [the video] I can assert that she spoke well and that the majority agreed with her" (523 upvotes).

Indeed, while the woman was initially booed at, people also clapped after she finished her remark, and this popular reaction looked more uplifting than the assurances of the MPs Pudelek mentioned.

In conclusion, on Pudelek Brexit was an engaging topic because in many ways it felt very close to home. The domestication of the issue appeared almost seamless, given that numerous Poles were directly affected by the EU referendum results. Lots of others were caught in a paradox between the wish to have the possibility of living and working in the United Kingdom, and a nationalist belief, shared with Leavers and with PiS, that immigrants are to blame for a country's troubles.

3.4 *United States 2016 Presidential Campaign*

The US presidential election, the most globally influential of the three studied votes, received the most traction in all three outlets. If this recognition was not unexpected, it manifested the international dominance of the United States, including the ability to draw the attention of online tabloid audiences in different countries. Yet despite the uniqueness of the US, it is striking that the most popular themes in Gawker, Mail Online, and Pudelek were, again, negative, this time towards both Donald Trump and Hillary Clinton – although Trump received considerably more coverage. This suggests that online tabloid audiences were largely disillusioned about politicians, and that the feeling was transnational. In the American case, the two other main themes concerned general impressions about the campaign, next to sex-related topics. And while unenthusiastic opinions filled the comments, accusations of sexual misconduct made by both sides during the 2016 US presidential campaign produced distinctive online tabloid fodder, making the campaign itself feel tabloid-like. As such, it was a (not) kidding goldmine, with commenters repeatedly voicing disbelief that particular actions, especially Trump's, had actually taken place.

3.4.1   Gawker[101]

3.4.1.1   *Negative Attitudes towards Donald Trump/Republicans*

Since Gawker writers were openly anti-Trump, the American online tabloid's dominant theme, of *negative opinions concerning Donald Trump and/or the Republicans*, was to be expected. "The New York Times Endorses Hillary Clinton, Promises Separate Trump Takedown"[102] (265 comments), an unusually restrained piece for Gawker, written by Lauren Evans and published on 24th of September, provided a good illustration of this approach. The piece discussed the approval of Hillary Clinton made by the daily, *The New York Times*, which listed "the many things that Hillary Clinton has done right over her long and respectable career, laying out a robust list of achievements grounded in their own merits, and not just how they relate to the toxic, nebulous ideas of her doll-handed opponent." However, the daily also articulated "her flaws, like favoring the Iraq war and her role in the U.S. intervention in Libya," Evans summarized. The author stressed that *The New York Times* was not the only paper to endorse Clinton; a similar declaration was made by the *Cincinnati Enquirer*, which was an unusual move for a daily known for its Republican sympathies. As for Trump, according to Evans *The New York Times* announced it would provide an assessment of the candidate a couple of days later. "May (…) Trump's takedown leave no survivors," the author ended her piece scathingly. Instead, the reader comments ranged from general-focus rhetorical questions,

"I can't fathom how anyone can possibly be undecided in this election" (Kris-the-Needlessly-Defiant, 373 upvotes),

to quite analytical. For example, one popular comment soberly scrutinized the power of *The New York Times*'s support:

"A NYT endorsement of Hillary is welcome but thoroughly unsurprising. Ultimately (and sadly) I don't think it matters who endorses Hillary, because Trump supporters are fueled in large part by a feeling of persecution. As such, any and all criticisms of Trump are dismissed out of hand as additional proof that the media is biased against him, which only further

---

101   The Gawker website was live until 22nd of August 2016. Its authors were then moved to other Gawker Media websites, later renamed Gizmodo Media Group. Articles analyzed here that were written in the two months preceding the 8th of November election, were published on other Gizmodo Media Group websites.

102   https://web.archive.org/web/20210918114028/https://jezebel.com/the-new-york-times-endorses-hillary-clinton-promises-s-1787038538.

lionizes him in the eyes of his believers. Even if Fox News, Breitbart, and the ghost of Ronald Reagan endorsed Hillary, Trump supporters would turn on them too" (Tabby Gevinson,[103] 137 upvotes).

Others focused on Hillary Clinton:

"I'm not worried so much about her prep because if there's anything she does, it's her homework, but I AM worried that expectations are so high for her and really all anyone is hoping for from Trump is that he doesn't shit in his hand and fling it at Lester Holt. And Mark Cuban"[104] (WhimsicalEthnographies in a reply to another comment, 123 upvotes);

"In my super red Southeastern state, there's a lot of people moaning about not knowing who to vote for / whether to vote. I think Trump broke them, but they can't admit Clintons the better option after decades of voting Red. I'm taking it as a good sign because any other year, I'd see a lot more Clinton is literally the devil stuff than I have so far" (Rosalind Franklin's Frankenkitty, 175 upvotes).

The latter comment was a response to Kris-the-Needlessly-Defiant about undecided voters. However, a post written by Tabby Gevinson in a reply to a different commenter, turned out to be particularly farsighted:

"As someone who hate-reads right-wing media I'm almost 100% certain that there will be violence if and when Trump loses, especially since a disturbingly high percentage of his supporters appear to believe that if he does lose it will be because Democrats stole the election" (Tabby Gevinson, 102 upvotes).

Although a miss by one presidential election cycle, the comment anticipated the January 2021 attack on Capitol Hill that took place in the aftermath of the 2020 presidential election, which, after a single term, Donald Trump lost to Joe Biden.

---

103   The nickname alludes to Tavi Gevinson, a writer and actress who became famous as a preteen at the end of the 00s for her fashion blog, Style Rookie. She later edited her own online magazine for teenage girls, which specialized in pop culture and feminism.
104   Lester Holt is an NBC news anchor and journalist who moderated one of the presidential debates between Clinton and Trump. Mark Cuban is a billionaire entrepreneur, owner – among others – of NBA team Dallas Mavericks, and a major investor on Shark Tank, a business reality TV show. Cuban endorsed Hillary Clinton in the 2016 presidential election.

"Audio Reveals Trump Bragged About His Daughter's Body, Ogling Naked Beauty Pageant Contestants"[105] (794 comments), written by Hannah Gold and published on 8th of October, a month before the election, offered another illustration of negative attitudes towards Donald Trump during the campaign. "Here we go again again again. Extensive, misogynist audio of self-described pussy-grabber Donald Trump has surfaced, and America continues to listen to his dumb voice dribbling putrid anecdotes about the sex he wants to have, can't have, did have, and wouldn't deign to have with a woman over the age of 35," the article began. The writer then presented an overview of years of interviews between Donald Trump and Howard Stern, a media personality most known for his radio show, The Howard Stern Show. The interviews had been collected by CNN, proving, according to Gold, that Trump "comes across a man who would really like to have sex with his eldest daughter" Ivanka, a former model. For instance, Trump admitted Ivanka could be described as "a piece of ass," he refused to date women older than 35, and "inspected" naked contestants in his beauty pageants because – in Trump's own words – he could "sort of get away with things like that." Despite the graphic descriptions of Trump's preferences concerning women, two of the most popular comments focused not on the Republican candidate but on Hillary Clinton and the second presidential debate that was scheduled for the next day. One commenter wrote enthusiastically,

> "It's easy to imagine Hillary Clinton wiling the evening away with some close friends, laughing over champagne over all of this mishegoss. Until you realize (...) she's a goddamn boss and she's still prepping for tomorrow night's debate because she's a professional" (OMG!PONIES!, 399 upvotes);

to which another commenter replied,

> "call her Hermione Clinton in my head now [an allusion to Hermione Granger, Harry Potter's smart friend] because you just know that even though she could beat Trump without studying a goddamn bit, she still studies because she wants to be the best she can possibly be" (ms.eliot, 296 upvotes).

---

105 https://web.archive.org/web/20210726164748/https://jezebel.com/new-audio-emerges-of-trump-bragging-about-his-voluptuo-1787578389.

A different commenter wondered if Trump's inappropriate behavior would influence his results in Utah:

> "Anyone else thinking this and his 'pussy' comments totally tank him in Utah? Three of their Republican leaders were among those who pulled support for him today, he is polling terribly there for a Republican, and Mormons hate him. His views on immigration and refugees make him unpopular, and his vulgarity has always been a major issue for a religious majority that prides themselves on their 'decent, hard-working people' image." (TheBurnersMyDestination, 258 upvotes).

Two other top comments, however, referred to Trump's comments on sex and attractiveness. One was a pasted tweet from Bill Pruitt, a producer of Trump's reality show, The Apprentice:

> "As a producer on seasons 1 & 2 of #theapprentice I assure you: when it comes to the #trumptapes there are far worse. #justthebegininng"[106] (WhimsicalEthnographies, 333 upvotes);

the other alluded to Trump's daughter's age:

> "Silver lining: Ivanka (born October 30 1981) is 22 days from being free of her Dad's attention" (VeryVicky2, 348 upvotes)

– a harsh reference to the candidate's lewd remarks concerning his own daughter.

The article, "What Is Up With Trump's Ill-Fitting Suits? A World-Famous London Bespoke Tailor Explains,"[107] (993 comments), written by Ellie Shechet on 11th of October offers a slightly different, sartorial take on the theme of negative attitudes towards the Republican candidate. The piece began with a list of Trump's derogatory comments on women's looks, and a photo of the candidate standing in a suit and tie during one of the presidential debates, with the questionable elements of his attire marked and described. Shechet then turned to discuss Trump's clothing, and interviewed an expert from Savile Row, London's street famous for men's tailors. The interviewee pointed out what could be changed to make Trump appear "smarter," including the fabric and

---

106   See: https://twitter.com/billpruitt/status/784872190587998209.
107   https://web.archive.org/web/20210801175311/https://jezebel.com/what-is-up-with-trumps-ill-fitting-suits-a-world-famou-1787666547.

cut of his suits. The commenters generally agreed with the expert opinion, and dove into further analysis of the candidate's fashion choices. For example,

> "My girlfriend and I were talking about this during the debate. Just like his homes, his suits look so, so, so cheaply made. He likely spends a ton of money on each suit, only to look like he's wearing a suit that belongs to someone else. Very happy for this breakdown" (Olivia Pope's Wine Glass, 555 upvotes).

Others were less kind. According to one commenter,

> "He looks dumpy and his ass looks like a burlap sack filled with snakes. Still, better than this ridiculous creep" (JujyMonkey: unstable genius,[108] 477 upvotes).

"This creep" referred to a photo of the Republican Ted Cruz wearing a trench coat over his suit, which the commenter added to the post.

> "Oh look! It's Vincent Adultman, heading off to a long day at the business factory!" (CharltonHestonsColdDeadHands's, 890 upvotes),

was another commenter's reply. The author referred to a different trench-dressed character, this time fictional. Vincent Adultman is three boys stacked on top of one another, featured in the adult animated black comedy Bojack Horseman. Carrying on with opinions on Trump's looks, Darklighter wrote in response to another comment:

> "Nah, it's not just that he's fat. I'm fat, and a $600 made-to-measure suit makes me look plenty sharp. Trump's just an idiot with no sense of aesthetics (among other, larger, glaring flaws)" (Darklighter, 617 upvotes).

The final argument, another reply to Darklighter's comment, expanded not just on Trump's appearance and fashion choices, but also on his taste for interior design:

---

108 The alias is another example of online tabloid commenters' exceptional foresight: Donald Trump called himself a "very stable genius" in a tweet posted on 6th of January 2018. See: https://twitter.com/realDonaldTrump/status/949619270631256064. It was a response to Michael Wolff's book, *Fire and fury: Inside the Trump White House* (2018), in which the author questioned whether Trump was mentally stable.

"'Trump's just an idiot with no sense of aesthetics.' Case in point, his condo décor" (FusiliJerry, 451 upvotes).

The comment was accompanied by a photo of a rococo-like room filled with gold and marble in the presidential candidate's penthouse in his own Trump Tower, located on New York's 5th Avenue. Trump was ridiculed, in line with Bourdieu's (1998) classic work on distinction, for his poor taste as a marker of his general lack of sophistication. However, while derisive, this interpretation was beneficial to Trump, since he campaigned by presenting himself as the anti-elite candidate, the very opposite of Hillary Clinton. The election showed that his strategy proved successful.

3.4.1.2   *Conversations between Commenters*
As in the other campaigns and outlets, here, too, *conversations between commenters* made up a frequent theme, highlighting the importance of interaction. One such example is "Producer Says There's Footage of Trump Saying the N-Word"[109] (813 comments). The article was written by Gabrielle Bluestone and appeared on 9th of October. In a follow-up to Bill Pruitt's tweet about "Trump tapes," mentioned earlier, another producer, Chris Nee also went on Twitter to accuse Trump of using the n-word. (The tweet has been since deleted but is quoted in the piece.) Bluestone reported that Associated Press had conducted anonymous interviews with the crew, editors, and contestants in the show, who confirmed Trump's "lewd and sexist" behavior.[110] In retaliation, The Apprentice executive producer and Trump supporter, Mark Burnett threatened them with a five million penalty fee for leaking footage. But to make things even more complicated, as a form of persuasion Nee addressed her tweet to Mark Cuban, the billionaire entrepreneur and Clinton supporter, who had starred as an investor in another business reality TV show produced by Burnett, Shark Tank. Sticking to the topic of finance, the conversation in the comments section began with a post written in the form of a plea to Mark Cuban to invest five million dollars in the penalty fee:

> "Please please Mark Cuban. I've never asked you for anything. This is all I want" ($7Coffee – aka Pat Toomey[111] is a Shit Weasel's, 1,234 upvotes).

---

109   https://web.archive.org/web/20210610205927/https://jezebel.com/producer-says-the res-video-of-trump-saying-the-n-word-1787592521.

110   See an archived version of the article: https://web.archive.org/web/20161004201418/http: //bigstory.ap.org/article/2778a6ab72ea49558445337865289508/ap-how-trumps-apprent ice-moved-capitalism-sexism.

111   Pat Toomey is a Republican politician who served as US Senator representing Pennsylvania from 2011 to 2023.

It was accompanied by a gif with two young men praying comically.[112] To this, a commenter replied,

> "If it is possible/real Mark Cuban will absolutely make this investment. I have never seen someone get so much glee out of the demise of Trump except maybe Hillary" (I'm Fart and I'm Smunny, 567 upvotes).

Another commenter added in the same vein,

> "Surely Mark Cuban can dig around his couch cushions and come up with the 5 million. For America" (Sneakys, 579 upvotes).

On a different note, however, the first commenter, $7Coffee... followed up with "Also" and an embedded tweet from Aasif Mandvi, an actor and comedian known, among others, for his performances in the late-night satirical news program, The Daily Show:

> "When #Trump insults #POC, #Muslims, #immigrants & #Disabled, #GOP don't care. But he insults "hot white women" & he's now #dispicable"[113] ($7Coffee – aka Pat Toomey is a Shit Weasel's, 772 upvotes).

It should be noted that this was not the only top comment pointing at the selective nature of public outrage. For instance, one commenter zoomed in on the overt racism of Trump and the unspoken racism of other fellow US citizens:

> "Here's what's frustrating about this: We already knew he was a racist. He's already dehumanized black americans, latino americans, muslim americans. (...) I'm tired of this trope amongst white america of wondering if maybe someone is secretly a racist? It's like we have to find out that they say either, 1) 'I hate black people' and/or 2) the n-word, before we are able to be like, 'Well, he's a racist, case closed'" (angriest-squirrel, 720 upvotes).

This last comment illustrates the notion of scandal that was discussed earlier in this chapter: one's behavior can be considered scandalous only if it causes widely shared moral outrage. Thus, if enough people agree with racist or sexist

---

112 The gif is a clip from Big Time Rush, a musical comedy television series about the adventures of a boy band, which was aired at the beginning of 2010s.
113 See: https://twitter.com/aasif/status/784865385170493440.

comments, no principled reaction will follow. Donald Trump's conduct is a telling example of this social behavior and exposes a shift in what people consider morally justifiable in politics, especially when it is presented in the ambiguous (not) kidding frame.

The conversational theme could also be found in another article written by Gabrielle Bluestone, "The New York Times Says Trump's Reputation Is Too Fucked Up to be Libeled"[114] (639 comments), published on 13th of October. According to the piece, after *The New York Times* published accounts of two women who claimed they had been sexually harassed by Donald Trump, his lawyers demanded the article be retracted since, they claimed, it targeted the presidential candidate's reputation. Contrary to their expectations *The New York Times* replied, "Nothing in our article has had the slightest effect on the reputation that Mr. Trump, through his own words and actions, has already created for himself."[115] The sentence inspired commenters:

"Holy crap. This was ice cold," wrote The Real Unsharer (333 upvotes);

but it was a comment made by The Ghost of James Madison's Rage Boner that sparked a number of top-voted replies. The Ghost... wrote,

"As I said on another post, this is the sort of burn media lawyers work their entire careers in hopes of being able to deliver. McCraw [*The New York Times* vice president and assistant general counsel] has probably already framed that letter and put it on his wall" (The Ghost of James Madison's Rage Boner, 1,044 upvotes).

weebleswobble responded in a similar tone:

"His Christmas card this year is literally just going to be a screen shot of that paragraph" (weebleswobble, 467 upvotes);

as did reachoutbitch:

---

[114] https://web.archive.org/web/20220125055307/https://jezebel.com/the-new-york-times-says-trumps-reputation-is-too-fucked-1787762318.

[115] For the full response of *The New York Times* to Trump's attorneys, see: McCraw 2016.

> "I can just hear all the attorneys in the firm yelling 'ooooooooooooo ooooooooooooooooooooooooooooooooooooooooooosnaaa aap!!' at this letter" (reachoutbitch, 336 upvotes).

A different commenter added a short, enthusiastic remark,

> "It was goddamn glorious, wasn't it?" (Hamlet goes against fascism, 329 upvotes),

and two gifs: one included John Stewart and Stephen Colbert, both satirical news program hosts, fake-sipping coffee on the street and saying "Wow!" emphatically; another showed Britney Spears clapping on the television music talent show, X Factor. In short, the top commenters were unanimously triumphant that Trump's reputation had been legally affirmed as poor.

"Nate Silver's Very Very Wrong Predictions About Donald Trump Are Terrifying"[116] (805 comments), written by Matt Novak and published on 4th of November, four days before the election, demonstrates the conversational theme, too. Basically, the article is a timeline of predictions concerning the chances of Trump's victory, which were made by the statistician, Nate Silver, mockingly titled by Novak as "Our National Oracle™." The forecasts, all quoted directly in the article, began in June 2015 with Trump predicted to have "a better chance of cameoing in another 'Home Alone' movie with Macaulay Culkin" – the Republican candidate had appeared in Home Alone 2 – "than winning the Republican nomination."[117] Yet on 4th of November the prognosis became quite different, with a "word salad," as the journalist put it mockingly, published by Silver in Politico: "The idea that she's [Hillary Clinton] a prohibitive, 95 percent-plus favorite is hard to square with polling that has frequently shown 5- or 6-point swings within the span of a couple weeks, given that she only leads by 3 points or so now."[118] The commenters, however, did not agree with Novak's argument. For example, one commenter questioned the assumed incomprehensibility of Silver's November analysis and criticized the journalist's bias towards the statistician:

> "This literally isn't at all difficult to understand and it's embarrassing to criticize him if you can't understand a pretty basic concept there. Further,

---

116   https://gizmodo.com/nate-silvers-very-very-wrong-predictions-about-donald-t-178 8583912.
117   See: Enten 2015.
118   See: Shepard 2016.

all your critiques on him are based on his not expecting Trump to win the nomination. (...) Also, no one expected that the media would whore itself out for Trump, and thus given him a huge advantage over the other candidates" (dayindayout112, 523 upvotes).

To this, Novak replied,

"If you can't definitively say what his prediction is right here right now, I'm not sure what use his model is for anyone" (Matt Novak, 60 upvotes).

Still, dayindayout112 countered with a link to the statistician's website, FiveThirtyEight:

"????????? (...) He's [Silver] currently giving Clinton a 65% chance to win and Trump 35%. (...) That's all available after literally one click on the 538 website" (dayindayout112, 405 upvotes).

avewavewvqwave was not convinced by Novak's line either:

"In his [Silver's] own words, they don't make predictions. They just analyze trendlines to tell you what the polls are saying. He has said repeatedly he's not in the business of making predictions" (avewavewvqwave, 74 upvotes).

The article author replied again, this time with a quote from Silver:

"August 11, 2015: 'Our emphatic prediction is simply that Trump will not win the nomination'" (Matt Novak, 74 upvotes).

Nonetheless, a subsequent reader's reply was similarly critical:

"The article you took that quote from ["Our empathic prediction."] has nothing to do with predicting anything. It's entirely about the problems with polls and how Trump was running his campaign. (...) It seems you failed to grasp the context of the article you linked to" (scribble, 85 upvotes).

When reading this article as a conversation between the Gawker writer and his readers, rather than a journalist's monologue with ignorable noise in the comments section, we can notice that the most upvoted comments did not focus on the likelihood of either candidate winning. Instead they discussed the limitations of statistical models, which had been glossed over by the article's author – a sophisticated critique as such. Secondly, this interaction serves as another example that on Gawker conversations which took place between the article authors and commenters could be remarkably factual, not just centered on friendly banter. Thirdly, this also illustrates how, as the discussion unfolded, commenters on Gawker could persuasively undermine the arguments of the journalist by providing credible sources to prove their own point. As part of this process, the substance of the article's topic was extended beyond the piece itself and spilled over into the comments, with the author and the commenters in open conversation similar to those held on online discussion forums, not gossip news websites. Such open exchanges – which at least temporarily flattened the hierarchy between the online tabloid writer with access to a brand-named space to write on and earn money, and the commenters writing underneath for free – were not seen on Pudelek or Mail Online; they were uniquely Gawker.

3.4.1.3   *Sex and Sexism*
Finally, a third recurring theme on Gawker involved *sex and sexism* – sometimes both at the same time. The most (in)famous example in the campaign was Trump's statement about grabbing beautiful women "by the pussy." Thus, on 7th of October the online tabloid published an article by Anna Merlan, titled "Donald Trump Bragged In 2005 That Being Famous Let Him Grope Women, 'Grab Them By the Pussy'"[119] (584 comments). The piece referred to an audio recording published by *The Washington Post*, in which the presidential candidate had been found bragging about his sexual conquests: "[W]hen you're a star they let you do it. They let you do anything ... Grab them by the pussy. You can do anything." The quote was taken from a conversation with Billy Bush, George W. Bush's cousin and, then, host in an entertainment television show, Access Hollywood. In the post, Merlan mentioned *The Washington Post*'s previous findings which included Trump's tax evasions, but for the most part she quoted extensive, and lascivious, excerpts from the audio recording. Also included in the article was Trump's tweet response, who called the conversation "locker room banter," and blamed the former President Bill Clinton for similar behavior, alluding to the 1998 sex scandal involving the White-House intern, Monica Lewinsky. Adding further context to the sexist language

---

119   https://web.archive.org/web/20210616171719/https://jezebel.com/donald-trump-bragged-in-2005-that-being-famous-let-him-1787545711.

used by the Republican candidate, the journalist referred to Trump's 2015 Fox News interview with Megyn Kelly which took place during the Republican Party primaries: "A good reminder that when Donald Trump yells about Megyn Kelly having blood coming out of her wherever, he's actually cleaning up his language." Briefly put, allusions to menstrual blood were a step up compared to sexual assault. It should be noted that the article had two updates, both posted at the bottom. The first was a short video from a CBS morning show in which Ivanka Trump defended her father as having a "respectful relationship with women;" the second briefly discussed a civil lawsuit filed against Trump in 1997 by a makeup artist, Jill Harth who accused him of having groped her at his home. However, the lawsuit was dropped. Not for the first time on Gawker, the most popular comment in response to the article turned out to be the most prophetic:

> "I heard a lady on NPR [National Public Radio] the other day who was pro-Trump because Hillary, 'spent the whole debate flirting with the camera.' I'm 100% certain she will buy this 'locker room talk' BS" (DarthPumpkin, 390 upvotes).

Another commenter echoed the sentiment:

> "Twenty bucks says this does more damage to Billy Bush than to Trump" (Darklighter, 367 upvotes).

perdue replied to DarthPumpkin, offering a reason for Trump's unwavering popularity and the impossibility of scandal to "stick" to the Republican candidate:

> "People like that NPR lady are so completely divorced from facts, reality, or anything Trump actually says or does at this point that I think his comment about being able to shoot someone in broad daylight with no consequences is true"[120] (perdue, 273 upvotes).

Nevertheless, adding the context of the second presidential debate, which was scheduled two days later, one commenter posted optimistically,

---

120   In January, at one of his campaign speeches Trump said, "I could stand in the middle of Fifth Avenue and shoot somebody, and I wouldn't lose any voters, OK? It's, like, incredible." See: Dwyer 2016.

"god bless the wapo [*The Washington Post*] sunday is going to be amazing" (code name v, 320 upvotes),

and added a gif with Tyra Banks, a model and producer, saying, "I can't wait to see how this turns out" on RuPaul's Drag Race television show. Finally, another top-upvoted comment went back to Trump's original "grab them by the pussy" quote, offering a general, matter-of-fact remark on human relationships:

"I can't really imagine that in even the most mutual, long term, consensual relationship being 'grabbed by the pussy' is a positive thing" (PootMcFruitcakesJr, 334 upvotes).

The sex and sexism theme was also manifest in an article published on 19th of October, titled "Condoleezza Rice's Response To Donald Trump Calling Her a 'Bitch' Is Just About Perfect"[121] (653 comments), written by Megan Reynolds. The piece opened with a backstory which took place ten years earlier: "In 2006 Donald Trump, a sentient pile of dirty sheets covered in poop, called former secretary of state Condoleezza Rice a 'bitch' in a speech" at an event of an education company in New York. The basis for this derogatory and chauvinist description of George W. Bush's Secretary of State was that Rice "never makes a deal," Trump clarified later. The speech resurfaced less than a month before the presidential election thanks to CNN.[122] Rice's reply to Trump was short: "Exactly. Can't wait until November 9!," Reynolds ended on a hopeful note. Trump's knowledge of diplomacy was the focus of two of the most popular comments. One commenter asked rhetorically,

"Is there anyone on earth who knows less about government and/or diplomacy than the orange goblin?" (justfornowtwo, 371 upvotes);

"The people planning to vote for him(?)" (hocuspocusoctopus says wash your damn hands, 609 upvotes),

another commenter responded in kind. Other top upvoted comments discussed Trump's sexism. For example, a commenter who presumably was not a fan of Condoleezza Rice, wrote nonetheless:

---

121 https://web.archive.org/web/20161020200949/https://jezebel.com/condoleezza-rices-response-to-donald-trump-calling-her-1787957410.
122 See: Kaczynski and Massie 2016.

"Wow ... I ... I like her very much right now. At this moment. Right now" (violentglitterorgy3, 347 upvotes);

while a different commenter posted angrily about the fundamental impossibility for women to be respected by Trump:

"She's a bitch for understanding diplomacy? She's a bitch for not casting spells over other governments and just compelling them to obey us? Trump's invented a new dichotomy no woman can ever live up to: bitch/witch. If you're not one, you're the other, or sometimes both" (SarsAttacks'll take the wine with the gravy, 307 upvotes).

However, the most popular comment offered a personal story, which concerned the normalization of sexual abuse. The commenter wrote,

"When I was about 22 ish (…) a 60ish man put his hand down my skirt and squeezed my ass at a charity function. My then boyfriend tried to make me tell someone, but all I wanted to do was leave. I'm going to continue to share this story, because I was scared and embarrassed and every time I fucking read about what Trump did to women I remember that fucking asshole who put his hand down my skirt and grabbed my ass. This is normalized, and that is a huge problem" (opheelia, 704 upvotes).

The conclusion in the last comment described the vicious social and political reality quite well: a society used to stories of sexual harassment and violence, including those committed by former presidents, would not be easily outraged by yet another example of such behavior.

The news host Megyn Kelly appeared once again in one of the most commented stories, and once again on the theme of sex. On 26th of October Megan Reynolds published the article, "Watch Newt Gingrich Lose His Shit When Megyn Kelly Calls Donald Trump a 'Sexual Predator'"[123] (872 comments). The author described a heated discussion between the news host and Trump's supporter, which was made available for the readers to see in a video embedded at the top of the article. When asked by Kelly about the presidential candidate's sexual allegations, Gingrich went "from zero to 100, pointing a finger at the camera and flapping his jowls," and accused Kelly of being "fascinated by sex."

---

123   https://web.archive.org/web/20161027162919/https://jezebel.com/watch-newt-gingrich-lose-his-shit-when-megyn-kelly-call-1788220309.

As Reynolds recounted, Kelly's response was: "You know what Mr. Speaker, I'm not fascinated by sex. But I am fascinated by the protection of women, and understanding what we're getting in the Oval Office." In their review of the post, one of the commenters opined Gingrich looked actually pleased with his performance:

> "Newt was proud of this! He tweeted about it! We live in an upside down world" (Masha's Bear, 377 upvotes).

To prove the point, the commenter pasted Gingrich's tweet with a link to the news segment.[124] Two other popular comments referred to Gingrich's response to Kelly, "I'm sick and tired of people like you using language that's inflammatory and not true." Sloth_stormborn wrote:

> "'I'm sick and tired of people like you.' Women. He means women" (Sloth_stormborn, 1,130 upvotes);

to which sui_generis responded,

> "'I'm sick and tired of [the majority of the population].'[125] Well, they're pretty sick and tired of you too, Newtie" (sui_generis, 397 upvotes).

Other top upvoted comments focused on the ambiguity of rooting for Kelly, who was working at Fox News at the time. For instance, Deadly wrote, receiving significant approval from other commenters:

> "Please let this election end already. It just feels so weird rooting for Megyn Kelly for something" (Deadly, 1,410 upvotes).

A different commenter remarked in a similar fashion:

> "Oh Megyn Kelly, how I simultaneously despise and cheer for you 'You can take your anger issues and spend some time working on them' I'm dead" (Witchy woo, 741 upvotes)

---

124 Link to Newt Gingrich's tweet: https://twitter.com/newtgingrich/status/791110323889516544. The link to the conversation pasted in the tweet is no longer working, but the video can be found here: https://youtu.be/j2bFYQZcAwU.
125 Square brackets were used in the comment.

– the quoted sentence was Kelly's final reply to Gingrich on the show. The Fox News exchange was extraordinary also because Kelly was working at a television news channel known for being famously pro-Republican and, later, pro-Trump. It was thus highly unexpected to see one of the channel's "faces" question the Republican candidate. However, sexual harassment proved a dealbreaker for Kelly; in 2017 she quit Fox News and moved to NBC.[126]

When we take a broad look at Gawker coverage of the US presidential election, we can easily notice that the attitudes were extremely critical of Trump. But while the articles emphasized his lack of morals, the commenters pointed out how little this mattered. On 8th of November it turned out that they had been right.

3.4.2 Mail Online
3.4.2.1 Negative Attitudes towards Hillary Clinton/Democrats

Mail Online was a very different story. Unlike its US counterpart, the sympathies of the British online tabloid, and the sympathies of its commenters in particular, were far closer to Donald Trump than to Hillary Clinton. What's more, while the Republican candidate's lecherous behavior was considered a flaw in private life, the Democrat was viewed as failing in her public performance. This is why *negative attitudes towards Hillary Clinton and/or the Democratic Party* were among the most popular themes in the UK online tabloid in the final two months leading to the November election. A prime example of this is "Donald's Great Escape: Trump keeps his campaign alive with barnstorming comeback after confronting Hillary with four Clinton 'sex victims' – and she FAILS to nail him over sleazy tape scandal"[127] (7,219 comments), written by David Martosko, Geoff Earle and Liam Quinn. It was published on 10th of October, a day after the second presidential debate. The piece had a grand opening, enthusiastic about the Republican Party candidate: "The debate night that will be discussed for generations in Political Science classes – and Women's Studies seminars – ended with Republican Donald Trump landing more punches than Democrat Hillary Clinton, and successfully deflecting attention successfully [sic] away from a two-day-old crisis about graphic sexual language ["grab them by the pussy"] that threatened to derail his White House bid." The reporting continued with a twist: "In the first debate (...) Clinton sat back and let Trump hang himself. But on Sunday her quiet patience gave him room to roam and

---

126 Kelly's contract was terminated by NBC in 2019; she currently hosts a show on Sirius XM radio station.
127 https://www.dailymail.co.uk/news/article-3830041/Second-debate-Hillary-Clinton-Donald-Trump-gets-underway.html.

dominate." The article offered a detailed description of the debate, accompanied by dozens of photos of the candidates and their families interspersed throughout the text. The journalists also reported that the two candidates did not shake hands upon entering the stage. Moreover, Rudy Giuliani, the former New York mayor, and a strong supporter of Trump, remarked – correctly, as it turned out later – that the debate would "switch the momentum" in favor of the Republican candidate. On the one hand, the writers described Clinton as "a superior bureaucrat" with "mature knowledge of foreign policy minutiae," standing against Trump who, on the other hand, was gaining momentum "in what has become the Year of the Outsider." Other issues mentioned by the journalists included Trump wanting to see Clinton in jail for using a private server in her official emails, next to his description of Clinton as ineffective in her role as Secretary of State, because President Obama's "red line" drawn for Syria's President, Bashar al-Asad in case he used chemical weapons against his own citizens, turned out to be empty talk. In stark contrast, Clinton's opinions about Trump were barely noted. It should be emphasized that overall Trump received significantly more attention from the journalists than his competitor, and this disproportion could also be observed in the article's bright-blue subheadings, which divided the piece into several parts, offering the gist of the debate "plot." And so, under the first such subheading, "DONALD TRUMP'S FIERY OPENING ON BILL CLINTON'S PAST" Trump was said to deflect accusations about sexually abusing women; instead he invited three women who claimed they had been raped by Bill Clinton, to sit in the front row in the debate hall. A picture of Trump's wife, Melania was also added in the bright-blue section; she was wearing a bright-pink pussy blouse, which was widely interpreted as an allusion to the recording of her husband's lewd comments. Another subheading ran "DONALD GETS DEFENSIVE OVER HOT MIC CONTROVERSY" and, further down in the article, the first subheading for Clinton, "HILLARY GOES ON THE ATTACK," accusing Trump of targeting women, "immigrants, African-Americans, Latinos, people with disabilities, POWs, Muslims, and many others." In response, under the subheading "TRUMP'S TIRADE ON 'HATEFUL' HILLARY," the Republican candidate attacked Clinton for using divisive language after she had called half of Trump's voters as belonging in "baskets of deplorables." Under the next subheading, "TRUMP TALKS TOUGH ON HILLARY'S EMAILS," he accused Clinton of lying; while under "THE DONALD, OUTNUMBERED?" the Republican candidate complained that he was being targeted both by his competitor and by the debate hosts. "SUNDAY'S SCANDALOUS BUILD UP AND THE GOP'S TROUBLED WEEKEND" was the final bright-blue subheading in the article, and referred to the infamous recording of Trump with Billy Bush that had been revealed by *The Washington*

Post. According to Mail Online, after its release Trump's campaign "found itself sucker-punched." Despite this, the article ended on a happy note for Trump, with the candidate's tweet thanking his supporters, save for "some Republican 'leadership' (...) self-righteous hypocrites." In line with this, the top comments emphasized Trump's victory in the debate. For example:

> "Trump won the debate. It's clear as day" (Stamford Bridge Guy, London, UK, 8,967 upvotes);

> "That was a total destruction by Trump. It was fantastic!" (LibsRTards, Texas, US, 5,364 upvotes);

and

> "Trump rocked it" (Dan Purcell, Somewhere, US, 6,849 upvotes).

Some, however, pointed at Clinton, albeit without much sympathy for the Democratic candidate. One popular comment recounted the ways she had been interrupted by her competitor:

> "Trump came out swimming tonight. 'It's a good thing Trump isn't in charge of the law in this country.' – Hillary Clinton 'Yeah, because you'd be in jail.' The first best line of the debate tonight. Great Job Hillary ..Bam! Tonight I saw the Trump I wanted to see on stage." (Jayla, brooklyn, US, 6,148 upvotes).

A different comment made innuendos into Clinton's past,

> "The libs forget that Hillary has a past too and it goes all the way back to the 70's!" (Francisco_dAnconia, Galts Gulch, US, 4,744 upvotes).

This was likely an allusion to a conspiracy theory, according to which a law firm which the Democratic candidate had worked for at the time helped transfer money to the Nicaraguan Contras, thus playing a part in the Iran-Contra scandal.[128]

Another vivid example of the theme is "Hillary's nightmare: Feds get a warrant to start search for classified info in 650,000 emails – thousands of them

---

128 For a list of conspiracy theories connected to Hillary Clinton, see: Murphy 2014.

from her private server – on sexting Weiner's laptop. Clinton faces ongoing FBI probe even if she's elected President"[129] (3,448 comments), written by Wills Robinson and published on 30th of October. The piece focused on FBI's warrant to analyze emails from Clinton's aide, Huma Abedin and from Clinton herself, for which she had illegally used a private server while in office as Secretary of State. The emails were found on a laptop owned by Anthony Weiner, a former Congressman and Abedin's husband, whom Mail Online had exposed sexting a 15-year old girl a month earlier. (Weiner was later sentenced to jail and registered as a sex offender.) The warrant to search Clinton's emails was given after the FBI director James Comey decided to reopen Clinton's private server probe, even though it had been already investigated and closed by the FBI in July. Robinson duly noted that Clinton was only one percentage point ahead of Trump, which was an 11-point drop within a week; he also pointed out that Abedin had not joined Clinton at her most recent rallies. The article reported Trump's enthusiastic reaction to these developments, too: "Huma! They just found a lot of them! We never thought we were going to say 'Thank you' to Anthony Weiner!" In addition, Trump blamed Clinton for poor judgment, which he did by quoting her own campaign chairman, John Podesta. His critical remark on the Democratic candidate's "bad instincts," was leaked by WikiLeaks in October 2016 along hundreds of other emails – a result of hacking carried out by Russian military intelligence.[130] Abedin, the article recounted, claimed that she had "no idea how the emails ended up on her husband's computer," since "she rarely used it." At the same time, FBI personnel were said to have been pleased about the reopening of the probe, given that Clinton barely got "a slap on the wrist" for using a private server for official matters, which constituted a major security breach. The lengthy piece provided details on Abedin's cooperation with the FBI, Clinton's meetings with her supporters, and Trump's excitement about reopening the probe. As always, the article included numerous photos, this time paparazzi shots of Abedin on a street in New York, a selfie of half-naked Weiner, as well as official photos of Clinton and Trump campaigning. A couple of bright-blue boxes described backstories for the piece: "ANTHONY WEINER SEXTING SCANDAL" with quotes of the lecherous messages sent by Weiner to the teenage girl; "THE CLINTON EMAIL CONTROVERSY," which began in 2009 after the domain name clintonemail.

---

129 https://www.dailymail.co.uk/news/article-3887790/Hillary-s-nightmare-scenario-Weiner-s-laptop-holds-650-000-emails-thousands-Clinton-s-private-server-search-WEEKS-Democrat-faces-ongoing-FBI-probe-s-elected.html.

130 A detailed investigation of Russian hacking of the Democratic National Committee was conducted by Associated Press; see: Satter et al. 2017.

com was created; and "THE TALE OF HILLARY CLINTON'S PRIVATE SERVER," which started even earlier, in 2008 with the installation of an Apple server in the Clintons' home basement. Predictably for Mail Online commenters, the top responses shared Trump's view of Clinton and her husband. Despite the fact that the online tabloid is British, most of the comments were marked as coming from the US; but one was also from the UK:

> "It's almost poetic that Hillary's campaign is being destroyed by a Weiner that isn't Bill's. Lets hope all the skeletons fall out of the Clinton closet. DRAIN THE SWAMP" (Spacer88, Northampton, 3,484 upvotes).

Other commenters maintained a similar tone:

> "Hillary's going down faster than Bill's pants" (Deplorable Dagny T, Transcontinental Railroad, US, 2,780 upvotes);

> "She is truly an embarrassment to the Republic on which we stand!" (Bamabell, Atlanta, US, 2,134 upvotes).

Another commenter deliberated on the newly-found emails:

> "Where is everyone saying there weren't any emails just used it for printing documents and it was all lies. 650k emails and she doesn't remember using the laptop!? LMAO this is fantastic" (baabaabaa, somewhere, US, 1,805 upvotes).

Finally, a popular Trump chant emerged in the top comments as well:

> "LOCK HER UP" (Trump4POTUS, Texas, US, 1,480 upvotes).

"Deplorables 2: Hillary shouts herself hoarse in tirade at Trump supporters calling them 'negative, dark and divisive with a dangerous vision' after a heckler shouts 'Bill is a rapist' at rally"[131] (3,679 comments), written by Geoff Earle and published on 2nd of November, six days before election day, offers another vivid example of negative opinions concerning Hillary Clinton. The piece examined Clinton's rally, her third that day in Florida, during

---

131 https://www.dailymail.co.uk/news/article-3896014/Hillary-unloads-Trump-s-conspiracy-theories-goes-vision-behavior-supporters-effort-goat.html.

which a protester shouted, "Bill Clinton is a rapist" and waved a neon green sign with the same words painted on it. In reaction to this, the journalists reported, "Clinton raised her voice and pointed a finger at the protester as she exclaimed: 'I am sick and tired of the negative, dark, divisive, dangerous vision and the anger of people who support Donald Trump.' (...) Her voice became hoarse as she delivered the address." The title of the piece, however, referred not to the Florida rally but to her comment from September on Trump supporters belonging in a "basket of deplorables." Although this set the tone for the article, "deplorables" were not mentioned anywhere in the text. As will be discussed in more detail in Chapter 3, a possible reason for this inconsistency is that at Mail Online, the editors, and not the article authors, choose headlines and photos, all of which have a considerable influence on the tone of the reporting. As for the article itself, further down Earle noted that during the rally Clinton was introduced by the "civil rights legend" John Lewis; then the journalist went on to describe her "withering attacks" on Trump concerning his "conspiracy theories" (the quotation marks were used in the article), sexual assaults and tax evasions. Regarding the latter, the piece ended with an explanation of the mechanism Trump had used to avoid paying taxes in the 1990s, a "maneuver so questionable, his lawyers warned him the IRS [Internal Revenue Service] might come after him should he be audited." Despite this, the commenters were skeptical of Clinton's campaign. One of the top comments stated plainly,

> "I hope America votes Trump" (John A C, Birmingham, UK, 4,702 upvotes).

Another commenter, claiming to be in Japan, criticized Clinton's performance:

> "The pointing. The screeching. That cackle at the most random, inappropriate times. Who wants to vote for 8 years of THAT?" (Light Yagami, Tokyo, Japan, 3,204 upvotes).

Others paid attention to Clinton's supporters, whom they openly despised:

> "She's sick and tired of the behavior of Trump supporters? She needs to look at how her supporters behave. She needs to own up to the baiting of Trump supporters by Democratic paid goons" (nowhere but here, here and there, 2,779 upvotes);

and

"I suppose she is trying to suggest to her mentally challenged supporters that she is being investigated by the FBI over 'conspiracy theories?' She becomes more unhinged each day" (smookie, Los Angeles, US, 3,364 upvotes).

One top comment, however, offered an analytical stance:

"As an observer from across the pond I never thought I would say this, provided Mr Trump keeps hammering home his policies and sells a brighter future for ALL Americans, then he could pull this off. Clinton is leaving the door wide open by attacking him all the time and if Mr Trump keeps to the script of policies then he looks more Presidential" (Marion1947, Gosport, UK, 2,300 upvotes).

This prediction eventually turned out to be correct.

3.4.2.2   *Negative Attitudes towards Donald Trump/Republicans*
Even though in Mail Online Hillary Clinton received more negative opinions than Donald Trump did, *negative views of the Republican Party candidate* were also a recurring theme in the online daily. A fitting example of this was published on 27th of September, after the first presidential debate. Typically for Mail Online, the article, written by David Martosko, Geoff Earle and Khaleda Rahman, bore a lengthy title; this time it was "Clinton brands Trump a racist AND a sexist: Donald complains about 'nasty' comments after Hillary torments him over backing for 'birther' question, discrimination and treatment of women"[132] (6,093 comments). "Clinton called Donald Trump a racist and a sexist – to his face," the journalists wrote, stressing that the accusation was similar to the charge made by Megyn Kelly over a year earlier during the Republican Party primaries. Trump answered with a "jab" at Rosie O'Donnell, a popular comedian to whom Trump had "said very tough things." He also added, "I think everybody would agree that she deserves it, and nobody feels sorry for her." Similarly to previously mentioned presidential-debate coverage, the subsequent paragraphs in this article, too, had subheadings, which highlighted the topics of discussion. The first one, "RACE: FROM HEALING AMERICA'S WOUNDS TO BOTH SIDES' 'BIRTHER' SMEARS," concerned Trump's false claims that President Barack Obama had been born outside the United States

---

132   https://www.dailymail.co.uk/news/article-3808968/Grinning-Hillary-Clinton-opens-hostilities-presidential-debate.html.

and was therefore illegally elected. According to Mail Online, in response "Trump delivered one of his most disjointed answers of the night." Clinton argued that he pushed the lie because his supporters wanted to believe it. (A bright-blue box was inserted in the middle of the paragraph, bearing the title "THE STANDOUT QUOTES FROM THE FIRST PRESIDENTIAL DEBATE.") The next subheading emphasized the Republican candidate's chauvinism: "SEXISM: FROM CLAIMING PREGNANCY IS 'INCONVENIENT' TO CALLING A WOMAN 'MISS PIGGY.'" Clinton accused Trump, among other things, of calling a beauty-contest participant "Miss Piggy" and "Miss Housekeeping," "because she was a Latina." Instead of a reply, Trump changed the subject: "I saw the polls come in today, and with all of that money, over $200 million is spent, and I'm either winning or tied. And I've spent practically nothing." Another subheading ran "HACKING: CLINTON SAYS RUSSIA HACKED THE DNC [Democratic National Committee]... BUT TRUMP CLAIMS IT COULD'VE BEEN A 400-POUND LONER." In the first sentence the reporters alarmed that the debate "devolved into a contentious slugfest" with Trump repeatedly cutting Clinton off. He derided (as it later turned out, wrongly) the idea of Russian hacking of the DNC, which revealed that the Party's National Committee had tried to undermine Bernie Sanders's campaign in favor of Clinton in the Democratic primaries. Instead, Trump mockingly speculated about the hacker conducting the cyber attack while sitting on a bed. "TAXES: CLINTON GOES AFTER 'TRUMP UP, TRICK DOWN' ECONOMICS ... AND MENTIONS LOAN FROM HIS FATHER" was the next subheading. The journalists reported Clinton "landed the first attacks of the night" when Trump claimed that she would sign "one of the biggest tax increases in history." By contrast, he promised to reduce taxes for companies which, according to the Republican candidate, would be "a job creator like we haven't seen since Ronald Reagan." The final subheading in the piece posed a fundamental question, "BUT WILL THEY ACCEPT THE RESULT? CLINTON SAYS YES ... AND TRUMP EVENTUALLY CONCEDES HE WILL 'ABSOLUTELY SUPPORT HER.'" The writers informed about the health of the candidates, too: Clinton "avoided making headlines with physical maladies" after having collapsed two weeks earlier; Trump, however, not only "had the sniffles" but "people in the auditorium could hear it." Finally, the article ended with information about guests invited to the presidential debate hall, including families, advisors, as well as people intended to shed a bad light on the opponents. Trump invited Mark Geist, a survivor of the 2012 terrorist attack on the US embassy in Benghazi. Clinton, then Secretary of State, was accused of initially misleading the public by claiming that the violence had not been planned but, instead, had been an escalation of anti-American protests sparked by an anti-Muslim online video.[133] Clinton, on the other hand, invited the billionaire entrepreneur Mark Cuban, as well as a domestic violence survivor with cerebral palsy, who condemned Trump for insulting a disabled journalist in 2015. Among the dozens of photos and several videos from the debate, Mail Online also included two screenshots of Snapchat videos with Trump and his family which were uploaded to the candidate's account right before the debate, and a couple of photos of protesters standing outside, who held signs calling for more socially and environmentally progressive politics, while criticizing the two political parties (e.g. "corporate parties"), and Trump (e.g. "Trump is a p***y"). In line with the overall tone of the article, most of the top comments were if not sympathetic towards Clinton, then explicitly critical of Trump. For example:

"Trump just failed Bigly!" (assatis7, Worcester, UK, 1,0391 upvotes);

"Trump makes any intelligent person's brain bleed" (PrincessElenaSophia, Southern California, US, 5,732 upvotes);

and

"Wow. Just wow. Trump is a delusional, pathological liar. Tonight's debate was confirmation of that fact" (Sam777, USA, 7,096 upvotes).

Aside from the criticisms targeted at the Republican candidate, one of the most upvoted comments cheered Clinton:

"HAHAHA CIinton NAILED HIM ... what an embarrassment for Trump" (Wordsworthbloke, An American in London, UK, 6,571 upvotes);

but another was pessimistic about the American political scene as such:

"The US is so polarised I don't think this is going to make much of a difference, people who hate hillary will continue to, the same for trump" (Fat-Tony, Newport, 5,438 upvotes).

"Giuliani and Christie call Trump a 'genius' for avoiding paying taxes for almost two DECADES – while campaign says tax returns published in the New York

---

133 For a detailed analysis of the events see e.g.: Kiely 2012.

Times were 'illegally obtained'"[134] (3,899 comments) offered a different take on the negative attitudes concerning Trump. Written by Liam Quinn together with Nikki Schwab, and published on 2nd of October, the article referred to a piece in *The New York Times*,[135] according to which in 1995 Trump had declared a loss of 916 million dollars; this allowed him to avoid paying taxes for 18 years. Rudy Giuliani responded to these findings on CNN, saying, "The man is a genius, he knows how to operate the tax code for the benefit of the people he's serving." Furthermore, he compared Trump to Apple's Steve Jobs and to the wartime British Prime Minister Winston Churchill, both of whom had been "thrown out of office (...) and came all the way back." Another Trump supporter, the New Jersey governor Chris Christie argued that this case only showed "what an absolute mess the federal tax code is, and that's why Donald Trump is the person best positioned to fix it." According to the online tabloid, *The New York Times* received hardcopies of the documents allegedly sent from Trump Tower. Bright-blue boxes followed. The first, "WHAT THE NEW YORK TIMES FOUND" explained how in the mid-1990s the financial troubles of Trump's casinos allowed him to post a huge financial loss in his tax file. The authenticity of the documents was confirmed by the Republican candidate's accountant at the time. Another box presented "TRUMP CAMPAIGN'S FULL STATEMENT" with a daring opening, "The only news here is that the more than 20-year-old alleged tax document was illegally obtained, a further demonstration that *The New York Times*, like establishment media in general, is an extension of the Clinton Campaign, the Democratic Party and their global special interest." However, the next sentence in the short statement put Clinton in the limelight: "What is happening now with the FBI and DOJ [Department of Justice] on Hillary Clinton's emails and illegal server, including her many lies and her leis [sic] to Congress are worse than what took place in the administration of Richard Nixon – and far more illegal." The statement assured that "Mr Trump knows the tax code far better than anyone who has ever run for President and he is the only one that knows how to fix it." Clinton's campaign released a statement as well, which was mentioned not in a separate bright-blue box but in the body of the article: "In one year, Donald Trump lost nearly a billion dollar [sic]. (...) He stiffed small businesses, laid off workers, and walked away from hard working communities. And how did it work out for him? He apparently got to avoid paying taxes for nearly two decades – while tens of millions of

---

134 https://www.dailymail.co.uk/news/article-3817902/Donald-Trump-avoided-paying-taxes-two-decades-declared-loss-1-BILLION-1995.html.
135 See: Barstow et al. 2016.

working families paid theirs. He calls that 'smart.'" This last sentence referred to Trump's remark during the first presidential debate that not paying taxes made him smart. Interestingly, though the article reported on taxes, only in the middle of the lengthy piece did the authors mention Trump's breaking with "campaign tradition" by refusing to release his tax returns. In contrast to Trump, the Clintons had been making their tax record public since the late 1970s, when Bill Clinton was elected the Governor of Arkansas, the journalists emphasized. The next bright-blue box stated, "TRUMP HASN'T PAID TAXES BEFORE" and went into detail about his reports of losses in the late 1970s, 1984, and 1995. What's more, Quinn and Schwab reported that in 1984 New York City challenged Trump's claims and after a legal battle he was forced to pay taxes on over 1 million dollars of income. The article ended with numerous tweets written by Trump, revealing his hypocrisy concerning taxes, for example by accusing Barack Obama and Amazon of not paying enough. In line with this, the most upvoted comments on the article were unanimously negative towards Trump:

> "He was bragging about it during the debate saying it made him 'smart'. Vile squirrel head" (vinblancman, London, UK, 1,749 upvotes).

One top comment even suggested the candidate's possible ties to Russia:

> "If it is legal and he is proud of being 'smart' Trump could show his tax returns to the people. But he refuses. He's a con man, conning the people. He's probably hiding how much he owes Putin and the Russian maf ia. Anyone voting for Trump is a sucker. He's a fasc ist" (jlist, Brighton, UK, 2,281 upvotes).

Condescending critics of the Republican candidate's sympathizers were present as well:

> "Trump supporters are the lowest of society. The dirt and filth of humanity" (Clémence Pellétier, Montreal, Canada, 2,040 upvotes).

Other commenters challenged the idea that Trump was indeed "smart." For example,

> "he's a genius for losing almost a billion dollars and now it's come to light that he doesn't pay taxes. I'm sorry but it's a prime example of how the rich get cut backs while the middle class and poor get taken advantage

of. If I pay taxes Trump should also. He's the problem with AMERICA"
(Paradise777, Florida, US, 1,991 upvotes).

Finally, making a long story on hiding tax records short,

"He won't show it because he doesn't want anyone to see that he is broke"
(jollyone, Wailea Maui, 1,718 upvotes).

If Trump did not have the wealth he claimed to own, the argument about his business acumen making him a better fit for the presidential seat would collapse. Trump managed to hide his tax record until 2020, and when *The New York Times* finally obtained it, journalists discovered that there were good reasons for keeping it secret: Trump had been making "chronic losses" for decades.[136]

A still different example of the theme of negative attitudes towards Trump could be found in a piece published on 8th of October, titled "Trump is CHEERED outside Trump Tower: Defiant Donald greets supporters in New York after Melania condemns him and senior GOP figures withdraw their support for his crude hot-mic comments"[137] (6,867 comments), written by Liam Quinn and Kalhan Rosenblatt. There, the authors reported on Trump's activities in the aftermath of the release of Access Hollywood tapes. Despite widespread outrage, which included some members of his own party asking him to drop out of the race, the Republican candidate was "cheered by dozens of fans in an extraordinary scene outside Trump Tower in New York." What's more, this happened "just hours after Melania called her husband's lewd remarks about women from a 2005 video 'unacceptable and offensive.'" The journalists noted that Trump made his lascivious remarks just several months after having married Melania, and that the candidate's children were suddenly silent, even though they had been otherwise very active in Trump's campaign. Still, in an interview in *The Wall Street Journal*[138] quoted by Mail Online, Trump assured he would not quit because, as he put it, the support he was receiving was "unbelievable," and "because Hillary Clinton is a horribly flawed candidate." Two bright-blue boxes followed, both with lists: "WHO ARE THE REPUBLICANS THAT HAVE WITHDRAWN THEIR SUPPORT FOR DONALD TRUMP OR CALLED ON HIM TO DROP OUT?" comprising forty names, and "WHICH

---

136 See: Buettner et al. 2020.
137 https://www.dailymail.co.uk/news/article-3828525/Certainly-interesting-24-hours-Trump-attempts-cast-aside-lewd-hot-mic-fiasco-JOKE-senior-Republicans-call-drop-race.html.
138 See: Langley 2016.

REPUBLICANS HAVE DENOUNCED DONALD TRUMP OR CONDEMNED HIS COMMENTS?" with thirty-two names. Quinn and Rosenblatt emphasized that "dozens of Republicans also condemned the Donald's remarks," including senator John McCain – who had not been fond of Trump in the first place – as well as Trump's own running mate Mike Pence. In a tweet, Joe Biden, then Vice President, likened Trump's actions to "sexual assault."[139] The article was packed with screengrabs of other disparaging tweets from members of the Republican party, snapshots from the Access Hollywood recording, and photos of the Republican candidate, including some showing Trump being given the finger by crowds in front of Trump Tower. The piece ended with quotes from the recording, which had sparked the "potentially election-losing scandal." In keeping with the tone of the article, the most popular comments were not sympathetic to the Republican party candidate either. One was short:

"Creep" (the philosopher, staffordshire, UK, 2,468 upvotes).

Another was more loquacious:

"If you haven't learnt how to talk at, FIFTY NINE years old – you haven't learnt how to talk at, 70 years old. A grown man talking like a hormone-ridden teen. The man is immaturity, through and through. A vile t h u g with money – pappi's money" (LawdHelpUsAll, Massachusets, US, 3,336 upvotes).

However, a different top upvoted comment reflected on Trump's wife and daughter:

"Poor Ivanka and Melania living with this all their life's Melania is at lest committed to his money and puts up with him but poor Ivanka lol" (Free the world oo, Igloo, Antarctica, 2,579 upvotes);

while another popular comment offered an analysis of Trump's gloomy prospects:

"Trump (...) is the worst debater I have ever witnessed, and the next debate is Sunday. Then this 'Friday afternoon news dump' of Trump ... for the umpteenth time ... disparaging women in a vile way ... (...) No

---

139 See: https://twitter.com/JoeBiden/status/784851147513270272.

debate monitor is going to lose credibility by not addressing it, Hillary will hammer him with it all night, and he will be in the position from which he absolutely has NEVER had a decent recovery, the defensive. (…) They've been smearing Hillary for 20 years and she's a smart woman. Did you think she learned nothing? She just schooled them on how it's done. ZERO chance he recovers" (du Vallon, Midwest, US, 3,840 upvotes).

Finally, one commenter appealed to Trump mockingly,

"PLEASE don't drop out, Donald. We need to see you lose by EPIC proportions on election day" (Stella, Dallas, US, 3,816 upvotes).

Contrary to these predictions, the second debate was far less damaging for the Republican candidate than the commenters had anticipated.

3.4.2.3 Sex and sexism

Similarly to Gawker, another top theme in Mail Online was *sex and sexism*. The Access Hollywood "grab them by the pussy" scandal was one that caught the most attention, but there were other instances of the theme as well. For example, the issue of abortion could be noticed in a piece which covered the third and final presidential debate, held in Las Vegas. Titled "Trump's bombshell: He rocks final debate with Clinton by REFUSING to promise to accept the results after bad-tempered 90 minutes begins AND ends without a handshake"[140] (8,155 comments), the lengthy article, interspersed with dozens of photos of the candidates, their families, and guests invited to the debate, was written by David Martosko, Francesca Chambers, Geoff Earle, Nikki Schwab and Hannah Parry, and published on 20th of October. Aside from the highlights mentioned in the headline, the journalists recounted the presidential debate in detail, including an interesting exchange which may have tilted voter sympathies in favor of Trump: "[The Republican candidate] said 'millions' of people are on voter rolls 'who shouldn't be registered.' News reports and independent investigations have found deceased Americans with active registrations, along with illegal immigrants who use driver's licenses to obtain ballots. 'That's horrifying,' Clinton responded, aghast at the idea of a presidential candidate questioning an election's validity." But Clinton's reply was not made in reference to Trump's accusations of enabling illegal voting. Instead,

---

140 https://www.dailymail.co.uk/news/article-3853760/The-big-freeze-big-fight-Trump-Clinton-s-final-debate-kicks-NO-handshake-Donald-brings-Hillary-s-accusers-Las-Vegas-shame-her.html.

it was response to his claim, "I'll keep you in suspense, okay?" after Trump had been asked by the moderator, Chris Wallace from Fox News if he would accept the election results if he lost.[141] While this misinterpretation is noteworthy, the journalists did mention Clinton's observation that Trump had accused the outcomes of his own Republican Party's Iowa Caucuses of being "rigged" when they did not suit him. Moreover, they reported Clinton's statement made after the debate that no one had contested election results in the United States since the country's foundation, until Trump threatened to do so. (And in fact did, in January 2021.) Subheadings were added further down in the article, as in the previous accounts of the presidential debates. The first was "FIREWORKS AND TENSION IN VEGAS ARENA," under which the journalists declared Trump the clear winner of the debate. While admitting that Clinton was still leading in the polls by about five percentage points, they – correctly – emphasized the potential of "invisible" voters not included in the surveys. "The Drudge Report, an influential right-leaning news website, put the margin at 81–19 in favor of Trump. But another conservative outlet, Breitbart News, surprisingly scored it 62–38 in Clinton's favor," the authors added. Immigration was the first heated topic of the debate, yet according to Mail Online, the "tensest moment" concerned Trump's "manhandling" of nine women. "Those stories have been largely debunked," Trump rebutted. "I didn't even apologize to my wife, who is sitting right here, because I didn't do anything!," he stated. Still, "CLASHES ON VIOLENCE AND WOMEN" was the next subheading. Trump was reported to have accused the Clinton campaign of planning to commit election fraud and inciting violence at his rallies. Clinton's reply did not refer to this, instead she focused on Trump's attitude towards women: "Donald thinks belittling women makes him bigger. He goes after their dignity, their self-worth." Trump responded, "Nobody has more respect for women than I do," and accused his competitor of running a "very sleazy campaign." The following subheading featured the "'CRIMINAL ENTERPRISE' ATTACK ON CLINTON FOUNDATION." Trump claimed the Clinton Foundation had adopted a pay-for-play scheme, in which it accepted "contributions from nations that expected preferential treatment" from Hillary Clinton, including "regimes that abuse gays and women," the journalists stressed. Trump then switched the topic to abortion and accused the Democratic candidate of favoring "near-infanticide." According to Trump, "late-term partial-birth abortions" were equal to "ripping babies from mothers'

---

141 For the full debate transcript, see: https://www.debates.org/voter-education/debate-tran scripts/october-19-2016-debate-transcript/.

wombs." Remarkably, Clinton's reply was not mentioned.[142] Citing Trump, "'BAD HOMBRES HERE'" was the following subheading. There, again, Trump attacked Clinton, this time for having failed in building a wall on the US-Mexican border, and simultaneously declaring she wanted to keep "open trade and open borders." The latter was a quote from Clinton mentioned by the moderator. "SUPREME COURT SHOWDOWN" followed; in that section Trump declared that Roe v. Wade, the basis of countrywide abortion rights in the United States would be overturned during his presidency. (He managed to fulfill this promise after appointing conservative Supreme Court judges, although Roe v. Wade was overturned in 2022, when Trump was no longer in office.) To boot, he warned that gun rights would be "gutted" under Clinton's presidency. In the next subsection, "WIKILEAKS LEADS TO 'PUPPET' CLAIMS" the journalists expanded on Trump's refusal to criticize the Russian President Vladimir Putin, and quoted an exchange between the two candidates: "'Putin, from everything I see, has no respect for this person,' Trump said, gesturing to Clinton. 'Well, that's because he'd rather have a puppet as president of the United States,' Clinton countered. 'You're the puppet!' Trump counter-punched." When asked directly, Trump condemned Russian hacking of the DNC that led to WikiLeaks revealing John Podesta's emails, but doubted whether the attack had in fact been committed by Russia. Interestingly, the reporters emphasized that while Trump "leaned on" the country's supreme law, Clinton mentioned the US Constitution only once. This could have been read as a criticism of Clinton's alleged disregard for the founding document. Next, "RUDY: ASK FOR A RECOUNT LIKE GORE DID" was the title of the second-to-last subsection, and presented comments from campaign members after the end of the debate. These included "That's what happens in third world countries," which was Podesta's review of Trump's threats he would reject the election result if he did not win. Giuliani, however, used the example of the 2000 Democratic presidential candidate, Al Gore, to argue the opposite: "If it's a close election and there are indications of fraud, he

---

142   Clinton's response was: "Well, that is not what happens in these cases. And using that kind of scare rhetoric is just terribly unfortunate. You should meet with some of the women that I have met with, women I have known over the course of my life. This is one of the worst possible choices that any woman and her family has to make. And I do not believe the government should be making it. You know, I've had the great honor of traveling across the world on behalf of our country. I've been to countries where governments either forced women to have abortions, like they used to do in China, or forced women to bear children, like they used to do in Romania. And I can tell you: The government has no business in the decisions that women make with their families in accordance with their faith, with medical advice. And I will stand up for that right." See: https://www.debates.org/voter-education/debate-transcripts/october-19-2016-debate-transcript/.

will do what Al Gore did, he'll challenge it." Still, both Giuliani and the journalists omitted the fact that the recount in Florida was stopped by the Supreme Court, and the ruling allowed the Republican candidate, George W. Bush to claim election victory. Finally, the last subsection title exclaimed, "MODERATOR WALLACE CALLS FOR CALM." Unrelated to the heading, a list with different guests invited to the debate by the candidates followed, including, on Trump's side, Barack Obama's half-brother and a news reporter who claimed Bill Clinton had sexually assaulted her; on Clinton's side one could find the billionaire entrepreneur Mark Cuban, Hewlett-Packard CEO Meg Whitman, next to "two illegal immigrant teens, two labor union leaders and a vice president of the Navajo Nation," the authors reported. At the very end of the article, the journalists concluded that Clinton had won the first debate but the second and third ones "quickly degenerated into highly personal, mudslinging attacks that pushed substantive policy issues to the side." The implicit suggestion was that the less substantial the debate, the bigger win for Trump. Yet despite, or perhaps because of the "mudslinging attacks," this time the top comments were visibly pro-Clinton. For example:

"Hillary did great again" (MimosaEliana, San Diego, US, 11,181 upvotes);

"Hillary shone tonight" (PageSage, Northern California, US, 13,082 upvotes).

The most upvoted comments were also highly critical of Trump:

"She is absolutely demolishing this two bit clown" (Josh Baron, Kansas, US, 12,507 upvotes);

"See whooped his tail tonight!! Everything is rigged against in life is rigged against him The Apprentice didn't get any [Grammy awards] it was against him the court system is against him he's paranoid you want a paranoid person running the country?!" (my thoughts, still.there, US, 11,662 upvotes).

The top comment, however, argued that Trump was betraying his own country:

"NO ONE can defend Trump's indefensible defense of Putin AND his refusal to ultimately accept the will of the voters. This man and his followers are proving to be a treasonous bunch. Vote Hillary" (KR629, US, 14,628 upvotes).

Even so, the end result was different.

Another example of the sex and sexism theme, and another with a wordy title, was "Trump furiously denies offering porn star $10k to spend the night with him a year after marrying Melania: The Donald says he would have 'no interest in ever knowing' latest accuser, who says pajama-clad tycoon groped and kissed her in hotel room"[143] (3,738 comments). The piece was written by Jennifer Smith with David Martosko, and published on 22nd of October. The journalists specified that it was Trump's eleventh denial of "damning accusations" made by different women. As earlier, he dismissed Jessica Drake's allegation concerning events that supposedly took place at a golf tournament in 2006 as "totally false and ridiculous." To prove her charge the woman showed a photo of her posing together with Trump, but the Republican candidate's spokesman called it "one of thousands taken out of respect for people asking to have their picture taken with Mr. Trump." He then added the campaign context: "Just another example of the Clinton campaign trying to rig the election." The article recounted Drake's story, according to whom Trump had invited her to his room and, once she left, his associates started calling her offering 10,000 dollars if she came back to his suite. Next to the body of the text, a bright-blue box presented "TRUMP CAMPAIGN STATEMENT IN RESPONSE TO DRAKE'S ACCUSATIONS." Further down in the article, the journalists noted that Wicked Movies, for which Drake worked, is "one of the largest porn production companies in the U.S." and that Drake campaigned against the mandatory use of condoms in all porn scenes. This could have been interpreted as a reason to reject her accusation – in the popular imagination a porn star, who had campaigned for condom-less sex, did not sound credible blaming a presidential candidate for improper sexual behavior. Still, the porn actress received support from Gloria Allred, a lawyer known for her engagement in cases concerning the sexual abuse of women. The article closed with another bright-blue box, alarmingly titled "TRUMP'S TIMELINE OF ACCUSERS: THE WOMEN WHO SAY HE ASSAULTED THEM BETWEEN 1980 AND 2007." It included names, photos and short descriptions of accusations made by thirteen women, including businesswomen, models, and a contestant on Trump's reality show, The Apprentice. This time, in contrast to the bad behavior reported in the article, the commenters were sympathetic towards the presidential candidate. Two of the most popular opinions doubted the veracity of the porn actress's accusation:

---

143   https://www.dailymail.co.uk/news/article-3863174/Trump-offered-10k-spend-night-says-porn-star-Adult-actress-claims-Donald-propositioned-inviting-two-women-penthouse-suite.html.

"Yeah right! A p o r n star would have taken the cash!" (JW8619, Houston, US, 2,651 upvotes);

"Sure he did. He's gonna offer you more than 10 x the going rate? I don't think billionaires work that way" (qe222, st pete, Azerbaijan, 1,466 upvotes).

Two others criticized Clinton's campaign for focusing too extensively on women accusing Trump of sexual misconduct. One argued analytically,

"Dems over played their hand on this. They've marched out too many 'victims' and now it's just laughable and falling on deaf ears" (Hoochmooch, Phoenix, US, 3,140 upvotes);

and the other echoed this opinion:

"Enough! This is laughable. Please just stop. So many women around a billionaire and all of them victims. Give me a break. Stop running these smut stories dm [*Daily Mail*]" (frankie2112, Hawaii, US, 1,954 upvotes).

Finally, one top comment stated simply,

"You know, I just don't care. I'm voting for Trump" (jigaratta, Woodstock, US, 2,367 upvotes).

It was a striking but, based on the comments, understandable response voicing indifference to what was seen as an oversaturation of the same charge. After some time, instead of being infuriating, sexual allegations started sounded boring; they were no longer "new". The juxtaposition between the journalistic tone of this article and other similar ones, and the popular comments concerning Trump's sexual violations, reveals the gradual change of attitudes of the Mail Online audience. Although generally pro-Trump, the commenters were initially enraged by the Access Hollywood recording scandal. Yet, the more instances of Trump's lewd behavior emerged, the less persuasive they became. The issue of improper conduct towards women turned into an insignificant personal flaw in Trump's private life. In contrast, the attacks on Clinton were based on the flaws of her public performance, confirmed by the reopening of the FBI email probe. Perhaps this is why they "stuck" more effectively.

Having said that, the Democratic Party candidate's troubles with her private email server were, too, strongly connected to a sex scandal; her aid's Huma

Abedin's husband, Anthony Weiner had been found sexting with minors. This was the focus of "Huma Alone: Hillary's exiled aide breaks cover to visit campaign HQ as she pleads ignorance over emails on her sexting husband's laptop, but faces JAIL if it's proved she lied to FBI"[144] (3,698 comments), written by Wills Robinson and published on 30th of October. The piece largely repeated information from a previous article on the matter: that Abedin denied having any knowledge about emails to Clinton on Weiner's computer; that Clinton was campaigning in Florida without her; and that the FBI reopened the probe into Clinton's emails after finding them on Weiner's laptop while investigating his sexual misconduct. Abedin claimed she had handed over all her devices which she had used to email with Clinton and was unaware of any emails on her husband's laptop. At the same time, polls showed that Clinton's lead over Trump shrank to only one percentage point, compared with twelve a week earlier – likely, a reaction to the reopened case. Further in the article, a bright-blue box briefly reminded about the "ANTHONY WEINER SEXTING SCANDAL," describing the 15-year old's allegations about Weiner's lewd texts and rape fantasies. The author then went on to report Clinton's "war against Comey right to her own supporters during a rally" in Florida. "It's pretty strange to put something like that out with such little information, right before an election. In fact, it's not just strange it's unprecedented and it's deeply troubling," the candidate said to the crowd. Referring to the location of the meeting, Robinson noted that Clinton's Florida rallies included one in Volusia County, which used to be a Democratic stronghold until Mitt Romney's victory there in 2012. Moreover, emphasis was put on Clinton's "business of retail politics," such as shaking hands with people and attending a tailgate party with local university students. Then, the article returned to Clinton's emails. John Podesta, her campaign chairman, called the reopening of the case "long on innuendo and short on facts," and confirmed that Abedin has "been fully cooperating and we of course stand behind her." Meanwhile, a campaign manager for the Democratic candidate noted that the FBI probe was, paradoxically, boosting support for Clinton. Still, as the journalist wrote, Trump was having a "field day" because of Comey's decision, while Clinton assured "I'm confident, whatever they are, they will not change the conclusion reached in July." More bright-blue boxes followed, one with a timeline of "THE CLINTON EMAIL CONTROVERSY," another with a timeline of "THE TALE OF HILLARY CLINTON'S PRIVATE SERVER." The piece also included several photos of Abedin, most of them paparazzi shots, a

---

144 https://www.dailymail.co.uk/news/article-3886250/Huma-Abedin-holed-New-York-home-day-FBI-reopens-case-against-Clinton.html.

naked selfie of her husband, Anthony Weiner, numerous photos from Clinton's campaign and, at the bottom, photos of Trump grinning during his own rallies. In the comments section the readers adopted a reserved approach to Clinton and Abedin's predicament. For instance, one of the top comments summed up the Democratic candidate:

> "This woman must be the poorest judge of character, ever! She couldn't surround herself with a more hideous cast of characters if she tried" (Harriet, Toronto, Canada, 1,913 upvotes).

Another commenter asked,

> "Do you suppose there are love letters between Huma and Hillary on that laptop ???" (InquiringTexan, My Island, US, 2,094 upvotes).

A different top comment – a Gawker-style pop culture observation – concentrated on Anthony Weiner's semblance to a nerdy character from Saved by the Bell, a 1990s US sitcom:

> "Hillary undone by Screech. You could not make it up" (Rick007, Gold Coast, Australia, 4,355 upvotes).

Also, in connection with Weiner, one popular comment analyzed the troubled relations between Clinton and her aide:

> "This lady is essentially on, Garden Leave, now. What a bad marriage can do. Sheesh. All her hard work, years of service – now, reduced to being a pariah. Hillary may still be loyal towards her, in the end – but right now, she must be absolutely livid with, Huma. (and that louse of husband of hers.)." (LawdHelpUsAll, Massachusets, US, 3,507 upvotes).

Finally, a commenter asked, not without merit,

> "What are the bombshell findings? Even Hillary wants you to reveal it. If this turns out to the 'weapons of mass destruction' nightmare, there will be he!! to pay" (saintlady, Nashville, US, 2,297 upvotes).

In sum, Mail Online coverage of the US presidential campaign was the most detailed and the most negative in tone, compared to the other two outlets. At the same time, one could observe that accusations of the campaign's poor quality, especially the petty fights in place of discussion during the presidential debates, appeared to work in Trump's favor. The worse the exchanges, the better off the Republican candidate seemed, as if the social rules of scandal and moral outrage did not impact him – though they were certainly harmful to Clinton. This is understandable if we take into account the "elite" vs. "non-elite" labels discussed at the beginning of this chapter. Clinton, a longtime member of the political top class, was expected to behave in a proper, moral way. Trump, posing as a person of the people, did not have to. The strategy paid off.

3.4.3 Pudelek

In the Polish online tabloid, the US presidential campaign received almost as much interest as the Polish one, held over a year earlier. However, this time the coverage was less issue-driven, and focused on general comments and photo galleries instead. Nonetheless, as in the other two online tabloids, on Pudelek, too, negative attitudes concerning Clinton and Trump were clearly more visible than positive ones. This points at a general feeling of frustration with politics, and it seemed more widespread than hopes for change that elections could bring.

3.4.3.1 *General Comments*

The theme of *general comments* in the US presidential campaign could be found on Pudelek, for example, in the article titled "30-year-old claims he is an illegitimate child of Bill Clinton and ... a prostitute!"[145] (195 comments), published on 13th of October. The piece described the sudden emergence of Danney Williams, a man who claimed he was an illegitimate son of Bill Clinton, and had been raised by his mother, a prostitute in Arkansas where Clinton had been governor. "You are seeing a black Bill Clinton," he explained. "When I comb my hair I see Bill with curly hair." The piece mentioned that Williams's own children were told they had a famous grandfather, even though Williams admitted that he was ignored by his alleged father, who "took care of his daughter Chelsea." In contrast to Chelsea Clinton's plush upbringing, Williams had to drop out of school to work, Pudelek reported. The article included numerous photos of Williams juxtaposed with pictures of Clinton from different points in their lives, in addition to pictures of Williams's mother and children. What's more, a YouTube video, which had been published two days earlier, was embedded at the bottom of the article. Titled "Banished: the untold story of Danney Williams," it bore a subtitle which was a thinly-veiled accusation of racism,

---

145 https://www.pudelek.pl/artykul/99102/3-latek_twierdzi_ze_jest_nieslubnym_dzieckiem_billa_clintona_i_prostytutki/.

aimed at the Democratic presidential candidate, Clinton's wife: "Hillary: Do Black Lives Matter?" Yet despite the revelatory story, the commenters did not notice similarities between Bill Clinton and his alleged black son. One comment stated insightfully,

> "in the us you can find a person claiming to be someone's son, daughter, grandson, dog, cat at any given time … 99% cases are people who simply want attention" (850 upvotes);

> "Not similar at all" (702 upvotes),

wrote another. Two top comments, however, voiced their doubts:

> "for me he is not similar at all, but who knows, in politics like in showbusiness, everyone with everyone" (452 upvotes);

which was followed by

> "As if he were the only one. He probably has siblings all around the world" (519 upvotes).

Finally, a different popular comment voiced skepticism about the peculiar timing of the disclosure:

> "News like this pop up every couple of days in the US. Weirdly enough they guy announces this during the campaign of the wife and only now;-) Suuuuuuuuure.." (144 upvotes).

"Ivanka Trump fans spent 90 thousand dollars to look like her! (PHOTOS)"[146] (89 comments) published on 4th of November, presented another take on the general theme, this time centered on the Republican presidential candidate's daughter. The piece began with a quote from a plastic surgeon – "Ivanka is in fashion. On the other hand, no one wants to look like Melania" – then went on to remind readers that the presidential election was four days away, and turned to Donald Trump, whom the journalist described as being known for his "rich sexual life, which produced four children, many ex-wives and victims of sexual

---

146   https://www.pudelek.pl/artykul/100154/fanki_ivanki_trump_wydaly_tysiecy_dolarow_zeby_wygladac_jak_ona_zdjecia/.

abuse." According to Pudelek, Ivanka, the most popular of Trump's children, was an inspiration for women to such an extent that they wanted to become her lookalikes. In fact, two of them had talked about their surgeries on an ABC television show, Nightline. However only one of them planned to vote for Trump, the article reported. As could be expected, the piece included several photos of the women before, after, as well as during their surgeries. The last photo was of Ivanka Trump herself, shown standing in front of cameras. She was holding "Stuff" men's magazine, the cover of which she graced in a short bodycon dress. As for her fans who had undergone surgery, the commenters were neither impressed with their aspirations, nor with the effects. The most upvoted comment was particularly harsh:

> "Fuck, people, really?! They should have brain surgery instead" (494 upvotes).

Others followed suit:

> "Spend so much money to look worse than before the surgery." (343 upvotes);

> "Madwomen with no brains. They're bored and here's the effect" (78 upvotes).

On a different note, one popular comment complimented Ivanka (confusing her name with that of her mother's):

> "Ivana is naturally very charming but, first of all, she takes care of her beauty" (255 upvotes);

while another comment, inspired by the article, offered a highly unfavorable opinion about Americans in general:

> "This is usa, they think there are no other countries in the world :D with kim kardashian,[147] a b***h … they turned a sex doll into a word-class celebrity, they eat fat in burgers ignoring their health, and think that new

---

147   Kim Kardashian is one of the most popular celebrities in the world. She became famous after a sex tape with her onetime boyfriend was released in 2007. Later, Kardashian starred in a series of television reality shows about her own family, which furthered her own and her family's celebrity status.

york is the us capital, chicago is central america – why is anyone surprised!?!?!?" (40 upvotes).

For the commenters, the plastic surgeries of the two women were evidence of their ridiculousness and vanity, but also, on a broader level, a symbol of decaying American culture.

"The most important photos from Barack Obama's second term (PHOTOS)"[148] (72 comments) offered yet another example of the general theme (and the photo-gallery theme as well). In fact, the piece was so politically detached that although it was published on election day, 8th of November, the post – seven sentences and twenty-three click-through photos – ignored the current presidential candidates entirely and focused on the retiring President instead. The short writeup included information that Obama became President of the United States in 2009 when he was 47 years old, and was reelected for the second term in 2012. His policies, the article explained, concentrated on "finding allies and ending military conflicts in Iraq and Afghanistan." Obama was flatteringly described as "a model father and husband, as well as a participant in social life, easy-going and full of humor, close to his voters." The photo gallery was no less sympathetic, with pictures of Obama during different international trips as head of state, next to photo shoots with other world leaders and artists. The final image, however, pictured Obama supporting Clinton during a rally in 2016 – the only sign of election day. Still, despite the puff piece, the commenters took an analytical view of the United States' military activities during Obama's presidency:

"the crap in the middle east began with Bush junior but the blame is put on Obama :/ Bush even admitted in his book that 'he thought weapons of mass destruction were there ... but there weren't' haha idiot Hussein was hanged." (106 upvotes);

"this campaign [in Iraq?] is said to have cost 6.5 million bucks, you could fill a budget hole with that and not push the world into poverty" (54 upvotes).

Other comments, in the style typical for Pudelek, set the US election in a more familiar Polish context:

---

148 https://www.pudelek.pl/artykul/100258/najwazniejsze_zdjecia_z_drugiej_kadencji_ba racka_obamy_zdjecia/foto_1.

"Trump wants to be president ... because he wants to. Besides, he is a person without opinions, without a spine. Something like [Paweł] KUKIZ." (36 upvotes).

Another comment worried about the US election in the context of the recent Polish and British votes:

"I am terrified by these comments [on Pudelek]... later it will turn out like with PiS and Brexit :(" (43 upvotes).

In response to a different commenter's fundamental question,

"What do we need america for" (14 upvotes),

another Pudelek commenter replied dryly:

"What does the world need Poland for?" (46 upvotes).

No answer was given.

3.4.3.2   *Photo Galleries*
Pudelek often posts *photo galleries*, and numerous visual pieces were also related to the US presidential campaign. However, many of them were pictures not of Hillary Clinton or Donald Trump but of Barack and Michelle Obama, who were consistently put in a flattering context in the online tabloid. As one of the Pudelek writers I talked to explained, the viewers loved looking at the Obamas, because they are a good-looking, likeable power couple that reminded them of royalty (and of the Kennedys). Nevertheless, images of the 2016 presidential candidates and their families received some attention from Pudelek's photo editors, particularly in the context of fashion. One such example is "Katy Perry dressed as Hillary Clinton and Orlando Bloom as ... ? (PHOTOS)"[149] (103 comments). The topic of the article published on the 29th of October was a celebrity-filled Halloween party hosted by the actress Kate Hudson. Most attention was paid to the pop singer Katy Perry who not only dressed as Hillary Clinton but was accompanied by Bill Clinton and Donald Trump lookalikes. The latter, with a MAGA hat sitting atop a mop of orange-red

---

149   https://www.pudelek.pl/artykul/99863/katy_perry_przebrana_za_hillary_clinton_a_o rlando_bloom_za_zdjecia/.

hair, deliberately fake suntan, a smiling mask, and huge gloves (Trump was often mocked for having small hands),[150] turned out to be the singer's boyfriend, the actor Orlando Bloom, Pudelek reported. Numerous photos of the costumes were pasted throughout the piece, but the commenters did not appreciate them much:

> "So-so" (324 upvotes),

stated one of the top comments;

> "it was supposed to be funny? didn't work out" (356 upvotes),

expressed another. In contrast, one top upvoted comment shared a personal experience of dressing up:

> "I was Pippi [Longstocking] at almost every costume party during childhood. Freckles, 2 ponytails and that's all for makeup 😊 and here, a different person" (126 upvotes).

Two other top comments were concerned with different topics. One commenter posed a self-critical rhetorical question,

> "Saturday evening and I'm on Pudelek ... no coment" (440 upvotes).

Another was, presumably, less rhetorical:

> "Where can you find a guy?" (475 upvotes).

Judging by the number of upvotes it is possible that numerous other readers had similar dilemmas.

On 7th of November, a day before the election, the online tabloid published a piece titled "Fashion according to Hillary Clinton: Armani blazer for 50 thousand and Ralph Lauren suits (PHOTOS)"[151] (216 comments). The author reported that Clinton had asked Anna Wintour, the editor-in-chief of US Vogue for help in choosing her campaign outfits because, in contrast to the male wardrobe, "proper" clothing for female candidates for the presidential seat

---

150 See e.g.: ABC News 2016.
151 https://www.pudelek.pl/artykul/100097/moda_wedlug_hillary_clinton_marynarka _armani_za__tysiecy_i_garnitury_ralpha_laurena_zdjecia_s/foto_1.

has not been well specified. Given it was mostly Trump's attire, such as his big red tie and ill-fitting suits, that had been the object of numerous discussions (including a meticulous analysis on Gawker, mentioned earlier), it is noteworthy that on Pudelek not Trump's but Clinton's outfits were put to the test of "appropriateness." This suggests that even if, as Pudelek claims, "the dress code for male nominees has been polished to perfection," they are perhaps freer to break them. Clinton was said to have been inspired by the likes of the German Chancellor Angela Merkel (deemed "too monotonous") and Michelle Obama (deemed "too adventurous"). But even with the help of Wintour, the Democratic candidate did not always get it right, for instance, when she wore an Armani blazer that cost 50,000 złoty (ca. 17,000 dollars) while speaking about income inequality. The photo gallery, placed on top of the page, presented ten photos of Clinton in different outfits during rallies and presidential debates. Curiously, the final photo included Clinton and Trump posing together with Cardinal Timothy Dolan, the Archbishop of New York – possibly a Catholic reference to Pudelek's at least officially predominantly Catholic audience.[152] Despite Clinton's efforts, Pudelek commenters were not convinced by the candidate's fashion choices:

> "How much is that blazer? You must be joking!" (361 upvotes),

was followed by:

> "The one from Armani looks like a sack of potatoes. A very expensive sack" (266 upvotes).

Others emphasized the hypocrisy of the Democratic candidate in regard to money, given Clinton's potential voters:

> "Hmmm how can someone like that talk about problems of the poor and unequal income?" (384 upvotes),

as well as in relation to her own marriage:

> "After this stunt with Levinsky [sic] she is still staying with Bill? The things cash can't solve" (305 upvotes).

---

152 According to official statistics, 85 percent Poles declare themselves Catholic. At the same time, in the recent decades the number of churchgoers has been gradually shrinking and is currently around 37 percent. See: Statistics Poland 2022.

As usual for Pudelek comments, the most popular one added a Polish context to Clinton's fashion choices:

> "And they scolded First Lady Duda for a 1,000 złoty [ca. 300 dollars] woman's suit" (508 upvotes).

Indeed, at the time, Agata Duda, the wife of President Andrzej Duda was being criticized for wearing pricey outfits. While far less expensive or designer-branded than those chosen by Clinton, they were nevertheless beyond the reach of many Poles.[153] Given this perspective, for Pudelek commenters Clinton's wardrobe budget looked outrageous.

A different oft-commented example of the photo theme visible during the presidential campaign on Pudelek was "Ivanka Trump: the new biggest star in USA? (PHOTOS)"[154] (136 comments). As the photo gallery with the Obamas, this one, too, was published on election day. Also, similarly to the "royal" visual allusions made to the retiring presidential couple, here the subheading placed directly under the title ran, "Donald Trump's daughter has been advertised as 'American Kate Middleton'. Won't she lose fans after the election?" Thus, the British monarchy, specifically the good-looking, likeable, and dutiful future Queen, was suddenly inserted into an election campaign held in a democratic republic. Presenting Ivanka as hard-working but also princess-like – parallel to Kate Middleton – could potentially give her father more stature. On Pudelek, over two dozen photos of Ivanka, including selfies, air kisses, and other posed photos, were pasted in the click-through gallery at the top of the page, with the last two images coming from her father's presidential campaign. In a few accompanying paragraphs, Trump's daughter was described as one of his five children and "one of the most popular celebrities in America." Pudelek listed her modeling contracts with US fashion designers and magazines, next to information that she gave birth to her third child while campaigning for her father. Nonetheless, with a heavy dose of irony, Pudelek pointed out that while Ivanka was being presented as a US version of Kate Middleton, her career looked "more like that of Kim Kardashian." The short piece ended with a question to the readers: "Do you think she will finally beat her in terms of popularity after the election?," but the commenters ignored the question. Instead, they shared favorable reviews of Ivanka's looks:

---

153 The median salary in Poland in 2016 was around 1,100 dollars.
154 https://www.pudelek.pl/artykul/100297/ivanka_trump_nowa_najwieksza_gwiazda_usa_zdjecia_s/foto_1.

"pretty" (182 upvotes);

"beautiful, but she was very pretty already as a teenager" (432 upvotes).

It is unclear, though, whether the second comment was an excuse, an accusation, or a statement of fact. Two other popular comments focused on Ivanka's alleged surgical procedures:

"NOSE JOB" (97 upvotes);

"pretty, and if she had a 'job' [plastic surgery] it was really done well" (266 upvotes).

One top upvoted comment changed the subject to Hillary Clinton's daughter, Chelsea, putting her in a bad light:

"By contrast: Chelsea Clinton spent part of the money that was supposed to go to a charity to fund for her own wedding !" (320 upvotes).

The source of the allegation mentioned by the commenter emerged in consequence of the DNC hack – it was found in one of the leaked emails from a former Clinton Foundation employee to John Podesta. Although the accusation of mismanaging funds was never confirmed, some voters began to question the transparency of the foundation's operations[155] and of the Democratic candidate herself.

3.4.3.3 Negative Attitudes towards Hillary Clinton/Democrats

Negative opinions concerning Hillary Clinton was the third most popular theme on Pudelek, though it is worth noting that negative opinions concerning her competitor followed close behind. While the articles themselves were often neutral in tone, sometimes even sympathetic to Clinton, they received highly critical comments from Pudelek's readers, who were clearly more supportive of Trump. The notion of the Republican candidate as the "elite-basher" in contrast to Clinton was embraced by many commenters, despite the numerous attempts made in Pudelek articles to undermine this belief. For example, the piece "Donald Trump as a puppet stuffed with money in Pussy Riot video!"[156]

---

155 See e.g.: Kessler 2017.
156 https://www.pudelek.pl/artykul/99900/donald_trump_jako_kukla_wypchana_pienie dzmi_w_teledysku_pussy_riot/.

(108 comments), published on 30th of October, described the Russian feminist performance group's video clip, mockingly titled "Make America Great Again." In it, they presented a dystopian version of the United States led by Trump. According to Pudelek's retelling of the video, anyone who disagreed with Trump – shown as a money-stuffed puppet – was "arrested and degraded to the level of a 'subhuman,'" while "immigrants, people of color, and women who had an abortion (...) were marked and punished." The article added some context on Pussy Riot, emphasizing that some years earlier the group had publicly "insulted" the Russian President Vladimir Putin, for which its members faced seven years of jail, but because of this they also gained international support. (The group members were sentenced to two years in a prison colony, but Pudelek did not mention this.)[157] The article included several stills from the music video as well as the full video itself, embedded from YouTube. The commenters were not impressed by the work. Two of the top comments openly criticized Pussy Riot:

"Building theories to fit the facts, aka self-promotion on the wave of [anti-]Trump hate!" (189 upvotes);

and

"I am neither for Trump nor Hillary but this is just pathetic" (227 upvotes).

Another comment sympathized with US citizens because of the tough choice they were facing:

"i feel sorry for MERICA ... hard to choose anyone ... all have their issues and unfortunately the choice of either bears irreversible consequences ... for the world." (275 upvotes).

A different top upvoted comment doubted whether the situation would be any better if Clinton won, and alluded to the conspiracy theories concerning the Clinton Foundation:

"Hillary is no better with her foundation" (329 upvotes).

---

157 See e.g.: Elder 2012.

In short, the commenters viewed the Pussy Riot video as anti-Trump propaganda, which backfired on Clinton. Still, among the most popular replies one set the foreign topic in a Polish context, and wished for a dystopian artistic interpretation of the ruling PiS party:

> "Perhaps a video about our government there would be lots to laugh about" (72 upvotes).

"Clinton on Trump: 'He is a loose cannon who could put everything at risk!'"[158] (103 comments), published on election day, is another illustration of the theme. The short article opened with a grand-sounding statement that Clinton could become the first woman president in the history of the United States. The Democratic candidate managed to maintain a small lead against Trump in a "thrilling" "campaign finale," the piece reported. It ended with an extended quote from her rally speech, the following fragment highlighted in bold: "we will have some work to do to bring about healing and reconciliation after this election." The article included several photos of Clinton, all flattering, showing her standing behind a lectern during her rally speeches. In response, one of the most upvoted comments sounded both alarming and vague in terms of political sympathies:

> "The functioning of the World and its society depends ... on this election!" (99 upvotes).

But the rest of the top comments were pro-Trump, from lukewarm support:

> "he is a maniac and she is a puppet.. it will be bad no matter who they chose, but I think trump might be the lesser evil" (129 upvotes);

to seeing him as a symbol of "elite-bashing":

> "People see that she is being sponsored by the largest corporations which strive towards globalization, which manipulate the media All banks, currency manipulation [Swiss] frank, euro, land Prices. (...) They won't let him win because they must carry out their plan. The migration crisis war in Syria is also rooted in this." (118 upvotes);

---

158 https://www.pudelek.pl/clinton-o-trumpie-to-narwaniec-ktory-naraza-wszystkich-na-ryzyko-6366058769213569w.

"The elites won't let Trump win. He is a loose cannon, that's a fact. But for ordinary Americans, not pompous starlets and millionaires, from what he's saying HE WANTS WELL. Perhaps less in terms of foreign affairs. Clinton is entirely untrustworthy." (120 upvotes).

The most hopeful about the Republican candidate saw him as able to make a difference:

"I hope Trump wins, this would be interesting, when Hilary wins absolutely nothing will change. But I think the elites won't let him win, their snouts are too deep in the shared trough" (109 upvotes).

"Lady Gaga supports Hillary Clinton, too! 'This woman will restore peace in our country!'"[159] (165 comments), also published on election day, offered a different example of negative attitudes towards Clinton, specifically visible in the comments section. The article reported that before the vote Clinton was two percentage points ahead of "the controversial billionaire." This "good" result was at least to some extent the result of the support given to her by numerous stars, including Beyoncé, Jay-Z, Cher, Meryl Streep, and Jennifer Lopez, Pudelek enumerated. A series of photos of Lady Gaga performing at Clinton's rally the previous day accompanied the piece, and Pudelek noted that the performer looked like Michael Jackson, dressed in a dark military-inspired suit and aviator glasses. The commenters, however, slammed both the stars and the candidate, not shying away from conspiracy theories:

"Freemasons supporting freemasons" (564 upvotes),

and

"All illuminati" (411 upvotes)

were among the most popular comments. Others focused on the candidate:

"Hillary looks deranged" (412 upvotes)

was one such example among top upvoted comments. Another expanded on Clinton's need to rely on celebrity endorsements and her general unfitness for the role:

---

159 https://www.pudelek.pl/artykul/100331/lady_gaga_tez_wspiera_hillary_clinton_ta_kobieta_przywroci_pokoj_w_naszym_kraju/.

"Pathetic. Trump doesn't have to pay starlets of this sort for their support. Let's hope Americans don't get fooled by this pro-liberal and pro-system rubbish. Clinton = Third World War" (419 upvotes).

Nonetheless, a different top comment hated both Clinton and Trump:

"All of this doesn't change the fact that the level of both candidates is pathetic☝" (406 upvotes).

Regardless of this universally negative take, the unenthusiastic sentiment towards Hillary or her chances of winning shared by many Pudelek commenters were much in line with the comments discussed in Mail Online and Gawker. This could be noticed in the Polish online tabloid even though Pudelek's most popular pieces on the US presidential campaign focused on neutral or flattering photos of the candidates and of the Obamas, fashion, human interest stories, and celebrity endorsements. As could be already observed in the Polish presidential campaign, particularly the latter was poorly received by Pudelek commenters, since they viewed celebrities as members of the elite whom they distrusted. Finally, after Poland's presidential election and the EU referendum in the United Kingdom, this time, too, online tabloid articles, taken together with readers' comments, showed to be noteworthy, if unconventional and highly emotional, predictors of the vote results.

4 A Brief Summary, and Moving on to the Next Chapter

The findings presented in this chapter highlight key frames used in Pudelek, Mail Online, and Gawker – the game frame, the scandal frame, and the (not) kidding frame – which can be found in online-tabloid election campaign coverage and spill over to the comments regardless of country or particular political setup. What's more, all in all, the articles and comments reveal that in all the three cases anti-elite sentiments proved stronger than trust in authority, and negative attitudes towards the candidates were more prevalent than positive ones. In consequence, the votes led to results that swung the three nations towards more right-wing and nationalist politics. Finally, while this chapter focused on Pudelek, Mail Online, and Gawker content, the next chapter takes a closer look at the journalists themselves, their experiences of working in these outlets, as well as their views on journalistic professionalism. The interviews with online-tabloid journalists open additional doors to understanding online-tabloid framing: (not) kidding.

References

ABC News. (2016). The History Behind the Donald Trump 'Small Hands' Insult. *ABC News*, 4 March. Available at: https://abcnews.go.com/Politics/history-donald-trump-small-hands-insult/story?id=37395515.
Abrams, B. (2015). *Gawker: an oral history*. Online: Kindle Single.
Addison, A. (2017). *Mail men: The unauthorized story of the Daily Mail*. London: Atlantic Books.
Alpert, L. I. (2019). Daily Mail's online reinvention relieves pressure amid newspaper-industry woes. *Wall Street Journal*, 5 December. Available at: https://www.wsj.com/articles/daily-mails-online-reinvention-relieves-pressure-amid-newspaper-industry-woes-11575530597.
Anspach, N.M. and Carlson, T.N. (2020). What to Believe? Social media commentary and belief in misinformation. *Political Behavior*, 42, pp. 697–718.
Atkinson, M. D. and DeWitt, D. (2016). Celebrity political endorsements matter, *Celebrity Studies*, 7(1), pp. 119–121.
Baden, C. (2019). Framing the news. In: Wahl-Jorgensen, K. and Hanitzsch T. eds., *The handbook of journalism studies*. 2nd edition. New York: Routledge, pp. 229–245.
Barstow, D., Craig, S., Buettner, R. and Twohey, M. (2016). Donald Trump Tax Records Show He Could Have Avoided Taxes for Nearly Two Decades, The Times Found. *The New York Times*, 1 October, pp. 10F–11F.
Baum, M. A. (2002). Sex, lies, and war: How soft news brings foreign policy to the inattentive public. *The American Political Science Review*, 96(1), pp. 91–109.
BBC News. (2012). Mail Online overtakes NY Times as top online newspaper. *BBC News*, 26 January. Available at: https://www.bbc.com/news/entertainment-arts-16743645.
bg. (2020). „Fakt" z paywallem w internecie. „Może zarabiać więcej na mniejszej liczbie użytkowników, internauci płacą za różne treści." *Wirtualne Media*, 6 August. Available at: https://www.wirtualnemedia.pl/artykul/fakt-pl-platna-oferta-moze-wiecej-zarabiac-na-mniejszej-liczbie-uzytkownikow.
Boczkowski, P. J. and Mitchelstein, E. (2013). *News gap: When the information preferences of the media and the public diverge*. Cambridge, MA: The MIT Press.
Bourdieu, P. (1998). *Distinction: A social critique of the judgment of taste*. Cambridge, MA: Harvard University Press.
Buettner, R., Craig, S. and McIntire, M. (2020). Long-concealed records show Trump's chronic losses and years of tax avoidance. *The New York Times*, 27 September. Available at: https://www.nytimes.com/interactive/2020/09/27/us/donald-trump-taxes.html.
Buras, P. and Knaus, G. (2018). *Where the law ends: The collapse of the rule of law in Poland – and what to do*. Warsaw: European Stability Initiative and Stefan Batory Foundation.

Cadwalladr, C. and Graham-Harrison, E. (2018). Revealed: 50 million Facebook profiles harvested for Cambridge Analytica in major data breach. *The Observer*, 17 March. Available at: https://www.theguardian.com/news/2018/mar/17/cambridge-analytica-facebook-influence-us-election.

Capella, J. N. and Jamieson, K. H. (1997). *Spiral of cynicism: The press and the public good*. New York: Oxford University Press.

CBOS. (2019). *Postawy wobec islamu i muzułmanów. Komunikat z badań nr 148/2019*. Warsaw: Centrum Badania Opinii Społecznej.

CBOS. (2022). *Opinie o integracji i działaniach UE. Komunikat z badań nr 90/2022*. Warsaw: Centrum Badania Opinii Społecznej.

Chmielewska-Szlajfer, H. (2018). Opinion dailies versus Facebook fan pages: the case of Poland's surprising 2015 presidential elections. *Media, Culture & Society*, 40(6), pp. 938–950.

Christin, A. (2015). "Sex, scandals, and celebrities"? Exploring the determinants of popularity in online news. *Sur Le Journalisme, About Journalism, Sobre Jornalismo*, 4(2), pp. 28–47.

Clausen, L. (2004). Localizing the global: 'Domestication' processes in international news production. *Media, Culture & Society*, 26(1), pp. 25–44.

Czuchnowski, W. and Jałoszewski, M. (2016). Umęczony miłośnik kryminałów. *Gazeta Wyborcza*, 13 January. Available at: https://wyborcza.pl/politykaekstra/7,132907,19467142,umeczony-milosnik-kryminalow.html.

Czuchnowski, W. and Szostak P. (2022). Jak Ziobro kupował Pegasusa dla CBA. Precyzyjna operacja, kamuflaż na każdym kroku. *Gazeta Wyborcza*, 3 January. Available at: https://wyborcza.pl/7,75398,27966080,jak-ziobro-kupowal-pegasusa-dla-cba.html.

Delli Carpini, M. X. and Williams, B. A. (2001). Let us infotain you: Politics in the new media age. In: Bennett, W. L. and Entman R. M. eds. M*ediated politics: Communication in the future of democracy*. Cambridge, UK: Cambridge University Press, pp.160–181.

Denby, D. (2009). *Snark: A polemic in seven fits*. New York: Simon & Schuster.

Doctor, K. (2016). Did the media win the election?. *Politico*, 15 November. Available at: https://www.politico.com/media/story/2016/11/did-the-media-win-the-election-004854/.

Dunaway, J. and Lawrence, R. G. (2015). What predicts the game frame? Media ownership, electoral context, and campaign news, *Political Communication*, 32(1), pp. 43–60.

Dunin-Wąsowicz, R. (2013). Polacy w brytyjskim społeczeństwie obywatelskim: analiza formalnych stowarzyszeń i organizacji. In: Kucharczyk, J. ed. *Nic o nas bez nas. Partycypacja obywatelska Polaków w Wielkiej Brytanii*. Warsaw: Institute of Public Affairs, pp. 79–104.

Dunn, J. (2016). Here's what Univision is getting for its $135 million. *Business Insider*, 17 August. Available at: https://www.businessinsider.com/univision-buys-gawker-traffic-2016-8.

Dwyer, C. (2016). Donald Trump: 'I could ... shoot somebody, and I wouldn't lose any voters'. *NPR*, 23 January. Available at: https://www.npr.org/sections/thetwo-way/2016/01/23/464129029/donald-trump-i-could-shoot-somebody-and-i-wouldnt-lose-any-voters.

Elder, M. (2012). Pussy Riot sentenced to two years in prison colony over anti-Putin protest. *The Guardian*, 17 August. Available at: https://www.theguardian.com/music/2012/aug/17/pussy-riot-sentenced-prison-putin.

Engell, L. (2005). Falle und Fälle. Kleine Philosophie des Fernsehskandals. In: Gernhards, C., Borg, S. and Lambert B. eds. *TV-Skandale*. Konstanz: UVK, pp. 17–37.

Enten, H. (2015). Why Donald Trump isn't a real candidate, in one chart. *Five Thirty Eight*, 16 June. Available at: https://fivethirtyeight.com/features/why-donald-trump-isnt-a-real-candidate-in-one-chart/.

Entman, R. M. (1993). Framing: Toward clarification of a fractured paradigm. *Journal of Communication*, 43(4): pp. 51–58.

Entman, R. M. (2012). *Scandal and silence: Media responses to presidential misconduct.* Malden, MA: Polity.

erka. (2014). Grupa Wirtualna Polska ma nowy zarząd, 14 February. Available at: https://biznes.trojmiasto.pl/Grupa-Wirtualna-Polska-ma-nowy-zarzad-n77039.html.

Fiske, J. (1992). Popularity and the politics of information. In: Dahlgren, P. and Sparks, C. eds. *Journalism and popular culture*. London, UK: Sage, pp. 45–63.

Galtung, J. and Ruge, M. H. (1965). The Structure of Foreign News. *Journal of Peace Research*, 2(1), pp. 64–91.

Gans, H. J. (2004). *Deciding what's news: A study of CBS Evening News, NBC Nightly News, Newsweek, and Time*. Evanston, IL: Northwestern University Press.

Gąsior, M. (2013). Internauci śmieją się z czekoladowego orła z akcji "Orzeł Może," a prawica oskarża "Trójkę" o polityczne zaangażowanie. *Na Temat*, 29 April. Available at: https://natemat.pl/59603,awantura-o-akcje-orzel-moze-prawica-oskarza-trojke-o-polityczne-zaangazowanie-a-internauci-obsmiewaja-czekoladowego-orla.

Głuchowski, P. (2022). Prezes PiS pozywa za naruszenie jego prywatności. Czy Jarosław Kaczyński jest szantażowany?. *Gazeta Wyborcza*, 2 September. Available at: https://wyborcza.pl/duzyformat/7,127290,28853789,prezes-pis-pozywa-dziennikarza-youtubera-czy-jaroslaw-kaczynski.html.

González, R. J. (2017), Hacking the citizenry?: Personality profiling, 'big data' and the election of Donald Trump. *Anthropology Today*, 33(3), pp. 9–12.

Goodwin, M. J. and Heath, O. (2016). The 2016 referendum, Brexit and the left behind: An aggregate-level analysis of the result. *The Political Quarterly*, 87(3), pp. 323–332.

Graham, T. (2013). Talking back, but is anyone listening? Journalism and comment fields. In: Peters, C. and Broersma, M. eds. *Rethinking journalism: Trust and participation in a transformed news landscape*. New York: Routledge, pp. 114–127.

Greenwald, G. (2013). NSA collecting phone records of millions of Verizon customers daily. *The Guardian*, 6 June. Available at: https://www.theguardian.com/world/2013/jun/06/nsa-phone-records-verizon-court-order.

Gross, D. (2012). Romney iPhone app misspells 'America' to Web's delight. *CNN*, 30 May. Available at: https://edition.cnn.com/2012/05/30/tech/mobile/amercia-romney-iphone-app/index.html.

Gurevitsch, M., Levy and Roeh, I. (1991). The global newsroom: Convergences and diversities in the globalization of television news. In: Dahlgren, P. and Sparks, C. eds., (1991) *Communications and Citizenship: Journalism and the Public Sphere in the New Media Age*. London: Routledge, pp. 195–215.

Hanusch, F. and Tandoc, E. C. (2019). Comments, analytics, and social media: The impact of audience feedback on journalists' market orientation. *Journalism*, 20(6), pp. 695–713.

Harper, J. (2017). Protests against judicial reforms in Poland. *Deutsche Welle*, 16 July. Available at: https://www.dw.com/en/thousands-protest-judicial-reforms-in-poland/a-39713057.

Holiday, R. (2018). *Conspiracy. Peter Thiel, Hulk Hogan, Gawker, and the anatomy of intrigue*. New York: Portfolio/Penguin.

Holmes, S. and Krastev, I. (2020). *The light that failed: Why the West is losing the fight for democracy*. London: Pegasus Books.

Ingram, M. (2016). Gawker gets its first outside investment ever, from a Russian oligarch. *Fortune*, 20 January. Available at: https://fortune.com/2016/01/20/gawker-funding/.

Kaczynski, A. and Massie, C. (2016). Trump wished Condi Rice was a 'bitch' in 2006. *CNN*, 19 October. Available at: https://edition.cnn.com/2016/10/18/politics/rice-trump-2006-comments/index.html.

Kelsey, D. (2015). Defining the 'sick society': Discourses of class and morality in British right-wing newspapers during the 2011 England riots. *Capital & Class*, 39(2), 243–264.

Kelsey, D. (2019). News, discourse, and ideology. In: Wahl-Jorgensen, K. and Hanitzsch T. eds., *The handbook of journalism studies*. 2nd edition. New York: Routledge, pp. 246–260.

Kessler, G. (2017). Did the Clinton Foundation pay for Chelsea's wedding?. *The Washington Post*, 4 January. Available at: https://www.washingtonpost.com/news/fact-checker/wp/2017/01/04/did-the-clinton-foundation-pay-for-chelseas-wedding/.

Kiely, E. (2012). Benghazi timeline. *FactCheck.org*, 26 October. Available at: https://www.factcheck.org/2012/10/benghazi-timeline/.

Kollman, K. and Jackson, J. E. (2021). *Dynamic partisanship: How and why voter loyalties change*. Chicago, IL: The University of Chicago Press.

Kosinski, M., Stillwell, D. and Graepel T. (2013). Private traits and attributes are predictable from digital records of human behavior. *Proceedings of the National Academy of Sciences*, 110(15), pp. 5802–5805.

Kwaśniewski, A. (2012). Kto sprawuje rząd dusz. Pudelek, czy Gazeta Wyborcza. *Na Temat*, 15 February. Available at: https://natemat.pl/blogi/aleksanderkwasniewski/1017,kto-sprawuje-rzad-dusz-pudelek-czy-gazeta-wyborcza.

Langley, M. (2016). Donald Trump Says Campaign Not in Crisis, and There Is 'Zero Chance I'll Quit'. *Wall Street Journal*, 8 October. Available at: https://www.wsj.com/articles/trump-tells-wsj-i-never-give-up-and-getting-unbelievable-support-1475940443.

Lewis, S. C., Holton, A. E. and Coddington, M. (2017). From participation to reciprocity in the journalist-audience relationship. In: Peters, C. and Broersma, M. eds. *Rethinking journalism again: Societal role and public relevance in a digital age*. New York: Routledge, pp. 161–174.

Maltby, K. (2017). William and Kate have been duped into endorsing Poland's ugly nationalism. *The Guardian*, 21 July. Available at: https://www.theguardian.com/commentisfree/2017/jul/21/william-kate-poland-nationalism-royal-brexit.

Marshall, P. D. (2014). *Celebrity and power: Fame in contemporary culture*. Minneapolis, MN: The University of Minnesota Press.

Mazur, D. and Żurek, W. (2017). Rule of law in Poland. State of play in October 2017. Analysis by judge Dariusz Mazur and judge Waldemar Żurek. *Rule of Law*, 6 October. Available at: https://ruleoflaw.pl/so-called-good-change-in-the-polish-system-of-the-administration-of-justice/.

McCraw, D. E. (2016). The New York Times's Lawyer Responds to Donald Trump. *The New York Times*, 13 October. Available at: https://www.nytimes.com/interactive/2016/10/13/us/politics/david-mccraw-trump-letter.html.

McNair, B. (2019). Scandal and news values. In: Tumber, H. and Waisbord, S. eds. *The Routledge companion to media and scandal*. New York: Routledge, pp. 76–85.

New York Magazine. (2008). How to be a Gawker. *New York Magazine*, 12 February. Available at: https://nymag.com/intelligencer/2008/02/how_to_be_a_gawker.html.

Mellado, C. (2015). Professional roles in news content. *Journalism Studies*, 16(4), pp. 596–614.

Murphy, T. (2014). The definitive guide to every Hillary Clinton conspiracy theory (so far). *Mother Jones*, 9 June. Available at: https://www.motherjones.com/politics/2014/06/hillary-clinton-conspiracy-theories/.

O'Neill, D. and Harcup, T. (2019). News values and news selection. In: Wahl-Jorgensen, K. and Hanitzsch T. eds., *The handbook of journalism studies*. 2nd edition. New York: Routledge, pp. 213–228.

Peters, T. (2016). Brexit? There was an app for that. *Medium*, 25 June. Available at: https://medium.com/@uCampaignCEO/brexit-there-was-an-app-for-that-57d1d 658b4f1.

Phillips, A. (2015). *Journalism in context: Practice and theory for the digital age.* New York: Routledge.

Ricoeur, P. (1970). *Freud and philosophy: An essay on interpretation.* New Haven, CT: Yale University Press.

Rietdijk, N. (2021). Post-truth politics and collective gaslighting. *Episteme*, First View, pp. 1–17.

Rosenstiel, T. (2005). Political polling and the new media culture: A case of more being less. *The Public Opinion Quarterly*, 69(5), pp. 698–715.

Satter, R., Donn, J. and Day, C. (2017). Inside story: How Russians hacked the Democrats' emails. *Associated Press*, 4 November. Available at: https://apnews.com/article/tec hnology-europe-russia-hacking-only-on-ap-dea73efc01594839957c3c9a6c962b8a.

Sedgwick, E. K. (2003). *Touching feeling: Affect, pedagogy, performativity.* Durham, NC: Duke University Press.

Shepard, S. (2016). Is Nate Silver right? *Politico*, 4 November. Available at: https://www .politico.com/story/2016/11/is-nate-silver-538-right-230734.

Siles, I. (2019). Blogs. In: N. Brugger, N. and Milligan, I. eds. *The SAGE handbook of web history*. London, UK: Sage.

sk and mc. (2015). Jarosław Kaczyński boi się, że uchodźcy sprowadzą zarazę? Tak mówił na wyborczym wiecu. *Gazeta Wyborcza*, 13 October. Available at: https: //wyborcza.pl/7,75398,19014711,jaroslaw-kaczynski-boi-sie-ze-uchodzcy-sprowa dza-zaraze-tak.html.

Smith, D. (2010). *Gawker Media: Overview of where Gawker stood in 2007, and a historical analysis of blogs more generally.* Portland, OR: Measure Creative. Available at: https://www.slideshare.net/devonvsmith/gawker-media.

Socha-Jakubowska, P. (2015). Kto stoi za Pudelek.pl. *Wprost*, 13(1672), p. 33.

Socha-Jakubowska, P. and Krawiec, S. (2015). Pudelek opiniotwórczy. *Wprost*, 13(1672), pp. 30–32.

Spangler, T. (2016). Gawker tumbles to 3-year traffic low: amid sales talk, legal woes, and controversy, the site is one of several politics-based outlets in user freefall. *Variety*, 31 May. Available at: https://variety.com/2016/digital/features/gawker-traf fic-political-websites-1201785316/.

Statistics Poland. (2022). *Concise Statistical Yearbook of Poland 2022*. Warsaw: Statistics Poland.

Street, J. (2004). Celebrity politicians: Popular culture and political representation. *The British Journal of Politics and International Relations*, 6(4), pp. 435–452.

Su, L. Y.-F., Xenos, M. A., Rose, K. M., Wirz, C., Scheufele, D. A. and Brossard, D. (2018). Uncivil and personal? Comparing patterns of incivility in comments on the Facebook pages of news outlets. *New Media & Society*, 20(10), pp. 3678–3699.

Szuleka M., Wolny, M. and Szwed, M. (2016). *The constitutional crisis in Poland 2015–2016*. Warsaw: Helsinki Foundation for Human Rights.

Thomas, O. (2016). Gawker, Peter Thiel, and me. *Medium*, 8 June. Available at: https://medium.com/@owenthomas/gawker-peter-thiel-and-me-f80389b84fa3.

Thompson, J. B. (2000). *Political scandal: Power and visibility in the media age*. Cambridge, UK: Polity.

Tobitt, C. (2022). Martin Clarke Mail Online leaving speech: 'Being an editor makes you a monster'. *Press Gazette*, 24 February. Available at: https://pressgazette.co.uk/news/martin-clarke-mail-online-leaving-speech/.

Tocci, J. (2009). Geek Cultures: Media and Identity in the Digital Age. *Publicly Accessible Penn Dissertations*, 953. Available at: https://repository.upenn.edu/edissertations/953.

Tumber, H. (2004). Scandal and media in the United Kingdom: From Major to Blair. *The American Behavioral Scientist*, 47(8), 1122–1137.

Tumber, H. and Waisbord, S. (2019). Media and scandal. In: Tumber, H. and Waisbord, S. eds. *The Routledge companion to media and scandal*. New York: Routledge, pp. 10–21.

tw. (2021). Pudelek z mniejszą przewagą nad Plotkiem, mocno w górę sekcje 02.pl i Radiozet.pl. *Wirtualne Media*, 20 April. Available at: https://www.wirtualnemedia.pl/artykul/pudelek-z-mniejsza-przewaga-nad-plotkiem-mocno-w-gore-sekcje-02-pl-i-radiozet-pl.

van Krieken, R. (2012). *Celebrity society*. New York: Routledge.

van Zoonen, L. (2005). *Entertaining the citizen: When politics and popular culture converge*. Lanham, MD: Rowman & Littlefield Publishers, Inc.

von Sikorski, C., & Hänelt, M. (2016). Scandal 2.0: How valenced reader comments affect recipients' perception of scandalized individuals and the journalistic quality of online news. *Journalism & Mass Communication Quarterly*, 93(3), pp. 551–571.

Vorberg, L. and Zeitler, A. (2019). 'This is (not) entertainment!': Media constructions of political scandal discourses in the 2016 US presidential election. *Media, Culture & Society*, 41(4), pp. 417–432.

Wahl-Jorgensen, K. (2016). Emotion and journalism. In: Witschge, T., Anderson, C.W., Domingo, D. and Hermida, A. eds. *The SAGE handbook of digital journalism*. New York: Routledge, pp. 128–143.

Walecka-Rynduch, A. (2016). Polityczna rozrywka czy nowa retoryka? W stronę współczesnej widoczności medialnej polityków. *Annales Universitatis Paedagogicae Cracoviensis. Studia Linguistica*, (210)11, pp. 135–150.

Warren, C. and Barton, D-G. (2019). Scandal, media effects and political candidates. In: Tumber, H. and Waisbord, S. eds. *The Routledge companion to media and scandal*. New York: Routledge, pp. 433–444.

Westlund, O. and Ekström, M. (2019). News organizations and routines. In: Wahl-Jorgensen, K. and Hanitzsch T. eds., *The handbook of journalism studies. 2nd edition*. New York: Routledge, pp. 73–89.

Wolff, M. (2018). *Fire and Fury: Inside the Trump White House*. New York: Henry Holt and Company.

Wroński, P. (2012). Z Pudelkiem na barykady. *Gazeta Wyborcza*, 11 February. Available at: https://wyborcza.pl/7,75968,11125948,z-pudelkiem-na-barykady.html.

Wylie, C. (2019). *Mindf*ck: Cambridge Analytica and the plot to break America*. New York: Random House.

CHAPTER 3

Backoffice, or How Online Tabloid Journalists Write on Politics

1 Getting to Talk to Online Tabloid Writers. A Personal Methodological Note on Finding Sources in Different Journalistic Cultures

To understand the process that goes behind the political coverage in online tabloids, I interviewed twenty journalists and editors writing for Pudelek, Mail Online, and Gawker. I talked to nine authors from the Polish outlet, some of whom had worked there since the site's launch, and I conducted six interviews with journalists from the UK website. In cases of Pudelek and Mail Online my interviewees agreed to talk only under the condition of anonymity, with one exception at Mail Online; in contrast, the five Gawker writers spoke under their own names. Although Gawker's founder, Nick Denton did not reply to my emails asking for an interview, I managed to attend a talk with him at Joe's Pub in New York,[1] which turned out to be illuminating. Overall, I conducted the interviews in Warsaw, New York, London, and online between 2016 and 2019. Because of the time constraints in New York, where I conducted my research during two months before the 2016 presidential election and in the spring of 2019, and in London where I spent several months in 2017 and 2018, the number of interviews conducted with Gawker and Mail Online authors was smaller compared to those conducted with Pudelek authors in Warsaw where I was mostly based. With some of the authors I talked more than once, others sent me additional messages as follow-ups to our interviews. Several of these writers and editors continue to work for these outlets while others have moved elsewhere, including glossy magazines, traditional broadsheets, hard-news papers, and other online media outlets. As for Gawker writers, at the time the interviews were held they were writing for different websites within the Gizmodo Media Group. Still, among the authors who switched jobs, in some instances the new places remained consistent with the political standpoints presented by their previous outlets, while others crossed over to the other

---

1 The show, hosted by Catie Lazarus, was titled "Employee of the Month" and took place on 28th of October 2016.

side. For example, such was the case of Damien Gayle, the single Mail Online journalist who agreed to speak on the record. During our conversation he had already changed his newsroom for the left-wing British daily, *The Guardian*. Most of my interviewees aligned with the general stance of their outlets, with a few exceptions at Mail Online.[2] As will be discussed further in this chapter, journalists' non-partisan approach to the political lines of the news media they work for is based on the shared principle of unbiased, factual reporting, and professionalism. While they were strongly emphasized by the interviewees as basic journalistic values, on a practical level these qualities also make it easier to transfer from one news environment to another.

Persuading the authors to agree to an interview varied across the three online tabloids, and I mention this because I believe it also reveals something about the management styles in the three organizations. Pudelek authors took the longest to convince, which is a paradox given the physical proximity – their office is located in Warsaw. A possible reason for this is that most of the writers there are anonymous. I contacted the editor – then the only person with an email on the corporate website – but the person politely declined to be interviewed, asked me to send questions, and responded with a polished set of answers looking as if they had been written by the PR department. I then decided to contact one of the chief officers of the head company (then Grupa O2, currently Wirtualna Polska) who happened to be one of the founders of Pudelek. Unlike the Pudelek editor, he immediately answered directing me back to the same editor, but this time the person agreed to meet. This process took around three months. However, this first interview did not easily lead to subsequent ones. What worked best was word of mouth, friends of friends who sent me email addresses and phone numbers of Pudelek writers, asking me not to tell who I got them from (I didn't). Only after I managed to interview some of the oldest Pudelek employees did I gain enough trust for them to pass on contact information to their colleagues. They were all clearly frightened of speaking openly about the outlet and the company that ran it. It was also hard to ignore the top-down management style, typical for Polish companies: I needed a green light from the company's C-suite before anyone in the Pudelek newsroom agreed to talk to me. After that, personal contacts and chance encounters with "people who knew somebody, who knew somebody" did the trick. In many ways, this, too, is a typically Polish mode of operation

---

2 In his compelling book, *Mail men: The unauthorized story of the Daily Mail*, Adrian Addison (2017) shows that this is not uncommon. For instance, he points out the popularity of Tony Blair among the paper's staff during the 1997 general election, which contrasted with Tory sympathies of the editor-in-chief, Paul Dacre.

of bypassing official structures (see e.g.: Chmielewska-Szlajfer 2019). In the end, I managed to interview most of the original writers and editors who had worked at Pudelek before the introduction of major corporate changes in the organization, after the owner of Pudelek, Grupa 02's merger with Wirtualna Polska in 2014. Of the three outlets, interviews with Pudelek writers were conducted over the longest period, which took about two years. Mail Online writers were a different story, yet also hinting at the organizational style of the profession, this time in the United Kingdom. Although the authors' contact information was easy to find, they either did not respond or declined to be interviewed. My luck changed when I asked UK-based journalist colleagues for help. Their recommendations, coming from inside the profession, proved far more persuasive than formal emails sent from my university account.[3] Thus, unlike the top-down and bypass model at Pudelek, at the British online tabloid the doors opened thanks to horizontal-professional support of fellow journalists, initially from other outlets and later from within Mail Online. Again, all but one writer, Damien Gayle, agreed to talk only on the condition of anonymity. This was not surprising given the well-known culture of "bollocking" enforced by the then editor-in-chief, Martin Clarke.[4] Unlike authors from the other two outlets, Gawker writers turned out to be the most approachable and unanimously open to talking on the record. My interviewees included: Ashley Feinberg, Rich Juzwiak, Hamilton Nolan, Brendan O'Connor, and Gawker's co-founder Elizabeth Spiers. This stark contrast between Gawker authors and writers from these other outlets hints at a more individualistic work culture, often associated with the United States. At Gawker the writers, some of whom had started online as bloggers, were used to writing in their own name, thus creating their own brands (see e.g.: Marwick 2013). Gawker Media (later Gizmodo Media Group) took advantage of this and held a much softer grip on

---

3 Before I reached out to journalist colleagues, in my attempts to find Mail Online writers I broadly shared information about my research on different social media platforms, from Twitter and Facebook to the dating app, Tinder. Given the nature of the latter medium, I included a neutral photo of my face and in the "bio" section a description of my study explaining that I was searching for Mail Online authors to conduct interviews about their work. The Tinder search proved a mixed success: I did manage to talk to a former Mail Online author – who was then working at a popular broadsheet – but he was deeply offended that our meeting was not a date, even though I had explicitly stated the purpose of the meeting in our brief Tinder chat beforehand. After this encounter, I decided to rely on journalists' recommendations instead.

4 Martin Clarke, who stood behind the success of Mail Online, announced his resignation from the post of editor-in-chief and publisher at the end of 2021, after 13 years of work at the online tabloid. See e.g.: Gray 2021.

the opinions its employees were sharing with the outside world through the website. This approach could not have been more different from that of Mail Online, where the sense of professionalism among reporters implies factual neutrality, opinions being left to the editors crafting the titles, and to the columnists. But it was also different from the model at Pudelek, even though the writers there have been inspired by the Gawker style. However, in the Polish outlet they have been able to maintain the mocking attitude not by writing with their own bylines but by adopting *noms de plume*, which have been sheltering them from personal attacks by offended parties. Still, even this layer of security did not make them feel safe to talk. In contrast, the reason for Gawker writers' openness could have lied in the fact that they were paid for openly writing highly opinionated pieces, so it was not astonishing that they would voice their remarks to researchers as well. At the time I was conducting interviews the company was in turmoil, the Gawker website ceased operations at the end of August 2016 – and, as some of the writers stated plainly, these conversations gave them an opportunity to vent. In some ways, this scenario repeated itself at Pudelek: more writers decided to speak to me after major changes were implemented in the company – according to them for the worse – as a result of the 2014 company merger. There is an irony in the fact that the worsening work conditions for journalists proved beneficial for my own research.

2   Content and Comments

2.1   *Content 101: Newsworthy, Entertaining, Reactive*

Published news pieces are a feature of online tabloid journalism that is plainly visible to both professional and lay readers. While Chapter 2 presented an analysis of the most popular online-tabloid articles on politics during the 2015–2016 election campaigns, in this chapter I focus on the people who write the stories. I examine their own understanding and often complex motivations concerning the work they do (or, in some cases, did and have since moved elsewhere) at Pudelek, Mail Online, and Gawker. In the simplest terms, Gawker journalists considered their website uncovering, Mail Online authors view their outlet as reactive, while Pudelek writers point at their medium's educational aspect. Still, given the tabloid nature of the outlets it does not come as a big surprise that nearly all the interviewees emphasize their role is first and foremost to "entertain" the audience with issues that are "newsworthy." Newsworthiness, which will be discussed in the following chapter, is, essentially, anything established journalistic routines show to be important and interesting – especially topics referring to power. What's more, political, celebrity, and gossip content exist in a delicate equilibrium, mutually reinforcing each other: gossip is made more relevant by politics, while politics is trivialized by gossip. Accordingly, in terms of politics, the newsworthy-entertainment value lies in the strong ideological angle matched with emotional style, in which the online-tabloid pieces are written. This is why readers are less likely to find dispassionate pieces about political meetings where, for example, fiscal policies are decided upon. Even though these events are important and bear long-term consequences, for laypersons they are often difficult to understand and are anything but entertaining, hence make for poor tabloid material. In contrast, campaign rallies, particularly those during which candidates make personal remarks alluding to sexual misconduct or financial corruption, garner far more popular interest.[5] This is not to say that emotional features are limited to sensationalist outlets. Wahl-Jorgensen (2013) points out that on the other end of news-making, Pulitzer-Prize winning journalists, too, deliberately employ emotions in their writing but unlike impassioned tabloid writers, they "outsource" emotions to the sources they quote. In short: in news, whether "soft" or "hard," feelings sell stories. However, newsworthiness and entertainment are not all; another characteristic shared by Pudelek, Mail Online, and Gawker is publishing news that is "gaining heat" elsewhere and covering "the big stories of the day that everyone is talking about," as Elizabeth Spiers, Gawker's co-founder puts it. This can be a topic or event other news outlets are already highlighting, such as a catastrophe, an attack, or a discovery. It is the event's popularity elsewhere that motivates online tabloid journalists to inform their own readers about it. Thus, broad media visibility of a story is a reason for online tabloids to cover it as well. At the same time, while the news selection is influenced by other media, the audience also plays a major part. In fact, online tabloid journalists consider content published in their own outlets predominantly "reactive" to the responses of their audiences; the stories are continuously adapted to their needs, both predicted by the journalists and based on monitoring online data. Still, maintaining the reactive character of online tabloids is a balancing act: the writers and editors publish content based on their predictions what the audience may pay attention to, and the readers have certain expectations concerning the content and tone. If a piece, even a highly popular one in terms of clicks, veers from the usual editorial style – for instance, a Mail Online article less pro-Brexit than usual during the EU referendum campaign – many commenters are quick to reject the argument. But this, too, generates more clicks

---

5 It is worth noting Mellado's (2015) argument about politicians' sex scandals being merely infotainment. Yet given the significance of sexual accusations in political campaigns and in their consequences for governance in the recent years, it is hard to agree with this position.

and, hence, revenue, which shows that stepping out of the outlet's expected line may prove profitable. Nevertheless, the fact that such deviations from the typical ideological tone are rare suggests that the reactive nature of online tabloids is not purely data-driven, but is a result of the journalists' and readers' assumptions what the outlet should represent. One Mail Online author, whom I shall call Steven*,[6] states bluntly that the outlet's content is not just reactive but "opportunistic" and "cynical." At the same time, he emphasizes, the stories reflect "human nature." (And if the atmosphere is Hobbesian, it is particularly visible in the comments.) Yet Steven* adds that "Mail Online is a very nonjudgmental place" in that it does not demand much from its audience. Indeed, you do not need prior knowledge of political matters to read Mail Online, the outlet provides all the information it deems important, in an entertaining style.

Next to these basic rules regarding the selection of content in online tabloids – newsworthiness, entertainment value, topics discussed in other media outlets, and the reactive character of content – the three outlets share a number of similar traits regarding the writing and photo editing style. These can be noticed despite the differences in the tabloids' political outlooks, national focus and, in the case of Pudelek, language. In fact, the writing style requirements in online tabloid writing that are mentioned by the journalists largely overlap. And so, one of the first things that stands out is the punchy, emotional approach, which has been perfected by tabloids ever since their emergence in the second half of the 19th century. Today, the writing is often driven by photos and, as some authors underscore, the choice of topics is frequently dependent on the available images. Considering this, it is striking that the focus on photos in studies of journalism – especially in relation to news values – has been limited, as Caple and Bednarek (2016) highlight. After all, nowadays it is hard to even imagine a piece in an online tabloid or any other online outlet without images, and for a reason: "Some things can be expressed using text, other things can be expressed using photos," Paweł*, one of Pudelek's writers tells me. John* from Mail Online agrees, and focuses on the images that can be more important than the writing itself: "Some stories are only about the pictures, and people would essentially look at the top few pictures, which takes twenty seconds, and then leave. And the text was sort of a dressing for the pictures." His colleague, Ian* adds a historical perspective, arguing that the significance of imagery is not an invention of the internet era but is intrinsic to general tabloid style:

---

6 Asterisks are added to pseudonyms of journalists who wished to remain anonymous.

"The genius of Mail Online is that it's just old-fashioned tabloid reporting online, with lots of pictures. So, it's just news that you want to read, and lots and lots of pictures that you want to look at. And that was always the big thing. (...) It was very different type of reporting [than in non-tabloids]: you write the headline, you pick the picture, you crop the picture, you write the picture caption, you do everything on that. (...) But the success of it is very simple, it was a story that people are interested in, with a picture, and that's what Mail Online is."

What online tabloids understand exceptionally well is that the photo often *is* the story, hence the popularity of "Photos!" headlines discussed in Chapter 2. When, however, a piece includes more reporting than merely an extended description of the images, a big picture is almost always located directly under the headline. The reason is simple: a photo captures the eye. From the point of view of semiotics, online-tabloid treatment of image and text is also a good example of Barthes's (1977) rhetoric of image at work: even if a picture is worth a thousand words, and in an online tabloid it is used to get the attention of readers, it is the big, bold headline that anchors the image's intended meaning. The caption eliminates ambiguity in interpreting what is being shown. Briefly put, in online tabloids the connection between image and headline is made to appear straightforward, seamless, and indisputable.

Writing the copy, too, follows specific online-tabloid rules. First of all, there are "strong verbs" ("escape" rather than "leave"; "fire" rather than "argue," etc.) used in most newswriting, which, Gayle explains, at Mail Online are additionally strengthened with "a good old adjective in there, or two (...), which [you] wouldn't necessarily do in a more upmarket newspaper – you'd probably go for slightly classier writing." He also adds, "Short sentences, strong verbs, swift moral judgements. (...) It was giving a kind of comicky, fun write-through." If Mail Online is about strong verbs, Spiers highlights Gawker's snarky tone, for which the outlet quickly became known, and this distinctive writing style was aligned with the outlet's original blog-like format. On the one hand, as Nolan explains, a "bloggy approach to the news" means the "constant writing [of] stories, piece by piece, instead of having to drop a huge story." On the other hand, because the sarcastic style is engaging and fun to read it has significantly influenced online writing as such. "I think the tone of it [Gawker] was widely adopted throughout the internet," Nolan summarizes. *The New York Times*'s Farhad Manjoo (2016) confirms: "even if you avoided Gawker, you can't escape its influence. Elements of its tone, style, sensibility, essential business model and its work flow have colonized just about every other media company, from upstarts like BuzzFeed and Vox to incumbents like CNN, *The New Yorker* and *The New York Times*."7

Like Gawker, Pudelek does not shy away from sarcasm and to some extent still retains an aughts-style blog look. Wojciech*, one of its original editors lists US gossip websites such as Popsugar, Egotastic, and Perez Hilton as the main inspirations for the Polish outlet, but the sarcastic style has a slight Gawker feel, too. Paweł* describes it in more detail: "This detachment (…), slightly ironic, it had great value. Sometimes it was *à rebours*, we wrote about issues you usually write about, but in cool tone, [conversely] for instance we wrote very emotionally about politics." His colleague, Maciej* underlines another characteristic of Pudelek's tone, after stating his own preference for "sensationalist-pathological" content:

> "We always do it in a form that strongly condemns such [pathological] behavior: 'It's shocking!', 'It's a scandal!', 'What is going through the minds of such people?!', 'Where are the authorities?!', 'Where are the parents?!', 'Where is the police?!', 'Where is the school?!,' if it's about teenagers. So, the way I understand this, there is an educational value in these articles."

The close similarities in online-tabloid writing styles are also stressed by Jagoda*, another Pudelek writer. She claims the influence of Mail Online on the Polish website's content and tone has been quite direct, as for years the British outlet has been a mandatory "morning inspiration reading" for Pudelek writers. Mail Online, for that matter, has been perfecting its own publishing style by taking into account the affordances of the internet. For example, instead of "having to drop a huge story" as, in the words of Gawker's Nolan, old-style journalism would have it, in Mail Online paragraphs are composed in a way that allows to get the gist in the opening section, while the subsequent segments serve to add more detail. (In this sense, it is the very opposite of clickbait, where the headline is vague and requires the reader to read several sections to understand the story.) This means that a person reading a Mail Online article while traveling may stop after the first one or two paragraphs with a sense what the piece is about. "[M]ost readers aren't looking at it as a package in the same way they would probably look at a printed paper," John* explains. "They don't think they have to read every story. On Mail Online you couldn't read every story, you would spend all day reading it," the journalist concludes.

---

7 See also: Elizabeth Spiers's (2023) *The New York Times* opinion piece on Gawker.

The bite-sized, image-heavy short summaries matched with the possibility of almost infinite scrolling on the web page present an interesting paradox concerning time: on the one hand, especially on Mail Online news is formatted to be viewed quickly. On the other hand, the option of scrolling further, either to get more details relayed in a particular article (in the UK outlet), or to continue reading in a virtually never-ending stream of loosely related articles (in all three outlets), shows that websites entice the reader to stay there indefinitely. From a historical perspective, this can be seen as another tabloid innovation intended to target people lacking time and space. The first such novelty was the one that gave tabloids their name: the soft-news papers' switch from broadsheet to the smaller "tabloid" paper size was made to appeal to factory workers who had to go to work in crowded buses, and lacked both time and space to read. Well over a century later, today's online tabloid formatting aims to attract anyone who is on the go with an even smaller format – the smartphone – and with a limited attention span. That is a lot of people. Unlike papers with their physical limitations of space, weight (and at times staining ink), online tabloids take advantage of the inexhaustible space of the web in the hope the reader will stay on the site for as long as possible.

2.2 Comments, Commenters, Language

Reader comments located directly under the articles are a mirror, occasionally a distorted one, to the articles written by journalists. They are also a commonplace feature on the web, which Reagle in his engaging book, *Reading the comments* labels "the bottom half of the Internet," filled with a lot of "dreck."[8] In fact, this "bottom half" translates into 45 percent Poles, 55 percent Americans, and 62 percent British citizens, who have been leaving comments online.[9] In the online reality, audience reactions have become an intrinsic part of the news page. For the most part unmoderated, in online tabloids reader reactions vary from emotional free flows to in-depth analyses, and the journalists' attitudes towards the commenters are, if anything, ambiguous. At the same time, these outlets are in many ways dependent on the commenters, since they generate additional clicks, which translate into revenue. In consequence, authors from all three outlets admit that their writing is reactive to their audience's online activity, although monitoring is largely limited to passive data measurement, such as information about unique visits and time spent on a particular article's

---

8   The phrase is a quote from Shane Liesegang, a game designer. See: Reagle 2015, pp. 2–3.
9   For Polish statistics, see: Dąbrowska-Cydzik 2019; for British statistics, see: Flash Eurobarometer 2016 (only individuals who had expressed their opinion online at least occasionally were taken into account); for US statistics, see: Stroud et al. 2016.

web page. In contrast, comments are active reader responses to the written and illustrated matter. In this sense, the shift in agency and visibility of online audiences compared to offline ones is fundamental. In newspapers, reader comments are significantly restricted, limited by the specific timing of printing paper issues. Furthermore, their visibility is conditional on the editor's choice which letter to print given the little space on a physical page. According to Reader (2012), such gatekeeping results in publishing "what journalists wanted [rather] than of what the writing public desired" (p. 495).[10] This is not the case in the online comments sections, freely accessible around the clock, even if the actual life span for a comment segment under a particular article lasts a day or two. On Pudelek and Mail Online the comments are only barely moderated,[11] and on Gawker the commenters relied on a unique content management system developed by Denton, named Kinja. Created as a tool to encourage meaningful conversation, Kinja made it possible to grant moderating privileges to article authors and popular commenters.[12] But even with such innovations and sales divisions' breakdowns of audiences tailored for advertisers, the commenters remain much of a mystery for journalists. For example, Alicja*, an editor from Pudelek, ponders:

> "For me, the biggest question is – (...) unfortunately I don't know how to check it because I don't know if we have such an option – who writes these comments? When I read these comments (...) I find it hard to believe that such things could be written by women [the majority of Pudelek's readers]. So, my guess is that it must be the forty percent of guys who are writing [them]. I have always been wondering about this."

The editor finds it astonishing that harsh, often extremely judgmental comments focused on celebrities and politicians can be made by women. On the one hand, her surprise is in line with statistics showing that men are more prone to violence than women. On the other hand, the astonishment appears less substantiated in light of research, which demonstrates that online commenters tend to adopt the tone of the original publications, as well as of other comments (see e.g.: Rösner and Krämer 2016). This means that the "strong" verbs and adjectives used by journalists are matched in kind by the

---

10 See also: Wahl-Jorgensen 2002.
11 On moderating comments at Mail Online, see e.g.: Moosa 2014.
12 While the initial reviews of Kinja were mixed, the content management system nonetheless continued to be used on other former Gawker Media websites (currently G/O Media). See e.g.: Tanzer 2014; Webb 2014; Mullin 2017.

belligerence of comments, regardless of their authors' genders. What's more, such strong-language style of comments can be found not only in tabloids but also in hard-news outlets. For example, Muddiman and Stroud (2017), who analyzed comments in *The New York Times*, found that "partisan incivility" is favored by commenters and tolerated by journalists because it increases audience engagement. Similarly, research on profane language in social media comments reveals that even though swearing is unpleasant to read, it is linked to greater honesty (Feldman et al. 2017). Briefly put, it appears that the more uncivil the language, the more truthful the message. Considering this, Nolan's take on Gawker commenters is not only more generous compared to that voiced by Pudelek's editor, but it is also confirmed in academic findings. The author explains,

> "I think we did have a lot of smart people (…) who must have been extremely bored at work, because they spent an insane amount of time leaving Gawker comments, which seems annoying when it's happening. But then you look back, it's better than other sites where there's no comments, and you just shout into a void."

Ashley Feinberg goes further, adopting a more provocative stance towards heated Gawker comments, and suggests a troll-like co-dependency between the writer and the commenters: "There's a section of [the comments] that is all just people angry and trolling (…). I like that a lot, personally, because I figure if no one's mad then what's the point? (…) And so, if no one gets mad at me after I write, I feel like I didn't do it correctly." Rich Juzwiak echoes this sentiment, though not from the point of commenters' anger but their sincerity, which was constantly challenged in Gawker's sarcastic writing: "I think people are used to this earnest sensibility. And so much of the pop culture that I love walks that line of ambiguity that I'm happy, actually, that some people didn't get it." Feinberg's and Juzwiak's remarks point at the snarky attitude of Gawker that was expected of its writers but also at its communal nature, where writers occasionally engaged in conversation with the readers in the website's comments section – still a largely unique concept. After all, it was the only outlet to actively and openly interact with commenters on its own website, and it was a deliberate strategy based on Denton's belief that "continuous conversation without institutional barriers" with readers should be the future of journalism.

Several Pudelek journalists mentioned that they, too, sometimes converse with their readers. However, they engage with the commenters only on the online tabloid's Facebook profile which was created in 2013, and when they join the conversation the writers use the official Pudelek account to remain anonymous. Because of this, an interesting paradox has emerged between the attitudes voiced in the anonymous comments on the Pudelek website and those posted on the social medium where the commenters are potentially identifiable. Maciej*, who is responsible for managing the Facebook page highlights this contrast: on Pudelek, he says, "we have people who very often support us – of course there are always instances when you see a wave of hate, when they totally disagree with what we're writing – but very, very often (...) they agree in our pointing out the nonsense [of the elite]." However, on Pudelek's Facebook page the behavior of commenters can be very different. There, despite – or perhaps because of – lesser anonymity the commenters find it much easier to contradict Pudelek authors, for instance by undermining the outlet's pro-choice stance on women's rights. One such example the Pudelek journalist mentions is a commenter who writes, "I prefer to cook lunch for my husband" rather than protesting for abortion rights. (After the 2020 ruling of the Constitutional Tribunal, abortion has been all but banned in Poland, as it is available only in the case of serious risk to the woman's health or when the pregnancy is a result of rape or incest.) He points out that these generally anti-progressive voices mainly come from young people who, according to Facebook data, live in small towns. This, however, does not mean that such opinions are not voiced on the online tabloid's website as well but there, judging by the number of upvotes, they are far less popular. One reason for this difference may be that people who comment directly on Pudelek are only seen and engage with others who visit the website. In contrast, individuals who comment on Pudelek's Facebook profile might find the article by chance, for instance because a post mentioning it popped up in their news feed. Another factor is that the audience on Pudelek is different from the audience which views the Facebook comments. Whereas on the online tabloid's website people who see other readers' opinions go there intentionally for particular tabloid content, on the social medium people who make remarks on Pudelek's profile are also visible to other, not-necessarily-Pudelek-reading Facebook users, who are linked by "friendships" and by "following" the same Facebook pages. In addition, Facebook commenters are far less anonymous because the platform allows its users to see the activity of others if the posts are labeled as publicly visible. This means that Facebook users' opinions can be seen by other Pudelek profile followers as well as by their broader network, which may be less aligned with Pudelek's views than the anonymous commenters posting directly on the online tabloid's website. Importantly, on Pudelek's Facebook page users comment under their own names (even if fictitious)[13] and to a broader audience. In this context, Rösner and Krämer's (2016) findings on anonymity and language use in online comments are particularly worth noting. The scholars show that opinions which agree or disagree with articles written by journalists may be less dependent on the anonymity of the commenters than on the audience they are targeting. Indeed, the behaviors of Pudelek commenters on the online tabloid's website – targeting other website viewers – and on Facebook – targeting a wider network of the platform's users – seem to prove their point. Still, another vital feature of comments is gatekeeping. Though usually attributed to journalists, in the case of online comments gatekeeping takes the form of post-factum meaning making (Vos 2019). In online tabloids, it is not uncommon for the significance of a news piece and, equally importantly, of the emotional approach and moral values attributed to the topic, to be shaped and occasionally transformed not so much in the article as later, in the comments section. (Examples of such comments were analyzed in Chapter 2.) Perhaps this is why a recurring comment found under posts in all three online tabloids goes along the lines of "I come here for the comments."

Lastly, unlike Gawker and Pudelek, Mail Online does not engage in conversation with their readers directly on the web. A possible reason for this is that the UK online tabloid simply does not have to, as the numbers of its visitors exceed to other two severalfold. But perhaps it is also because Mail Online was crafted out of a physical paper, *Daily Mail*, founded at the end of the 19th century, while Gawker and Pudelek were born digital at the beginning of the 21st century, during the peak popularity of blogs, a format that is personal, diary-like, and conversational. Both Denton and Spiers had already been bloggers before they co-created Gawker. For bloggers and blog readers, interaction on these websites was what gave them their appeal, so it felt natural to take the format of author-commenter exchange to online tabloids.

2.3 *Journalists on Commenters*

Although online tabloids remain in a symbiotic bond with the commenters – the activity of the latter brings revenue for the former – journalists tend to see this affinity more as a love-hate relationship. Among the three outlets, Gawker writers offer the most favorable view of their online comments section: "I think we had a pretty above average intelligent group of commenters compared to

---

13 Facebook has been enforcing its real-name policy since the 2010s; see: https://www.facebook.com/help/112146705538576.

most places on the internet," Nolan admits. He then expands on the historical reasons for this:

> "I remember, way back in the very early days of Gawker, they [Gawker employees] actually sent out invites by email for people to be commenters – a really exclusive thing. And so, it started out as the commenters [being] this sort of exclusive club, and it's all 'we're so smart.' (...) And then, as the site got bigger, we got more and more commenters (...). Nick [Denton] has put a lot of effort, and the tech people (...) did all these redesigns and different systems to try to produce a good comments section, which is one of the hardest things to do on the internet. Because if you look at the vast majority of websites, their comments sections are horrible."

Gawker's Kinja content management system played a major part in maintaining a stimulating place for comments, which at least partly matched the tone of Gawker pieces, but Nolan emphasizes that human content moderation is key. He points at *The New York Times* as an example how this should be done: "The only place that really had good comments sections – you can look at *The New York Times* and they have decent comments. But they have people whose job it is to go through [the comments]. It's hard to produce a good comments section organically." However, considering that Gawker had far fewer resources to properly moderate comments, the website's writers found it was doing markedly well. In comparison, comments on other news sites are "either nonexistent, or they're complete, 99 percent garbage. So I think a lot of writers probably kind of hate the commenters," Nolan summarizes.

Pudelek journalists adopt a different approach to comments, focusing primarily on their role in boosting the site's popularity – rather than just revenue – which translates into the outlet's influence on what people know and discuss. For example, several journalists underscored the fact that the online tabloid was "the first mainstream outlet that wrote about issues such as ACTA," specifically the anti-ACTA protests that were held in Poland at the end of 2011. (The topic was discussed in Chapter 1.) Maciej* explains that the buzz generated in the comments section is a direct consequence of publishing pieces on "hot" political issues: "We will always write about things like these, and we will always reach people who don't think about them every day, as the comments show. (...) We point a finger at issues that should be paid attention to." Jagoda* adds,

"The topics that were the best in terms of clicks were those which allowed people to vent, to voice their hate because they either envied someone for having something, or they loathed someone, or they noticed that someone was dividing them. This was particularly the case of political topics, where we typically showed: this is the person who is dividing our society."

At the same time, the journalists acknowledge that Pudelek attracts many commenters simply because posting opinions on the website is easy and, unlike numerous other news and gossip websites, does not require creating an account. There is also the rare chance of Pudelek highlighting a comment. Every now and then, the editors publish user comments they like as Comment of the Day or Comment of the Week posts. Yet despite such efforts the number of comments has been declining from several thousand per post at the beginning of the 2010s to several hundred a couple of years later. This could be particularly noticed after the merger between Grupa o2 and Wirtualna Polska, which led to changes in both tone and staff of the online tabloid, including the departure of its co-founder and editor-in-chief, who had been largely responsible for Pudelek's distinct style. However, the falling numbers of comments can also be attributed to outside changes, particularly the fact that people increasingly choose to voice their opinions on social media, where they can be seen and interact with more people. Pudelek writers are aware of this but are confident about their outlet's influence. Tomasz*, also a journalist, points this out clearly:

"People whose pictures are on newspaper covers, who have power in this country, told me the following: 'Yes, I read [Pudelek] because you are a [web] portal that can't be ignored.' Everybody claims that no one reads [the online tabloid] but I can ask any person sitting here [a café in Warsaw] and they will tell me what was published on Pudelek yesterday."

The mass appeal of online tabloids is hard to ignore. Even if people claim to prefer hard news, they end up reading soft (or junk) news – an illustration of the "news gap" described by Boczkowski and Mitchelstein (2013). And then there are the comment-generating typos, which Pudelek articles are often filled with. Even though all my interviewees assured me that this is the result of the fast pace of work and too little editorial staff, a popular conspiracy theory found in the comments claims that the spelling and occasionally factual errors are intentional. Regardless of the reasons, the end result is a success: typos cause more (outraged) comments.

If Gawker writers adopted a tough-love attitude towards its commenters and Pudelek authors share mixed views on their commenting readers, Mail Online journalists are the least generous in their portrayal of online commenters. Bill* states candidly that they are "really shit," and adds that he avoids looking at readers' comments, because some of them are "outrageous." However, other journalists can be critical of the written matter they themselves produce. For example, Steven* says, "In a way, [at] the Mail Online, I think they're aware of how lowbrow, how stupid a lot of the content is, (...) although they're not embarrassed by that. That's what people read, that's fine." At the same time, he stresses that Mail Online content is "freed from an ideology about what's that about, and what's legitimate." Rather, "it just gives people what they want to read, and that's why it's successful." Thus, the writer confirms his colleagues' view on the online tabloid's reactive nature, which, in turn, is driven by audience attention. But who are these people who read Mail Online, according to its writers? "[M]ainly really young women," Gayle replies; "fairly self-righteous, I guess, middle class types" who are "fairly working class as well" and "obviously, very opinionated," Bill* adds. (The last characteristic can be easily attributed to all three online-tabloid commenters). John*, however, depicts Mail Online audience as "a young person who's sort of not from the left," and "probably someone who voted Tory, reluctantly, voted to leave the EU, but reluctantly, doesn't support gay marriage, doesn't support immigration, but doesn't think we should kick them [immigrants] out or anything." The same writer notes an interesting contrast between left-wing and right-wing-leaning young people, which is worth mentioning:

> "It's a very broad brush, but among young people, on the whole, the ones who are really politically passionate and committed are the ones on the left. The ones who are in the center and the right, I think, often (...) are a bit more unsure of what their political beliefs really are, and [are] a bit less committed."

If this is this case, it means that the online tabloid caters to young people who are more politically confused and less politically active. Still, Ian* puts emphasis not on political awareness but on gender: "Lots of women read it because it's easy, like it's the equivalent of men checking sport. (...) I don't think they would like it if it was too overly populist right-wing." In a similar vein, Gayle expands on the section of the outlet that predominantly caters to women, namely show-business:

"[W]e got the sense that we were kind of playing second fiddle to the showbiz team, which was a smaller team but, actually, I think, accounted for probably more traffic overall to their stories. (...) Whenever I see people reading the Mail Online on their phone on the tube or wherever, they're always looking at the showbiz stories, they're never looking at the news stories."

The mix of celebrity and gossip next to political content in online tabloids is not accidental and exists in a delicate balance, which can be viewed from two perspectives. Firstly, it can serve as a factor alleviating the "harder," more political topics. But because the distinctive tabloid writing and visual style is applied both to politicians and show-business personalities, secondly, political actors and complex political topics are made to fit the same entertaining, easy-reading mold, discussed in Chapter 2. Yet as Hersh (2020) writes convincingly, politics is not the same as a sports game to cheer on. Treating politics as a hobby which boils down to getting the news and venting about it, regardless of how emotionally engaging, mostly leads to further passivity. Thus, heated language used in online tabloids can be seen as a game of pretend hate, as in "hating" the opposing sports team, but it is difficult to tell at which point the animosity stops being playful and turns into openly hateful – another example of (not) kidding. According to the classic Thomas theorem, "If men define situations as real, they are real in their consequences" (Thomas and Thomas 1928, p. 572). Here, a situation described in a news piece is made real by the commenters as they either strengthen or redefine its original meaning, and the real consequences may be found in the comments' typically heightened emotions – and at the ballot box. Indeed, the journalists I talked to find that reader comments often cross the line from playfulness to hatefulness, and a survey conducted on Polish online commenters corroborates this notion (Dąbrowska-Cydzik 2019). Its findings reveal a remarkable paradox: while only one percent of online commenters intend to hurt readers with their remarks, 64 percent are certain other commenters do this on purpose. At the same time, 56 percent of online commenters post their thoughts to show outrage concerning the opinions or behaviors of others. Conversely, 39 percent hopeful commenters publish their remarks to change something for the better, thus engaging in a form of click activism. Despite the optimism of such commenters, Hersh argues that in reality they merely engage in "political hobbyism," which requires significant emotional input but offers little efficacy.

For reasons both ideological and financial political coverage plays an important role in Pudelek, Mail Online, and Gawker. This also tells them apart from many other gossip outlets, which only offer show-business and human-interest stories. At Mail Online, born out of the paper daily, the news section with political reporting has been treated as an extension of the print paper albeit with a more liberal bent (which will be discussed later). In the case of Gawker, Spiers explains that the US outlet started out as a New York media-industry gossip site. However, political coverage that came later proved successful in attracting a bigger national – and international – audience. Finally, at Pudelek the moment of political awakening came during the 2011 anti-ACTA protests. Many of the journalists I talked to emphasize that reporting on this EU bill proposal and presenting an unequivocally negative opinion about it, proved a political turning point for the website. After this, politics became Pudelek's regular topic of interest. Its writers estimate that around one third of the stories published on the website concern politics but, in contrast to the daily political coverage served at Gawker and Mail Online, on Pudelek the frequency of such news is more dependent on the political calendar. For example, an increase of political pieces can be noticed during election season. Moreover, there is an important financial aspect in publishing political stories because they generate lots of comments which bring revenue, even if some readers claim to despise political news. (They occasionally voice their discontent, such as the disgruntled commenter who wrote, "This is a gossip site, I come here to read about celebrities and not some important topics!") Still, Pudelek writers are divided on the reasons for publishing political content on the website. Some, as Tomasz*, favor a more reactive approach, akin to Mail Online:

> "It's not a question of us being pro- or anti-[government] because this is not our task. We deal with what fires people up. If they are fired up by Donald Tusk, we write about Donald Tusk. If they are fired up by Jarosław Kaczyński, we write about Jarosław Kaczyński. If they are fired up by Obama, we write about Obama. If they are fired up (...) by Donald Trump, we write about Donald Trump. It's only about what is trending on the internet, what is a hot topic – on Pudelek, too, because Pudelek covers hot topics."

But then the journalist adds a perspective that is less traffic-oriented and more concerned with Polish public life. The links between politics and show-business, as he somewhat reluctantly admits, should not be overlooked:

> "[W]e are being told who is cool and who is not cool, and this polarization influences the comments, because in the comments people can argue in a meaningful way, or not. Politics is a part of our life, and you can't ignore it completely, although personally I would like to be able to ignore

it. But you can't if you see Doda [a Polish popstar] being photographed with Antoni Macierewicz,[14] with (...) Kaczyński, with [PiS's slogan] 'Good Change'."

While the reactive, trending-topic-focused approach to politics certainly drives attention, it is contradicted by other articles on Pudelek in which journalists reveal their own political views. These range from the first anti-ACTA article written by Pudelek's then editor-in-chief to more recent pro-LGBT+ and pro-women's rights pieces. On the one hand, this divergence of opinions on the reasons for publishing such content in the online tabloid – reactive to the needs of the audience versus educational – suggests a degree of editorial freedom on the part of the writers. On the other hand, it shows that Pudelek is stuck somewhere between Mail Online-style opportunism, at least as it is labeled by its own journalists, and Gawker-style finger-pointing. Still, it is worth remembering that each of these three approaches, which in their extreme forms may be (reductively) described as reactive (Mail Online), educational (Pudelek), and uncovering (Gawker), is implemented to attract the audience. Obviously, none of these approaches are neutral. Revealing secrets is a delicate endeavor, in which issues such as whom the secret concerns and who can be impacted need to considered. But the educational tone is, too, employed to instruct about value-laden issues the journalists find important, be it LGBT+ rights or the fact that politicians often are ridiculous, rather than, for example, focusing on Catholic values. Thirdly, the reactive approach is adopted in response to something or someone, in this case to audience expectations, so that the readers keep coming back for more, including the possibility of venting in the comments. It is also worth bearing in mind that these three approaches are not adopted in a normative void but in regard to audience assumptions about the outlet's character. After all, journalists from Gawker, Pudelek, and Mail Online all stress that many of their readers click on their websites directly, which means they do not find themselves there by accident. Thus, one of the key tasks of these online tabloids is to not fall out of their perceived character, and if an infrequent change of tone occurs it has to be done in a way that does not alienate more readers than it attracts.

2.4   *Commenters on Journalists*

If journalists are in a love-hate relationship with the commenters, the commenters love them back even less. They mercilessly point out factual errors

---

14   See: footnote 43 in Chapter 2.

(especially on Gawker) and question the writers' credentials (especially on Pudelek). As evidenced by Maciej*, they do not remain unnoticed. He complains about being criticized by the commenters for showing the flaws of people in public view:

> "For example, people always ask in the comments: 'And who are you? Show yourselves!' as [if they were saying], 'you're judging!' (...) We don't have an inferiority complex, and we are not ashamed of anything. But we took on this role, we kind of settled ourselves in it."

Elsewhere, the journalist refers to the criticisms concerning errors in the published pieces and, consequently, assumptions about the poor education of Pudelek's writers:

> "I am always very annoyed by comments which state that an intern must have written this nonsense, these mistakes. 'Who is writing there?,' 'You can't call this a journalist!' This type of stuff. I don't reply, of course, because there is no point in taking part in such discussions. But a month ago a colleague of ours received her doctorate, another is an academic lecturer, and still another one, who recently left for a more normal job, is also pursuing a doctoral degree."

The journalists I talked to at Pudelek were the most highly educated group of the three outlets. According to Dorota*, another writer at the Polish outlet, there was a period during which among a staff of six, two members were PhDs and two were pursuing doctoral degrees. (Some of the journalists used the work at the online tabloid as a source for their own academic research.) In contrast to Gawker and Mail Online, at Pudelek the possibility of working remotely, at least until the merger between Grupa o2 and Wirtualna Polska, made it easier for the journalists to engage in other projects, including pursuing academic degrees.

The criticism of commenters, however harsh, does not mean that readers shun away from delivering scoops – an activity that may be called online-tabloid reader whistleblowing. Journalists from all three outlets confirm that they work with material provided by readers; in fact, some Gawker writers acknowledge that the best scoops they got came from reader tips. Occasionally, journalists find useful trails in the comments, for instance when a commenter corrects the article's author who misidentified a person in a photo included in the piece. One of the editors admits that the commenters are usually right. Cezary*, also a Pudelek writer, praises the commenters' wit in creating mocking nicknames for people described in the articles, which are sometimes picked up by the writers in subsequent pieces. Pudelek also has a clickable tongue-in-cheek "send tip" sign on the top of the page which anyone can use. As for Gawker, the writers admit that it was not unusual for them to follow trails based on the scoops they received in their email boxes. For example, Feinberg explains: "I'd gotten good tips from commenters. Sometimes commenters would [say], 'I worked at this place,' just offhand. 'Well, can you shoot me an email? I'd like to ask about that.' And I've gotten really good stuff from there." Nolan adds some detail on the matter: "People can send you internal documents, people can forward you emails that other people send. And people have their own motives. But 'is it true?' is the base standard." Mail Online authors, too, confirm that they occasionally work with material sent by readers, particularly photos and videos, which are usually taken using mobile phones. However, most of the material in the British online tabloid comes from wires, and the writers spend their days reworking them into pieces fit for Mail Online. Yet, once in a while online tabloid readers manage to get their findings into the journalistic pieces, above the anonymous comments sections – both literally and symbolically.

Even so, Mail Online writers claim not to interact with the commenters. When Pudelek writers interact with them, they do it anonymously on the outlet's Facebook page or by posting de facto comments as separate posts, in a form of appreciation. In contrast, on Gawker exchanges between writers and readers were open and engaging; this interactive approach was deliberate, envisioned from the start by Denton. In "Employee of the Month," a talk show held at Joe's Pub in New York in October 2016[15] – two months after Gawker folded – Denton explained his vision behind the conversational quality of Gawker to the show's host, Catie Lazarus:

> "I like the idea that if you tell a story, that you should be answering questions about it or that there should be possibility for further discussion, that my writers and readers can be in a constant, constant conversation. And the comments on the Gawker sites were always my real passion. I liked the idea of writers going in and talking with readers. I didn't [want] what we see right now, which [are] the comment zones or forums like Reddit. [They] are just seen – and largely are – just cesspools, just full of hate and trolls, and just the worst of current society. (...) [A] symposium

---

15   For an audio recording of the conversation, see: https://itunes.apple.com/us/podcast/employee-of-the-month/id487274151?mt=2&i=1000377715549.

between writers and readers, a party in which writers and readers can participate together – that's always been my dream."

This principle, simple yet difficult to carry out, was nonetheless put into practice by Gawker writers. Nolan describes the process in a straightforward manner:

> "If you write something, you can go into the comments section, you can (…) promote comments that are good, you can interact with the people if you want to try to start the conversation. So, you can, if you're the writer, make a little bit of effort to promote the good comments and (…) get rid of the bad comments – you can have a really good comments section. It's a time-consuming thing, people don't always want to do that."

He then sums up the writer-commenter relationship on Gawker: "I think commenters get on people's nerves a lot, [but] overall, especially when we died they weren't so bad, they were alright." Indeed, after Gawker folded at the end of August 2016, many of the comments posted on other Gawker Media websites voiced support for the journalists and the site itself. What's more, although for years the online tabloid had been getting less than stellar press, frequently accused of meanness, after it closed it was all but redeemed. *The New York Times*, *The New Yorker*, *The Atlantic*, *Vanity Fair*, *Wired*,[16] and numerous other major outlets offered a more sympathetic stance towards the online tabloid once it was no longer there. The reason was not that Gawker's content suddenly gained value in the eyes of these influential mainstream outlets but how it had been brought down by a single very wealthy man. Gawker's bankruptcy by the hand of Peter Thiel became a clear warning that this could happen to other media in the United States.

3 Newsroom Agendas

Gawker, Mail Online, and Pudelek were launched as services which rewrote stories from wires and added their own commentary. According to the journalists, it is still mainly a "desk-led" operation. Thus, on any given day, the writing begins with reading what has been already published in other media outlets

---

16   See: Chen 2016; Manjoo 2016; Manthorpe 2018; Margolick 2016; Thompson 2018; Watson 2019.

and checking the news received from wires. Next, stories are creatively rewritten – "lifted" from other sources, as one Mail Online writer puts it – or in some cases developed by the journalists themselves, who are expected to publish around six stories a day. Writers at Gawker and Pudelek, specifically those more senior, are typically allowed to publish what they want. Authors who write for Mail Online are directed by the editors but, in contrast to the *Daily Mail* paper, they usually do not get corrections from the editors before publication. The reason for this is simple: speed. The online rush to get the news out first gives writers more freedom but at the cost of little time. Such daily decisions take place in the distinct setup of a newsroom – physical or remote, but also organizational, and symbolic – occupied by individuals engaged in the journalistic profession within which they perform particular roles (Hanitzsch and Örnebring 2019). These in turn inform their work routines and practices, such as gatekeeping and gatewatching news – while the former concerns the selection of information for publication, the latter concerns monitoring and amplifying news already published elsewhere (see: Bruns 2011; Shoemaker and Vos 2009; Vos 2019; Westlund and Ekström 2019). (This, too, will be expanded on later in this chapter.) All these day-to-day activities are immersed in the collective ideals shared within the profession, such as objectivity, truthfulness, and public interest (Tandoc and Duffy 2019). Like other members of the trade, online tabloid journalists largely follow these beliefs, even if in some cases they are taken to the extreme. For example, based on the principle of "the public deserving to know," Gawker authors focus on revealing secrets above anything else. In this context, "above anything else" frequently means directing people's emotions – negative more often than positive – towards people who did something they had rather kept hidden, regardless of the consequences of such disclosures. However, online-tabloid journalists are not the only ones who "disregard the implications of the news," as Gans points out in his influential book, *Deciding what's news* (2004, p. 183); hard-news writers do this as well, even if in the name of objectivity rather than entertainment. Finally, the fact that the profession's general ideals are shared by its online tabloid subset is not particularly shocking if we take into account that these writers, too, switch media they work for, occasionally changing tabloids for broadsheets, and navigating between entertainment and opinion media. These journalistic perceptions and activities will be explored in the next sections.

3.1 Newsworthiness and Traffic

Four decades ago, in his study on news in the United States Gans (2004) presented four theories of story selection: journalist-centered, organization-centered, event-centered, and technology-centered. While today all still remain relevant, in the context of online tabloids – and online news in general – the fourth approach strikes as exceptionally important. Thus, given the importance of technology, when one asks what is worthy of being "fit to print" at Gawker, Mail Online, and Pudelek, the shortest answer is not so much a great piece of opinion writing on a major event but: a photo. An eye-catching image is key, and it should be supported by a strong headline, followed by the copy. This is why politicians looking odd or doing unusual things are solid online-tabloid choices, especially if they are embroiled in a scandal or if the photo can get a scandalous-sounding caption. According to Ian*, what matters is "just speed and lots of pictures, you know. You gotta have catchy headlines and [a] good picture, otherwise nobody's reading it."

A good online tabloid piece needs to be visually strong, which means the photos not only serve the role of magnet but also of visual evidence. In consequence, stories not accompanied by photos are virtually nonexistent. Apart from attracting the eye, photographs provide the gist of the fact – this happened! – in case the writing is not convincing enough to stand on its own.[17] It does not hurt for a story to be polarizing, for example by presenting a very strong point of view, because this generates reader comments and leads to more clicks. Indeed, political topics serve this aim particularly well. In terms of Pudelek's political coverage, some writers go so far as to say that editorial decisions are fundamentally populist, in that the outlet offers what the audience wants to read. Similarly to Mail Online's "reactiveness," this implies that if someone "talks nicely [and] is nice, the person is written about in a nice manner. If someone is inconsistent and hypocritical, a story about this follows," Paweł* explains. Yet populism might also mean providing topics people like to argue about. Cezary* describes Poland's First Lady, Agata Duda as solid material for such pieces:

> "We want people to be outraged. If Agata Duda is known among Pudelek readers – and sections of society in general – as distant, that she doesn't speak up, that in truth she is something of a figurehead, I think we write about her to aggravate the readers a bit and to point out that she pretty much is a figurehead."

The journalist suspects that links to Pudelek's political pieces are shared on right-wing and other political fan pages, and that their users come back to

---

17   The popularity of the phrase "Pics or it didn't happen," coined on the internet, is also an example of the importance laid on photographic evidence.

Pudelek to "troll" in the comments section. But this, too, is good for business. Creating pieces for readers to argue about on the screen is an online development in political news-making, which, according to Cook (2005), is centered on emphasizing conflict.[18] If the idea is not new, on the internet it is enhanced: in contrast to one-directional media such as television and newspapers, on websites the conflict narrative seamlessly trickles down from the news articles to the comments section.

Another feature specific for online-tabloid writing that attracts reader attention is mentioned by Bill* from Mail Online. He states plainly that these are "things which are generally accepted as weird." It can be a new historical finding that goes against set ideas or a mysterious crime story, but it can also reveal politicians doing peculiar things, for instance Nigel Farage going to dinner with his son instead of participating in the final EU referendum debate.[19] Gawker's Denton lays out the matter in even more basic terms: "I have a simple editorial litmus test, which is: is it true, and is it interesting?"[20] However, this begs the question: for whom is it supposed to be interesting? Nolan answers with a journalist-centric perspective: "The honest definition of newsworthy is what journalists judge to be newsworthy;" this self-serving tautology is widely adopted within the profession. Still, in an influential study Golding and Elliott (1979) deconstruct newsworthiness as a more specific set of eleven criteria which journalists implicitly employ when deciding whether an event is indeed worthy of becoming the news. Among them are drama, visual attractiveness, entertainment, importance, and size referring to the number of people involved and/or their popularity – all clearly noticeable in online-tabloid writing.[21] Nonetheless, newsworthiness is not all, and Nolan stresses that the job of journalists is a balancing act between wanting to tell everyone about "crazy shit" received in tips and questioning whether, aside from being alluring, they have "a redeeming hook" that would justify the publication. Such conflict of interest often occurs when readers submit their accounts concerning private sexual behaviors of public persons. If the tip describes sexual harassment, Nolan argues, the story is newsworthy. Alas, one such story published in July 2015, titled "Condé Nast's CFO Tried To Pay $2,500 for a Night With a Gay Porn

---

18 See also: Harcup and O'Neill 2017; Philips 2015.
19 This news story was discussed in Chapter 2.
20 The quote is from an interview conducted in June 2015. See archived version: https://web.archive.org/web/20150613103404/http://www.capitalnewyork.com/article/media/2015/06/8570075/gawker-fight-its-life-hulk-hogan-sex-tape-suit.
21 See also: Gans 2004; Harcup and O'Neill 2017; O'Neill and Harcup 2019.

Star"[22] did not go well. Numerous Gawker readers sided with journalists from other media outlets in criticizing Gawker for publicly outing a private individual, who was a married man with children.[23] As a result of the widespread condemnation, the piece was deleted by Denton the next day. This was the first instance of taking down a post on Gawker, and the website's creator argued that the times have changed since Gawker's beginnings, hence the removal:

> "The story involves extortion, illegality and reckless behavior, sufficient justification at least in tabloid news terms. The account was true and well-reported. It concerns a senior business executive at one of the most powerful media companies on the planet. In the early days of the internet, that would have been enough. 'We put truths on the internet.' (...) But the media environment has changed, our readers have changed, and I have changed. (...) I believe this public mood reflects a growing recognition that we all have secrets, and they are not all equally worthy of exposure. I can't defend yesterday's story as I can our coverage of Bill O'Reilly, Hillary Clinton or Hulk Hogan. (...) The point of this story was not in my view sufficient to offset the embarrassment to the subject and his family."[24]

At that time Denton could not have known that the coverage of Hulk Hogan would turn out to be what brought Gawker down in court. Meanwhile, the Condé Nast story led to a change in Gawker's editorial lead. Max Read left after a disagreement with Denton about deleting the piece, and he was replaced by Alex Pareene, a "big politics guy" according to Nolan. The journalist found this hire a safe editorial choice after the crisis; it was also a sensible one in terms of traffic given the upcoming US election campaign.

Undeniably, another key factor for internet outlets is traffic. It indicates whether an online story becomes news – whether it is read, commented on, and shared. Papers rely on purchased ads and subscriptions which, at least in theory, give them the financial freedom to also publish pieces that are less attention-grabbing than others but considered important by the editors. Instead, online tabloids are dependent on live audience clicks, and because

---

22 The original post was deleted; see archived version: https://web.archive.org/web/2015071
7013027/gawker.com/conde-nasts-cfo-tried-to-pay-2-500-for-a-night-with-a-1718364339.
23 See e.g.: Huffington Post (Arana 2015); *USA Today* (Mandaro 2015); and *Washington Post* (Wemple 2015).
24 See archived version of Denton's post: https://web.archive.org/web/20150717213840/http:
//nick.kinja.com/taking-a-post-down-1718581684.

journalists are very much aware of this they make an effort to please the readers. Mail Online's Steven* states matter-of-factly, "That's the name of the game, really. You're trying to provide something for people to read, not trying to write for nobody to read it, right?" Gawker, for that matter, was so metrics-driven and fixated on attracting new visitors that the company installed a live online board which ranked writers generating the most unique visitors in the previous month. Petre (2015), a journalism scholar who studies the influence of metrics on newsrooms, found that this not only led to more competition in the office but steered writers "to go with what works, or had proven to work in the past" (p. 21). This boiled down to publishing content such as "unhinged" letters, cute kids, and animals. In addition, because of the importance of metrics which at Gawker rewarded pieces that were short and up-to-the-minute, journalists tended to write more often at the cost of putting off lengthier, more time-consuming pieces. However, despite all the shortcomings of the metrics-centered approach, the irony is that as long as the authors get the numbers right, they enjoy far more independence in choosing their own topics compared to legacy media. Nolan sums this up frankly: "I've been here a long time, I know everybody, and they let me write what I want. You can only ask for so much in journalism." Nevertheless, this reveals a striking paradox in editorial autonomy across hard and soft news: the freedom to write something that does not generate a lot of traffic but is dependent on the editor's approval is contrasted with the freedom to write whatever the author is interested in but having to generate significant traffic. Still, when I interviewed Gawker writers in 2016, they claimed to not feel the pressure of the leaderboard, perhaps because they started working there under a different, less traffic-oriented editor. For example, Feinberg explains, "When A.J. [Daulerio] was editing [Gawker] there was a lot of pressure to get traffic." But when she started working at Gawker in 2015,[25] "the only pressure I felt to get more traffic was self-motivated. There was never any sort of mandate that we have to get this many uniques [unique hits]. (...) When Tommy Craggs[26] became the executive editor [in 2014], his mandate was that [we] focus more on doing good work and 'don't work on traffic right now, that will figure itself out.'" This notion is echoed by Brendan O'Connor, who expands on the topic of metrics:

---

25 Before switching to Gawker, from 2012 until 2015 Feinberg worked at Gizmodo, a technology-focused Gawker Media sister site.
26 Tommy Craggs left Gawker together with the editor-in-chief Max Read after Denton deleted an article about the Condé Nast CFO.

> "There was definitely a period of time before I joined [Gawker], where there was an emphasis on cultivating as much traffic as possible by any means possible. I mean, there is still a big board that shows (…) the most popular posts at any given moment. But (…) there are no consequences associated with that. (…) If as a staff you do good traffic, you publish a few big scoops or a really lively essay, or something like that, then (…) everybody gets a specific [monthly] bonus."

While Gawker's leaderboard and its influence on the outlet's writers was a matter of discussion in other media outlets (see e.g.: Mullin 2015; Phelps 2012, it was certainly not the only newsroom interested in traffic. Martin Clarke, Mail Online's famous (now former) editor-in-chief, too, has been very much a metrics person. "Martin Clarke is conservative, as is Paul Dacre,"[27] Ian* states, "but I think he's mostly public about numbers, clicks and hits. (…) And what we were trying to do was be sort of consumer-led and focused on ordinary people." This *modus operandi* has been key for the online outlet because, according to the journalist, Mail Online audience is younger, more "populist conservative" in comparison to the "tribally conservative" readers of the paper. Other writers emphasize that this difference has been reflected in online content, and the growing numbers of readers show that this more populist, audience-reactive approach is effective. Abundant reader comments make up the other end of this success as they are important traffic generators, but they are difficult to handle. An editor responsible for moderating Mail Online's comments section tells me he spent six months sifting through around a million comments, many of which were hateful and racist. It was "a numbing task," he summarizes. At Pudelek, too, "resentment" towards politicians and other public figures that surfaces in the journalistic pieces is reactive and for the most part aimed at generating traffic. Such content is also the consequence of monitoring audience attitudes, which show up first in the readers' comments. Maciej* declares, alluding both to celebrities and politicians, "no one in their right mind should read comments about themselves." He admits that some comments are deliberately deleted from the website: "those that are very problematic for the [online] service, for example such comments that could make someone sue us. We do this but it gives us no pleasure." In sum, if at Gawker authors could write anything as long as they generated traffic, and at Mail Online journalists walk a fine line between factual reporting and conservative bias, the strategy

---

27 Paul Dacre was the editor-in-chief of the *Daily Mail* paper from 1998 until 2018. He is now the editor-in-chief of DMG Media, a holding company for Associated Newspapers, the owner of *Daily Mail* and Mail Online, among others.

of attracting audiences to the Polish outlet has a still different touch: brazen anti-elitism. In contrast to the UK and US outlets, at Pudelek this broad approach against people in power has been not so much politically based as considered a means to keep readers coming. Similarly, the increasing focus on Polish celebrities in connection with politics has been a way for the outlet to attract more users. This strategy has proven effective to such an extent that, as Maciej* stresses, "A really big section of our readers gets knowledge about the world from Pudelek. They click on Pudelek first, then they go to WP or Onet, or Gazeta."[28] He provides additional details on the most popular times during the day for readers to click on Pudelek: "It peaks around eight or nine [in the morning], then in the evening around nine or ten. There is also a smaller peak during lunchtime." The writer concludes: "If they're not doing anything work related, they're relaxing" – with Pudelek. What's more, Paweł* highlights readers' evening habits: "People sitting in bed with their laptops and reading Pudelek made the biggest numbers throughout the day, apart from mornings." Next to discussing people's daily schedules of Pudelek browsing, other journalists describe a typical Pudelek reader: a female office worker in her thirties, with disposable income. This strongly influences content, such as entertainment and fashion. But, as the numbers of comments and comment votes show, the audience clearly loves (to hate) political topics as well. All of this is good news for business.

3.2 Newsroom Routines

In discussing everyday newsroom tasks, Shoemaker and Reese (1996) provide a useful definition of routines in journalism, namely "those patterned, routinized, repeated practices and forms that media workers use to do their jobs" (p. 105). At Gawker, Mail Online, and Pudelek writing a story might begin with reading information sent by wires, checking news published in other outlets, or looking at already trending news in the online tabloid itself. Elizabeth Spiers emphasizes that "in a place like Gawker in particular, where the writers are allowed to go decide what they're gonna go hunting for, there is a site lead on every site and there are some broad editorial directions." She then adds, "The voices are so strongly articulated on Gawker. You could almost take off the bylines and you would be able to recognize a Hamilton [Nolan] story." Mail Online, however, is almost the opposite of Gawker, with a strong top-down

---

28 Wp.pl (Wirtualna Polska, the owner of Pudelek), Onet.pl and Gazeta.pl are among the most popular online news portals in Poland.

hierarchy in which writers are the very bottom. Steven* provides some more detail on the organization of work at the British outlet:

> "The setup of the Mail Online is such that you have a group of journalists who are in the office, working from the office, repackaging information from the wires, and from other outlets, occasionally, making a phone call here and there, sometimes sending an agency reporter [to a] house to knock the door. But on the whole it's time in the office."

Although Mail Online journalists may pitch ideas to their editors, few of them are used because they have to go through a vetting process from the bottom up. In contrast, ideas sent from the top are developed immediately. "It tends to be you're told where to go and what to do," Steven* sums up. Gayle explains that topics taken from wires or other outlets, including those trending on social media (but also, for instance, Drudge Report) were consulted by the editors with Martin Clarke, whose own interests were "almost a hundred percent search-engine led." The journalist describes the process: after the idea was accepted, the editors took "a brief blank to the wire copy and they'd decide what they wanted the story to be. So they'd actually write a headline for the story before the reporter had written the story." The headline is important not just because it is the first thing – next to the photo – that a viewer sees on the website, but because it is supposed to include a value judgement. It provides direction how a particular piece of information should be treated in terms of good and evil, justice and injustice. "There's a moral stance in every single story that's published on the site," Gayle emphasizes. Several other writers add that home news tends to be significantly more editorialized than foreign news, where they have slightly more independence. The possible reason for this may be that local news is more directly related to readers' lives and so, according to the editors, moral judgment there is more vital than in distant topics with no palpable relevance to the audience's everyday. At the same time, it is not just the editorializing that is responsible for the tone of Mail Online articles. Wire agencies, too, try to fit in the Mail Online mold and tend to "hype" stories that are tailored for the outlet, "because they know that a certain kind of story will get attention from Mail Online editors," Gayle argues. Such typically attention-grabbing pieces may focus, for example, on illegal immigrants or people misusing benefits.

Pudelek is a very different story from Mail Online, which grew out of a well-established paper and relied on its organizational experience, though one may find some similarities with Gawker, especially in the two online tabloid's beginnings. Still, at Pudelek for many years the organization of work reflected the Polish post-1989 bootstrap entrepreneurial spirit, which translated into long work hours and barely-there management; this changed after the 2014 Grupa o2 merger with Wirtualna Polska. Before corporate changes were introduced, Pudelek writers and editors were scheduled to work seven days a week including holidays, with a day's break every four or five days, and no paid leave. At the same time, the entire staff was dispersed in different cities in Poland and worked remotely, relying on Tlen ("oxygen" in Polish), an instant messaging service, for work communication.[29] (In comparison, Slack was used at Gawker but people could also physically see each other at the Manhattan office.) This setup additionally secured the anonymity of the writers, who had little incentive to attend show-business or political events, typically held in Warsaw, during which they could be identified. An interesting, and largely unanticipated, consequence of this obscurity was that online commenters began to treat "the poodle" as a distinct personality. Cezary* observes with amazement,

> "I think that Pudelek's anonymity makes the [online] service one of the few in Poland, or even in the world, which people address [directly], 'Poodle'. As if it were a strange entity, as if there weren't people like me but some sort of 'Poodle' on the other side of the computer screen. When we write we try to do this using our own voices, to show some human emotions. But at the same time we want to be part of this immense 'Poodle' being, so that they [the stories] remain Pudelek."

Because the original editor-in-chief, who was also the cofounder of Pudelek, was hands-off in terms of organizing work, the authors and editors organized themselves instead. They coordinated work shifts and secured substitutes if someone needed to take time off. Referring to Frédéric Laloux's (2014) theory of self-management in organizations, Paweł* describes this setup, also in the broader context of competition among Polish online portals:

> "[The editor-in-chief] didn't know who he would work with, we did. We had our work shifts divided. We simply did all management at the grassroots level, like some teal organization. (...) We managed this mechanism perfectly, we really did. Everyone [else] (...) had their own [web] portals normally staffed, but it was total guerilla here – which was also supposed to get results equal to the entire competition."

---

29   Tlen and Pudelek were both owned by o2.pl.

And, as in many cases of Poland's bootstrap entrepreneurship, it worked. Pudelek became the top celebrity and gossip site, competing only with Plotek.pl, which is owned by a major online portal, Gazeta.pl.

Typically, Pudelek's newsroom comprises around ten to fifteen people; a similar number of staff worked at Gawker. Mail Online is a much bigger operation, though, with a noticeable turnover. One of Mail Online journalists confessed he saw people quit after a single day. As for Pudelek, its writers start their day by going through the news published elsewhere earlier in the morning, including Mail Online, and social media accounts of famous people, from social-media influencers to politicians. At the beginning, Pudelek's main column in the center of the page was managed by the original editor-in-chief, while the smaller side columns were largely left to the journalists. Yet after the corporate transformation, managing the main column became the task of newly-hired publishers, and some authors argue that because of this the outlet has lost its unique voice. Still, on a regular day, after the topics are accepted, journalists write their pieces and add agency photos. They describe the process as straightforward, although ease comes with experience – finding stories fit for Pudelek becomes an "intuitive" routine. In their own opinion, much of the authors' work boils down to editorializing, that is inserting opinions to materials sourced from elsewhere. For example, Alicja* says, "The strength of Pudelek is that you can read between the lines. When you have an interview with someone somewhere, you can always pick a quote, write around it." Nonetheless, as in the case of Gawker, an intuitive understanding of the medium may lead to serious mistakes. One such example is a, now edited, Pudelek gallery from 2016 in which different US presidents were compared to animals. Barack Obama, the President at the time, was juxtaposed with a monkey.[30] The post did not go well with the readers. Popular comments published under the piece ranged from accusations of flat-out racism to jokes that Pudelek should consider itself lucky for being based in Poland, because it would not survive a trial in the United States. One writer tells me that this was a case of mindless copy-pasting of a similar gallery published in one of the many English-language outlets Pudelek writers are expected to check for inspiration. Alicja*, however, offers a different explanation of the error:

> "[The gallery] was made by a young girl and it hadn't occurred to her what she had done. (…) I told her that the first thing someone thinks when they

---

30　See archived version of the story, with the Obama-monkey photo pair already deleted: https://web.archive.org/web/20161112133249/http://www.pudelek.pl/artykul/100233/zwierzaki_ktore_wygladaja_jak_prezydenci_usa_zdjecia/.

see something like this from the outside is 'Jesus, racists!' I was talking to her and I thought she would cry. She had been so involved in making this news piece, she thought it was a great pair. (...) She was fresh, she didn't have much journalistic experience (...) but she had always dreamt of working here."

Another mistake described by the journalist was of a different kind, this time resulting not in reader outrage but potentially hurting the company's advertising profits. She recalls an incident when the website had to delete a post which made fun of a tone-deaf advertisement. The act of self-censorship concerned an article mocking a quick loan commercial made for Orange, a major mobile company. In the ad, a television personality encouraged people to take out a loan from Orange for 1000 złoty (around 330 dollars at the time), a hefty sum for most people in Poland, to buy a sweatshirt. Offended by Pudelek's publication, Orange threatened to pull ads from all websites owned by Wirtualna Polska, and the online tabloid, reluctantly, removed the piece. Still, a perfect illustration of the so-called Streisand effect, where the more someone tries to hide something the more popular it becomes, even without Pudelek's ridiculing post the campaign was widely criticized on the media, and Orange quickly pulled the ad (Business Insider Polska 2017). The effect was nonetheless chilling, and the journalists have since become more careful whose toes they step on. Though editorial and advertising departments are kept separate, Pudelek writers confirm they are prone to self-censorship because of the fear of losing advertisers (see: Westlund and Ekström 2019). Yet even given these constraints, journalists writing in other, particularly print media are sometimes jealous of Pudelek's relative freedom. One of them, who later moved to Pudelek, explains: "We always laughed that we are a bit envious of those [journalists] at Pudelek because they can write what we can't, what we really know." However, similarly to Mail Online, this freedom is also tied to speed. Online journalists do not so much have the liberty to write more if they want to – they have to write more. According to the generally accepted belief, the internet never sleeps and the writers are expected to file, on average, between five to eight stories a day. This is way above the submission rate in slower-paced, offline-based papers. Thus, when compared to authors writing for paper outlets, the job of an online journalist appears almost never-ending. Mail Online's Steven* sums this up bitterly:

"I'm still quite envious of my colleagues because the people who are on the paper basically stand around all day going to where the story's happening, doing a few interviews. But then towards deadline they text that back, to put everything everybody's reported, to look at what they've got, and write it up with the benefit of perspective. (…) Then after deadline that evening, they can go out and get drunk. And if anything happens (…) you know deadline is the next day. Whereas from the online point of view, (…) my colleagues [in the paper] file once a day, I might file five, ten, fifteen, twenty times a day with different developing lines, different news stories. And then in the evening if something happens I have to go get the newest [update] and file all that again."

Still, the price to pay for the slower speed is the declining number of sold print issues across the news industry. In contrast, online outlets are doing increasingly well at least in traffic, if not in terms of the journalists' workload.

3.3 Newsroom Changes

The fast pace of work is the daily drill of journalists working in online outlets, but it is not the only aspect of the news-work reality they have to take into account. In all three online tabloids, the everyday tasks writers describe are carried out in work environments that are in flux, sometimes radical. For instance, Pudelek journalists frequently mention the organizational chaos they had to contain themselves; this changed after the company merger and the introduction of more corporate-style organization in the newsroom. Another major corporate change was firing Pudelek's original editor-in-chief, which left the outlet's staff in shock since they valued his leadership, even if they describe the relationship with their main editor as difficult. The US online tabloid, after an impressive rise, fell from its online-tabloid glory because of the Hulk Hogan defamation lawsuit that was secretly financed by Peter Thiel. According to many, the billionaire entrepreneur succeeded in taking the website down as an act of personal vendetta (which was discussed in detail in Chapter 2). In the third case, namely Mail Online, changes have been more subtle. Journalists explain that for the most part they came as a result of staff adjustments. At the beginning, the online side project of the *Daily Mail* paper was made by outsiders who, on the one hand, were less visibly ideological and, on the other hand, were more experienced. This, they point out, was necessary to convince Westminster insiders to start talking to the online arm of the not much liked tabloid. Eventually, with employee changes and the editor-in-chief's, Martin Clarke's "bollocking sessions" of screaming and cursing at his editors, the outlet grew to be more in tune with the print operation.[31] The election campaign

---

31 Adrian Addison (2017) vividly describes Martin Clarke's "bollocking" in *Mail men: The unauthorised story of The Daily Mail*.

coverage analyzed in the previous chapter was published in the three online tabloids as these changes were taking place, and working there during these transformations set an important context for many of the journalists I talked to. Gawker lost its voice suddenly; Pudelek's shift in tone was rapid, although with new corporate oversight such outcomes were to be expected. At Mail Online changes happened gradually, with outsiders slowly being replaced by new hires better fit to the outlet's line. It is particularly worth noting that when asked about their work, newsroom changes are one of the aspects of the job that journalists focus on most. This is understandable as the shifts they describe have led to less freedom of writing, which after all is a fundamental journalistic value. This has been enforced either by pushing a populist-conservative agenda, by corporatization and self-censorship based on dependence on advertising deals, or, most radically, by closing an outlet.

"Pudelek was pure anarchy, led spontaneously," Wojciech*, one of the online tabloid's first writers tells me. It was "anti-elite but pro-capitalism because back in the day we thought capitalism was alright," he adds. Wojciech* has since changed his views on the economy. "The idea for Pudelek was to create a medium, not a product to push e-commerce" which, he argues, it eventually became after the 2014 company merger. From the start, the website was deliberately structured to resemble a blog because there "you don't want to miss a single entry." Its name, a nod to celebrity culture it aimed to comment on, was inspired by Paris Hilton's dog. Yet the goal of Pudelek, the journalist explains, was high-reaching: to become "a staple." While Wojciech's* point of reference is *Przekrój*, the oldest postwar illustrated social and cultural magazine in Poland – it was founded in 1945, soon after the end of the Second World War – Pudelek's content was decidedly more tabloid-like. Still, it quickly became the most popular Polish online gossip outlet. After Pudelek's co-founder and original editor-in-chief was fired, a new person came in his place in 2016. This marked the beginning of a new period in the newsroom, not only because the original creator of the online tabloid's success was gone but because the new editor-in-chief employed people who were outsiders. Before, all hires at Pudelek had been done using word of mouth, which made the team tightknit. (However, one early employee tells me she was hired after having sent two useful tips.) As Paweł* underlines, this was crucial when the original editor-in-chief was still there because,

> "the key to everything was trust. Everyone had to go through fire and water for others. The work was demanding, often thankless, and we had to count on each other since [the editor-in-chief] gave us no support. We had to organize ourselves independently."

What's more, under new management strong differences emerged between the first generation of Pudelek writers and the more corporate second-generation, which sometimes led to conflict. The old, insider-hire authors claim ironic detachment from the effects of their work. Unlike them, the new and often younger outsider employees are, the old-guard journalist argues, "model Pudelek consumers, totally excited about the content," after having spent years enthusiastically reading the online tabloid. Indeed, Cezary*, a fairly new hire tells me, "I've wanted to work at Pudelek for a very long time, it's kind of my dream job." But Wojciech*, a first-generation editor harshly sums up this over-eager attitude: "Someone who is interested in show-business shouldn't work at Pudelek. The first thing that disappears is being cool." What these new authors lack is the tongue-in-cheek attitude that was previously reflected in the language of the tabloid. They make up for it with more straightforward zeal concerning women's and LGBT+ rights, which had been previously presented with more humor. "Now you simply see someone panting at the keyboard," Paweł* remarks dryly. In addition, corporate changes have influenced the daily work itself. Meetings of the entire team have become a regular event in the physical office space, although they had been a rare occurrence earlier, and when they did take place, it was mostly online. Another change was that everyone received, and has to use, their corporate email. "This was a corporate standard already back then but for us the demands were outlandish," Dorota* confesses. While one aspect of the transformation at Pudelek was content, the second was related to staff and organization of work, the third vital element concerned the visibility of the online tabloid. As a result of the merger Pudelek began to be featured on Wirtualna Polska's main website, which is one of the top two online portals in Poland.[32] The boost in audience numbers has been substantial. At the same time, Pudelek is an important asset for the company, being its second most-visited website, after Wirtualna Polska's main page, a new-generation author points out. Perhaps this is the reason for another uniquely corporate bonus, mentioned by a different Pudelek editor, namely designating a special lawyer to deal with the online tabloid's matters. These more often than not have to do with accusations of slander. "To finish law and end up as Pudelek's lawyer! That's beautiful," Jagoda* observes, this time without sarcasm.

Unlike Pudelek, Mail Online has been functioning in a corporate environment from the very start, although at the beginning it operated as a less tightly controlled internet side project of the *Daily Mail* paper. Ian* explains that an

---

32 Wirtualna Polska's main competitor is Onet.pl. Both are among the oldest portals on the Polish web: Wirtualna Polska was launched in 1995, while Onet.pl went online a year later.

early political news editor pitched the online outlet to Members of Parliament "as almost nonpolitical, a lot less political than the *Daily Mail* newspaper." Mail Online was intended to be different:

> "It would be less partisan. It would be more focused on what mattered to people: [whether these were] consumer issues, whether that was energy crisis, or cost of petrol. (...) We worked quite well together pushing this. We would say to people, we're not *Daily Mail*, we're Mail Online, less partisan. We would write stories about the Labour Party and the Tory Party, and that would be focused on just straightforward tax expenses, money in your pocket. We would try and write it straight."

According to the journalist, this strategy proved successful for the political news section of Mail Online, also because the online outlet's newsroom and the journalists' beat were physically disconnected from the paper:

> "We were very much distinct from the [*Daily Mail*] headquarters which is over in Kensington. We hardly ever went there, we stayed here [in Parliament], we didn't deal with the editor very much, and we had a news editor who we liked. So we were sort of separate, we carved out our own niche, in a way. But I think neither of us were *Daily Mail* people."

Gayle, too, admits that despite the differences between his own views and those of the editors, working at Mail Online could be enjoyable, particularly when it concerned rewriting boring news into exciting online-tabloid material:

> "We used to take, for example, local news from the [United] States, stuff that had been published on the local TV and local newspaper over there – and in America they have a really turgid style of newspaper writing. You could take one of their stories, which were really badly written and completely missed the whole point of the story, find something down in there, the penultimate paragraph of their story – that was actually the entire point of the story and was the most exciting part of it – pull that up to the top, and then suddenly you've got a really, really good UK-style tabloid news story."

His jab at US reporting is not isolated. Other Mail Online writers, too, remark that newsmakers on the other side of the pond take themselves too seriously. Even Gawker writers like to highlight Denton's prior experience at *Financial Times*, next to his general British news sensibility, as key for the online tabloid's success. To boot, Spiers lists *Private Eye*, the British satirical and current-affairs magazine as her inspiration.

Editorial independence at Mail Online was allowed because political reporters were generating good traffic with their "straight journalism." It managed to avoid, as some of them put it, *Daily Mail's* "vicious" and "one-sided" "instinctive conservative spin" and "snap right-wing moral judgement." The audience was clearly attracted to "straight" reporting, and the online outlet steadily grew in popularity. However, as Mail Online gained traction it gradually became more ideologically aligned with the paper, and newly hired reporters were more dependent on the hands-on editor-in-chief, Martin Clarke. Gayle describes the change coming with new hires, in this case a UK news editor: "She came over and brought a bit more of the *Mail's* discipline – the print edition's discipline – over to the online. From then on, the stories started to become more right-wing." The journalist adds that after a time he was banned from writing home news and, instead, was relegated to covering foreign news, which is less politically slanted. Still, even there he mentions instances of spinning stories to fit the outlet's agenda. For example, Gayle's editor, faced with a Reuters report which showed that anti-Qaddafi rebels in Libya were not exactly the "good guys" portrayed by the online tabloid, dismissed the report saying, "We don't want any of that." Bill*, another reporter mentions that in a story about a criminal who had been receiving modest monthly benefits, the editor inflated the sum more than fivefold. "Those headlines were clearly put up to irritate the reader," he sums up the editorial intervention.

Conservative editorializing is a regular feature mentioned by all Mail Online writers I talked to. On the one hand, it concerns tampering with content, the most blatant example being the addition of suggestive headlines and pictures, but also inserting supplemental information that alters the meaning of the original copy filed by the reporter – such as the bright-blue boxes discussed in Chapter 2. In this way, the political slant "sticks" to otherwise impartial reporting. For instance, a reporter explains how a "straight" piece on the consequences of Brexit for EU citizens was transformed by editors by including more one-sided news in the original copy: "They didn't really change anything I wrote, but by adding extra information from this other reporter it gave it more of a slant towards Brexiteers." According to the journalists, at Mail Online conservative editorializing is carried out by pushing typical right-wing populist topics favored by the editors, such as condemning illegal immigration, fraud, and misuse of benefits, while endorsing everyday sexism towards women. "The Mail [Online] has always had a kind of misogynistic attitude towards women," Gayle argues, "and the way that it treats women, the way it talks about women is misogynistic and sexist. It denigrates them for having cellulite or for not looking 'beach-body ready'." Paradoxically, despite its often-demeaning approach to women Mail Online also tends to "call out homophobia," as one of the writers puts it, which is a clear nod to the online tabloid's younger and more liberal readers. Yet this shows that if hatred towards non-heterosexuals is no longer accepted, the objectification of female bodies still is. Even so, examples discussed in the previous chapter show that in terms of the female body scrutiny goes across the political spectrum. It can be found in photo descriptions of the looks of Hillary Clinton and her aide Huma Abedin, but also of Melania, Ivanka, and Tiffany Trump. Perhaps this female-objectifying political impartiality is possible because it concerns the United States and not the United Kingdom, or perhaps because the British EU referendum campaign coverage was mostly focused on men. This, too, is news framing.

Another typical right-wing topic, a benefit-fraud story, is mentioned by John*:

> "Someone who is claiming some sort of disability or incapacity benefit, and they are pictured or filmed jumping on a trampoline or carrying heavy boxes, or whatever it is that proves that, actually, they were perfectly physically capable all along."

In his description, the writer draws attention to the editorial interventions that reveal what Mail Online chooses to show (and, respectively, to hide from) its readers (see: Dayan 2005). On such example is lawbreaking: "It's certainly true that the perspective was always firmly on the crime rather than on any potential mitigation or on the experiences of the person ... of the criminal or of the relatives, or anything like that." John* points at the direct responsibility of the individual, rather than the social context, that is viewed as a core conservative value. Yet Gayle adds a broader, national us-versus-others perspective to explain Mail Online's increasingly inward-looking, conservative angle:

> "This idea that we're being bled dry by people minting the benefits system, health tourism. Focus on religion and Islam. All the familiar tropes of right-wing [politics]. (...) Brits versus the world. This started to occur; I don't know whether there was some executive order to make it this way."

Finally, there was the "bollocking" done by Martin Clarke. According to my interviewees it intensified with time and Mail Online's success. Gayle notes that it was a variation of the printed daily editor-in-chief Paul Dacre's "vagina monologues," during which he called everyone a "cunt." The reporter expands on this management style, based on good wages and fear:

"[Clarke] would give his senior staff really severe bollockings. You'd see them coming out of his office after their morning conference and they'd all look kind of shell-shocked, as if they'd just done eighteen months in the trenches or something like that. A lot of the time they would come out and then start bollocking reporters, to pass it down the chain."

The writer adds that because of the oppressive atmosphere some journalists quit after several days. Still, although Mail Online is known for its difficult work environment it remains an attractive place for journalists because of the competitive pay. And, however cruel it may sound, journalists know that if "you can make it there you'll make it anywhere."

Gawker, the last to be discussed in this section, was the first of the three outlets to emerge online, and was the only one that suffered a sudden and fatal legal blow as a direct result of its popularity. Nevertheless, the beginnings of the online tabloid were modest, a two-person operation focused on New York media gossip, created by friends, Nick Denton and Elizbeth Spiers. Denton dealt with the operations, while Spiers focused on writing. "I would take whatever he [Denton] said into account and do whatever I was going to do anyway," Spiers explains. "We also didn't think it was going to be a business at that point, so there was no fear of experimenting. (...) We were surprised that it was taking off," she adds. The format was a blog, a setup adopted by Pudelek a couple of years later. However, before this happened Gawker was also one of the first blogs to insert ads. In a fake-it-till-you-make-it spirit, Spiers says,

> "There wasn't really a mechanism [to] put ads on the site, you ended up hard-coding and doing it yourself. (...) We didn't see any reason why you couldn't put a banner ad on a blog, just because nobody had done it. So Nick [Denton] put a Corcoran[33] banner on Gawker, thinking that the advertisers for a site about New York would probably be New York real-estate companies. He didn't ask for their permission to do it, they weren't paying us for it, but it just clicked through to their site. He figured that would be signaling, and it worked! A little while after he put that banner out, competitors called, wanted to know how much that spot was. And so that's how the ad banner was born. But, you know, at the time, in 2001, 2002, that stuff didn't exist."

---

33   Corcoran Group is a US real-estate company.

This was not the only reason for Gawker's growing influence. Another was the fact that because the outlet focused on New York media, journalists started reading it and then writing about it. This became a perpetual cycle, to Gawker's benefit. But as the online tabloid grew it became something more, which according to Denton was "the expression of the rage of the creative underclass."[34] He continues:

> "I think it was a kind of an inchoate expression of the sense that the system was rigged, that no matter how hard you worked or how talented you were, if you didn't know the right people, you didn't have a big enough trust fund, you didn't have the kind of luxury to be creative. That you were going to get stuck in one of those shitty jobs that pays a bunch but, you know, all your money is going to go out on rent, and your future looks kind of hopeless."

In this sense, Gawker became a site one clicked on not just to get the latest snarky gossip. By being in on the Gawker joke, in other words by sharing the online tabloid's sensibility, readers could feel together in a reality that was working against them, as the American Dream of success through hard work in creative jobs turned out to be increasingly out of reach. This is also perhaps why Gawker became a trusted place for people to send tips. Nolan explains:

> "It was the one place that everybody would think of when people had something. When people had a tip that they knew that no one else would publish, everybody would send [it] to Gawker because it was in the public's mind: it's that kind of place."

Tips sent to Gawker that were unfit for other media often contained NSFW (not-safe-for-work) content, such as explicit photos, as well as scandalous information about people's lives. Nolan admits that as far as newsworthiness was concerned, dealing with tips sent by readers required calm: "If you get a tip, and you open [it], and you're [thinking] 'oh my god!' The first thing you want to do is run out and tell everybody here in the office, look at this crazy shit! And then, oh, we wouldn't publish that." The tip that eventually brought Gawker down was sent in 2012 and included a video with Hulk Hogan having sex with his best friend's wife. Hogan sued and eventually won over

---

34   See: *New York Magazine* (2008); the article focuses on the voice of Gawker, which includes the expression later used by Denton in the "Employee of the Month" interview.

$100 million in a court case held in Florida, his home state, largely thanks to Peter Thiel's financial backing. Had the case been heard in New York, Gawker would have likely won based on the First Amendment, which guarantees the freedom of speech. Despite Thiel's claim that the trial was "one of my greater philanthropic things that I've done" (Sorkin 2016), the fact that a media outlet could be eradicated by a vindictive billionaire sounded alarming to many, especially in the media (see e.g.: Savan 2016). When the case was still in court, Niehoff (2016), a professor at the University of Michigan Law School worried that Hogan's case could "inspire a strategy of privacy-bait-and-switch, where a celebrity lures the media into reporting on a presumptively private topic and then ambushes them with a lawsuit seeking millions of dollars when they do so." Although this prediction did not materialize (yet), in recent years Strategic Litigation Against Public Participation, or SLAPP, cases aimed at censoring media and whistleblowers, have become increasingly popular both in the US and elsewhere. Nolan sums up these developments bitterly, "Those kinds of lawsuits are a legacy of what Peter Thiel did." While Gawker's case is extreme in that it concerned scandalizing, sexual material involving a celebrity, it highlights the potential chilling effect of SLAPP-type cases used to silence media.[35] Meanwhile, after Gawker folded in 2016 its writers were dispersed among other remaining sites, such as Gizmodo, Deadspin, and Jezebel, owned by Gawker Media. Still that same year the company was bought – albeit without the Gawker website – by Univision, a Spanish-language network, and was renamed Gizmodo Media Group. Three years later, Univision sold the company to Great Hill Partners, a private equity firm, which rebranded it again, this time as G/O Media. As for Gawker itself, the website was relaunched by Bustle Digital Group in 2021 with the goal of making a "nicer" version of the infamous online tabloid. Ironically, this outcome was foreseen by Denton. Back in 2016, in the "Employee of the Month" interview he said,

> "Gawker owned by some corporate media entity it would be... it would be something very different, it would've been something watered down. It maybe would have been reinvented as an entertainment, a light-hearted entertainment site."

However, the project failed, and in 2023 the website folded again.[36]

---

35   It is worth noting that the European Commission presented a proposal of anti-SLAPP regulation in 2022: https://www.europarl.europa.eu/RegData/docs_autres_instituti ons/commission_europeenne/com/2022/0177/COM_COM(2022)0177_EN.pdf.
36   See e.g.: Smith 2021; Spangler 2023.

These three cases show that strong voices of their original creators are essential for the outlets' initial, but not necessarily long-term, success. Gawker folded because its notoriety was taken advantage of by an extremely wealthy man in an abstruse court system, where in the end money proved stronger than the freedom of speech. A short-lived, less snarky resurrection of Gawker five years after its closure turned out a failure, possibly because the readers expected a more old-style version of the website, or perhaps they were not waiting for Gawker to come back at all and have gone elsewhere. At Mail Online, many of the original outsider political reporters, who initially built the outlet's credibility, where later replaced by journalists better adjusted to the right-wing angle of the editor-in-chief. Nonetheless, Mail Online's popularity has been steadily growing. Finally, Pudelek went through a generational change as well, which was spearheaded by a corporate merger. New journalists who came from outside were unable to retain Pudelek's old, detached, and mocking tone precisely because they were too uncritically enthusiastic about the outlet. Yet even after the firing of the original editor-in-chief the Polish online tabloid has maintained its popularity. Though the posts are now written with less sense of self-irony, it is still the most critical and most popular gossip tabloid on the Polish web.

3.4 *Professionalism*

If there is one thing that links writers and editors across the Polish, British, and US online tabloids it is the notion of professionalism, even if it means different things to different people. Briefly put, journalistic professionalism falls into three categories: firstly, professionalism means providing accurate content; secondly, professionalism is viewed as a set of skills valued within the news industry; and thirdly, professionalism is delivering what the audience wants. This threefold definition encompasses the writing produced (content); the position of journalists in the news media industry (insiders in a professional field); and meeting the needs of the readers (outside audience). What's more, articles that journalists produce are assessed both by the outside audience and by insiders – the industry professionals – and are molded to fit the expectations of both groups. Yet it is important to note that the ways that insiders assess the professional value of content may be starkly different from the judgments made by typical lay readers.

A vivid illustration of the latter can be found, for example, in the comments section on Pudelek, where anonymous commenters regularly accuse the article authors of being uneducated ignoramuses. In contrast to this outsider opinion, online tabloid journalists move not only horizontally inside the industry, switching tabloids, but also vertically between soft and hard-news outlets, publishing

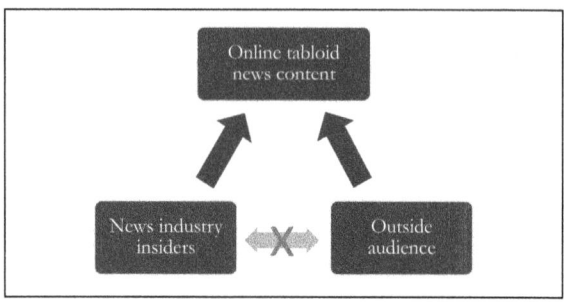

FIGURE 5   Assessment of professionalism in online tabloids

in places ranging from Pudelek, Mail Online, and Gawker to *Gazeta Wyborcza*, *The New Yorker*, and Politico.

Journalists may or may not personally share the views of the online tabloids they write for, which they broadly describe as populist conservative (Mail Online); anti-elite and progressive (Gawker); and anti-elite and liberal-conservative (Pudelek). At the same time, they find accurate reporting, regardless of their own opinions, a key element of their sense of professionalism. For example, Spiers evokes the beginnings of work at Gawker in terms of factual correctness: "[When] we started, we fell into journalistic appearances without really thinking about it, because the point was we wanted to put information on the site that was interesting, but we had to make sure it was accurate." Getting the facts right, irrespective of the tabloid line, is crucial for journalists to feel they are doing their job well. And while "accuracy" is a word I heard often from the writers I talked to, none used the word "objective" to describe their work, perhaps because the concept of objective journalism is often criticized as an ideal impossible to achieve in practice. For example, Gawker's Feinberg openly voices her reservations concerning this principle, and points out the tension between abstract ideals of objectivity and the reality of news made by living and breathing individuals: "I think that the idea that you can be objective is dishonest. I don't think anyone can be objective about anything, and I think it's much more honest to be actually explicit about your biases."[37] Even if voiced by an online-tabloid writer, this remark underlines a fundamental dilemma: to what extent can a journalist claim to be describing reality, when that reality is intrinsically tainted by the author's own beliefs? The sociologist, Gaye Tuchman (1972) offers a key contribution to this issue by problematizing the

---

37   See also: Koliska et al. 2023.

concept of journalistic objectivity, based on her ethnographic research conducted in newsrooms. The scholar shows that journalists who claim objectivity in fact follow routine procedures – of presenting conflicting truth-claims, supporting evidence, quotations, and separating facts from opinions – which allow them to avoid criticism and being sued for libel (see also: Tandoc and Duffy 2019). Given that all writers have their own beliefs, prejudices, and social backgrounds, these procedures help them claim impartiality. That the idea of journalistic objectivity has not aged well is evidenced by the fact that over 40 years after Tuchman's study, the term my interviewees use instead is "professionalism." After decades of growing criticism and distrust towards news media, the latter term sounds both less ambitious and safer.[38] This also suggests a change in the perception of journalism: from delivering objective news, a universalist if unattainable ideal (or "paraideology" according to Gans) of reporting the world to others as it is, to focusing on proper conduct within the occupation.

The concept of journalistic professionalism, which Mellado defines broadly as "the responsibilities of journalism and the news media in society" (2015, p. 599), has received much interest from scholars. It is usually analyzed from the point of view of journalistic organizations and practices of people performing the roles of journalists, in the context of their own profession and in relation to other institutions (e.g. Aldridge and Evetts 2003; Anderson and Schudson 2019; Zelizer 2005).[39] However, these inquires either overlook tabloid – not to mention online tabloid – journalism, or at best swiftly relegate it to the role of scandalizing infotainment. Little attention is paid to the substance of political coverage present in these outlets, which is a void I try to fill in this book. Still, some general scholarly findings on journalistic professionalism are helpful in scrutinizing online tabloids as well. For example, in the view of Hanitzsch and Örnebring (2019) the independent, dispassionate, and predictable – in other words professional – manner in which journalistic work is done is such only to a certain degree. In real life, news-making is never perfectly autonomous, detached, or foreseeable. What's more, journalistic professionalism is grounded in particular contexts, such as shared norms, rules, and practices of conducting this type of work. Tabloid journalists, in this sense, are no different. For example, Bill* describes the approach to writing in Mail Online: "Most

---

38   Reuters Institute Digital News Reports offer comprehensive analyses of changes in trust towards news: https://reutersinstitute.politics.ox.ac.uk/digital-news-report/; see also: Ihlebæk and Figenschou 2023.

39   For a comparative perspective, see: Mellado et al. 2013; Waisbord 2013; de Vreese et al. 2017.

people [who] work there are fairly media types. You know, a bit left-wing a bit right[-wing]. (...) Our personal internal beliefs don't come into the stories because it's not really about what we think, it's about getting the story out there." Nevertheless, their work is typically seen as inferior compared to hard news because of the sensationalizing, celebrity-filled content – even though precisely this is expected from a professional tabloid writer. Moreover, professionalism relates to the ways the work is organized and, more broadly, to the organizations themselves. Consequently, Pudelek, Gawker, and Mail Online are examples of gradual organizational professionalization. But there is more to it: as several writers at the British online tabloid emphasize, its "slick," state-of-the-art technology is considered one of the most advanced in the industry, envied by less well-to-do outlets. Despite this, the organizational and technological characteristics of professionalism in online tabloids are largely ignored in research, though not in the news industry itself. On the contrary, because of these advantages work experience at Mail Online is considered an asset for other news employers, and its graduate trainee scheme is widely sought for, often irrespective of the interns' political outlooks.

Thus, when examining the notions of journalistic professionalization, a complex matter as such, more paradoxes emerge when online tabloids are brought into the picture. As mentioned before, on the one hand, from the point of view of a professional news organization, advertising-related censorship, described by Pudelek authors, undermines the ideal of journalistic independence from outside and inside influences, that is advertisers and the sales department. Yet, on the other hand, journalists from non-tabloid media are jealous of their online tabloid peers' freedom to write what they want and how they feel about it, and to brazenly spill secrets otherwise only known to insiders. Secondly, in terms of professional norms, rules, and practices, Pudelek, Mail Online, and Gawker writers all stress their adherence to these practices – for instance, by checking their sources – if less so to rules and norms, for example by publishing salacious information about public persons that is not related to their performance. Still, in the reality of the journalistic profession it is enough for online tabloid writers to practice their job well to successfully switch outlets, including publishing in highly regarded non-tabloid media. But from a normative point of view, by challenging the common rules of the profession online tabloid journalists open up bigger questions about its fundamental values, and test the limits of what is considered right and wrong within the journalistic trade. For example: in what instances is hiding information about a public person's private life beneficial to the public? The practical response of hard-news media has been to quietly acquiesce, at least to a limited extent, and to provide more and more coverage about misconduct in the private lives of politicians and other people in power.⁴⁰ This clearly shows that within the journalistic profession understanding of what is beneficial to the public has been shifting. However, while online tabloid transgressions both reinforce and subtly shift professed general journalistic values, tabloids themselves are kept at the profession's ethical margins as its loud rotten apple, the "other" that hard-news outlets can distinguish themselves from.⁴¹ (In contrast, the sales of the latter are anything but marginal.) At the same time, even with such divisions in the journalistic profession, Hanitzsch and Örnebring (2019) argue that a shared sense of membership allows for acts of institutional solidarity across news genres. Indeed, expressions of sympathy towards Gawker voiced by different news media outlets after the online tabloid went bankrupt illustrate of this. They are more understandable, though, if one realizes that the Peter Thiel-backed fall of the US online tabloid demonstrated how easy it is to break a news medium if one has the money. This poses a very real threat to the journalistic profession as a whole.

Boundary work is another related issue within the journalistic profession that is illuminating when we attempt to identify the position of online tabloids alongside other news media (Deuze and Witschge 2018; Zelizer 1992). Boundary work is generally understood as a discursive, authority-shaping process in which journalists differentiate themselves from non-journalists as well as from other fellow-journalists, depending on their beats and news organizations. This approach is helpful in understanding the professional space occupied by online-tabloid journalists who write about politics because they transgress two distinct spheres: that of gossip and entertainment, considered trivial, and that of politics, considered fundamental for sustaining an informed public. This crossing of boundaries between high and low in tabloid political coverage is particularly significant given the importance placed on political journalism. For example, Anderson and Schudson make a powerful statement that "journalists who cover politics (...) have the highest professional standing and an especially marked cultural authority" (2019, p. 144). However, Darras (2005) offers a different take: journalists gain professional recognition for their proximity to power, especially the political kind. This puts online (and not only online) tabloid journalists who write about politics in a confusing position within the profession, between the highs of writing about politics and

---

40   The popularity of the #metoo movement in news outlets illustrates this change well.
41   This is as a meta-take of sorts on Thompson's (2000) and McNair's (2019) argument about media revealing political scandal and hypocrisy, discussed in Chapter 1. Here, however, I focus not on the news story but on the news makers.

lows of writing about it in a sensationalizing outlet. Yet their own accounts of changing employers in the news industry show that what counts in practice is not whether they come from tabloid or non-tabloid media but their ability to write factually, fast, in an engaging style, and to maintain reliable sources. Case in point, according to the British journalist, Harold Evans (2000) journalistic skills that matter the most are acquired in the "College of Osmosis," that is in the newsroom and on the job. Thus, ambiguities in defining professionalism in the context of online tabloids and boundary work are the result of conflating distinct elements of journalistic professionalism: the professionalism of an individual and of a particular news outlet recognized within the journalistic industry; and outside popular opinion about the professionalism of different journalists and news outlets. Briefly, if somewhat reductively, put, the former are practical and technical; the latter are based on commonly perceived values.

3.5   *Politics, Principles, and Secrets*

Political coverage in the three online tabloids is like Schrödinger's cat: both serious and not, depending on who is looking (e.g. a regular reader familiar with the style or an outsider) and when (e.g. before or after elections). Moreover, even if online tabloid journalists claim to be nonpartisan in their political writing, this does not necessarily mean they are so perceived, particularly when a news outlet is recognized for having a clear political bent. Nevertheless, for Gawker's Feinberg understanding truth in politics is not a matter of partisan sympathies but, rather, requires revealing politicians' hidden intentions, regardless of their party affiliation. The surface level of politics, she explains, is fake:

> "I think that politics is a very superficial kind of world. If you don't dig in, it's impossible to get the other tones of what people are actually saying, unless you know where they're coming from. You don't know that unless you dig into (...) what they do outside of what is publicly shown."

Whereas Feinberg aims at uncovering hidden contexts in political performance, Pudelek's Tomasz* explains his view on discussing politics, in keeping with the expected snarky style: "We only deal with things that are either really funny or shocking." But then he, too, adds in a more somber tone:

> "We don't say: listen, [Paweł] Kukiz yuck, [Donald] Tusk yay. We show you: listen, Kukiz did this, Tusk did that, you choose. Or rather, you think about it. (...) But if someone claims we are lefties or that we support the right-wing side, that's ok because in reality we are probably somewhere in the middle, like any other journalist. Although we are totally unobjective

in judging stars, we try to be objective in what is happening around us, since imposing anything on anyone neighbors on politics."

Maciej* sums up the matter frankly: "We never laugh at someone because they are ugly but because they don't think." If Gawker writers claim to look behind the curtain to reveal instances of abuse of "the privilege of power," as Feinberg aptly puts it, and Pudelek, in a similar vein, points its mocking finger at anyone they label elite, Mail Online's approach is different. Unlike the two, it provides strongly nation-centered coverage exposing how Britain and Britishness are constantly under attack by those who exploit the system. This concerns not only foreigners taking child benefits for families which are living abroad, but also hospital bosses earning hundreds of thousands of pounds while people wait years for surgery. The populist conservatism voiced by Mail Online echoes the populist conservatism of its readers, and it is not one sympathetic to small government. This means, for instance, that the deterioration of the welfare state may be used as a convenient pretext to sow fear. Gayle bitterly summarizes this overall approach of the online tabloid:

"I think Mail Online will never be satisfied with the world no matter which way it looks because it thrives on conflict, it thrives on hatred and dissonance. (...) This goes to some extent for all newspapers, because we're all in the business of trying to make stories interesting and exciting to read. The Mail more so than anyone, I think, tries to frighten its readers. It tries to make the world look like a scary place, and that [people] need to read the Mail so they know just how scary it is so they can keep safe, by voting conservative."

In the end, according to Mail Online, Britain's safety lies in the hands of the Tories, and depends on nation-focused conservative values. At the same time, however, it plays a role in transforming them by being "opportunistically" "reactive" to the more liberal younger audience. Hence, Mail Online engages in a difficult balance of carefully including certain outside elements in the conservative narrative, while rejecting others. For example, supporting LGBT+ rights while objectifying women, or singling out "good" and "bad" immigrants, discussed in Chapter 2, illustrates this tension well. In comparison to Mail Online, Gawker was not necessarily scaring its readers – although the online tabloid might have scared the people it wrote about – but it was not in the business of positive news either. As O'Connor puts it, "We just don't really do positive stuff. Either it's news (...) or it's a thought-provoking essay about why something is bad. (...) Nobody at Gawker understood their role as producing good things to the world." From this point of view, the world is a glum place: in the eyes of the writers, Pudelek is in the business of ridiculing the powerful; Gawker – showing how bad the world is; and Mail Online – sowing fear of it.

This may be the reason why in all three online tabloids unforgiving political coverage exists next to – and to an extent competes with – light-hearted celebrity gossip and other entertainment news. On Pudelek commenters like to complain, "Too much politics! We want Doda's boobs," one of the writers points out, referring to the Polish popstar. But the numbers show that, in contrast to these protestations, political topics are hugely popular. At Mail Online the rivalry between news and showbiz sections is direct: on the mobile version of the website's main page one can select "mobile friendly news," "mobile friendly showbiz," or "classic homepage." Nonetheless, a Mail Online political reporter has little patience for celebrity news: "We're the fig leaf for all the mountains and mountains of crap, of celebrities [on] the website every day." But linking the two spheres is not only a matter of their proximity on a page, but of substance. Feinberg explains her approach to merging the high of politics and low of celebrity at Gawker: "I've been encouraged to pursue narratives that you create in the political world that might be more suited to celebrity coverage, traditionally. Applying that to politics and hard news gives you a very different product." To illustrate this, the writer gives an example of an article about Donald Trump's daughter, Tiffany – less popular than the model-cum-entrepreneur Ivanka – which discusses the fact that she was included in a photo-op during one of her father's presidential campaign speeches.[42] "I'm a lot more interested in the periphery of the whole spectacle of it," Feinberg says. She admits that this type of reporting is considered "too lowbrow for traditional newspapers," but stresses that ignoring these marginal features results in an incomplete picture of the political realm. Her peers from other online tabloids would likely agree.

In fact, according to many of my interviewees, political outlooks that are visible in the outlets are based on a more general online-tabloid news principle: politics is first and foremost a media event. As one Pudelek journalist emphasizes, in Poland this realization coincided with the entrance of celebrity-like figures to the political stage in the 2015 presidential campaign, such as Paweł Kukiz, a rock star, and Magdalena Ogórek, an unknown quickly turned into a celebrity. He argues that when they appeared in politics, the difference between political and show-business discourse began to blur. Wojciech,* from the same outlet, makes an even stronger claim, this time about US politics.

---

42   https://deadspin.com/trump-eventually-remembers-daughter-1788240268.

He maintains that Donald Trump won the presidential election in the United States because of the way he used show-business acumen in his political campaign. For Wojciech*, in politics Trump behaves like Pudelek (or, more generally, an online tabloid): scandalizing, gossiping, and mocking others. As such, this demonstrates a contemporary transformation of celebrity politics, especially when compared to Street's (2004) or Marshall's (2014) studies, where the division lines between the two spheres were clear. If less than two decades ago celebrity endorsements of politicians and political causes were considered major crossover feats, today it does not hurt for political hopefuls to learn how to perform in a reality-television environment. To understand this shift, Bourdieu's (1998) classic concept of field is particularly useful, as the sociologist places both politics and journalism in the larger field of power. Given that celebrity gossip journalism offers its own visibility, which may, too, translate into a form of power, it makes sense for an individual functioning in the subfield of politics to be also purposely present in the subfield of gossip journalism. In consequence, such spillovers between subfields can lead to changes in the broader field of power. What's more, as Benson and Neveu write in their explorations of Bourdieu's work on journalism, "journalistic fields (...) under certain conditions may actually transform power relations in other fields," (2005, p. 9). The growing closeness of politics and celebrity-style coverage visible in online tabloids seems to illustrate this well. Indeed, Pudelek's Paweł* asserts,

"Politics is not directed as a serious discussion on matters of the state but is a media event. It is made with the same principles, the same comedic potential as (...) concerning a star displaying her underwear. When Magdalena Ogórek appeared in a dress that looked like a nightie[43] it wasn't so much about her as it was a symptom that all of this is the same spectacle. The difference is that some people later go to a film set and others go to the Sejm. But all these appearances had the exact same rules, the same dynamic, and the same effects in terms of discussion [on Pudelek]."

While Pudelek authors are motivated to write about politics at least in part because of the clicks it produces, politicians admit that although Pudelek is a gossip tabloid, they cannot afford to pretend it does not exist. A telling example of the acknowledgement of the outlet's influence is an official repudiation

---

43 In April 2015, Magdalena Ogórek, then still a presidential candidate supported by SLD (Democratic Left Alliance), went to a fashion show wearing a white minidress with spaghetti straps. See e.g.: https://www.pudelek.pl/artykul/78713/magdalena_ogorek_na _imprezie_u_przetakiewicz_zdjecia/komentarze.

that was sent by the Presidential Palace after the online tabloid had asked whether Andrzej and Agata Duda were getting divorced.[44] According to a Pudelek writer, politicians have figured out what celebrities already know, namely that success is measured in visibility, and if this requires being seen in a show-business context, so be it. Jagoda* points out matter-of-factly that covering politicians as celebrities goes hand in hand with the general tabloidization of news: "We've been making politicians into celebrities, and this began selling wonderfully. [Jarosław] Kaczyński with a cat or Kaczyński with a straw basket; (...) [Andrzej] Duda on skis, Duda on a motorboat. (...) It turned out that people simply love seeing these politicians in everyday situations, and this is something they can't find anywhere else." Another aspect of this matter is that, according to Shoemaker and Vos (2009) journalists have a preference for deviance, and in online tabloids the lives of celebrities are deviant by default. Hence, the act of celebrifying politicians is a process of entwining political power with celebrity-like eccentricity, in order to present an attractive news story. Even if this eccentricity is quite mundane, like skiing, tabloid-style attention makes it into a celebrity media event. Furthermore, while there is nothing new in politicians trying to convince citizens that they are ordinary Joes and Janes, to gain votes, the difference today is, firstly, that they actively expose themselves to snarky treatment from online tabloids; and, secondly, that it goes together with readers' emotional comments on the same webpage. In the heterogenous mix of politics, entertainment, punchy headlines, unforgiving photos, and comments, the ambiguity of (not) kidding comes to life. Because the news is written with professional accuracy it can be considered factual, yet because it is filled with sarcasm it can be explained as merely playful. To illustrate this, Ian* argues that "British journalism can be a little bit like a gentlemen's game. You know, it's all a bit of a laugh, a sort of 'oh, don't take that too seriously.' (...) I don't think there's any coincidence that the *New York Post* and *Daily News* are often edited by Brits" – the same went for Gawker. But the (not) kidding frame is a gentlemen's game gone wrong, where the rules are no longer clear, we cannot be sure whether we are indeed still merely playing, and the real-life influence of politics on people's lives is effectively obscured.

Despite the emphasis on celebrity and sarcasm, online tabloids want to serve an educational role as well. This, at least, is something that a number of Pudelek writers emphasize. Cezary* explains that they write with "a big-city

---

44   https://www.pudelek.pl/artykul/91412/agata_i_andrzej_duda_rozwodza_sie_kancelaria_odpowiada_pudelkowi_to_plotka_nie_bedziemy_tego_komentowac/.

Grażyna in mind,"[45] who appreciates traditional values and is increasingly open towards gays as well as other issues she finds progressive. What's more, Maciej* offers another reason for writing about politics, which makes Pudelek look almost like a public service:

> "Many people start their day with Pudelek. Over a million people come to us daily, so we assume that if they start their day with us, before work, having breakfast and coffee, it's cool to also show what happened beyond the small Polish world. Actually, there is often a lack of juicy showbusiness stories, especially from Poland, so we need to make up for it with something. And frequently such juicy stories come from politics and breaking news."

Tomasz* echoes this sentiment:

> "Our role is to show people: listen, this is also happening. Besides Doda's boobs the President had an accident, say, his tire exploded. (...) If something interesting is taking place in the political realm, we notice it. (...) And we are living in interesting times, which is impossible to ignore."

Many journalists would agree that their role is at least somewhat instructive – they provide information about the outside world. But if Pudelek authors publish stories on politics because they find them "juicy," which usually means scandalous enough to gain clicks, Gawker writers saw their role as more specific: exposing the secrets of people in power, regardless of the consequences. "I do not think that journalists have a responsibility to protect the interests of public figures," O'Connor tells me. Indeed, this was the reasoning behind the exposure of Condé Nast's CFO, Peter Thiel, and Hulk Hogan. Besides, what is uncovered often relates to individuals' sexual lives or family relations. In some cases the stories reveal hypocrisy between publicly stated morals and private actions (e.g. Hulk Hogan claimed to be a faithful husband but had sex with his best friend's wife), in others they simply make public what individuals holding power would prefer to keep private (e.g. Peter Thiel's homosexuality). For online tabloid journalists these, too, are important public matters that justify disclosure, since people who have power over others should be subject to essentially limitless scrutiny precisely because of the power imbalance. In this

---

45   The name Grażyna is the Polish equivalent of American Karen, which is used to label stereotypical middle-class women with a sense of entitlement, and has been immortalized in internet memes.

sense, by revealing secrets of the powerful, journalists aim to take away some of their power, and by doing so lessen the disproportions between the powerful and the powerless. One could argue this is a noble pursuit, especially given the implicit argument that if the former dictate the lives of the latter, journalists help the vulnerable by undermining the stature of the mighty. Here, speaking truth to power means displaying the moral corruption of the elite. Undeniably, in some instances revealing secrets concerning sexual comportment did have a direct influence on politics, for example in the case of the sexual misconducts of Donald Trump, Bill Clinton, and, earlier, John F. Kennedy. Particularly JFK serves as an inspiration of sorts for many of my interviewees, and Nolan offers a strong opinion about uncovering such secrets of politicians:

> "If you want to be the holier than thou person, you can say: we're only going to publish things with a redeeming public good. If it's something about a politician, it has to affect a piece of legislation in order for it to be newsworthy. But the fact is (…) JFK was running around doing all types of dirty shit, and it was never published. And all the journalists knew he was having all these affairs but that was just considered an indiscrete thing, you would never publish that."

He follows with a question: "Does this serve the public interest better, for powerful people to be able to have a ton of open secrets that the public will never be privy to?" For Nolan, and for Gawker, the answer is no. Even if one chooses to agree with him, the remaining issue is how do secrets of people in power infringe on those who are powerless? As signaled earlier in this chapter, the assumption made by online tabloid writers creates no distinction in terms of circumstance: what is important is not that people holding power have secrets, but the mere fact that they do makes them hypocrites at best, and criminals at worst. Thus, their secrets are intrinsically immoral.

One of the founding stories about Gawker I heard from several writers concerns a news-media ritual: after work journalists go to a bar and tell each other the unvarnished versions of news, which are never published. Denton's idea was to expose this journalistic insider information or, in the words of Nolan, "Just tell the truth and don't worry about offending people." The issue, however, is weightier than ignoring affronts of the exposed. The basic principle behind this idea is that readers should be treated as equals and, thus, should be equally in the know. Yet journalists may have the tendency to consider their actions "inherently moral" simply because they believe they enforce the public's "right to know," as Shoemaker and Vos (2009) argue. What's more, they aptly stress that this approach can in fact be "a defense against journalists' violations of ethics" (p. 72). Nonetheless, Gawker's O'Connor adopts a moral standpoint, viewing secrecy as both elitist and "a way of preserving that professional class that can itself become classified into an institutional power." In this, he echoes the argument of the communications scholar, Timothy Cook (2005) who makes a persuasive argument about news media power in the political field: "Far from holding up a mirror to external political actions, the news media are directly involved in instigating them" (p. 165), the scholar states strongly. What's more, the very act of choosing news for publication, even if in the name of objectivity, is inevitably arbitrary, which means it is political – what you see is what you know, and this informs action. Ultimately, as Schudson elucidates, distortions based on selection are intrinsically "built into the structures and routines of news gathering" (2003, p. 33). Thus, contrary to O'Connor's hopes, revealing secrets does not make journalistic selectivity any less present. Rather, it is another arbitrary choice, which brings attention to chosen, previously hidden indiscretions. But the principled stance presented by online tabloid journalists is not limited to revealing secrets. One of Pudelek's editors makes a much broader claim, and asks, "Why should anyone be a gatekeeper for democracy?" The question is fundamental. By filtering information to be published, journalistic gatekeeping limits what people can know about the world. The essential activity of choosing news worthy of publication requires first picking and then processing a narrow selection of information. It is based on the journalists' "gut feeling," which is a mix of intuition and understanding of news media conventions that come with experience (Cook 2005; O'Neill and Harcup 2019). This process is both functional, since there is only so much news one can produce and consume even on a website, hence some form of elimination is necessary, and normative because the choices made are based on journalistic values and often focus on the violations of norms. Despite Pudelek editor's reservations, gatekeeping (selecting news), gatewatching, (highlighting news), and gatebouncing (eliminating news from public debate), as Vos (2019) puts it, are among the prime tasks of journalism, including online tabloids. Still, the editor has a point: the gatekeeping powers of journalists are becoming increasingly diluted because of the sheer multitude of news media outlets out there.

Although broadening the range of news by providing content that has been previously hidden from outsiders may allow them to be more in the loop, the remaining key question is how does this relate to democracy? One major belief that can be found in the statements of online tabloid journalists is that democracy requires full transparency of every individual in a position of power, be it political, financial or, especially today, technological. But an additional form of power that is also subject to scrupulous online tabloid examination is the power of attracting media attention. It is a domain of celebrities, "persons who are known for their well-knownness" – examined by Boorstin in his classic work, *The Image* (1964) – and revamped in the internet age by social-media influencers. While online tabloids play a major role in both providing and deriding this form of power, politicians may adopt some elements of celebrity-like form in order to be seen. (The irony is that people who hold the power of providing news do not come under the same scrutiny, especially if they remain anonymous.) On the one hand, the principle of transparency of those in power is an idea many journalists and readers would agree with. On the other hand, another, ostensibly contradicting, assumption is that it is not the job of online tabloids – or any news medium for that matter – to restrict themselves in their publications to what is commonly considered beneficial for a democracy. Online tabloids treat politics as entertainment and entertainment brings revenue. The broader social implications of such framing of politics seem to matter less than financial calculations, even if as a result the democratic foundations on which these news businesses operate may shift – after all, Gawker was shut down because it turned out that money is indeed more powerful than free speech protections. In the end, (not) kidding is a fundamentally ambiguous stance adopted by online tabloids, which provides an effective shield against any potential accusers who would like to blame them for the deteriorating state of democracy (or journalism, for that matter). In spite of this, these outlets provide news on politics, especially during election season. Even if the goal is to amuse the audience, delivering information on politics which the readers may use as citizens at the ballot box, makes online tabloids powerful actors in a democratic system.

References

Addison, A. (2017). *Mail men: The unauthorized story of the Daily Mail*. London: Atlantic Books.

Aldridge, M. and Evetts, J. (2003). Rethinking the concept of professionalism: the case of journalism. *The British Journal of Sociology*, 54(4), pp. 547–564.

Anderson, C. W. and Schudson, M. (2019). Objectivity, professionalism, and truth seeking. In: Wahl-Jorgensen, K. and Hanitzsch T. eds., *The handbook of journalism studies. 2nd edition*. New York: Routledge, pp. 136–150.

Arana, G. (2015). Gawker's outing of Condé Nast's CFO is gay-shaming, not journalism. *HuffPost*, 17 July. Available at: https://www.huffpost.com/entry/gawker-conde-nast-david-geithner_n_55a90c56e4b0c5f0322d0b2c.

Barthes, R. (1977). *Image – Music – Text*. New York: Hill and Wang.

Benson, R. N. and Neveu, E. (2005). Introduction: Field theory as a work in progress. In: Benson, R. N. and Neveu, E. eds., *Bourdieu and the journalistic field*. Malden, MA: Polity Press, pp. 1–28.

Boczkowski, P. J. and Mitchelstein, E. (2013). *The news gap: When the information preferences of the media and the public diverge*. Cambridge, MA: The MIT Press.

Boorstin, D. J. (1964). *The image: a guide to pseudo-events in America*. New York: Harper Colophon Books.

Bourdieu, P. (1998). *On television*. New York: The New Press.

Bruns, A. (2011). Gatekeeping, gatewatching, real-time feedback: New challenges for Journalism. *Brazilian Journalism Research*, 7(2), pp. 117–136.

Business Insider Polska. (2017). Orange przeprasza za reklamową wpadkę. Po krytyce internautów zdjęto spot na YouTube. *Business Insider Polska*, 26 February. Available at: https://businessinsider.com.pl/biznes/media/orange-i-reklama-z-agnieszka-jastrzebska-firma-przeprasza-internautow/hdjlbfp.

Caple, H. and Bednarek, M. (2016). Rethinking news values: What a discursive approach can tell us about the construction of news discourse and news photography. *Journalism*, 17(4), pp. 435–455.

Chen, A. (2016). Gawker was a great place to become a journalist. *The New Yorker*, 13 June. Available at: https://www.newyorker.com/news/news-desk/gawker-was-a-great-place-to-become-a-journalist.

Chmielewska-Szlajfer, H. (2019). *Reshaping Poland's community after Communism: Ordinary celebrations*. New York: Palgrave.

Cook, T. E. (2005). *Governing with the news: The news media as a political institution*. Chicago, IL: The University of Chicago Press.

Darras, E. (2005). Media consecration of the political order. In: Benson, R. N. and Neveu, E. eds., *Bourdieu and the journalistic field*. Malden, MA: Polity Press, pp. 156–173.

Dayan, D. (2005). Mothers, midwives and abortionists: genealogy, obstetrics, audiences and publics. In: Livingstone, S. ed., *Audiences and publics: When cultural engagement matters for the public sphere. Changing media, changing Europe*. Bristol, UK: Intellect Press, pp. 43–76.

Dąbrowska-Cydzik, J. (2019). Polak twierdzi, że hejtują inni, on tylko wyraża opinię. *WirtualneMedia*, 20 March. Available at: https://www.wirtualnemedia.pl/artykul/co-to-jest-hejt-kto-obraza-innych-raport.

de Vreese, C., Esser, F. and Hopmann, D. N., eds. (2017). *Comparing political journalism*. New York: Routledge.

Deuze, M., and Witschge, T. (2018). Beyond journalism: Theorizing the transformation of journalism. *Journalism*, 19(2), pp. 165–181.

Evans, H. (2000). *Essential English for journalists, editors, and writers*. London: Pimlico.

Feldman, G., Lian, H., Kosinski, M. and Stillwell, D. (2017). Frankly, we do give a damn: The relationship between profanity and honesty. *Social Psychological and Personality Science*, 8(7), 816–826.

Flash Eurobarometer 437. (2016). Report: Internet users' preferences for accessing content online. *European Commission*, March. Available at: https://data.europa.eu/data/datasets/s2123_437_eng.

Gans, H. J. (2004). *Deciding what's news: A study of CBS Evening News, NBC Nightly News, Newsweek, and Time*. Evanston, IL: Northwestern University Press.

Golding, P. and Elliott, P. (1979). *Making the News*. London: Longman.

Gray, A. (2021). MailOnline publisher Martin Clarke to step down. *Financial Times*, 3 December. Available at: https://www.ft.com/content/4ef0cdc6-7c2b-4da9-8327-f3428887cef9.

Hanitzsch, T. and Örnebring, H. (2019). Professionalism, professional identity, and journalistic roles. In: Wahl-Jorgensen, K. and Hanitzsch T. eds., *The handbook of journalism studies. 2nd edition*. New York: Routledge, pp. 105–122.

Harcup, H. and O'Neill, D. (2017). What is news? News values revisited (again). *Journalism Studies*, 18(12), pp. 1470–1488.

Hersh, E. (2020). *Politics is for power: How to move beyond political hobbyism, take action, and make real change*. New York: Scribner.

Ihlebæk, K. A. and Figenschou, T. U. (2023). Journalism as a strategic action field: How to study contestations and power dynamics between professional journalism and its challengers. *Digital Journalism* [published online].

Koliska, M., Moroney, E. and Beavers D. (2023). Trust through relationships in journalism. *Journalism Studies* [published online].

Laloux, F. (2014). *Reinventing organizations: A Guide to Creating Organizations Inspired by the Next Stage of Human Consciousness*. Brussels, Belgium: Nelson Parker.

Manthorpe, R. (2018). How Peter Thiel and Hulk Hogan broke Gawker: UpVote 24. *Wired*, 3 August. Available at: https://www.wired.co.uk/article/ryan-holiday-conspiracy-peter-thiel-gawker-hulk-hogan.

Margolick, D. (2016). Nick Denton, Peter Thiel, and the plot to murder Gawker. *Vanity Fair*, 6 November. Available at: https://www.vanityfair.com/news/2016/11/nick-denton-peter-thiel-plot-to-murder-gawker.

Mandaro, L. (2015). Gawker apologizes, removes article on CFO. *USA Today*, 17 July. Available at: https://eu.usatoday.com/story/money/2015/07/17/gawkers-apparent-outing-cfo-meets-internet-backlash/30280505/.

Manjoo, F. (2016). The Gawker worldview lives on. *The New York Times*, 25 August, pp. B1, B4.

Marshall, P. D. (2014). *Celebrity and power: Fame in contemporary culture*. Minneapolis, MN: The University of Minnesota Press.

Marwick, A. (2013). *Status update: Celebrity, publicity, and branding in the social media age*. New Haven, CT: Yale University Press.

McNair, B. (2019). Scandal and news values. In: Tumber, H. and Waisbord, S. eds. *The Routledge companion to media and scandal*. New York: Routledge, pp. 76–85.

Mellado, C. (2015). Professional roles in news content. *Journalism Studies*, 16(4), pp. 596–614.

Mellado, C., Márquez-Ramírez, M., Van Leuven, S., et al. (2023). Comparing journalistic role performance across thematic beats: A 37-country study. *Journalism & Mass Communication Quarterly*, pp. 1–30.

Moosa, T. (2014). Comment sections are poison: handle with care or remove them. *The Guardian*, 12 September. Available at: https://www.theguardian.com/science/brain-flapping/2014/sep/12/comment-sections-toxic-moderation.

Muddiman, A. and Stroud, N. J. (2017). News values, cognitive biases, and partisan incivility in comment sections. *Journal of Communication*, 67(4), pp. 586–609.

Mullin, B. (2015). The New York Times gets its own 'Big Board'. *Poynter.org*, 9 June. Available at: https://www.poynter.org/reporting-editing/2015/the-new-york-times-gets-its-own-big-board/.

Mullin, B. (2017). Kinja, the publishing system at the heart of Gawker, lives on under Univision. *Poynter.org*, 16 June. Available at: https://www.poynter.org/tech-tools/2017/kinja-the-publishing-system-at-the-heart-of-gawker-lives-on-under-univision-update/.

New York Magazine. (2008). How to be a Gawker. *New York Magazine*, 12 February. Available at: https://nymag.com/intelligencer/2008/02/how_to_be_a_gawker.html.

Niehoff, L. (2016). Hulk Hogan v. Gawker: A fight between privacy and free speech. *HuffPost*, 16 March. Available at: https://www.huffpost.com/entry/hulk-hogan-gawker-lawsuit_b_9477556.

O'Neill, D. and Harcup, H. (2019). News values and news selection. In: Wahl-Jorgensen, K. and Hanitzsch T. eds., *The handbook of journalism studies*. 2nd edition. New York: Routledge, pp. 213–228.

Petre, C. (2015). The traffic factories: Metrics at Chart beat, Gawker Media, and The New York Times. *Columbia Journalism Review*, May. Available at: https://www.cjr.org/tow_center_reports/the_traffic_factories_metrics_at_chartbeat_gawker_media_and_the_new_york_times.php.

Phelps, A. (2012). What makes something go viral? The Internet according to Gawker's Neetzan Zimmerman. *Nieman Lab*, 11 June. Available at: https://www.niemanlab.org/2012/06/what-makes-something-go-viral-the-internet-according-to-gawkers-neetzan-zimmerman/.

Phillips, A. (2015). *Journalism in context: Practice and theory for the digital age*. New York: Routledge.

Reader, B. (2012). Free press vs. free speech? The rhetoric of "civility" in regard to anonymous online comments. *Journalism & Mass Communication Quarterly*, 89(3), pp. 495–513.

Reagle, J. M., Jr. (2015). *Reading he comments: Likers, haters, and manipulators at the bottom of the web.* Cambridge, MA: MIT Press.

Rösner, L. and Krämer, N. C. (2016). Verbal venting in the social web: Effects of anonymity and group norms on aggressive language use in online comments. *Social Media + Society*, 2(3), pp. 1–13.

Savan, L. (2016). Does Hulk Hogan's lawsuit against Gawker really threaten freedom of the press?. *The Nation*, 21 March. Available at: https://www.thenation.com/article/archive/does-hulk-hogans-lawsuit-against-gawker-really-threaten-freedom-of-the-press/.

Schudson, M. (2003). *The sociology of news.* New York: W. W. Norton & Company.

Shoemaker, P. J., and Reese, S. D. (1996). *Mediating the message: Theories of influences on mass media content.* White Plains, NY: Longman.

Shoemaker, P. J. and Vos, T. P. (2009). *Gatekeeping theory.* New York: Routledge.

Smith, B. (2021). Can There Be Any Room Online for a Nice Gawker?. *The New York Times*, 6 September, pp. B1, B4.

Sorkin, A. S. (2016). Tech billionaire in a secret war with Gawker. *The New York Times*, 26 May, pp. A1, B8.

Spangler, T. (2023). Gawker Is Shutting Down (Again). *Variety*, 1 February. Available at: https://variety.com/2023/digital/news/gawker-shutting-down-1235509262/.

Spiers, E. (2023). One day they'll say this was the best (and worst) thing I ever made. *The New York Times*, 3 February. Available at: https://www.nytimes.com/2023/02/03/opinion/gawker-media.html.

Stroud, N. J., Van Duyn, E. and Peacock, C. (2016). News commenters and news comment readers. *Center for Media Engagement*. Available at: https://mediaengagement.org/wp-content/uploads/2016/03/ENP-News-Commenters-and-Comment-Readers1.pdf.

Street, J. (2004). Celebrity politicians: Popular culture and political representation. *The British Journal of Politics and International Relations*, 6(4), pp. 435–452.

Tandoc, E. C., Jr. and Duffy, A. (2019). Routines in Journalism. In: Powers, M. ed., *Oxford Research Encyclopedia of Communication.* Oxford, UK: Oxford University Press.

Tanzer, M. (2014). Gawker Media staffers are still ambivalent about Kinja. *BuzzFeedNews.com*, 12 August. Available at: https://www.buzzfeednews.com/article/mylestanzer/gawker-media-staffers-are-still-ambivalent-about-kinja.

Thomas, W. I. and Thomas, D. (1928). *The child in America. Behavior problems and programs.* New York: Alfred A. Knopf.

Thompson, D. (2018). The most expensive comment in internet history?. *The Atlantic*, 23 February. Available at: https://www.theatlantic.com/business/archive/2018/02 /hogan-thiel-gawker-trial/554132/.

Thompson, J. B. (2000). *Political scandal: power and visibility in the media age.* Cambridge, UK: Polity.

Tuchman, G. (1972). Objectivity as strategic ritual: An examination of newsmen's notions of objectivity. *American Journal of Sociology*, 77(4), pp. 660–679.

Vos, T. (2019). Journalists as gatekeepers. In: Wahl-Jorgensen, K. and Hanitzsch T. eds., *The handbook of journalism studies. 2nd edition.* New York: Routledge, pp. 90–104.

Wahl-Jorgensen, K. (2002). The normative-economic justification for public discourse: Letters to the editor as a "wide open" forum. *Journalism & Mass Communication Quarterly*, 79(1), pp. 121–133.

Wahl-Jorgensen, K. (2013). The strategic ritual of emotionality: A case study of Pulitzer Prize-winning articles. *Journalism*, 14(1), pp. 129–145.

Waisbord, S. (2013). *Reinventing professionalism.* Malden, MA: Polity Press.

Watson, L. (2019). The real threat to journalism is not Donald Trump. *The New Republic*, 25 October. Available at: https://newrepublic.com/article/155497/real-threat-jou rnalism-not-donald-trump.

Webb, S. (2014). A new digital community? An analysis of Gawker's commenters-to-contributors approach. *Journal of Magazine & New Media Research*, 15(2), pp. 1–15.

Wemple, E. (2015). Conde Nast exec story: Gawker is keeping its sleaze game in shape. *Washington Post*, 17 July. Available at: https://www.washingtonpost.com/blogs/erik -wemple/wp/2015/07/17/conde-nast-exec-story-gawker-is-keeping-its-sleaze-game -in-shape/.

Westlund, O. and Ekström, M. (2019). News organizations and routines. In: Wahl-Jorgensen, K. and Hanitzsch T. eds., *The handbook of journalism studies. 2nd edition.* New York: Routledge, pp. 73–89.

Zelizer, B. (1992). CNN, the Gulf War, and journalistic practice. *Journal of Communication*, 42(1), pp. 66–81.

Zelizer, B. (2005). Definitions of journalism. In: Overholser, G. and Jamieson K. H. eds., *The Press.* Oxford, UK: Oxford University Press, pp. 66–80.

CHAPTER 4

Conclusion
Online Tabloid Voices and Democracy

Gawker, Mail Online, and Pudelek journalists openly state they provide entertainment, and political news coverage is no exception. Yet in doing so they walk a thin line between presenting politics as amusement, something to joke about, and something quite different altogether – a serious affair with crucial social, economic, and cultural consequences, not to mention effects on political power and governance. What these online tabloids deliver is a balancing act of banter and solemnity found in facetious headlines and pictures, hard news, and showbiz-like reporting. These, in turn, are augmented by readers' impassioned comments which, as the online tabloid writers attest, influence the outlets' direction, reactive to their audience's needs. This dependency can be observed in the ultimate (not) kidding game that online tabloids play with their readers: political issues described there can be both joking and serious, conditional on the users' reactions. While there is no direct measure of influence of online tabloids on people's political decisions, these outlets reach far more viewers than other news media. Even though readers often say they treat them as pure entertainment, if they do not get their news somewhere else as well, they are stuck with the political coverage these online tabloids offer – and are left with this information when making political decisions. In fact, a study by Wojcieszak et al. (2024) conducted in Poland, the Netherlands, and the United States reveals that two thirds of political content people get online come from non-news websites. This is no small number. What's more, the scholars found that "exposure to political content outside news predicts increased participatory intentions (e.g. protesting or signing a petition)" (p. 142) in Poland and the United States.[1] This suggests that the influence of online tabloid political coverage may, too, reach beyond mere entertainment and inspire political action, including voting. Because of their tongue-in-cheek tone and undemanding mix of hard and soft news such as show-business, crime stories, and sports, for many people online tabloids remain the main providers of news on politics. And these readers, too, make decisions who and what to vote for, at least in part based on the political news they read, regardless of whether this

---

1 This aspect was not measured in the Netherlands.

CONCLUSION

content is kidding or not. Consequently, their political choices affect their local communities, their countries, and resonate in other parts of the world.

In this book, I showed that online tabloids, these elephants in the room, deserve a serious look, especially in relation to politics. Among the many paradoxes concerning these media, they are perceived as the least credible news sources, yet they remain some of the most popular journalistic outlets. In a troubled news media environment, increasingly challenged by alternative, often disinforming sources, which are particularly widespread on social media (see e.g.: Ceylan, Anderson and Wood 2023; Persily and Tucker 2020), the success of online tabloids should not and cannot be ignored if we want to get a better understanding how political news journalism functions today. My goal was to uncover, at least in part, how these popular outlets work with political material, hence, I studied dominant journalistic narratives next to commenter voices on Pudelek, Mail Online, and Gawker in the 2015–2016 vote campaigns: Poland's 2015 presidential campaign, United Kingdom's 2016 EU (aka Brexit) referendum campaign, and the United States' 2016 presidential campaign. Considering their sheer popularity and interactive appeal, I argued that scholars cannot afford to discount online tabloids in research on politics and the public sphere. Their authors and the commenting readers play an important part in shaping people's opinions. Readers' remarks on politics can be found on the tabloids' webpages, and their decisions on democratic governance – in the ballot box. Thus, online tabloids provide unique spaces combining professional journalistic authority with non-expert reader inclusion. This is achieved thanks to the accessible, often black-and-white, entertaining, scandalizing, photo-filled, and conversational character of the websites. On the one hand, by treating politics as if it were just like any other media event, online tabloids obscure politics' practical influence on people's lives. On the other hand, in contrast to other news outlets, online tabloids are inviting spaces for people not particularly interested in political matters, making it easy for them to share their opinions and feelings on these topics – and occasionally find these remarks highlighted in the news headlines later. These outlets become critical spaces of enquiry by providing a unique mix of journalistic authority and reader inclusion. At the cost of making political coverage sensationalizing, simplifying, and celebrifying, they expose the process of negotiating popular political sentiments. Ultimately, in a real-world mix of Habermas's, Mouffe's and Schütz's concepts on democratic participation, these online tabloids create a plebeian public sphere of sorts. There, the agon – "the conflictual consensus" – and the popular passions of people who are not well-informed "enough" are nonetheless seen in their potential for political agency.

1 Producing Knowledge and Inclusion in Journalistic Authority

For audiences who want to be entertained by the outside world rather than solely informed about it, online tabloids successfully provide appropriately formatted political coverage. This is not accidental, given increasing news avoidance (Newman et al. 2023; Toff at al. 2023) and because "news" usually means bad news. Ultimately, journalists are not in the business of passing selected information to the audience but of producing knowledge about the world. If hard news is negative and somber, online tabloid news can be negative, too, but at the same time tends to be funny, outraged or otherwise emotionally gripping. This aspect may appear as merely a matter of style, but it bears major consequences. Because emotions are performative, as Wahl-Jorgensen (2019) stresses, they "fuel and direct our political energies and inform our rational decision-making" (p. 172). The 2015–2016 votes in Poland, the United Kingdom, and the United States which, led by voters' discontent with the status quo, shifted politics in a populist right-wing direction, are a good illustration of this. Even if online tabloids played a peripheral role in influencing voters, the (not) kidding frame of cynicism, outrage and ridicule could nevertheless be seen at work. But online-tabloid knowledge production is not limited to solely stirring emotions; equally significant is the fact that attention begets importance. Put in the simplest terms, what you see is what you know, and people's attention informs their understanding of reality – whether these are detailed policy analyses or celebrity trivia. In a world oversaturated with content, avoiding news is, too, a form of managing attention, and the choice to focus on one thing is also a choice to ignore something else. As such, this is a step further compared to Dayan's (2005) traditional news media "midwives" and "abortionists," which the scholar describes as, respectively, highlighting and killing stories. Today, after this first act of selection carried out by journalists, the second act is performed by the audience who comment on the content journalists offer. In the three studied online tabloids, the production of knowledge – a fact-based process of creating meanings and highlighting their significance – translates into giving similar importance to matters both vital and trivial. From a certain point of view such a selection may appear impartial – after all, everything is a spectacle, the journalists argue – but Schudson (2003) rightly emphasizes that each journalistic choice is innately a distortion of reality.

Consequently, if journalists are visibility authorities who are involved in emphasizing certain facts while discounting others, they provide what Dayan (2013) elsewhere calls "monstrations." These are not so much pieces of information as fact-based performative acts, which focus on "(1) asserting or denying the existence of given interactions; (2) imposing judgment on their protagonists; and (3) displaying respect or disrespect toward them" (p. 148). Placing this concept in the context of online tabloids, journalistic stories – as monstrations – can be viewed as propositions, the meanings of which are further negotiated, visibly, in the comments, and analyzed, invisibly (for outsiders), using audience metrics. However, if readers are in fact treated as equals like online tabloid journalists assert, this means it is then their job, the second act, to either dismiss the (not) kidding journalistic pieces as shallow media events or to sift through the content to construct their own orders of importance. For example: was Melania Trump's appearance wearing a pussy-bow blouse at a campaign rally, after her husband had been accused of sexual misconduct, significant? Was Polish *Newsweek's* magazine cover revealing Jarosław Kaczyński, the leader of right-wing PiS, hiding behind the mask of Andrzej Duda, the party's presidential candidate? Or a woman stating in a televised discussion that her disabled mother could not get a council house because of too many immigrants living in the United Kingdom? Decisions on the importance of publicly available knowledge provided by news media are based on the assumed presence of facts, their possible implications, and the audience's moral stance towards them. Given the deliberate ambiguity of the online tabloid (not) kidding frame, it is for the readers to decide whether the news is a joke or not. In turn, the subsequent stories are "reactive" to these audience decisions. This means it takes journalistic pieces – effects of paid work conducted by professionals – together with reader comments – effects of reading and responding to the articles in the audience's free time – to get a popular perspective on the significance of an event and on its moral judgement.

2 Voicing Popular Passions and Exposing (Im)morality

By putting emphasis on emotions and, implicitly, on moral values that underlie them, online tabloids take up the role of voicing popular passions. These, according to Mouffe (2013), are vital for democratic life. The philosopher argues that they are indispensable for collective identities to materialize, such as those concerning different political candidates and other causes that can be decided in citizens' votes. However, next to these passions Mouffe also stresses the fundamental importance of "radical negativity" in a democracy, an approach which reveals itself in the constant potential for conflict. This takes place in the public domain, which is a space where "conflicting points of view are confronted" (p. 92). In this respect, the role of online tabloids appears ambiguous: on the one hand, by treating politics simply as another form of media events they make it look frivolous, thus weakening the potential for building radical negativity envisioned by Mouffe. But, on the other hand, by uncovering the pettiness and hypocrisy of politicians, they may help for such radical negativity against people in power to take shape. Again, echoing Thomas, in the (not) kidding frame the meanings are negotiated in their consequences, in a continuous interaction loop between journalists, the articles they write, audience metrics, and reader reactions. What's more, journalists often take upon themselves an adversarial role that is "critical of the powers that be" (Pihl-Thingvad 2015, p. 394; see also: Hanitzsch 2007) and requires autonomy in their workplaces – more noticeable at Gawker and Pudelek, less so at Mail Online. Still, they are more likely to care about this function than journalists from "traditional" outlets. In a study of newsmakers in the United States, Weaver et al. (2007) indicate that, compared to print and broadcast journalists, their online peers are more likely to find the adversarial speaking-truth-to-power role important. (At the same time, "traditional" journalists focus on less confrontational roles: of the neutral disseminators of news and news interpreters). Hence, borrowing from McLuhan (1964), it appears that it is the online medium that strengthens the adversarial message.

But popular passions can be also noticed in the importance laid by Pudelek, Mail Online, and Gawker on morality, as they eagerly point out examples of the opposite, that is immoral and unjust behavior. Online tabloids thrive on transgressions of individuals in power because people believe that those bestowed with authority over others should behave better than the average person. History shows that they rarely do. This is why, if according to Lord Acton (1907), "power tends to corrupt," the role of the Fourth Estate is to keep it in check. Hard-news media do so with solemnity. Online tabloids use a mix of outrage and farce instead, to the audience's enjoyment, and the popularity of the latter shows that people like reading about the misconducts of those with means and influence. Within the frame of (not) kidding, and paraphrasing the title of a popular *Us Weekly* column that was launched in 2002, politicians – they're just like us! (Graham 2016). But as stars photographed on the street for a celebrity gossip magazine are not like ordinary people, neither are politicians, even if all sometimes leave the house in sneakers. Though the lives of the rich, famous, and powerful may feel both desirable and often unattainable, online tabloids "at least" expose their moral imperfections. This reveals yet another paradox these outlets bring to light, even if only implicitly: people in power either pay the price for their position by becoming morally flawed or by being morally flawed from the start, a disposition which then brings them to power. For everyone else, moral superiority is available as consolation, and can be voiced in the comments. Furthermore, as Entman (2012) argues persuasively, even politicians who are caught red-handed often do not have to pay for their moral shortcomings, since scandals are hushed and people tend to forget them. Hence, even if only for a brief moment of the readers' alertness, the comments sections located directly under news stories of injustice, are spaces ready for them to vent. The question is whether this function boils down to maintaining the existing social order or whether the comments sections may turn into fertile ground for sharing discontent to shape other, conflicting political identities, as Mouffe proposes. My previous research on civic engagement using anonymous small-town online forums suggests, optimistically, the latter (Chmielewska-Szlajfer 2019).

3 The L(e)ast Credible Source and Democracy

Online tabloids can be easily seen as the least credible sources of information, especially when compared to hard-news sources. However, from a different point of view they are the last credible sources beyond which no press laws apply. It may appear an unorthodox conclusion, but thanks to online tabloids' entertaining, sensationalizing content, as well as the (not) kidding frame, these highly popular outlets serve as the final vestiges of journalism shielding readers from outright disinformation, exceptionally prominent on social media. Online tabloids garner large audiences because the stories that focus on issues with significant social, economic, and political consequences are placed next to human-interest and celebrity topics that offer respite from the former. Thus, as if it was not yet clear, online tabloids are undeniably successful in keeping readers' eyeballs focused. Thanks to this – even though the idea may sound outrageous to people who blame tabloids for, well, the tabloidization of news – there are two lessons that can be learned from online tabloids on political reporting.

Firstly, online tabloids emphasize the importance of interaction between journalists and the audience directly on the website. It is an approach that was most developed by Gawker but can be also found, for example, on the website of the British broadsheet daily, *The Times*. Other online outlets, such as *The New York Times*' web version, highlight reader comments the editors find most interesting. Nonetheless, conversing with commenters is a very different, and significantly more engaging, form of interaction compared to singling out reader comments. Furthermore, since anonymous comments tend to be more aggressive than non-anonymous ones, news outlets may want to encourage commenters to create identifiable profiles, for example linked to their Facebook or LinkedIn accounts. It is worth noting that some forms of interactions between journalists and commenters are already present online, albeit elsewhere. For instance, in Poland various conversations between journalists and commenters take place on social media, notably Facebook and X (formerly Twitter). But news outlets can move these exchanges back to their own websites, if for no other reason than at least to generate ad revenue for themselves, rather than passing it over to social media platforms. In addition, in light of the decreasing trust in news media, a more dialogical approach may lead to larger reader confidence in journalists, once they do not only write their pieces for others to read but also respond to comments.

Secondly, news could be made constructively "reactive" if journalists allow themselves to be inspired by reader comments and are open about it. This, too, can be found in social-media discussions between writers and commenters. However, ties between the two parties may be strengthened if journalists acknowledge helpful, thought-provoking comments, for instance in the form of notes at the bottom of the article. This is not a proposition to bring down the divisions between professional and amateur, civic journalism. Rather, it is a suggestion how to do justice to the meaningful, mutually beneficial interactions that are already taking place, and to bring them back to the authoritative journalistic source: the news outlets.

•••

Ultimately, online tabloids demonstrate that democratic values are the object of people's passions – this is the reason why political topics are so popular in the first place. People want democracy, as well as the principles of justice and fairness to work. This can be clearly noticed in the enraged comments when politicians do not behave properly: when they lie, cheat, break the law, or – more generally – turn out to be hypocrites, which online tabloids love to report. At the same time, readers feel less overwhelmed by political coverage when they encounter it in soft-news spaces, including sensationalizing, celebrifying online tabloids. One reason for this may be that such outlets embrace big emotions and bold moral statements, which are far easier to understand and far more entertaining to follow than specialist analyses. Another is that the populist language of online tabloids seems more personal and more direct in connecting with the audience. In short, online tabloids are more inviting and less demanding of their readers than non-tabloid media. This skill – attracting large audiences – and its costs – providing sensationalizing content – should not be easily dismissed. The ability of journalists to meaningfully communicate with their audiences is exceptionally important today, as we are witnessing both growing news avoidance and democratic backsliding in different parts of the world. Neither Poland, the United States, nor the United Kingdom are immune to it, albeit each country in its own particular way. From 2015 until the end of 2023, Poland was ruled by PiS, a right-wing party which openly undermines the rule of law, independence of the judiciary, and independent media. In the October 2023 parliamentary election, PiS again received the most votes, although this time not enough to form a government. The pattern repeated itself in the spring 2024 local elections. Donald Trump's 2016–2020 presidential term was marked, among others, by praise of neo-fascist groups inside the US, such as the Proud Boys, autocratic rulers outside the US, including Vladimir Putin, and a fundamental disregard for democratic process. It had its shocking culmination in Trump's endorsement of the 6th of January 2021 attack on the Capitol by rioters outraged that Joe Biden had won the presidential election. Given this, the fact that Trump is the presidential candidate of the Republican Party for the upcoming 2024 election shows the deeply troubled state of the modern world's oldest democracy. In the United Kingdom, the Conservative Party which has been in power since 2010, and whose Prime Minister David Cameron was responsible for the EU referendum, has been bearing the grunt of the negative economic consequences of Brexit the Tories had largely endorsed. Boris Johnson's erratic 2019–2022 tenure as Prime Minister and his breaking of social distancing regulations during the Covid pandemic in the so-called Partygate scandal did not help either. Lastly, a footnote: bearing in mind the notable disinterest of Gawker and Mail Online in Poland's politics during the 2015 presidential campaign, it is an ironic twist that Keir Starmer, the leader of the Labour Party made headlines across major British media – Mail Online included – when at the beginning of 2023 he warned that the United Kingdom will be poorer than Poland by 2030 (Wilcock and Beckford 2023). Foreign topics are generally discussed in the news in a way to make them look more familiar, and here is a Polish victory of sorts: from the object of indifference to a reference point for the United Kingdom's humiliation, in consequence of its own poor judgment in the 2016 referendum that left many Polish immigrants in the UK with a bitter aftertaste.

Mouffe writes that the "prime task of democratic politics is (…) to 'sublimate' (…) passions by mobilizing them towards democratic designs" and "by creating collective forms of identification around democratic objectives" (2013, p. 9). As I showed in my exploration of politics and online tabloids, Pudelek, Mail Online, and Gawker are examples how such outlets voice popular passions concerning political life. While they use moralizing language which Mouffe is wary of, by highlighting the shortcomings of politicians and governance, online tabloids uncover people's expectations and hopes concerning a well-functioning democratic state. By exposing democratic deficiencies, online tabloids and their commenters indirectly reveal how they wish politicians to behave and democratic institutions to function: justly, considerately, caringly. Although few would disagree with these ideals, they can mean different things to different people when details are involved. For Mouffe, this is a good thing. Hence, if popular passions are already here, there is a chance collective identities will materialize.

From the onset, tabloids have been among the most read papers and, transported into the online reality, they remain the most popular news sources. They are unique in their unabashed, revenue-driven embrace of strong emotions. They claim to follow their readers and deliver what they want. Just this is enough to pay heed to what they write about political life. At the end of the day, popular passions are formed not so much in expert debates as in a mix of high and low, in-depth and entertaining, serious and sensationalizing discussions. Those who care about democracy, cannot afford to ignore these voices.

References

Ceylan, G., Anderson, I. A. and Wood, W. (2023). Sharing of misinformation is habitual, not just lazy or biased. *Proceedings of the National Academy of Sciences*, 120(4), pp. 1–8.

Chmielewska-Szlajfer, H. (2019). *Reshaping Poland's community after Communism: Ordinary celebrations*, New York: Palgrave.

Dayan, D. (2005). Mothers, midwives and abortionists. Genealogy, obstetrics, audiences & publics. In: Livingstone, S. (ed). *Audiences and publics: When cultural engagement matters for the public sphere*. London: Intellect Press, pp. 43–76.

Dayan, D. (2013). Conquering visibility, conferring visibility: Visibility seekers and media performance. *International Journal of Communication*, 7, pp. 137–153.

Entman, R. M. (2012). *Scandal and silence: Media responses to presidential misconduct*. Malden, MA: Polity.

Graham, R. (2016). One of Us: "Stars – They're Just Like Us" and the future of always-"on" celebrity coverage. *Slate*. Available at: https://slate.com/human-interest/2016/09/the-invention-of-us-weeklys-stars-theyre-just-like-us-feature.html.

Hanitzsch, T. (2007). Deconstructing journalism culture: Toward a universal theory. *Communication Theory*, 17, pp. 367–385.

Lord Acton. (1907). Letter to Bishop Mandell Creighton, April 5, 1887. In: Figgis, J. N. and Laurence, R. V. (eds.). *Historical essays and studies*. London: Macmillan.

McLuhan, M. (1964). *Understanding media: The extensions of man*. Cambridge, MA: The MIT Press.

Mouffe, C. (2013). *Agonistics: thinking the world democratically*. London: Verso Books.

Newman, N., Fletcher, R., Eddy, K. et al. (2023). *Reuters Institute Digital News Report 2023*. Oxford, UK: Reuters Institute for the Study of Journalism.

Persily, N. and Tucker, J. A. (2020). *Social media and democracy: The sate od the field, prospects for reform*. Cambridge, UK: Cambridge University Press.

Pihl-Thingvad, S. (2015). Professional ideals and daily practice in journalism. *Journalism*, 16(3), pp. 392–411.

Schudson, M. (2003). *The sociology of news*. New York: W. W. Norton & Company.

Schütz, A. (1946). The well-informed citizen. An essay on the social distribution of knowledge. *Social Research* 13(1/4), pp. 463-478.

Toff, B., Palmer, R. and Nielsen, R. K. (2023). *Avoiding the news: Reluctant audiences for journalism*. New York: Columbia University Press.

Wahl-Jorgensen, K. (2019). *Emotions, media and politics*. Malden, MA: Polity.

Weaver D., Beam R., Brownlee B., Voakes P. and Wilhoit C. (2007). *The American journalist in the 21st century: US news people at the dawn of a new millennium*. London: Lawrence Erlbaum Associates.

Wilcock, D. and Beckford, M. (2023). Keir Starmer warns Brits will soon be worse off than people in Poland, unless the UK's 'low wage, high tax, doom-loop' is broken as the Labour leader tackles the Tories over their economic record. *Mail Online*, 27 February. Available at: https://www.dailymail.co.uk/news/article-11797939/Keir-Starmer-warns-Brits-soon-worse-Poles-UKs-low-wage-high-tax-doom-loop.html.

Wojcieszak, M., Menchen-Trevino, E. and von Hohenberg, B. C. et al. (2024). Non-News Websites Expose People to More Political Content Than News Websites: Evidence from Browsing Data in Three Countries. *Political Communication*, 41(1), pp. 129–151.

Index

1989   1–2, 12–13, 17, 18, 66, 82–84, 223

Abedin, Huma   154, 170, 171, 231
abortion   68, 164–166, 181, 204
abortionists   56
Access Hollywood   46, 162–164, 169
accuracy   236, 244
ACTA   26, 42, 43, 206, 210, 211
actor   73, 74, 142, 177
actress   91, 92, 137, 168, 176
advertising   12, 225, 227
agonism   9, 28
al-Asad, Bashar   152
Alexander, Jeffrey C.   28
Allan, Stuart   23–25
Allred, Gloria   168
Americans   164, 174, 201
Anderson, Chris W.   237, 239
animals   219, 224
anonymity   9, 193, 195, 204, 205, 223
Anti-Counterfeiting Trade Agreement. *See* ACTA
anti-elite   46, 51, 56, 67–68, 86, 141, 180, 182, 184, 221, 227, 236
antisemitism   79, 83
Apprentice, The   46, 87, 139, 141, 168
attention   5, 20, 22–25, 27, 28, 40, 48, 52, 53, 55, 59, 62, 66, 67, 84, 85, 118, 119, 127, 135, 151, 156, 164, 176, 197, 199, 201, 208, 211, 217, 231, 237, 244, 247, 256
audience   5, 6, 11, 12, 21, 22, 24, 29, 40, 43, 45–48, 51–55, 59, 61, 63, 80, 87, 93, 95, 99, 102, 104, 135, 169, 178, 196–198, 201–205, 208, 210, 211, 216, 218, 220–222, 228, 230, 235, 236, 241, 248, 254, 256–260
audience metrics   257, 258
authority   8, 9, 184, 239, 255, 256, 258

bankruptcy   41, 214
Banks, Tyra   148
Barthes, Roland   199
BBC   24, 91–94, 99, 134
boyd, danah   5
benefits   222, 230, 231, 241
Beyoncé   183

bias   3, 4, 6, 52, 101, 144, 220
Biden, Joe   137, 163, 261
Bieńkowska, Elżbieta   76
Black Lives Matter   29, 173
Blair, Tony   97, 194
blog   39, 42, 137, 199, 200, 205, 227, 232
Bloom, Orlando   177
Bluestone, Gabrielle   141–143
Boczkowski, Pablo J.   54, 207
Bollea, Terry. *See* Hogan, Hulk
bollocking   195, 226, 231
Boorstin, Daniel J.   248
boundary work   239, 240
Bourdieu, Pierre   141, 243
Brański, Michał   42
Breitbart News   137, 165
Brexit   5, 46, 57, 84, 86–100, 102, 104–113, 116, 118, 120–122, 124–127, 129–135, 197, 230, 255, 261
Brexit referendum. *See* EU referendum
British pound   116
broadsheet. *See* news, hard
broadsheet, format   11, 13–15, 19, 21, 22, 193, 195, 201, 215, 259
Bubba the Love Sponge (Todd Clem)   40
Bush, Billy   146, 152
Bush, George W.   148, 167
Bustle Digital Group   234

Cambridge Analytica   3, 108–109
Cameron, David   2, 48, 53, 57, 87–90, 94–98, 100, 123, 261
campaign app   113
campaign rally   197, 257
candidate   2–5, 37, 45, 47, 48, 51, 53, 70, 74, 77–83, 87, 113, 136, 138–141, 143, 144, 146, 147, 149, 151–154, 157–173, 175–178, 180, 182–184, 197, 243, 257, 261
celebrity   6, 7, 22, 24, 40, 43, 45, 53, 66–69, 74, 80, 81, 91, 114, 174, 183, 184, 196, 209, 224, 227, 234, 238, 242–244, 248, 256, 258, 259
censorship   130, 225, 227
Cher   183
Chmielewska-Szlajfer, Helena   74, 195, 259

Christie, Chris   159–160
Churchill, Winston   160
circulation, print   14, 15, 17–18, 25, 37, 39, 42
citizens   3, 12, 26, 27, 54, 74, 105, 106, 118, 122, 123, 132, 134, 142, 152, 181, 201, 230, 244, 248, 257
Civic Platform. *See* PO
Clarium Capital   40
Clarke, Martin   44, 195, 220, 222, 226, 230, 231
class, middle   11, 208, 245
class, working   208
clickbait   20, 24, 200
climate   29, 106
Clinton, Bill   25, 146, 152, 156, 161, 167, 172, 173, 176, 246
Clinton, Chelsea   172, 180
Clinton, Hillary   3, 25, 46–48, 51, 52, 55–57, 93, 109, 112, 135–138, 141, 144, 151–162, 164–173, 175–184, 231
CNN   16, 24, 138, 148, 160, 200
Colbert, Stephen   144
Comey, James   154, 170
commenters   46, 47, 49, 54, 55, 60, 67, 69, 70–73, 75, 78, 81, 83, 94, 98, 101, 105–114, 116–127, 129, 131, 132, 134, 135, 137–151, 155–156, 161, 164, 168, 169, 171, 173–184, 197, 201–214, 223, 235, 242, 255, 259–261
commenters, paranoid   55
Communism   13, 17, 52, 62, 72, 79, 80, 82–83, 126
Conboy, Martin   6, 23
Condé Nast   16, 39, 40, 42, 217–219, 245
conflict   6, 9, 28, 66, 84, 99, 175, 217, 228, 257
Conservative Party   2, 46, 86, 91, 95–100, 102, 124, 194, 208, 229
Cook, Timothy E.   217, 247
Corbyn, Jeremy   57, 89
corruption   48, 54, 56, 84, 197, 246, 258
Couldry, Nick   22
court   6, 126, 129, 166, 218, 234, 235
Cruise, Tom   40
Cruz, Ted   112, 118, 140
Cuban, Mark   137, 141, 159, 167
Cummings, Dominic   97
Cunningham, Howard   111
czerwoniaki   16

Dacre, Paul   194, 220, 231

Daily Herald   13
Daily Mail   6, 10, 13, 14, 19, 43–45, 104, 205, 215, 220, 226, 228–230
Daily Mirror   13–15, 22
Daily News   15, 16, 244
Daily Show, The   142
daughter, presidential candidate's   70, 138–139, 172–173, 179, 180, 242
Dayan, Daniel   8, 9, 231, 256
Deadspin   41, 234
debate   3, 5, 6, 21, 29, 47, 51, 72, 74, 77–78, 87–89, 91, 93–103, 137–140, 147, 151–153, 157–159, 161, 164–167, 172, 178, 217, 247, 262
democracy   6, 9, 21, 27, 29, 50, 247, 248, 257, 260–262
Democratic Corporatist model of media and politics   12, 13
Democratic Left Alliance. *See* SLD
Democratic National Committee. *See* DNC
Democratic Party   118, 119, 151, 158, 160, 169
demonstrations   26, 43, 124, 125, 128, 129
Denton, Nick   38–40, 50, 193, 202, 203, 205, 213, 217–219, 229, 232–234, 246
deplorables   152, 155, 156
Diana Princess (Diana Spencer)   23
disinformation   3, 6, 103, 118, 259
DNC   158, 166, 180
Doctor Who   106–107
Dolan, Timothy   178
doll. *See* puppet
domesticating. *See* familiarizing
downvote   63, 91
Drake, Jessica   168
Drudge, Matt   23
Drudge Report   23, 25, 165, 222
Duda, Agata   129, 179, 216, 244
Duda, Andrzej   1, 2, 4, 46, 48, 52, 53, 55, 57, 66–74, 77–79, 81, 83–84, 87, 129, 130, 179, 244, 257
Duda, Kinga   71
Duffy, Lisa   134
Durkheim, Émile   5, 28, 50

economy   20, 60, 79, 105, 116, 227
editor   8, 9, 29, 39, 40, 44, 104, 141, 156, 176, 193–197, 200, 202, 203, 207, 212, 215, 218–223, 226–230, 235, 247, 259

editorializing 222, 224, 230
editor-in-chief 2, 39, 44, 177, 195, 207, 210, 220, 224, 226, 227, 230, 231, 235
election campaign 4, 5, 8, 9, 24, 27, 37, 41, 43, 45, 48, 63, 67–71, 74, 76, 78, 81, 84–88, 91, 96–104, 108, 112, 113, 115, 124, 132, 135, 138, 141, 146, 147, 151, 153–156, 158–162, 165–172, 176, 177, 179, 184, 196, 218, 225, 226
election day 37, 155, 175, 179, 182, 183
election, parliamentary in Poland 1, 2, 85, 261
election, presidential in Poland 1, 2, 4, 29, 37, 57, 60, 62, 66–68, 70, 74, 76, 79, 80, 81, 82, 84, 86, 184
election, presidential in the United States 3, 4, 27, 29, 37, 39, 54, 57, 59, 60, 62, 63, 93, 108, 113, 135–138, 151, 173, 243, 261
elite 11, 12, 15, 17, 20, 22, 37, 46–49, 52, 54, 56, 62, 66, 69, 72, 73, 80, 83, 86, 87, 90, 172, 184, 241
emails 40, 152, 154, 155, 160, 166, 169, 170, 180, 193, 195, 213
Employee of the Month 193, 213, 233, 234
entertainment 7, 20–23, 25, 26, 48, 51–54, 67, 146, 197, 198, 215, 217, 221, 239, 242, 244, 248, 254
Entman, Robert M. 47, 50–52, 258
Esser, Frank 1, 6, 20, 22, 27
EU referendum 1–4, 10, 29, 57, 58, 60, 87–104, 106, 108, 110, 112, 113, 116–118, 121, 122, 124, 126, 128, 131, 135, 184, 217, 261
EU referendum campaign 37, 60, 63, 87, 91, 100, 104, 197, 231, 255
European Union 2, 26, 48, 55, 59, 60, 66, 67, 84–85, 89, 91, 92, 97, 99, 100, 104, 106, 111, 122, 124, 126, 129–131, 132
Euroskepticism 82, 85, 95
Express Wieczorny 17, 18
Extinction Rebellion 29

Facebook 6, 24, 54, 73, 88, 108–110, 195, 203–205, 213, 259, 260
Fakt 18, 19, 42, 45
familiarizing 61, 124, 127
family 25, 51, 78, 93, 102, 121, 132, 152, 158, 159, 161, 164, 166, 174, 245
Family Guy 121

Farage, Nigel 47, 48, 57, 66, 95, 102, 103, 106, 115, 131, 217
fascist 113, 115, 261
fashion 81, 137, 140, 173, 176–179, 184, 221, 243
FBI 154, 160, 169, 170
Feinberg, Ashley 195, 203, 213, 219, 236, 240–242
female. See women
finance 15, 43, 54, 141
Financial Times 14, 19, 38, 229
Fiske, John 49
Florida 156, 167, 170, 234
Fox News 24, 137, 147, 150, 151, 165
frame 7, 28, 38, 48, 49, 53, 55, 184
frame, (not) kidding 7, 28, 29, 50, 101, 143, 184, 244, 256–259
frame, game 5, 47, 48, 100, 104, 184
frame, scandal 37, 47–52, 53, 184
framing 5, 28, 47–49, 55, 66, 127, 131, 231, 248
fraud, electoral 68, 165
freedom of speech 26, 43, 234, 235
Freud, Sigmund 56

G/O Media 202, 234
Gans, Herbert J. 21, 61, 62, 215, 237
gaslighting, political 47
gatekeeping 202, 205, 215, 247
gay 40, 73, 165, 208, 217, 245
Gayle, Damian 194, 195, 199, 208, 222, 229–231, 241
Gazeta Wyborcza 2, 5, 18, 19, 43, 72, 78, 236
Gazeta.pl 18, 221
Generoso, Pope Jr. 15
Germany 12, 27, 92, 100, 114, 115
Gevinson, Tavi 137
gif 112, 142, 143, 144, 148
Gingrich, Newt 149–151
Giuliani, Rudy 152, 160, 166
Gizmodo Media Group 29, 41, 58, 136, 193, 195, 219, 234
Gold, Hannah 138
Good Change 4, 48, 84
Gore, Al 166
gość 67
Gove, Michael 87–89, 97
government 17, 72, 75, 81, 82, 100, 106, 113, 123, 125, 129, 131, 132, 134, 166, 241, 261
Great Hill Partners 234

Greenwald, Glenn 113
Gripsrud, Jostein 6, 20, 21
Guardian, The 14, 25, 128–131, 194

Habermas, Jürgen 6, 7, 9, 25, 28, 255
hacking 25, 154, 158, 166
Hallin, Daniel C. 8, 11, 12, 27
Hamilton, Alexander 15
Hanitzsch, Thomas 215, 237, 239, 258
Harmsworth, Alfred. *See* Lord Northcliffe
heading. *See* headline
headline 22, 24, 45, 68, 91, 93, 97, 101, 105, 126, 132, 134, 156, 164, 199, 200, 216, 222, 230, 244, 254, 255, 261
Hilton, Paris 227
Hilton, Steve 102
hires 227–228, 230
Hitler, Adolf 48, 97, 114
Holiday, Ryan 39, 41
Hudson, Kate 176
Hulk Hogan (Bollea Terry) 6, 40, 41, 218, 226, 233–234, 245
Hungary 13, 66
hypocrisy 27, 48, 51, 102, 120, 161, 178, 239, 245, 258

identity 28, 61, 257, 259, 262
immigrants 92–95, 102, 135, 164, 222, 241, 257
immigrants, Polish 91, 134, 261
immigration 87–89, 91–95, 100, 121, 132, 134, 165, 208, 230
infotainment 20, 25, 52, 197, 237

Jackson, Michael 183
Jay-Z 183
Jews 56, 70, 118, 129–130
Jezebel 41, 234
Jobs, Steve 160
Johnson, Boris 46, 48, 51, 57, 66, 89, 97–99, 101, 261
Jolie, Angelina 91, 92
Jones, Alex 118
journalism 8, 11–13, 20–23, 27, 29, 49, 54, 55, 76, 196, 198, 203, 219, 221, 230, 236, 237, 239, 243, 244, 247, 248, 255, 259, 260
justice 28, 49, 259–260
Juzwiak, Rich 195, 203

Kaczyński, Jarosław 55, 68, 69, 71, 73, 124, 127, 244, 257
Kaczyński, Lech 69, 83
Kardashian, Kim 174, 179
Karski, Jan 130
Kelly, Megyn 149–151, 157
Kennedy, John F. 176, 246
Khan, Sadiq 99–100
Kinja 39, 202, 206
Kolbe, Maximilian 17
Komorowski, Bronisław 1, 2, 46–48, 55–57, 63, 66–75, 77, 78, 80, 82, 83, 130
Kukiz, Paweł 50, 66, 71, 74, 76, 77, 79–83, 242
Kulczyk, Jan 79
Kurier Czerwony 16–18, 22
Kushner, Jared 39
Kuźniar, Jarosław 68
Kwaśniewski, Aleksander 43, 126

Labour Party 89, 96, 100, 261
Lady Gaga 183
Laloux, Frédéric 223
Law and Justice. *See* PiS
Lawson, Nigel 102
lawsuit 40, 41, 45, 147, 226, 234
layout 11, 17, 27, 42
Lazarus, Catie 193, 213
Le Pen, Marine 113, 115
leaderboard 219–220
Leadsom, Andrea 99
Leave campaign. *See* Leavers
Leavers 2–4, 10, 46, 48, 53–56, 60, 67, 84, 86, 87, 91, 93, 95–104, 108, 117, 135
left-wing 8, 15, 81, 194, 208
Lepper, Andrzej 82
Leveson Inquiry 25
Leveson, Brian (Lord Justice Leveson) 25
Lewinsky, Monica 23, 25, 146
LGBT+ 8, 211, 228, 241
Liberal model of media and politics 11–13, 27
Libya 230
lies 87, 99, 155, 158, 160
like. *See* upvote
Lis, Tomasz 68, 70
lock her up 155
London 9, 100, 106, 116, 124, 132, 139, 193
Lopez, Jennifer 183

Lord Acton (Dalberg-Acton John E. E.) 258
Lord Astor (Astor John J.) 95
Lord Northcliffe (Harmsworth Alfred) 10, 13
Lord Rothermere (Harmsworth Jonathan) 14
Lord Sugar (Sugar Alan) 100
Luft, Krzysztof 77

Machiavelli, Niccolò 52
Macierewicz, Antoni 69, 82, 211
Maleńczuk, Maciej 82–83
Maltby, Kate 128–131
Mancini, Paolo 8, 11, 12, 27
Manjoo, Farhad 199
March for Science 106
Marwick, Alice 195
Marx, Karl 56
MAXQDA 29, 59
May, Theresa 125
McCain, John 163
McLuhan, Marshall 258
McNair, Brian 6, 25, 27, 48, 239
media event 242–244, 255, 257
#metoo 239
Mellado, Claudia 45, 197, 237
meme 112, 119, 121, 245
men 21, 134, 142, 202, 208, 231
Merkel, Angela 92, 178
metrics. *See* traffic
Michalczewski, Dariusz 69
Michnik, Adam 2
Middleton, Kate 179
midwives 256
migrant crisis 85
migrants, bad 241
migrants, good 241
Military Information Services 48, 70
misinformation. *See* disinformation
monarchy 101, 179
morality 28, 49, 258
moralizing 8, 261
Mouffe, Chantal 9, 25, 28, 29, 255, 257–259, 261–262
Mroczek, Marcin 74–76
Murdoch, Rupert 13–15, 24
Muslims 74, 123–124, 159

National Enquirer 14, 15, 38

National Health Service. *See* NHS
nationalism 113–114, 118, 126, 133
Nazis 131
New York 16, 39, 40, 141, 148, 152, 154, 161, 162, 178, 193, 210, 213, 232–234
New York Herald 11
New York Post 15, 244
New York Times, The 15, 16, 19, 39–41, 44, 131, 136, 136, 143, 160, 162, 199, 200, 203, 206, 214, 259
New Yorker, The 29, 200, 214, 236
News of the World, The 25
news outlet 4, 5, 7, 8, 10, 22, 48, 49, 51, 55, 62, 194, 197, 203, 235, 239, 240, 255, 259, 260
news story 62, 217, 239, 244
news, fake 5, 70
news, foreign 61, 62, 64, 124, 222, 230
news, hard 1, 6–8, 10, 19–22, 24, 27–29, 48, 53, 193, 203, 207, 215, 219, 235, 238–239, 242, 254–256, 258, 259
news, soft 20, 21, 48, 54, 201, 207, 219, 235, 254, 260
news, wires 213–215, 221–222
newsroom 194, 215, 219–221, 224, 226, 227, 229, 237, 240
Newsweek Polska 68, 257
newsworthiness 26, 196–198, 215–217, 233
NHS 100
Nietzsche, Friedrich 56
Nixon, Richard 50, 160
Nolan, Hamilton 195, 199, 200, 203, 206, 213, 214, 217–219, 233, 234, 246
non-elite 11, 21, 37, 47, 53, 66, 69, 75
(not) kidding 7, 29, 50, 101, 135, 143, 184, 209, 244, 248, 254, 259

O2 19, 42, 194, 195, 207, 212, 223
Obama, Barack 130, 152, 157, 161, 167, 175, 176, 178, 184, 224
Obama, Michelle 176, 178, 179, 184
objectivity 5, 94, 215, 236, 237, 247
O'Connor, Brendan 195, 219, 241, 245–247
Ogórek, Magdalena 81, 242, 243
Olejnik, Monika 70, 83
Onet.pl 18, 19, 24, 221, 228
Orbán, Viktor 63
Örnebring, Henrik 10, 11, 215, 237, 239

outrage 26, 48–50, 54, 71, 121, 124, 142, 149, 162, 172, 209, 225, 256, 258, 261

Paczkowski, Andrzej 16, 17
Palin, Sarah 40
Papacharissi, Zizi 9, 10
paparazzi 23, 154, 170
parasite 56, 124
Pareene, Alex 218
Pariser, Eli 5
PayPal 40
paywall 37, 45
Pence, Mike 163
Perez Hilton 42, 200
Perry, Katy 176
Petry, Frauke 115
photo galleries 53, 124, 172, 175, 176, 178, 179, 224
PiS 1, 2, 4, 46, 48, 51, 57, 66–69, 74–75, 78, 81–85, 113, 123, 124, 126–129, 132–134, 135, 182, 257, 261
plastic surgery 175
PO 1, 2, 57, 67, 72–75, 81, 82, 127
Podesta, John 154, 166, 170, 180
Poland 1, 2, 6, 8–10, 12, 13, 16–18, 24, 26, 27, 29, 37, 42, 43, 50, 57, 59, 62, 63, 66, 73–86, 113, 122–126, 128–179, 184, 204, 206, 216, 221, 223–225, 227, 228, 242, 254–256, 260–261
Polarized Pluralist model of media and politics 12, 13
Poles 43, 70, 84, 91, 122–124, 129–135, 178, 179, 201
Politico 144, 236
polls 1–5, 7, 8, 48, 50, 79, 86, 87, 89, 91, 97–100, 144, 165, 170
Poniedziałek, Jacek 73
popular passions 9, 28, 255, 257, 258, 261–262
populism 10, 11, 48, 49, 51, 66, 82, 216, 220, 227, 230, 236, 241, 256, 260
porn 168
Pospieszalski, Jan 76
post-truth 87
presidential look 52
press, elite. *See* news, hard
press, popular. *See* news, soft
Private Eye 230

professionalism 11, 29, 194, 196, 235–240
profit 17, 22, 28, 39, 50, 54, 120, 198, 225
prostitute 40, 172
protest 26, 43, 123–125, 130, 156, 158–159, 204, 206, 210, 242, 254
Pruitt, Bill 139, 141
Przekrój 227
public sphere 6, 7, 9, 11, 21, 22, 25–29, 255
public sphere, plebeian 7, 255
punk-rock 80, 81
puppet 55, 68, 69, 166, 180, 181
pussy 48, 54, 60, 138, 146, 148, 152, 164
Pussy Riot 180–182
Putin, Vladimir 109, 166, 181, 261

racism 21, 29, 50, 54, 95, 100, 102, 124, 132, 142, 157, 172, 220, 224
rape 152, 170, 204
reactive 5, 46, 51, 99, 196–198, 201, 208, 210, 211, 220, 241, 254, 257, 260
Read, Max 218, 219
Reagle, Joseph M. 201
red tops 16
Reddit 16, 113, 115
refugees 74, 85, 91, 92, 124, 132
Remain campaign. *See* Remainers
Remainers 2, 3, 10, 47, 48, 55, 56, 60, 86, 87, 88, 94, 97–102
remote work 212, 215, 223
Republican Party 59, 67, 112, 118, 136, 144, 147, 151, 153, 157, 163, 165, 261
revenue 14, 16, 24, 39, 45, 49, 55, 198, 201, 205, 206, 210, 248, 260, 262
Rice, Condoleezza 148
Ricoeur, Paul 55, 56
right-wing 1, 8, 13, 17, 45, 51, 66, 70, 74, 76, 78, 114, 115, 131, 184, 216, 230, 231, 235, 256, 257, 261
rock star 80–84, 242
Romney, Mitt 113, 170
routines, journalistic 196, 215, 221
royals, British 25, 101, 128–131, 179
Russia 13, 40, 69, 83, 109, 154, 158, 161, 166
Russian influence 3x, 69

Sambrook, Richard 24
Sanders, Bernie 50, 66, 118, 158
Saramonowicz, Andrzej 75

scandal   12, 23, 25–28, 37, 46–55, 60, 68, 75, 113, 123, 142, 146, 147, 153, 164, 169, 170, 172, 197, 216, 239, 261
Schudson, Michael   11, 237, 239, 247, 256
Schütz, Alfred   255
Scientology   40
secrets   6, 41, 56, 76, 83, 162, 211, 215, 226, 238, 245–247
sensationalism   17–22, 24, 48, 66, 197, 200, 238, 240, 255, 259, 260, 262
sensationalizing. *See* sensationalism
sex   1, 19, 22, 40, 54, 135, 138, 139, 146–148, 150, 151, 154, 164, 168, 233, 245
sex scandal   25, 51, 54, 55, 146, 169, 197
sexism   27, 48, 52, 55, 80, 142, 146, 148, 164, 168, 230
sexting   154, 170
sexual abuse. *See* sexual assault
sexual assault   23, 135, 143, 147, 149, 151, 156, 163, 167–170, 197, 217, 246, 257
sexual harassment. *See* sexual assault
sexual misconduct. *See* sexual assault
show-business   7, 81–84, 208–210, 223, 228, 242–244, 254
Silicon Valley   6, 40
Silver, Nate   144–145
Skiba, Krzysztof   82, 83
SLAPP   234
SLD   81, 82
Smoleńsk plane crash   69, 72, 83
snark   40, 43, 55, 56, 121, 199, 203, 233, 234, 240, 244
Snowden, Edward   113
soap opera   21, 74–76, 84
social media   3, 5, 6, 24, 45, 54, 108, 110, 195, 203, 207, 222, 224, 248, 255, 259, 260
Solorz, Zygmunt   79
Spears, Britney   144
Spiers, Elizabeth   39, 40, 195, 197, 199, 200, 205, 210, 221, 230, 232, 236
Spy   339
Starmer, Keir   261
Staszczyk, Muniek   80
Staszewski, Kazik   80
statistics   21, 39, 146, 178, 201, 202
Stern, Howard   138
Stewart, John   144
Stokrotka   83

Strategic lawsuit against public participation. *See* SLAPP
Streep, Meryl   183
Street, John   52–53, 243
Stuart, Gisela   99, 100
subheading   46, 125, 152, 157, 158, 165, 166, 179
subscriptions   12, 14, 15, 18, 39, 40, 218
suit   103, 139, 140, 183
Sun, The   13, 14, 25, 43, 101
Super Express   18, 19
Syria   74, 85, 91, 152

tabloid. *See* news, soft
tabloid, format   11, 39, 199, 201, 232
tabloid, history of   10–19
tabloidization   6, 19–24, 27, 244, 259
tax evasion   146, 156
taxes   156, 158, 159–161
Thiel, Peter   6, 40, 41, 214, 226, 234, 239, 245
Thomas, William I.   209, 258
Thompson, John B.   27, 50, 239
tips   23, 212, 217, 227, 233
Tlen   223
Tocqueville, Alexis de   10
Tories. *See* Conservative Party
traffic   210, 218–220, 226, 230
troll   6, 113, 203, 217
Trump Tower   141, 160, 162, 163
Trump, Donald   3, 4, 25, 27, 39, 46, 48, 51, 53–57, 60, 66, 76, 87, 90, 93, 106–109, 112–115, 118–119, 135, 174, 243, 246, 261
Trump, Ivanka   138, 147, 173, 174, 179, 180, 231, 242
Trump, Melania   152, 162, 173, 231, 257
Trump, Tiffany   231, 242
Turkey   99
Turner, Graeme   21, 23
Tusk, Donald   127–130
TVN 24   79, 83, 126, 127
tweet   70, 71, 100, 107, 109, 131, 140–142, 146, 150, 153, 161, 163
Twitter   6, 24, 54, 141, 195, 260

UKIP   47, 93–95, 102, 103, 115, 134
United Kingdom   1–4, 6, 8, 18, 25–29, 37, 38, 47, 55, 59, 60, 62, 66, 84–100, 111, 113–116, 125–127, 131, 133, 135, 151, 155, 184, 193, 195, 201, 205, 221, 229–231, 255–257, 261

United Kingdom Independence Party.
　　See UKIP
United States   1, 3, 6, 8–18, 25–27, 29, 37, 38,
　　39, 50, 59, 62, 66, 90, 100, 102, 106, 111,
　　114, 115, 118, 135, 155, 157, 165, 166, 175,
　　179, 181, 182, 195, 214, 215, 224, 231, 234,
　　243, 254–256, 258, 261
Univision   234
upvote   9, 10, 29, 61, 62, 63, 69, 72, 74,
　　76, 78–84, 87, 90, 91, 94, 97, 105, 117,
　　118, 123, 124, 131, 133, 145, 150, 159, 161,
　　174, 204
Urban, Jerzy   73
USA Today   15, 16, 39, 218

Valleywag   40
verb, strong   199, 202
visibility   4, 8, 9, 52, 56, 60, 197, 202, 228, 243,
　　244, 256
voter   2–6, 9, 10, 47, 48, 51, 53, 55, 56, 67, 69,
　　86, 87, 89, 91, 92, 94, 97, 98, 100, 108,
　　109, 113, 118, 122, 133, 137, 152, 164–167,
　　178, 180, 256
voting   29, 77, 114, 123, 129–130, 164, 254

Wahl-Jorgensen, Karin   55, 197, 256
Waisbord, Silvio   26, 27, 50
Wałęsa, Lech   73, 82
Wall Street Journal   15, 39, 162
Walter, Mariusz   79
Warsaw   17, 130, 193, 194, 223
Washington Post   15, 146, 153
Weber, Max   52
Weiner, Anthony   154, 170–171
Wiechecki, Stefan "Wiech"   18
Wikileaks   154, 166
Wintour, Anna   177–178
Wirtualna Polska   19, 24, 42, 194, 195, 207,
　　212, 221, 223, 225, 228
Wojewódzki, Kuba   80
Wolff, Michael   140
Wollaston, Sarah   100
women   21, 29, 60, 138, 139, 143, 146, 149, 151,
　　152, 162, 165, 168, 169, 174, 175, 181, 202,
　　204, 208, 211, 221, 228, 230, 231, 241, 245
Women's Strike   29
wp.pl. See Wirtualna Polska
WSI. See Military Information Services
Wylie, Christopher   3, 110

www.ingramcontent.com/pod-product-compliance
Lightning Source LLC
Chambersburg PA
CBHW070614030426
42337CB00020B/3799